The Art and Practice of Economics Research

Acclaim for *The Art and Practice of Economics Research*

'Bowmaker's *The Art and Practice of Economics Research* is the book I wish I had when I was "growing up" as an economist. It is a series of interviews with economists: some are Nobel Prize winners, others the working economists who have helped build the modern science. The interviews are augmented with a brief synopsis of the contributions of the interviewee and are highly structured. Bowmaker probes both the motivation of economists – crucial to succeeding as a researcher – and the process of research itself. I will second a message that several of the interviewees gave: don't be afraid to admit failure and move on. For anyone who is or wants to be an economic researcher, or anyone just interested in how economics "works", this is a terrific and inspirational resource.'

– David K. Levine, Washington University in St. Louis, USA

'It is hard to imagine an economist in the world who would not enjoy this book. It is fascinating, gripping, and full of the wisdom imparted by age and by scholarly life's ups and downs. My favourite line, by one of the world's most interesting economists, is: "eventually … I developed the courage to work on the things that originally attracted me to economics". That sounds like a good motto for all of us – and for the profession.'

– Andrew J. Oswald, University of Warwick, UK

'Fascinating and revealing. Although each has followed his or her own road, these scholars share a passion for economics and a commitment to the research enterprise. To paraphrase Steve Levitt, one of those interviewed: if you see economics as just another job, then you'll never be good at it. The best economists lie sleepless, gripped by their questions.'

– Joshua Angrist, Massachusetts Institute of Technology, USA

'This is a wonderful book of interviews with some of the most respected economists in the world. It is full of insights into academic life, and clearly conveys the joy of doing economics research.'

– Jon Levin, Stanford University, USA

'*The Art and Practice of Economics Research* is an interesting collection of interviews with 25 leading economists covering all broad fields of the subject and critically examining many questions of our time. The relaxed frame of the interviews gives interested parties exciting insights into the thoughts and concerns of leading economists and might well inspire some of the best young minds to continue with economics in their later lives.'

– Ernst Fehr, University of Zurich, Switzerland

The Art and Practice of Economics Research

Lessons from Leading Minds

Simon W. Bowmaker

New York University, USA

Edward Elgar

Cheltenham, UK • Northampton, MA, USA

Published by
Edward Elgar Publishing Limited
The Lypiatts
15 Lansdown Road
Cheltenham
Glos GL50 2JA
UK

Edward Elgar Publishing, Inc.
William Pratt House
9 Dewey Court
Northampton
Massachusetts 01060
USA

A catalogue record for this book
is available from the British Library

Library of Congress Control Number: 2012938062

ISBN 978 1 84980 846 0 (cased)
ISBN 978 1 78254 019 9 (paperback)

Typeset by Columns Design XML Ltd, Reading
Printed and bound by CPI Group (UK) Ltd, Croydon, CR0 4YY

Contents

Foreword

In this book, Simon Bowmaker offers a remarkable collection of conversations with leading economists about research in economics. He has selected a broad sample of the great economists of our time, including people whose perspectives span most of the major subdivisions of economics research, from micro to macro, from theoretical to empirical, from rationalist to behavioral. Here each offers his or her personal view of how one can do great work to advance understanding of economic problems.

This is a critical time for the economics profession, when it is clear that our understanding of economics is not good enough. Nobody can be complacent about the received wisdom in economics at a time when financial crises and a global recession have crippled the economies of so many nations. Demand for new advances in economic analysis has never been greater, and each economist here expresses a personal and professional commitment to help meet this demand.

While recognizing the need to learn more, however, we should also recognize a broadly shared appreciation of the value of what economists have learned in the past. Recent decades have seen major advances in many areas of economics which are discussed by experts in this book and which can provide the basis for the future advances that are so greatly needed. Furthermore, the difference between American unemployment near 10 per cent in today's Great Recession and American unemployment reaching 25 per cent in the Great Depression of the 20th century may be credited to better macroeconomic management that has been based on macroeconomics research since 1930. So even while recognizing the need for better understanding of economic instability, people in this book regularly express great confidence in the methodology of economics itself. The economists here use a wide range of different methods and tools in their research, but they cannot be divided into any ideological or political categories. They all are united in the goal of building a better understanding of economic problems by careful disciplined analysis of economic decisions and behavior. All here express broad confidence that the analytical methods of economics today can offer the best toolkit for advancing our understanding in the future.

A student here can find many role models for a career in economics. Any scholar's greatest asset is his or her personal algorithm for deciding what to study next, and so each of us must rely on our personal intuition about what would be interesting and what should be tractable in potential research questions. The economists here have many different ways of looking for creative insights and different styles of collaboration in research. But all express a view that the problems of economics are important, that the methods of economic analysis can provide powerful tools for studying these problems, and that there is much more work to be done. Nobody here has expressed any plan to retire from this quest for better understanding, but the student is welcome to join the quest.

Roger B. Myerson
University of Chicago, USA

Preface

This book contains 25 interviews with leading economists who are based in the United States and Europe. They are asked to reflect introspectively on their methods of working; provide insights into the process of scientific discovery, knowledge creation, and research dissemination in economics; and identify and evaluate specific contributions and findings from the discipline. The intended reader is someone at any stage of a research career in economics, whether you are a graduate student or a well-established scholar.

The interviewees were selected on several criteria, the most important of which were prominence within the economics profession, as measured by academic awards and citations, and diversity, as proxied by age, gender, research interests, research style, and institution. The interviews were all conducted face-to-face at 13 locations in the United States over the period June 2010 to August 2011.

Compiling this book was a deeply enriching and pleasurable experience. First and foremost, I learned an enormous amount about the work habits of some of the world's greatest economists. Second, it was an unexpected lesson in the complexities of the human condition. Failure, rejection, disappointment, frustration, courage, perseverance, and triumph are characteristics that burn brightly throughout this volume. Therefore, I hope that you find these interviews not only fascinating and stimulating, but also inspirational.

Acknowledgements

I would like to thank each of the interviewees in this book for their generosity in giving up their precious time to speak to me. I owe them a huge intellectual debt.

My colleagues at the Stern School of Business, New York University have provided tremendous support and assistance throughout this project. In particular, I am grateful to John Asker, David Backus, Luís Cabral, Allan Collard-Wexler, Tom Cooley, Heski Bar-Isaac, Joyee Deb, Ignacio Esponda, Alessandro Gavazza, Bill Greene, Kim Ruhl, Vasiliki Skreta, Dick Sylla, Laura Veldkamp, Paul Wachtel, Mike Waugh, Larry White, and Stan Zin. I would also like to thank Dan Hamermesh, Frank Heiland, John List, Steve Medema, Naci Mocan, Tim Salmon, David Skeie, Richard Upchurch, and Robert Wright for their help at various stages of this project. A special note of gratitude to my former PhD supervisor, Ian Smith.

Last, but not least, I am extremely grateful to Edward Elgar Publishing for sharing my enthusiasm for the idea behind this book.

Abbreviations

Many of the interviewees use the following abbreviations:

AER   *American Economic Review*
JPE   *Journal of Political Economy*
NBER   National Bureau of Economic Research
NIH   National Institutes of Health
NSF   National Science Foundation
QJE   *Quarterly Journal of Economics*

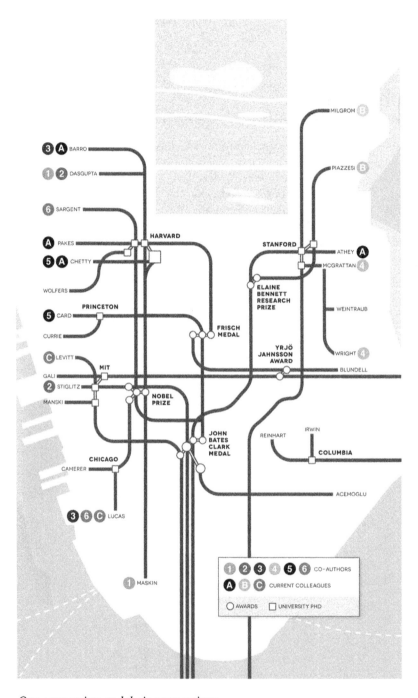

Our economists and their connections

Daron Acemoğlu (Massachusetts Institute of Technology)

Daron Acemoğlu was born in Istanbul, Turkey in 1967 and graduated with a BA in economics from the University of York, England in 1989 before obtaining both an MSc in mathematical economics and econometrics and a PhD in economics from the London School of Economics in 1990 and 1992 respectively. Between 1992 and 1993, he was a Lecturer in Economics at the London School of Economics and then moved to the Massachusetts Institute of Technology, where he currently serves as the Elizabeth and James Killian Professor of Economics.

Professor Acemoğlu's research interests include political economy, economic development, economic growth, economic theory, technology, income and wage inequality, human capital and training, labor economics, and network economics. His most-cited articles in chronological order include 'Was Prometheus Unbound by Chance? Risk, Diversification, and Growth', *Journal of Political Economy* (1997), co-authored with Fabrizio Zilibotti, 'Why do Firms Train? Theory and Evidence', *Quarterly Journal of Economics* (1997), co-authored with Jörn-Steffen Pischke, 'Why do New Technologies Complement Skills? Directed Technical Change and Wage Inequality', *Quarterly Journal of Economics* (1998), 'The Colonial Origins of Comparative Development: An Empirical Investigation', *American Economic Review* (2001), co-authored with Simon Johnson and James

Robinson, and 'Reversal of Fortune: Geography and Institutions in the Making of the Modern World Income Distribution', *Quarterly Journal of Economics* (2002), co-authored with Simon Johnson and James Robinson. His books include *Economic Origins of Dictatorship and Democracy* (Cambridge University Press, 2006), co-authored with James Robinson, *Introduction to Modern Economic Growth* (Princeton University Press, 2009), and *Why Nations Fail: The Origins of Power, Prosperity, and Poverty* (Crown Business, 2012), co-authored with James Robinson.

Professor Acemoğlu's academic awards include the 1996 *Economic Journal*'s best paper award for 'Consumer Confidence and Rational Expectations: Are Agents' Beliefs Consistent with the Theory?' co-authored with Andrew Scott, the inaugural T.W. Shultz Prize from the University of Chicago in 2004, the inaugural Sherwin Rosen Award for outstanding contribution to labor economics in 2004 from the Society of Labor Economists, the Distinguished Science Award from the Turkish Sciences Association in 2006, and the John von Neumann Award from Rajk College, Budapest, in 2007. He was also awarded the John Bates Clark Medal in 2005, given every two years by the American Economic Association to the best economist in the United States under the age of 40. Acemoğlu was elected as a Fellow of both the American Academy of Arts and Sciences and the Econometric Society in 2006, and was awarded an honorary doctorate from the University of Utrecht in 2008. He is currently Co-Editor of *Econometrica*.

I interviewed Daron Acemoğlu in his office in the Department of Economics at the Massachusetts Institute of Technology. It was late-afternoon of Wednesday, 14 July 2010.

BACKGROUND INFORMATION

What was your attraction to economics?

In high school, I was very interested in social issues like inequality and differences between nations, and I got the impression from reading books that economics was all about answering those kinds of big questions. And so I applied to the University of York in England to study economics and political science. Once I was there, I quickly realized that I did not like political science and that economics was not exactly what I thought it was. But I was sufficiently intrigued by economics and continued with it.

As a student, which professors were most influential or inspirational?

I learned a lot from all of my professors at York. I was particularly fortunate as a second-year undergraduate to work with Peter Lambert, who taught me how to work on a research paper. And then at the London School of Economics as a graduate student, I was lucky to work with great researchers like Kevin Roberts, John Moore, and Charlie Bean.

Why did you decide to pursue an academic career?

In high school, I was thinking about an academic career because I wanted to dig deeper into those topics that I mentioned earlier. I did waiver at points about whether it was the right thing to do. In England, I got the impression that being an academic also meant being poor, which was true in 1989 when I graduated from York. But I really liked the intellectual investigation and freedom that being an academic provides.

As a researcher, which colleagues have been most influential or inspirational?

Early on in my career at MIT, I didn't work that much with senior colleagues. I felt more comfortable working with people who were my age, like Fabrizio Zilibotti, Steve Pischke, and Rob Shimer, who was a graduate student here.

MIT is a very friendly, kind, and supportive environment. Olivier Blanchard and Bengt Holmstrom, in particular, were great senior colleagues in terms of giving advice. Although neither do work that is very closely related to my research, it was good to get some perspective about how the profession works.

GENERAL THOUGHTS ON RESEARCH

There is an increasing emphasis in many economics departments on applied research. Is this true at MIT?

MIT has always been at the forefront of applied research, but theory does play some role. My view is that economics is an applied discipline and so the trend that you mention is a very good one. But sometimes when you have such movements, it takes a while for you to find your footing and, right now, we're going through a phase in economics where the exact mixture of empirical and theoretical work is very much in the air. I think there needs to be more synthesis about how to do that best.

What is the value of pure versus applied research in economics?

Pure research is probably a bigger chunk of research in economics than in many other scientific disciplines because empirical work is hard and multifaceted. But it enables us to have a better conceptual and methodological approach to applied questions that people care about.

How would you describe the dialogue between theory and empirics in economics?

As I've just said, economics is an applied discipline. But the set of questions we're asking are too complex unless we look at them through the lenses of a well-defined, narrow conceptual framework. The most important dialogue between theory and empirics is that theory provides the conceptual framework for us to pose well-defined empirical questions and enables us to interpret the answers. Empirics, on the other hand, does (or should) continuously challenge theory and make us re-evaluate whether we have the right ingredients. Another equally important role of theory is to enable us to go from specific empirical findings towards generalizations, that is, the so-called 'external validity' of empirical findings. In the context of complex human interactions, changes in the environment or interventions often lead to reactions and counter reactions. In many economic theories, we can capture those as the equilibrium, or general equilibrium, effects. And so we need to rely on theory to guide us to the important equilibrium effects and then provide us with insights on how to understand and evaluate them. Of course, ultimately we must use empirical methods to gauge the importance of these equilibrium channels as well.

I realize this is the ideal, and it doesn't always work exactly as I've just described in practice. There is less dialogue between theory and empirics in economics today than I would like to see, and this is both because economics is still a developing, young science and because we tend to be too narrowly specialized.

How would you characterize your own research agenda and how has it changed through time?

I started out as what people might call an applied theorist; always beginning from a specific question, but trying to provide theoretical answers. And as I went forth in my career, I became more of an empiricist. Right now, my work is half-theoretical, half-empirical. I haven't been much into doing both theory and empirics in one paper because it's not always easy to communicate. But I think ultimately that's what I'd like to do; combine both organically in a single body of work.

Do you think it is important to have broad research interests?

The answer is both "yes" and "no". The answer is "no" if you look at it from the very selfish point of view of how you become successful in the profession. The profession values narrowness for a good reason and a bad reason. The good reason is that narrowness is a way of becoming an expert in a particular area. The bad reason is that, as in every other human activity, being part of a group or camp is valued, and you can achieve that by being narrowly focused.

My own view is that depth is very important. If breadth comes at the expense of not understanding a particular area, or even the background of a particular question, then that's a bad thing. On the other hand, breadth has a very important, often underplayed positive: a lot of ideas come from analogies or by combining them from different realms. And so breadth brings a fresh perspective to certain problems. Also, I work on a broad set of topics because that's what I enjoy; it's a consumption good.

Do you think there is any difference in the types of work done by researchers at different stages of their careers based on tenure concerns, publication requirements or other pressures? Should there be a difference?

I'll answer the first question! [*Laughs*]. Before I had tenure, I was told that I was pursuing a strategy that would destroy me; I was working on too many topics and I should narrow it down. That's the advice that many people get. Without tenure concerns, I think there would be more diversity in what an individual does.

IDEA GENERATION

Where do you get your research ideas?

There isn't a fixed formula. Sometimes you read an article in the newspaper that gives you an idea about topic X, you start thinking about topic X, and then that suddenly gives you an idea about topic Y. I generate a lot of ideas by thinking in terms of analogies. And, of course, there is also the natural progression of science. Ideas are very often based on those of other researchers, and you push them further.

At what point does an idea become a project that you devote resources to?

Good question. Most of the time, I use natural selection. When I get an idea, I'm normally very busy, and so if it's a good idea, it will recur to me, and if it's not a good idea, it will die down. Sometimes an idea comes to mind that is so relevant that I can create the time to work on it, but usually it takes several years for me to go from the idea stage to the project stage. In many cases, I don't even know where it will lead. Any initial probing that I do, such as background reading, is to see whether the idea has any useful direction. And so many of the ideas that don't turn into projects are those that I don't feel will mature into something that's concrete; they are a little loose.

IDEA EXECUTION

What makes a good theoretical paper? Can you give an example?

I think there are two kinds of good theoretical papers, and the profession values one kind versus another a little more but, in my opinion, they're both extremely useful. One kind looks at the existing problem and resolves open issues or takes it to another level in terms of depth of analysis. The obvious example would be Arrow–Debreu competitive equilibrium. Going back to Walras and Smith, people had some intuition about why it had to exist, and that it should have some optimal properties, but Arrow and Debreu nailed it.[1] First of all, they closed some open questions like the existence of equilibrium using a theorem, but in doing that, they also took it to a higher and deeper level of analysis by defining what the commodities are and what the structure of equilibrium has to be. I'm just picking that example because it's one that will be familiar to many people, but it's an extremely valuable contribution.

Another kind of theoretical contribution poses a new question, brings some formalism to that question, and broadens our horizon. That could be because, in posing the question, it generates some surprising answers that one would not have expected or, just by formalizing the question and what it answers, it might change our perspective on the issue. Sometimes people make the comment that some of the mathematics in economics is superfluous because you can say certain things in words, not in math. There is some truth to that, but I think by saying them in math, you can often make those things more explicit, and that enables people to build on them.

What makes a good empirical paper? Can you give an example?

Again, I would say there are two kinds of good empirical papers. One I would call an answer paper, and the other a challenge paper. The answer paper is the more straightforward one. It will answer a well-posed empirical question: What is the elasticity of labor supply? What is the value of one more year of schooling to an individual or to society? What is the effect of subsidies on school building? But the question can be asked at different levels of depth, such as at a purely descriptive level, which wouldn't be my favorite, or you can add some theoretical structure so that the empirical exercise gives generalizable answers or external validity.

There are also challenge papers that reject a well-known theory or put a puzzle on the table. Those kinds of empirical papers are very useful because they encourage people to dig deeper into a field. For example, there is a fairly simple theory of the equity premium, and Mehra and Prescott have written an empirical paper, which is essentially descriptive, showing that the model doesn't fit the data.[2] Perhaps, it's a little 'inside baseball'; this type of research often has a bit of that feel. On the other hand, it has led to a very large literature, and we have learned something from that process of probing deeper.

When you hit a brick wall on a project, do you continue to work on the problem or do you take a break and work on something else?

I do one of three things. Sometimes you keep on pushing a bit more because, if you give up too early, you'll never tackle difficult enough questions. More often, I take a break and come back to it six months later or two weeks later. But the third thing is that you might hit a brick wall because the problem is not well posed, and so it's useful to think about how you would change the questions. One example would be the early work that I was doing on human capital in labor markets; training and technology adoption and their interactions, and how this might lead to human capital externalities and so to underinvestment. I came to those problems thinking about unemployment; I had a hunch that a firm's choice of technology and training of workers had a lot to do with unemployment. I still believe that's true, but once I started working on those topics, I realized that, firstly, unemployment was not so interesting from a theoretical point of view, and secondly, the papers that I was writing on the topic were just paying lip service to unemployment.

Related to the previous question, when a project isn't going to turn out as hoped, do you scrap it or aim to send the work to a second-tier or field journal?

I scrap a project for every one that I complete. It's very time-consuming to finish a project.

What has been the biggest change during your career in how researchers in your fields conduct research?

I developed the courage to work on the things that originally attracted me to economics, and I was fortunate that the profession was already undergoing changes in that direction. When I was in the PhD program at the LSE, there was a field called political economy, although it was only dealing with a subset of issues. But then I met Jim Robinson, who was like-minded, and we started investing more in the field, and I think it has been fairly well received. That's been the biggest change in my own career trajectory.

I would also say that the profession is much more open to answering other kinds of big questions. Of course, it's not an isolated event. The Gary Becker revolution, which showed that economics could ask social questions that were outside the subject's narrow realm, was very important, and the major work that people did in political economy before then was obviously quite a big precursor.

Other economists might say, "Oh, the biggest change is that we now have much better empirical tools." I think that's important, but it's not a qualitative change. People had empirical tools before, and were aware of their pros and cons. And so while it's great that we now have faster computers and can run bigger regressions, the bigger change in my view is the conceptual structure that we bring to a problem.

Has your training from England influenced the way that you conduct research?

Yes. In England, the tradition is very non-technical, so I learned a lot of intuitive economic thinking. That had a big influence on me. Also, apart from just a few complementary disciplines, you don't study anything other than economics during the three-year condensed program. I think that's a bit of a shortcoming, and I had to make up for it by studying mathematics and history by myself.

THE WRITING PROCESS

Which aspect of the writing process do you find most difficult?

Writing in general is difficult, and in economics it takes a lot of learning. You have to be clear so that you don't force the reader to read the text several times. And you have to be economical, despite the fact that papers in our profession are overly long. It's not an easy process, and I found it very painful at first.

What steps have you taken during your career to improve the quality of your writing?

I just worked on it over and over again; that's the only way you can do it. I think it also helps having read a lot. I find generally that two kinds of students have great difficulty in writing well. There are those who haven't read much in literature or in history; their ability to process long prose has not been developed because they haven't invested enough. And there are those who haven't written enough mathematics. You can immediately see that there's a mathematical immaturity in some writings and a mathematical maturity in some others, which, again, is an entirely acquired trait.

Who proofreads your writing?

Sometimes I'll ask my assistant or my co-authors, including graduate students, to proofread it for grammar but, most of the time, nobody does it. I think it might help if I had more proofreading.

How do you split up the writing tasks among co-authors?

That is very specific to the project and to the co-author. Some co-authors may not be very experienced at writing, so I may end up doing quite a bit of it.

COLLABORATION

When you work with co-authors, how do you decide whom to work with?

Early in my career, it was people from the same PhD program, but once I started going to conferences and meeting others with a lot of common points, that also developed into co-authorships. Then, as your time becomes increasingly scarce, it becomes a good option to co-author with students and split the work, otherwise you end up doing everything and it just becomes infeasible at some point. Of course, I'm blessed that MIT students are fantastic.

How do you prefer to interact with them (e-mail, phone, or face-to-face)?

Certain things are much easier face-to-face, but I'm not a big fan of writing papers that way. Being some distance apart is certainly not a big constraint in my view.

RESEARCH ASSISTANCE AND FUNDING

How do you use undergraduate and graduate research assistants?

I used undergraduate RAs early in my career, but I decided that wasn't for me. You need to be a very organized person to have undergraduate RAs because they make a lot of mistakes. And they don't get things unless you explain it in a very, very clear manner, and I'm just not very good at that.

I use graduate RAs for two purposes. One is that when I have a paper that has mathematical derivations, I hire a graduate RA to check over it. The other purpose is for data work. Because I started as a theorist, I never became extremely quick at manipulating datasets. And so I have always relied on graduate RAs to put the data together. Often if the graduate student is heavily involved in the project, I will make them a co-author.

How important is funding for getting your work done?

If I didn't have any funding, I wouldn't have any RAs, and that would be a problem. But it's not a do-or-die thing. It's not like in engineering or physics where you need a big lab and a hierarchy of post-docs, PhD students, and undergraduates, although some people in economics have turned it into that.

Do you have any advice for a young scholar on the funding process?

Not really. The NSF is organized a bit like a journal; you submit and you get rejected [*laughs*]. But over the last decade, I've seen lots of alternatives for funding become available. I haven't made much use of them, but a lot of my colleagues have taken funding from NIH or from private sources and foundations. Being entrepreneurial helps. But I think too much effort is spent on funding, which is perhaps an inevitable consequence of empirical research becoming more important.

SEMINAR PARTICIPATION AND NETWORKING

What are the benefits to attending a seminar that is closely related to your work versus one that is not closely related?

I like the ones that are not so closely related to my work; I find that I learn more from those. But I view all seminars as a learning experience, and I try to get as much out of them as I can.

How important is professional networking to success in research?

Unfortunately, it's very important and an inevitable aspect of human relations. It's worse in some fields because you have to network with funding bodies and so on. In economics, it's about being part of a club, and sometimes that matters in our profession.

How does the researcher without extensive networks succeed?

It's very difficult. There are some very talented people in the UK and other parts of Europe, but they follow leading research indirectly by reading journals. You don't always get the full picture when you just look at an article, and you don't become known by doing that. And people who are part of a network tend to get better treatment in journals.

To what extent is the absence of departmental colleagues working in one's research area a major disadvantage?

It depends on how narrow or broad is your area. If you're a theorist, and there's nobody else in the department who's doing any theory, then that would be a major disadvantage; you wouldn't get the right conversations and you wouldn't be exposed to the right ideas. But if you're a decision theorist in a department where there are game theorists and contract theorists, I don't think it would be a big deal. In fact, it's good to talk to people who have different perspectives.

COMMUNICATION OF RESEARCH

How do you find the right balance between communicating your research at an early stage versus the close-to-finished stage?

In economics, the issue is a little different from medicine, where being first is very important. Unfortunately, journals take a long time to publish articles in our field, and so you have no choice but to post them on your website. Then the question is when to do this. I think first impressions matter. If you do it too early, people will read your paper when it's not polished in a way that tells the story appropriately, and that might backfire. And so I don't post my papers until I'm fairly comfortable with them.

What are the unique challenges to giving a seminar and how do you overcome them?

The main reason why you give a seminar in economics is to advertise the work. Originally, I thought the point was to get comments, but I now believe it's the networking; people get to see the work, they get to understand it, and you get to clarify what they don't understand. And once the work becomes known in seminars, it gets easier reception in journals, and people are more likely to adopt it for teaching. You can write great papers and post them on your website or submit them to journals, but that won't have the same impact as a seminar.

PUBLICATION

How do you decide upon the appropriate journal to send your research to?

The incentive structure in the profession is such that highly coveted publications are very valuable – that's why they're highly coveted [*laughs*]. And so everybody has an incentive to send their articles to *Econometrica*, the *AER* and the *QJE*. When I feel that my papers have a shot, that's what I try to do.

How would you best describe your approach to dealing with a 'revise and resubmit' request from a journal? How about an outright rejection?

Rejections happen all the time and you get very upset at the referees who didn't understand your paper, and at the editor who didn't treat you very well. A 'revise and resubmit' is a good outcome; no paper ever gets in straightaway. And so I believe in trying as hard as possible to be responsive and clear in the revision to satisfy the referees. That's the respectful thing to do when people have actually taken time to read your paper, and also because sometimes they might have a point that you didn't see. My papers tend to improve after refereeing.

Do you think that the current structure of the publication process in economics facilitates or impedes scientific understanding and knowledge production?

I think it's important that there is a hierarchy of journals because nobody has the time to read even one thousandth of the papers that are being produced. But there are two major problems with the process. One is that the economics profession has a terrible record in terms of speed in dealing with papers; it's despicably bad. There's no justification whatsoever for a journal to take one year on a paper. It's totally irresponsible of the editors. I'm an editor myself, and I know that it's not that hard to make sure that you respond to things on time. It's awful behavior to be playing with people's careers, particularly junior authors. I just cannot understand it. The profession does well on many, many other dimensions, but this aspect of it just infuriates me.

The other thing is that refereeing sometimes becomes very strategic. I see this as both an author and as an editor. People are very open to work that is a minor improvement on a particular research line that they are pushing, and they are very closed to anything that's outside that line. Again, bad editorship comes in there; you can condone it implicitly by not doing anything about it. I think it makes it really hard for new ideas to break into good journals, and can result in articles in those journals being full of meaningless extensions of past work.

What has been your best and worst experience during the publication process?

I have had many experiences that were awful. As a junior author, I had a paper at the *Review of Economic Studies* that went to four rounds of revision in almost four years and then a new editor came in and rejected it right away. For somebody at the beginning of his career, I felt like everything was going to collapse.

My best experience was having my first paper accepted in one of the top journals. That was more than three years after finishing my PhD – quite a while – and so when the *QJE* published my paper on human capital externalities, I felt like I'd finally broken the barrier.[3]

REFEREEING AND EDITING

What are the benefits to refereeing?

None. I enjoy reading papers, but being a referee requires you to read very carefully a paper that you may or may not be interested in. Refereeing is public service; the profession could not function if nobody did it.

Why did you decide to become Co-Editor of Econometrica?

Again, I view it as public service. I think the profession suffers in the hands of bad editors and, if I express that opinion, I feel that it's incumbent on me to do something about it when offered the opportunity.

What are the benefits to editing?

I don't see any benefit whatsoever; people hate you because you reject their papers.

TIME MANAGEMENT

How do you divide up your working day, both in terms of quantity and timing of different kinds of work?

I feel like I have a fireman's approach – there are fires to be put out – but I've lost control. Most of the time during the day, I'm unable to do anything other than answer e-mail. And so I often have to stay up at night in order to get research done. I don't have good time management.

How do you balance multiple research projects?

I'm pretty good at that, actually. I form a hierarchy in my mind as to which project is more urgent, and I don't have difficulty in switching from one to the other.

What is the optimal number of projects that you could be working on at any one time?

Whatever it is, I know that I'm beyond it. It would definitely be more than one because you get bored with one; it becomes too engrossing and all consuming.

How many projects are you working on at the moment?

Probably about 20.

How do you balance your personal and professional lives?

What personal life? My wife is also an academic, so we're both used to our personal lives being encroached upon by obligations. Things often fall out of balance to the point where my personal life becomes a residual claimant. And now I have a two-month-old son, so sleep has become a residual claimant.

REFLECTIONS AND THE FUTURE OF ECONOMICS

What have been the most important findings and contributions in your research fields during your career?

Going back a little before my career started, I think the most important innovations were made in the 1980s. The incomplete information game theory revolution deeply changed economics. Many areas have been swept by that; for example, we have a greater understanding of organizations and contracts. And then came the work on endogenous technological change. That's still a very, very fruitful area for further research and many questions remain unanswered, but I think we now have a framework that goes beyond what the non-economists bring to the table. I would also say that the empirical literature was absolutely transformed by more use of micro data and greater attention to the issues of causality and interpretation of estimates.

The one that I would pick after my career started is the political economy perspective where, instead of policy being treated as exogenous or conducted by benevolent governments, we think of where policy comes from, where the institutions that lead to policies come from, how we can link them to their historical roots, and how they are related to long-run economic growth. That paradigm shift has been quite important in my view.

What are the biggest challenges facing your research fields?

I think we have a relatively poor understanding of how credit markets work, as the recent credit crisis has demonstrated. And I also think the general area of short-term macro is a wasteland. But I'm a little less optimistic about how much progress we're going to make there because the problems are so difficult.

What are the strengths and weaknesses of your own research?

I'll give you weaknesses. The biggest weakness is that I still don't understand most of the questions that I work on. That's what keeps me going. I'm deeply passionate about political economy, but if you ask me, "You've done all this work on political economy; if the World Bank or a government comes to you and says, 'How should we use your research in order to improve something?'" I would be very hard-pressed. There is a big gulf between concept and practice.

In the end, do you think the profession has helped to bring out and shape your research for the best?

I think so. It's a great profession for pursuing different things. It's relatively open, combines mathematical and theoretical ideas with data, and opens up lots of frontiers. It's also been blessed by having some amazing leaders in many different generations that have really helped it go forward. I have benefited tremendously from being in this area, and I can imagine that, if I had ended up choosing something else, I would have been much more miserable.

Do you have any professional regrets?

I wish I had learned more in my undergraduate and graduate days. I spend a lot of my time reading because there are big holes in my knowledge. I always look at our PhD program here at MIT and think, "Wow, I wish I'd taken that program." The London School of Economics was very good by European standards, and it's improved a lot, but it was really sub-par compared to the US institutions in terms of what it invested in the students. That was something that I was able to make up for with hard work, but I still feel, "Oh, God, there is a hole in my training here."

I just find the British system very strange. Economics is a technical discipline and, to come up to speed, you need to have lectures where you go through problems. I don't think it's the job of a teacher to give you comments on an essay in a tutorial. Obviously, some people will disagree with that, but you can put that in the book – I don't mind.

What are your professional ambitions?

Just to keep on doing what I'm doing. I like what I'm doing.

How would you describe the state of economics today? Are you optimistic about its future?

The financial crisis has been good for us – of course, it's been terrible for society and the world would have been a better place without it, so I'm not trying to minimize that – but it has been like a wake-up call for our profession. To a non-trivial fraction of the profession, it has been a reminder that we know very little, and that there are lots of important questions. It has also increased people's interest in economics. And so that makes me optimistic that there will be plenty of interesting research to come. I think the empirical tools of economics are really being used, and there is also a useful debate about how to combine empirics and theory. That was long overdue and, hopefully, it will have an impact on how economics is done. And I'm very encouraged by the fact that a lot of young, talented people are doing political economy, and thinking about institutions and the big questions in economics.

NOTES

1. Arrow, K.J. and G. Debreu (1954), 'Existence of an Equilibrium for a Competitive Economy', *Econometrica*, Vol. 22, No. 3 (July), pp. 265–290.
2. Mehra, R. and E.C. Prescott (1985), 'The Equity Premium: A Puzzle', *Journal of Monetary Economics*, Vol. 15, No. 2 (March), pp. 145–161.
3. Acemoğlu, D. (1996), 'A Microfoundation for Social Increasing Returns in Human Capital Accumulation', *Quarterly Journal of Economics*, Vol. 111, No. 3 (August), pp. 779–804.

Susan Athey
(Harvard University)

Susan Athey was born in Boston, Massachusetts in 1970 and graduated with a bachelor's degree in economics, mathematics, and computer science from Duke University in 1991, before obtaining a PhD in economics from Stanford University in 1995. She was an Assistant Professor of Economics at the Massachusetts Institute of Technology between 1995 and 1997, an Associate Professor of Economics at Stanford University between 2001 and 2004, and since 2006 has been a Professor of Economics at Harvard University.

Professor Athey's research interests include mathematical methods and tools for theoretical modeling, auctions, industrial organization, econometric identification, and organizational design. Her most-cited articles in chronological order include 'Single Crossing Properties and the Existence of Pure Strategy Equilibria in Games of Incomplete Information', *Econometrica* (2001), 'Optimal Collusion with Private Information', *RAND Journal of Economics* (2002), co-authored with Kyle Bagwell, 'Identification of Standard Auction Models', *Econometrica* (2002), co-authored with Philip Haile, 'Monotone Comparative Statics under Uncertainty', *Quarterly Journal of Economics* (2002), and 'Collusion and Price Rigidity', *Review of*

Economic Studies (2004), co-authored with Kyle Bagwell and Christopher Sanchirico.

Professor Athey's academic awards include the John Bates Clark Medal (2007) and the Elaine Bennett Research Award (2000), given every other year to an outstanding young woman in any field of economics. She was elected as a Fellow of the Econometric Society in 2004. President Obama named Athey as an Appointee for Member to the President's Committee on the National Medal of Science in 2011.

Professor Athey's current professional activities include being Co-Director of the NBER Working Group on Market Design, as well as acting as an Associate Editor of *Theoretical Economics* and the *B.E. Journal in Theoretical Economics*. Since 2007, she has served as Chief Economist to Microsoft Corporation.

I interviewed Susan Athey in her office in the Department of Economics at Harvard University. It was mid-morning of Tuesday, 13 July 2010.

BACKGROUND INFORMATION

What was your attraction to economics?

I got started in computer science, but I didn't get excited about research there. When I discovered economics, it seemed like a wonderful opportunity to apply abstract ideas and mathematical techniques to something really important. And I was exposed early on to a policy problem through a summer job. My mentor at Duke, Bob Marshall, showed me how to take a real-world problem about procurement auctions (that I discovered in a summer job), and translate it into a possibility to change policy in a way that would make procurement more efficient. He ended up testifying before a Senate sub-committee on the research that I assisted in, and that was transformative for me. I got to see how you start with a real-world problem and use mathematics to break it down and explain what the policy problem is, and come up with the proposed solutions. And then we had a chance to go in and influence public policy. In the end, I think that's a lot of what the power of economics is about, and it was incredibly appealing to me.

Was Bob Marshall your most influential professor as an undergraduate? How about as a graduate student?

Bob Marshall made a big effort to pick up promising undergraduates. He got me a full-time research assistant job with summer funding and a little office. He was really influential in getting me into economics, which I had never considered. And I also hadn't considered the possibility of being a professor before. He was a big believer in mapping the real world into mathematical models and using rigorous techniques to analyze the problems, while emphasizing the institutional details and making sure that your work was going to be relevant. That's something that I evangelize today; I believe it's an important part of my own research to dig into applications deeply, while solving real-world problems with full rigor.

One thing Bob did for me as an undergraduate was to show me Roger Myerson's papers on mechanism design, and Paul Milgrom's seminal work and his PhD thesis.[1] I was just amazed; all those problems in one beautiful mathematical framework that delivered enormously powerful insight. Interestingly, today I explain the Revenue Equivalence Theorem to top executives at major firms, and I think back to when I first discovered it and understood it as an 18-year-old undergraduate. I think Bob did a great job in showing me work that would be very appealing to me.

Then in graduate school, my advisors – Paul Milgrom, John Roberts, and Eddie Lazear – were all very influential, and gave me enormous amounts of time and very close mentoring. They were great role models, as well as very hands-on advisors. And the influence of Bob Wilson, the grandfather of Stanford GSB and Milgrom's advisor, was everywhere.

Why did you decide to pursue an academic career?

It was the chance to change the world through research. I didn't think going in that the life of a researcher was likely to appeal to me. I saw myself as being in maybe more of a more social type of work environment. But I found, to my surprise, that even the solitary aspects of research were incredibly enjoyable. That said, I collaborate in all of my projects. I don't even think about writing a paper by myself. And I've done a lot of work advising students. So, I feel like the academic career still gives me the chance for that sort of personal interaction; it's a good mix.

Of course, if you're at a top school, being a professor is a dream job. I'm now getting to reap the benefits. You get called for policy questions, and when you're a recognized world expert, there's a world of possibilities open to you from that platform, and amazing opportunities to take your ideas and put them into practice.

As a researcher, which colleagues have been most influential or inspirational?

My advisors – Paul Milgrom and John Roberts – have maintained an influence on me throughout my career. As junior faculty, I leaned on them very, very heavily for support and guidance, like getting through the publication process, which I didn't find easy initially. And in the last couple of years, I've been very active in market design. There are a number of senior leaders in the field of market design who I think have done a great job in showing how you can spend time solving important applied problems without sacrificing any of the rigor of research or the excitement or quality of research. And when I think about people who have been very successful at maintaining that balance, Paul Milgrom is a great example, as well as Al Roth, Jon Levin, and Rob Porter. They are using both theory and empirical work and applying them in practice.

GENERAL THOUGHTS ON RESEARCH

There is an increasing emphasis in many economics departments on applied research. Is this true at Harvard?

I think Harvard has a healthy mix, although we might do better to have one or two more pure theorists. I like working at all parts of the spectrum.

What is the value of pure versus applied research in economics?

Some kinds of pure research are part of a food chain that eventually feeds more applied research. Roger Myerson's classic mechanism design paper is very abstract and difficult to read, but it's influencing practice decades later.[2] And some of the ideas in the other papers from that area are still being read by engineers at Google or Microsoft or Yahoo! as critical reading before they go into business meetings. Of course, very few theory papers have that kind of an impact, but in some sense, all the pay-offs are in the tail, and we're trying to come up with conceptual frameworks which have a lasting impact and help organize your thinking.

Bengt Holmstrom likes to describe theory as like a laboratory; you want to have a beautiful theoretical model that can be used like a laboratory. And then you change one assumption, and then you change another assumption, and each time you change one assumption, you've isolated an effect and created some insight. I would think of that as pure theory, not applied theory, in the sense that an applied theory model is tailored for a particular application, whereas some of these more basic models are used over and over again, and applied in many different circumstances. But there's also room for theory that isn't part of the food chain and is more of a philosophical exercise.

How would you describe the dialogue between theory and empirics in economics?

When I go to find an economic problem, I like to organize my thinking about an applied problem using a conceptual framework, whether that's formalized as an explicit theory model or whether the problem is simple enough that it can be conceptualized verbally. I certainly think that having a clear and crisp conceptual framework of the data-generating process will greatly improve the quality of the work; the empirical methods that will be appropriate, the limitations of those methods, and the generalizability of the empirical results.

One of the things that I love about economics is that all the different approaches have their place and value. And when there's an economic problem, I come to it and ask about the best approach. Is it a randomized field experiment? Is it a structural model that's going to give me counter-factuals? Is it a combination of those two things? Is it a theoretical model because we don't really understand what's happening here? And one of the things that I love about market design is that most of the scholars in that area are not religious about methods, and most of them have developed expertise in applying multiple methods to problems; it's all about the best way to answer the question. Most sub-fields that are motivated by policy, and trying to get the right answer, tend to not think about methodology as a religion, but as a means to an end. And they will learn and develop expertise in the methodologies that are best suited to their applications.

How would you characterize your own research agenda and how has it changed through time?

I've gone through phases. I certainly had a period when I was more exclusively focused on theoretical research than I am right now. But, in some sense, the things that first appealed to me about economics when I was an undergraduate are exactly the things that I'm doing today. And so I'm finding real-world problems and using whatever tools in the spectrum of methodology are useful to tackle them. And I'm most excited when I'm doing something that's going to change the world. Right now, I'm working closely with Microsoft to implement changes to their online advertising options based on my research. That's incredibly exciting and motivating. And when I write a paper, I know I'm writing about something important, and I know I understand the real-world issues as well as anybody. I have a lot of conviction that what I'm doing is, in fact, useful in changing the world, as well as intellectually interesting research.

Do you think it is important to have broad research interests?

I think it's important to develop expertise. And so the question is what you develop expertise in. Early on, it's important to develop expertise in a field so that you can understand what it means to have a depth of knowledge, and to master a set of techniques and methods so that you aren't just applying what somebody else did, but understanding the limitations of what you're doing. Specialization is crucial to have any depth in your work and to make a lasting impact.

My research is probably too broad. And I've compensated for that by working harder [*laughs*]. I've worked very, very hard over time to develop multiple methodological expertises so that when I come to a problem, I can use whatever the appropriate tool is without sacrificing quality and depth. That took many years; to develop theoretical skills that were deep; to develop empirical skills that were deep; to develop structural modeling skills that were deep; and recently doing some field experiments. Each of those endeavors requires writing research papers, advising students, refereeing papers, and teaching; the whole spectrum of activities that are required to become a thoughtful and critical scholar of a certain area.

But if I'm going into an area where I still feel like I'm not deep enough, I will certainly bring on collaborators. So, I've collaborated with econometricians on papers that required deeper econometrics than I had. I could contribute fully on the conceptual parts, but my co-authors brought the knowledge of asymptotic theory, for example. I want the papers to be high quality. If I have an econometric theorem in my paper, I want it to be meeting the standards of the highest-quality econometrics. And therefore I wouldn't really attempt to do that without a co-author who had that depth.

Do you think there is any difference in the type of work done by researchers at different stages of their careers based on tenure concerns, publication requirements or other pressures? Should there be a difference?

I did empirical work while I was junior faculty and it was certainly a risk; it could have slowed me down towards tenure because it took so much time to develop the expertise that I didn't have coming out of graduate school. There was a lot of time spent learning every aspect of the process, and the clock was ticking. When you come up for tenure, you are only judged by the very best papers. And so if I had spent all that time on the empirical papers, but I hadn't gotten them into the very top journals, I don't think they would have helped my tenure case.

One thing about specialization that's very important to keep in mind for younger scholars is that unless you become very good at something, it doesn't really contribute to your tenure case. A side project can be quite fun and interesting, but if you're working in, say, industrial organization and you write a paper in macro, then the IO people may not even comment on that macro paper in their evaluation letters, and it may not count at all for your tenure case. For something to matter for tenure, it has to be good enough so that it's noticed by people who will write your letters. And it has to be a big enough part of your portfolio so that, in fact, letters are requested by experts in that area. You can easily end up in a situation where the IO people say, "She's a theorist who's interesting to us," and the theorists say, "She's an IO person who's interesting to us," but nobody says, "You're the best at what I do"; and you need that for tenure.

One thing that I advise people to do when they have broader interests, or they don't fit neatly into a box, is to look for a set of similar senior people at peer institutions. For instance, Rob Porter is an example of someone like me; he's done theoretical work on collusion and empirical work on auctions. I've done those things, and he will like my portfolio of work and be able to evaluate it. If there are enough similar senior people at peer institutions, then your portfolio is probably fine, even if it's eclectic.

I would say that in the market design area, there's a large group of people with that set of skills; for example, me, Jon Levin, Phil Haile, and Ken Hendricks. And as more people get tenure who have a similar portfolio, it becomes easier for junior people to follow this path that has a breadth to it and that doesn't fit into traditional fields. But without that, you can be lost [*laughs*].

IDEA GENERATION

Where do you get your research ideas?

They've come in two ways. The first one has been real-world problems. My very first research was looking at timber auctions as an undergraduate. Then in graduate school, my first theory paper was about mentoring and diversity, and that came out of my experience noticing that some of the male students were getting better research assistant opportunities because they were participating in men-only athletic events with faculty. That observation turned into an *AER* paper.[3]

My next set of papers were about organization theory. I was observing organizations in action and I was interested in incentives, how organization worked and so tried to model those.[4] And then my theory work came from working on applied theory and being somewhat dissatisfied with using special models and functional form assumptions. There was part of me that wanted to see the bigger picture, the abstract ideas that were behind the special results I was proving in applied theory papers. And so a lot of my pure theory came from noticing patterns and common problems that were coming up in applied theory that could benefit from a clearer conceptual insight.[5]

And my econometric theory was very similar. I'd be working on an empirical paper, and I'd say, "How can I think about the conditions under which this empirical approach would work?" And I would read papers with informal descriptions of the reasoning, and I would be dissatisfied. And so I would say, "Let me write this down, and if I do it formally, maybe then I'll understand." As I started writing things down, I would realize that there was a deeper, more general idea. And I felt that other people would benefit from having that clarity of conceptual insights in their own empirical work, and so I wrote it into econometric theory papers.[6] Almost all of my very theoretical papers have been motivated by trying to solve an applied theory problem, and realizing that I would have more clarity about the specific problem if I understood the generality.

Do your research ideas ever come from your consultancy work?

Oh, sure. Right now, I'm working on market design, where the goal is to design markets to make them work more efficiently. Some of the big successes of this field have been in public auctions. Why is that? Because they're often big, they're often important, they're actively designed, and the government asks for expert help. And so when you're asked for expert help, you tend to figure out what we know and what we don't know. And when you understand what we don't know, then you develop new theory and test it in order to see how it's going to work.

The most recent new wave of auction design has been coming from large firms in the private sector like Google, Microsoft, and Yahoo! Fortunately for us, they have been open and interested in getting the advice of academic economists to design their markets. It's a little bit more awkward because it's a private firm doing these things rather than a government, but the public policy implications are fairly similar. The size of the online search advertising market is somewhere around $30 billion, and the advertiser surplus and the consumer surplus that's mediated through that are on the same order of magnitude. You're talking about an overall economic value going through the platforms in the range of $100 billion.

It's important because it's big, but also because it affects public policy, as people find their information through search engines. And the way that the auction is designed affects what information people get, and it affects whether certain businesses even have access to consumers, because the businesses have to succeed in the auctions in order to be visible to them. Of course, the firms have their own private interests, but their decisions have large efficiency implications.

Right now, most of my ideas are coming out of that general area. I've been writing some empirical papers and applied theory papers, and it's been fascinating.[7] It's impossible to run out of ideas, because every day there's a new problem that comes up that needs to be solved.

At what point does an idea become a project that you devote resources to?

I tend to hold a pretty high bar on a project. Either I need to see the path to it being a strong submission to a top-five journal, or if it's a smaller idea, then I need to see a path to a specific outlet that I could publish in, like the *Papers and Proceedings*, which has been a nice outlet for shorter applied theory papers, or a conference might be a good outlet for shorter, more succinct points that I want to make.

If I don't see either of those outlets, then I'll typically write something up and leave it on my website, but I won't devote resources to taking it to publication. And that's partly because I have plenty of papers on my vita, but also because it's an enormous amount of work to put a paper through the publication process. It's not any easier to put a paper into a second- or third-tier journal than into a top journal; you still have to do the revisions, write the responses to the referees, and read the galleys.

I'm happy to explore lots of projects, but before I really jump into them, I keep refining and generalizing the idea until I see the path that's going to have a fairly major impact.

IDEA EXECUTION

What makes a good theoretical paper?

I think there are a number of categories of impact that a theoretical paper can have. One is that it's a method or a tool that will be applied by other people. If you're part of a literature, you'll often be aware of the need for a method or a tool; there's a result that's open, like an existence theorem or a comparative statics theorem. And so you can see clearly that if you solve this problem, people will use it.

A second category of paper is about providing insight – a new idea – and that's very hard. A good, experienced economist often is pretty familiar with a lot of ideas. The one question I ask about a theoretical paper is: Would you need to see the model after reading the abstract? For many applied theory papers, a good, experienced applied theory economist doesn't need to read the model. They could write the model in about a day once they read the abstract.

Papers like that can be still excellent and have a big impact, but the idea should be pretty important in terms of changing the world. If it's not, and you didn't really need the model, then you kind of wonder what you're doing [*laughs*]. And so, in some areas like, say, organization theory, incentive theory, or information theory, the basic trade-offs are well understood, and it's very hard to have a brand new idea. That's one reason why some of those areas of applied theory have slowed down and haven't been making the general interest journals as often.

I think there are also theoretical papers that are just very elegant. Those papers may not have much of a lasting impact, but the theory community will appreciate a paper on a fairly narrow point if it has a very subtle and elegant proof of a major theorem.

A final thing would be something that pushes the literature forward. For example, we understood a certain class of problems, and now we understand a more general class of problems. Or, there's a class of models that's very important from an applied perspective, and so here's two or three more important facts and theorems about that class of models. Those papers may not be transformative in the sense that they didn't invent a model, but they can be very important.

And I guess I didn't say a class of papers that everybody wants to write: inventing a new model and coming up with a new laboratory. Everybody wants to come up with an elegant, flexible model that can be applied in lots of different situations. That's a beautiful laboratory and incredibly valuable. But only a few people have succeeded in building these workhorse models. Bengt Holmstrom's moral hazard models are one example.

What makes a good empirical paper?

Again, I think there are various categories of good empirical papers. The first question is whether the methodology is right for the question, and the second question is whether the data can identify the question that you're asking. That same second question can be posed of a fairly simple, empirical model like a regression, and it can also be posed of a structural model, where you're trying to estimate the parameters of a theoretical model. In either case, the answer might be "yes" or "no" to whether the data can estimate accurately the parameters that you're interested in, or whether it is the assumptions that you've put into the model that are actually driving your parameter estimates.

And so a good empirical paper chooses exactly the right method for the question and an empirical setting where the data is rich enough and has enough variation to answer the question. And, of course, you would like it to answer a specific question that is important, or one that's going to push forward our general knowledge in economics.

When you hit a brick wall on a project, do you continue to work on the problem or do you take a break and work on something else?

A lot of times when you get to something hard, you need to find a couple of days to sit down and focus on it and don't do anything else. It's not productive to just take an hour here and there and keep circling around something that you've gotten stuck on before.

Do you scrap many projects?

Yes, I have tons of abandoned projects.

What has been the biggest change during your career in how researchers in your fields conduct research?

In the early '90s when I was in graduate school, I think pure theory and applied theory were more unified. They were coming up off the success of the '80s when Paul Milgrom's work on auctions was really central to theory, and when game theory and industrial organization were developing hand-in-hand. For a while, applied theory was making methodological contributions in the process of doing the work, but then after a lot of those basic ideas were worked out, some people wanted to go on and do more foundational work, and other people were really interested in the problems. And so I would say the field of theory has gotten a little more polarized or divided than it was in the early '90s.

I feel like there have been enormous advances in the quality of empirical work in all fields, but especially in industrial organization, over the last 20 years or so. A long time ago, people were very divided. There were those who did reduced-form empirical work and there were others who did structural empirical work. There was a lot of antipathy between the groups, and debates about what was the right way to go. But students are now better educated in all of the different kinds of empirical work. They have an appreciation for things like identification of models, being very clear about which assumptions are important for your conclusions, and which assumptions are simplifying assumptions. There's been a huge improvement in the clarity of thought, in tolerance, and in education across different approaches.

THE WRITING PROCESS

Which aspect of the writing process do you find most difficult?

Polishing – once you know what you want to say and then making sure every single detail is right. It's just so tedious, especially if you've developed something over a long period of time and you've changed notation. I like my papers to be very, very clean and elegantly written, but it just takes so much time to achieve that.

What steps have you taken during your career to improve the quality of your writing?

Economic theory in the area of mechanism design and auctions is pretty sloppy with notation. And early on, my own writing also inherited that sloppiness. But about two or three years into my career as junior faculty, I just had an epiphany that this was confusing and created needless ambiguity. And so I decided almost overnight that I wanted every paper to use better and correct notation. And once I noticed it and observed it, I got very frustrated when other people didn't do it as well. I think I really just came to appreciate the value of careful notation. For example, when you write an expectation, what's the random variable? That's a simple thing, but it can cause a reader to get completely confused. And one thing that I also learned to do was to get two or three technical graduate students to proofread all of my papers.

How do you divide up the writing tasks among co-authors?

That depends on the co-authors. I tend to want to have a substantial final edit, though. I'm probably more particular about writing clarity and grammar; I want every term to be formally defined, and I want to use the terms consistently.

COLLABORATION

When you work with co-authors, how do you decide whom to work with?

That's varied through my career, but, as I mentioned earlier, I want to have my work at the highest-possible quality. And so if I'm going outside of my area of core knowledge, I want to collaborate with a really outstanding person who has the right set of skills. Even if I thought I could spend the time to become the expert on a new area, it's more fun to be taught by someone else. And that's both on technical, as well as substantive, areas.

As I've gotten more senior, I do like to work with younger people who are more motivated to get papers out quickly, who are out at every conference publicizing the work, who are up to speed on the 'very latest', and who are buddies with the other young people who are doing the most work. I'd like to continue that trend of working with younger co-authors. I have young children, and so it's harder for me to travel.

How do you prefer to interact with your co-authors (e-mail, phone, or face-to-face)?

It's a lot of fun to work with people face-to-face, and especially for a new co-author early in a project. But once a project gets going, being face-to-face isn't important.

What are the main challenges associated with collaborative work and how do you overcome them?

Just keeping the projects moving forward. With multiple busy people, it is easy to let things go for months, especially once the fun part of conceiving the paper is done.

RESEARCH ASSISTANCE AND FUNDING

How do you use undergraduate and graduate research assistants?

I use graduate research assistants for a couple of different things, apart from the proofreading that I mentioned earlier. If I'm doing a theory project where I haven't got all the results that I want, I find it very useful to have people do simulations or examples. I will have a conjecture, and to see if it's true, I'll ask them to find some parameter values, or to put in a functional form to see if they can find a counter-example. I think that's fun for students as well. It gives them a chance to engage in a theoretical project and really think about the problem.

On empirical projects, I use graduate students very differently. They're invaluable; they can do everything from cleaning data to running regressions. When I'm doing work myself, I'm busy and going quickly, and not always documenting and keeping careful track. And so I'll often prototype some kind of empirical analysis, and then have a student assistant write a full program that starts from the beginning and loads in the data and every step is documented.

I do like to play with data myself and make sure I understand what I'm doing, and I get my ideas that way. But the graduate students really keep it organized, make sure there are no mistakes, and that it's all replicable. Because they have a lot more time, they'll often discover things that I wouldn't have discovered. And so I might give them very open-ended exploratory tasks, and they then discover anomalies in the data or other things. Undergraduates can be used that way, too, but they need a lot more structure.

One thing I have discovered recently is that some faculty have hired full-time research assistants, and Microsoft Research has done this for me. And I have learned that, while there's a lot of work to hire them and a fair bit of work to administer them, a full-time research assistant is much more than twice as productive as two half-time research assistants. They're just much more motivated and focused. And so, if it's possible, that's an incredibly useful way to go. But it's a huge risk because, of course, if the person doesn't work out, you spend a ton of money on nothing.

How important is funding for getting your work done?

For a long time, I would say it was only moderately important, but for empirical projects now it's much more so. Because I have full-time research assistants, I'm doing things I would never have been able to do otherwise; I'm taking on many more empirical projects, and projects that are much more data-intensive.

Do you have any advice for a young scholar on the funding process?

I've been on the NSF Panel and know that it's very competitive among young people. People needed to submit projects at exactly the right stage, so they had to have some part of the work really well developed and then some parts that hadn't been done yet. It was difficult.

Looking for good support from your institution is a very important negotiating tactic. Sometimes, young scholars are negotiating more on things like salary, which is less important. Getting an extra $1000 or $2000 isn't a big deal because you still can't hire a research assistant for that. But having enough money to actually hire a research assistant is a big difference in your productivity.

SEMINAR PARTICIPATION AND NETWORKING

What are the benefits to attending a seminar that is closely related to your work versus one that is not closely related?

One of the biggest challenges for me is too many seminars, because I work between fields. For a long time, I was doing double duty; I was going to IO and theory seminars, and also to both the student lunches and the faculty seminars. At some point, I realized I couldn't do double duty and get all of my other work done. And so then I started trying to split my time, but that leads to its own problems because, of course, the people in each field feel like you're shirking [*laughs*].

I do see a lot of young people spending so much time going to seminars. You have to put a limit on it, and figure out which ones are really important. You have your whole career for consumption. You have to spend some time locked in your office finishing your papers.

How important is professional networking to success in research?

I think it's very important. Again, because you don't have all the time in the world, you have to be very strategic and selective about it. One piece of advice I give to young people is to, about once a year, write down the list of 20 people who could write tenure letters for you. Figure out what conferences are they going to, and what institutions are they at. That helps set your priorities.

It's not that your whole life is about getting tenure letters, but it's also correlated with a lot of other things. The leaders in your field will be from peer institutions or better institutions than yours. Their choice of conferences to attend probably tells you something about what's important. You want to learn from those people, and from people like them. And so rather than giving 15 or 20 random seminars in a year, like I did during my junior faculty year on leave, you want those seminars to help advance your career among your pool of letter writers and referees.

Generally, you will find those letter writers and referees in the same place. If for some reason there's a divergence, you also have to think about who your referees are going to be. And young people sometimes think that the refereeing is random and anonymous, but, in fact, it is quite predictable. As an editor, you look at the references in the paper, and you try to find the experts in the area. It's actually pretty easy to figure out who the 15 or 20 people would be that might referee a particular paper.

Again, you might think that there's a bunch of referees and tenure letter-writers out there who, when given your paper or packet, will dutifully sit down and spend an entire day reading your paper or two days reading everything in your packet. That's just an illusion. A lot of people will do things very quickly, and they'll base a lot of their efforts on things they already know. And so if you've presented in front of them, if you've talked to them, if you've explained things to them, if you've gotten their questions, and incorporated their feedback in advance, you're going to be much, much more successful in the process. But you have a limited amount of time, and you've got to be in your office writing your papers, too. You have to figure out the highest-impact ways to achieve those objectives.

To what extent is the absence of departmental colleagues working in one's research area a major disadvantage?

It's certainly a disadvantage. You can get a much different kind of feedback from colleagues, and much earlier on. It's great fun to be somewhere where there are five or six people in your area. If you can get that, that's golden. But most people can't get that. And so there are two other things that are really important to me. One is a buddy, a younger person. They don't have to be exactly in my field, but someone who I can go to lunch with, talk to, bounce ideas off, or give me quality feedback. You don't need ten buddies, but if you don't have one, you'll be miserable. And the second thing you need is a senior person who is invested in you and wants you to succeed. Now, you may not get a perfect buddy and a great senior person in the same place, and then you have to trade those off. But those are the two things that are probably most important.

COMMUNICATION OF RESEARCH

How do you achieve the right balance between communicating your research at an early stage versus the close-to-finished stage?

I see young people making two kinds of mistakes: not presenting until something is done, and presenting something that's half-baked. Generally, you have to realize that when you go out and give a seminar, you need to be prepared that people in the audience will have their main impression of you formed by that seminar. If there's a group that you regularly present to, then it's a little bit safer, but the world is full of Bayesians – people will update a lot based on one signal. Something that you present doesn't have to be done, but you better be intelligent about it; you better be very clear on what you have done and what you haven't done. And the part that you have done had better be good. Senior people and good people will be very happy to give you feedback on things that aren't done. They'll respect the research process. But what you don't want to do is have something where the whole idea doesn't make sense, where you haven't thought it through, and where people will feel like you're wasting their time, or they'll just decide that you're stupid.

It's important for young people to practice. They practice for the job market, but probably underestimate the importance of doing it later. You see a lot of people mismanage their time. I find it very difficult to practice [*laughs*]. It's a difficult thing to discipline yourself to do, but, until you become really comfortable and fluent, it's crucial. And you also need to think from the perspective of the audience, particularly in terms of what questions people might have.

PUBLICATION

How do you decide upon the appropriate journal to send your research to?

First of all, you want to look at the response time of the journals. There are some journals that are very poorly run, and you just shouldn't submit to them as a young person. But that can vary by editor; a journal can be generally good, but one editor is better than another. And so if you can find out about the specific editor, that's the most important piece of information. Then I look to see if I'll get an expert editor. Is the editor going to be positively disposed to the paper? Will the editor know how to find good referees? Sometimes, that's a problem. *Econometrica* has often not had an expert in empirical IO, for example. You might have a complicated paper, and the editor is outside the field. If the referee says something that doesn't make sense, you can't count on the editor to be able to fully appreciate that, and discern the good comments from the bad ones. That's a pretty risky strategy, but sometimes you have to do it to go for a top journal.

Beyond that, you look at the associate editors. If you're coming from a very good school, the editor will probably send it to one of the associate editors. And so you can pretty well figure out who one of the referees will be, as associate editors have a lot of influence.

You also want to think about the audience of the journal. Again, you have your list of 20 potential letter-writers or referees. Look at where they're publishing. That's going to tell you something about what journals your target audience respects, and what journals they read.

When you're junior and trying to get tenure, all that matters are the people who evaluate you [*laughs*]. And so your audience is the set of experts in your area. As you advance in your career, you have a lot more flexibility about who you want to reach. And then there are trade-offs. I've been reaching more of the computer science community lately, so I've been giving a lot of talks at computer science conferences. As a result, I've been going to fewer economic theory conferences. My influence grows in one area and shrinks in the other. Once you're tenured, it's just a matter of personal preference of the group in which you think you'll have the most influence.

How would you best describe your approach to dealing with a 'revise and resubmit' request from a journal? How about an outright rejection?

You make sure that you thoroughly and carefully address every single referee comment, and prepare a very succinct and easy-to-read response to the editors. On occasion, you can ask for clarification from the editor, especially if you think there's a mistake in the referee report or if you have a real disagreement. Editors have many, many initial submissions, but they don't have many 'revise and resubmits' on their desks. Generally, they want to publish a good paper, so I think once you have a 'revise and resubmit', they will be more willing to work with you. You shouldn't be a pest, but if there's a real issue, you shouldn't be afraid to communicate with them for clarification. Again, you have to remember that the editor probably handled 20 papers on the day that he wrote your letter and may not have thought about it that hard. And so, rather than just sitting there and being frustrated, you can communicate.

I would not protest an outright rejection, unless you have a real, factual problem. You don't want to develop a reputation for protesting, although some people have protested successfully many times. But I don't advise it as a general principle. Generally, when you do get a rejection, you want to think hard about the referee reports. Sometimes, I have decided that I got the wrong referees; they weren't my audience. And so I'm going to send it somewhere else where the referees are the right audience. And maybe I need to revise my introduction and my cover letter to make sure that the editor gets the clue of who my audience is.

On the other hand, you don't want to be too thick-headed. Sometimes, referee reports are thoughtless and crazy, but a lot of times, there was something you could have done that would have reduced the chance of getting that report. Again, whether that is signaling better who the referees should be, or that the way you wrote and presented things allowed someone to persist in an incorrect assessment.

Do you think that the current structure of the publication process facilitates or impedes scientific understanding and knowledge production?

I find my own research being influenced just by the large fixed cost of publication. That's sad. I don't do projects that I think would be fun because the fixed costs are so large and also the delays are long. It's so hard to get motivated to come back to the paper after you're done with it – you've presented it, everybody's seen the results, everybody knows the results, people are citing the results, and still you're being tortured through this awful revision process that may or may not be that productive.

I'm not a huge fan of our current process. I wish it were faster, and I wish we had more outlets for shorter papers that have faster turnaround. In computer science, they have another model where people publish almost primarily in conference volumes that are very carefully refereed, but often they're getting their papers published within six months. It's kind of frustrating to see the pace at which they're going relative to our pace. On the other hand, the computer science articles are often shorter and much more incremental. I think that our format of longer, more substantive papers is fine. I like the fact that we spend longer on our papers, that they're more complete and often deeper. But I wish once you have spent two years writing it, you would be done with it [*laughs*].

What has been your best and worst experience during the publication process?

One thing I've noted is that different sub-fields have very different standards of refereeing. I've had papers that have sailed through the refereeing process that weren't my best papers, but the referees and editors loved them. And I've had papers that I thought were fabulous that have struggled in the refereeing process, even though they were clearly having an influence outside of that. The often negative correlation between the ease of publication and the quality of the paper is frustrating, even though the publication process eventually has been kind to me and I'm a beneficiary of being at a leading institution, which gives you much better treatment in the process. I think a few editors have worked very hard to create good experiences, and when that happens, I'm forever grateful.

But as junior faculty, I submitted a paper to the *Journal of Political Economy*. I had a year to get one referee report, which was a 'revise and resubmit'. And then I sent it back, and I waited another year to get a single referee report from a different referee that was a rejection on completely different grounds. That was a really big setback for me. I'll never forget it. It was just sloppiness and laziness on the part of the editor.

REFEREEING AND EDITING

How do you decide upon whether or not to accept a refereeing job? What are the benefits to refereeing?

Early on, refereeing helped me write my own papers because it made me understand the mindset of a referee. And so when I write a paper, I immediately think "Okay, what are the first two paragraphs of the referee report that are going to get this paper published in a top journal?" And if I haven't written that for the referee in the introduction and the conclusion, then I've screwed up [*laughs*]. There's nothing like being a referee to help you appreciate that.

I think refereeing is also very good for forcing you to think more deeply about papers and not just read them superficially. But there can be limits. For a while, I was probably refereeing about 30 papers a year, but when I had my first child, I slowed down on refereeing. I realized it was a lot more fun to go to the zoo on Saturday morning than it was to write a referee report [*laughs*]. It's good to have in mind a budget of how much time you want to spend on refereeing, and how many referee reports you want to do every year, and try not to go over that budget. Also, if it's a journal that I don't usually interact with, I feel that I don't really owe them a lot of service.

How do you decide upon whether or not to accept an editing position? What are the benefits to editing?

I thought very hard about whether I wanted to be an editor. And I was an editor most recently for a year, and I found it not to be that compatible with my work style, because it was difficult to meet my very high standards all the time. It was a constant guilt-inducing thing and I felt it was always hanging over my head. I think the people who succeed at it are able to compartmentalize it, are very organized, and they have a certain time every week they do it. That time is blocked, and they get in and they focus on it. And I wasn't able to be that structured. And so sometimes it would build up, and I would feel terrible about it. And then other times I would be really on top of it, but then it might interfere a lot with my research. I may revisit it later in my career when I would be willing to make more sacrifices.

When I think about editing, there are a couple of ways to influence the profession outside of your own research. One of them is to advise students, to teach, and to try to do a lot of mentoring. Another is to edit. And, of course, you have some people who've done a lot of both, like Rob Porter and Glenn Ellison. But I found that I had somewhat limited time, and so I thought if I was going to focus on one thing, I would rather do more direct mentorship of the students. And at a school like Harvard, I'm getting fabulous students.

TIME MANAGEMENT

How do you divide up your working day, both in terms of quantity and timing of different kinds of work?

I think as you get more and more senior, the time management gets to be harder and harder because everybody wants a piece of your time, and you have so many different things that are non-research pulling at you. And so now I rely on co-authors and research assistants to help me manage my research time. I have scheduled meetings with co-authors and with research assistants. I have deadlines. When a research assistant finishes something, I give them another task. That forces the research time to be spent, and it keeps the projects moving. And that's one reason to have young, motivated co-authors who are just making sure that the ball moves forward.

When I was younger, after dinner I did no administrative work and no refereeing. And so then my day ended up shifting; I would do research from 7:00 pm to 2:00 am every day. That time was blocked. I would know that I had five or six hours in front of me completely uninterrupted. And that was very, very helpful for me because I would tackle the harder, more difficult tasks that you would otherwise procrastinate on.

One thing that I've done that was extremely helpful, and I highly recommend, is that all of my student meetings are electronically scheduled through a sign-up sheet. I'll send out an e-mail to my students to say I'm having office hours and, during the year, it's at the same time every week. The students sign up (they don't e-mail asking for an appointment) and they come back-to-back. I might meet with 10 or 11 students in a row – boom, boom, boom.

If they have written work, I try to read that out of the time, but I'll also spend the blocks with them just sitting there reading the paper and commenting verbally. That saves me time, and it actually gives them better quality feedback on some things like exposition. You can write a comment that says, "This is unclear," but if they're sitting with me, I can explain to them why the paragraph isn't working, and I'll give them more color as to what the problems are.

At the end of the day, I go home exhausted. But if I didn't focus and concentrate my students in a specific time interval, I could ruin my entire week.

How do you balance multiple research projects?

I always have had too many [*laughs*]. It's nice to have a suite of projects where each of them requires a different kind of work, so that no matter what mood you're in that day, you'll be able to be productive on at least one research project.

How about the balance between your personal and professional lives?

That's also very difficult. I sometimes worry that I don't set a good example here, because people do see me working very hard, and I feel like I may have set unrealistic expectations. When I was junior faculty, I was working all the time and at a level that wasn't sustainable long-term.

I think that you have to figure out for yourself what the right kind of rest is, whether it's exercising every day or taking all day Saturday off; whatever the production process that works right for you. And all I can say is that you should spend a lot of thought on it [*laughs*]. There's no one right answer, but you should try different ways until you find a routine that works.

If you're sitting in your office, surfing the Web, doing your e-mail and not doing research, then there's something wrong with the way you're organizing your life. You then need to decide how you are going to change it. If I'm surfing the Web two hours every morning, then maybe I should have student meetings first thing in the morning for two hours, or that's when I should schedule my co-author meetings or my teaching. If you have any block of time that's systematically unproductive, find another way to use it, unless you figure out that actually that two hours is what your mind needs to settle down and get to work.

Once you have kids, it's much harder; there are a lot of sacrifices, especially when it comes to travel and evening events and so on. And I've tried to have certain times that are very well protected for my children. I don't schedule things too early in the morning, so I have a nice, relaxed morning with them and do drop-offs at school. I try to make the mornings not rushed and a pleasant time for them, and for me. In the evenings, sometimes I have conflicts, but again I try to make sure that I am there and completely focused on them, not trying to do multiple things, like doing laundry and picking up the house. It's kid time and that's all there is. My kids are pretty happy with that.

I'm very selective about travel. I skip things that are connecting flights, and when I go to conferences I take 'red eyes' to get home, which is hard. If it's a 'West coast', I try to do it on Friday, so I can fly out at 6:00 pm and then come back on a red eye on Friday night and be there on Saturday. They don't mind so much if I'm gone for dinner on a Friday or a Sunday night because they see me all weekend.

The other really important decision you can make when you're young is how you manage your money. And that's because you can spend money in ways that could make you much, much more productive. And that means you have to have not already committed that money to a large house or a new car or something else. Take nanny versus daycare. A high-quality nanny can save you enormous amounts of time versus daycare. They can cut the time you're spending on mundane non-child-related tasks, like doing the laundry, emptying the dishwasher and cooking dinner, so that your household time is almost 100 per cent devoted to the kids. They can travel with you so you can bring your kids on longer trips. And that's also how you can achieve a balance where your career and kids don't suffer. But it does cost money [*laughs*].

REFLECTIONS AND THE FUTURE OF ECONOMICS

What are the biggest challenges facing your research fields?

In the field that I'm working in actively right now, market design, the biggest challenge is just legitimizing itself as a field in which people can get jobs in the junior market and people can get tenure. I think we've had some good examples of that, like Parag Pathak and Michael Ostrovsky, who have just gotten tenure at top-three schools.

Micro theory has become fragmented. It has slowed down on major innovations; it's now more ordinary science and more specialized. It would really benefit from new paradigms and new methodologies that might unify a larger group of people and get them all excited about the same kinds of things.

As I said before, empirical industrial organization has made amazing progress, and I think the quality of work is extremely high right now. But the challenge it often faces is that the empirical projects are on specific industries and on more narrow, specific problems. There's accumulative contribution to knowledge from all these papers, but they're individually often not that well cited. And so the challenge for the field is to figure out how to market our work more broadly to the rest of economics so that the general interest matches the quality of the work.

Industrial organization theory has struggled a lot because it's been out of fashion. Many schools don't really want to hire an industrial organization theorist. The micro theorists think that it's applied theory, not pure theory. Applied theory has been in no-man's land, and it's been very difficult for young people to make careers doing it. And so the challenge is how to latch onto an applied field so that the work has a bigger audience and a longer-term impact. And I think in those cases, since most of the applied fields are pretty empirical, it's partly having the applied theory maybe link a little more closely to the issues that are of interest empirically, either directly or indirectly.

What are the strengths and weaknesses of your own research?

I'm proud of the fact that when I've tackled new methodologies, I've really gone deep. Despite the breadth, which is generally a liability and a huge challenge to overcome, I think the papers that I've written have been viewed as high quality. I've avoided being viewed as a dilettante who came in, didn't read the literature, didn't reference the papers, and just wrote something everybody in the literature already knew. That's really important, and it's something I've worked hard at, too.

In some areas, I think it's always hard to write a paper that is hugely influential. A lot of the areas that I work in naturally have somewhat smaller audiences, and so I've recognized that there is a trade-off. I have a large number of high-quality, carefully written papers that all are very influential within their literatures, but there's not one paper that's got a 1000 cites or something like that. Maybe I'll write a paper like that someday, but that's not my primary goal. There's a certain kind of research that I'm good at, that I like, that I'm attracted to, and that I'm motivated by. I'm going to try to be good at what I think I'm good at, rather than try to make myself into something that I'm not.

I've been slow getting my papers out sometimes, and that's partly because I'm working on a lot of different things, and also because, just like everybody, the miserable process of revisions is not appealing.

In the end, has the profession helped to bring out and shape your research for the best?

I've gone against the grain a bit. In some ways, the profession made it hard for me to do exactly what I wanted to do early on because I felt a lot of pressure to fit into certain boxes. I feel like, within certain research areas, there is a big tendency of people to discount work in other areas. Parts of the theory community, in particular, view it as almost selling out or abandoning the principles of theory if you do applied work. That tension has been difficult for me because I do like to do theory; that was my original home base. And similarly, when I've been doing empirical work, I didn't initially feel part of that home community, because I wasn't traditionally a pure empiricist. When you're doing something that's in-between, the profession can make it challenging to blaze your own path.

But, again, a few role models who had also made non-conventional decisions showed me that it was possible to follow my heart and do the research that really excited me. I can work 75 or 80 hours a week productively if I'm inspired. And if I'm supposed to do something one week that I don't want to do, like revise a paper where I'm basically done with the paper and I just have to do what other people want me to do, which, in my mind, makes the paper worse, I can get nothing done [*laughs*]. For me, productivity is a function of following my passion. I can't force myself down one path or another. And so to maintain my productivity, it's been very important to continue to be inspired by new things.

I think the positive side is that the profession has helped to create institutions around new sub-fields. For example, we have a working group on market design at the NBER, and we've had conferences at Stanford on market design that have helped validate that sub-field. Almost all of the researchers share my values. They don't think that it makes you a worse theorist to go out and change the world [*laughs*]. By creating those institutions, I hope that the next generation of scholars doesn't feel the same tensions that I felt, and that we don't have to tell them that they're sacrificing their tenure probabilities if they follow this particular path of mixing theory and empirical work, and being more organized around real-world issues like matching problems or auction problems than being a theorist or empiricist.

Do you have any professional regrets?

No big ones. I've been very lucky because I've taken some gambles that have maybe caused short-term grief or could have worked out badly, like moving from theory to empirical work, and investing in econometrics. Those are non-standard choices that I wouldn't advise other people to follow. But luckily they worked out for me, so in the end, I'm happy that I've followed my heart.

You always wish you could be better at time management. I still regret somewhat that I spent so much time in my most productive research times doing non-research things. If I look back at my late 20s and early 30s, I wish I'd written a few less referee reports. I also did a lot of department administration for a while. Some of that was really useful, but most of it wasn't.

A big regret that I have is that for a long time I judged myself component-wise against the best people at everything. I used to say, "This person's a great referee," or "This person's a great advisor," or "This person is doing all this department service." What I wouldn't do is realize that there was not one person excelling at all of those things at the same time [*laughs*]. There are a few people who can, but I don't think that should be one's aspiration. What I try to remind myself is that you have a long career, and you don't have to be the best at everything at every time.

What are your professional ambitions?

I think my most important ambition is to maintain my passion. That's one of the harder things to do as you get older; you get distracted, you get pulled in a lot of different directions, and you feel like maybe you've already done your best work. And so maintaining that passion may mean making changes at various points. I needed a change a couple of years ago, and now I'm really passionate about online advertising and Internet economics. That makes me want to work as soon as I get up in the morning, and it has me thinking about it when I go to bed at night. And so my ambition would be that five years from now if I'm bored with that, I can find something else that has me feeling the same kind of passion and energy.

The other thing is that I've spent a lot of time on students for a long while, and I'm probably spending a little bit less time on them now. But I really would like to look back and see that I've helped teach people how to think in various ways, and even though they might have taken it in their own directions, that I still had some influence on them, especially on their ability to be true to what attracted them to economics to start with. I think a lot of people come to economics for the same reasons that I did; they have some motivation or passion for changing the world. Sometimes, you have that beaten out of you. But you can try to keep that motivation or passion for doing rigorous work that, in the end, makes a difference, is real, and matters … and to believe that that's possible.

How would you describe the state of economics today? Are you optimistic about its future?

I am very optimistic. Economics is healthy, it's popular, and it's got a lot of real-world challenges. I think that we've been very influential in changing policy in all sorts of different areas. The tools that we use are often the best for a range of policy problems and business problems and real-world problems. And I'd say that when I've gone out into the world in the last couple of years, and I've been interacting with engineers and computer scientists and business people and firms all trying to solve problems, I've just been amazed at what my economics training has brought to the table: the ability to conceptualize empirical work, to design experiments, to put structure on decisions, to help forecast the future of an industry, and to guide anti-trust policy and privacy policy. There are so many problems that come to you, but I feel that I'm the best prepared of all the people in the room to address the questions. And my input and insight is valued and appreciated, and I have a lot of demand from people wanting to learn from that economic approach.

NOTES

1. Myerson, R.B. (1979), 'Incentive Compatibility and the Bargaining Problem', *Econometrica*, Vol. 47, No. 1 (January), pp. 61–74; Myerson, R.B. (1982), 'Optimal Coordination Mechanisms in Generalized Principal–Agent Problems', *Journal of Mathematical Economics*, Vol. 10, No. 1 (June), pp. 67–81; Myerson, R.B. (1984), 'Two-Person Bargaining Problems with Incomplete Information', *Econometrica*, Vol. 52, No. 2 (March), pp. 461–487. See Milgrom, Paul (1979), *The Structure of Information in Competitive Bidding*, New York: Garland Press (PhD Dissertation). Milgrom's seminal work is discussed in this volume's interview with him.
2. Myerson, R.B. (1979), 'Incentive Compatibility and the Bargaining Problem', *Econometrica*, Vol. 47, No. 1 (January), pp. 61–74.
3. Athey, S., Avery, C. and P. Zemsky (2000), 'Mentoring and Diversity', *American Economic Review*, Vol. 90, No. 4 (September), pp. 765–786.
4. See, for example, Athey, S. and J. Roberts (2001), 'Organizational Design: Decision Rights and Incentive Contracts', *American Economic Review*, Papers and Proceedings, Vol. 91, No. 2 (May), pp. 200–205; Athey, S. and S. Stern (2002), 'The Impact of

Technology on Emergency Health Care Outcomes', *RAND Journal of Economics*, Vol. 33, No. 3 (Autumn), pp. 399–432.

5. See, for example, Athey, S. and A. Schmutzler (1995), 'Product and Process Flexibility in an Innovative Environment', *RAND Journal of Economics*, Vol. 26, No. 4 (Winter), pp. 557–574; Athey, S. and A. Schmutzler (1995), 'Investment and Market Dominance', *RAND Journal of Economics*, Vol. 32, No. 1 (Spring), pp. 1–26; Athey, S. (2001), 'Single Crossing Properties and the Existence of Pure Strategy Equilibria in Games of Incomplete Information', *Econometrica*, Vol. 69, No. 4 (July), pp. 861–889; Athey, S. (2002), 'Monotone Comparative Statics Under Uncertainty', *Quarterly Journal of Economics*, Vol. 117, No. 1 (February), pp. 187–223.

6. See, for example, Athey, S. and P.A. Haile (2001), 'Identification of Standard Auction Models', *Econometrica*, Vol. 70, No. 1 (November), pp. 2107–2140; Athey, S. and G.W. Imbens (2006), 'Identification and Inference in Nonlinear Difference-in-Differences Models', *Econometrica*, Vol. 74, No. 2 (March), pp. 431–497; Athey, S. and G.W. Imbens (2007), 'Discrete Choice Models with Multiple Unobserved Choice Characteristics', *International Economic Review*, Vol. 48, No. 4 (November), pp. 1159–1192.

7. See, for example, Agarwal, N., Athey, S. and D. Yang (2009), 'Skewed Bidding in Pay-Per-Action Auctions for Online Advertising', *American Economic Review*, Papers and Proceedings, Vol. 99, No. 2 (May), pp. 441–447; Athey, S. and J.S. Gans (2010), 'The Impact of Targeting Technology on Advertising Markets and Media Competition', *American Economic Review*, Papers and Proceedings, Vol. 100, No. 2 (May), pp. 608–613; Athey, S. and G. Ellison (2011), 'Position Auctions with Consumer Search', *Quarterly Journal of Economics*, Vol. 126, No. 3 (August), pp. 1213–1270.

Robert J. Barro
(Harvard University)

Robert Barro was born in New York City in 1944 and graduated with a BS in physics from the California Institute of Technology in 1965 before obtaining a PhD in economics from Harvard University in 1970. Professor Barro has taught economics at Brown University, 1968–1972, the University of Chicago, 1972–1975 and 1982–1984, the University of Rochester, 1975–82 and 1984–87, and Harvard University, where he currently serves as the Paul M. Warburg Professor of Economics.

Professor Barro's research interests have focused largely on macroeconomics and economic growth, including the empirical determinants of growth, the economic effects of public debt and budget deficits, and the formation of monetary policy, but he is currently researching the interplay between religion and political economy and the impact of rare disasters on asset markets. His most-cited articles in chronological order include 'Are Government Bonds Net Wealth?', *Journal of Political Economy* (1974), 'A Positive Theory of Monetary Policy in a Natural Rate Model', *Journal of Political Economy* (1983), co-authored with David Gordon, 'Government Spending in a Simple Model of Endogenous Growth', *Journal of Political Economy* (1990), 'Economic Growth in a Cross Section of Countries', *Quarterly Journal of Economics* (1991), and 'International Data on

Educational Attainment: Updates and Implications', *Oxford Economic Papers* (2001), co-authored with Jong-Wha Lee. His books include *Nothing is Sacred: Economic Ideas for the New Millennium* (MIT Press, 2002), *Economic Growth* (MIT Press, second edition, 2004), co-authored with Xavier Sala-i-Martin, and *Macroeconomics: A Modern Approach* (Thomson/Southwestern, 2008).

Professor Barro was elected as a Fellow of the Econometric Society in 1980 and a Fellow of the American Academy of Arts and Sciences in 1988. He holds honorary professorships from Tsinghua and Wuhan Universities in China and from Universidad del Pacifico in Peru, and honorary degrees from the University of Macedonia, Greece and Universidad Francisco Marroquin, Guatemala. Barro is currently a Co-Editor of the *Quarterly Journal of Economics*, and is a past Editor of the *Journal of Political Economy* (1973–1975, 1983–1985).

I interviewed Robert Barro in his office in the Department of Economics at Harvard University. It was mid-afternoon of Thursday, 21 October 2010.

BACKGROUND INFORMATION

Why did you decide to pursue an academic career in economics?

I guess it started when I was an undergraduate at Caltech majoring in physics. I took a course from Richard Feynman. He was a very inspirational, brilliant figure, but his course also persuaded me I should not be a theoretical physicist, because I did not believe I would make any major contributions. I did not like applied physics, but there were a lot of positives out of that course in terms of mathematical reasoning and logic.

I took my first economics class when I was a junior. My brother was an economist and he gave me some ideas about the subject. Once I got into it, it was very clear to me that it was the field I should be in. I liked the combination of the technical material and the applied aspects, including policy.

As a student, which professors were most influential or inspirational?

I had only one professor of economics at Caltech: Alan Sweezy. His brother, Paul, is better known and was more of a Marxist economist, but Alan was basically a straight Keynesian. In retrospect, the amazing thing is that I liked the course even though it was taught completely out of Keynes's

General Theory. Aside from the question of intellectual merit, the *General Theory* does not make a very good textbook, but I thought at the time that it was exciting.

I applied to Harvard and MIT and some other places for graduate school. I almost went to MIT, but I ended up going to Harvard for the PhD program, because MIT did not guarantee me financial support beyond the first year. Harvard's department at the time – the mid- to late-'60s – turned out to be really bad. They had little strength in macroeconomics, but more generally, it was before Harvard made some major appointments that made a big difference, including Kenneth Arrow, Martin Feldstein, Zvi Griliches, and Dale Jorgenson. At the time I started graduate school, Harvard's Economics Department was close to a vacuum, but maybe that was what I needed. That is, it forced me to work things out mostly on my own.

The person who inspired me most in that period was Franco Modigliani, who was visiting Harvard from MIT. I enjoyed his class. He was working on a big macroeconometric model at the time, and he wanted me to work on it. Fortunately, that didn't work out, because a big macroeconometric model was not the right focus for me. But Modigliani was a positive figure, certainly the best macro professor I had, even though he was not involved with my thesis. Marc Nerlove, another visitor, gave me some good ideas on research. And Zvi Griliches, after he arrived and after I had already taken a job at Brown, was a great help with the research on my dissertation. Actually, he once told me that his major job was to run interference for me with respect to the rest of the department.

As a researcher, which colleagues have been most influential or inspirational?

Milton Friedman and Gary Becker would be the two outstanding people for me. I went to Chicago in the early '70s after I had been at Brown University for three and a half years. Milton was a bigger influence for me in terms of his approach to economics. Maybe the fact that all the Harvard professors thought that Milton's work was no good made me think that Milton must be brilliant, once I realized that the Harvard people did not know what they were talking about. But he was particularly an influence for me in terms of applied price theory and, in some ways, his impact is bigger there than in macroeconomics and monetary economics.

I met Gary Becker when I was on the job market. I gave a seminar at Columbia, where he was at the time, and since then we have had a lot of positive interactions. We did some work together, and I particularly admire the way he has stuck with serious research throughout his career. Most people who do good work tend eventually to go on to do something different, but often less valuable. Bob Lucas was like Gary in this respect – Bob has continued to do serious research throughout his career. Lucas's work was also very important to me, not so much in terms of direct one-on-one collaboration, but more in terms of the ideas in his research, especially the work in the '70s related to rational expectations.

GENERAL THOUGHTS ON RESEARCH

What is the value of pure versus applied research in economics?

In some sense, the best research is work that combines the two, but most research does not exactly follow that model. Economists tend to be pretty narrow in terms of what they are good at.

How would you describe the dialogue between theory and empirics in economics?

Some theoretical work lends itself naturally to empirical applications and some less so. You see that today in terms of trying to assess the financial crisis and why it was that most economists were too optimistic about not having a repeat of the Great Depression. A lot of modeling of financial markets being done right now is pretty theoretical; whether it turns out to be successful will certainly relate to its predictive power.

How would you characterize your own research agenda and how has it changed through time?

I have worked in a lot of different areas, mostly related to monetary economics and macroeconomics, but sometimes even applied price theory. My first large body of research tried to understand better the Keynesian model and how to improve it.[1] I then moved into the Lucas-inspired rational expectations macro model and the related real business cycle analysis (originated particularly by Ed Prescott).[2] At about the same time (the early to mid-'70s), the work I did on Ricardian equivalence was consistent in approach with the rational expectations research.[3] I also did a lot of applied work related to the rational expectations model, in particular, trying to explain business fluctuations by monetary shocks that were unanticipated.[4]

I then worked on long-run economic growth, mostly focusing on the empirical implications from the Solow growth model.[5] I never understood why Solow did not appreciate this research more, but I think he and I just have never gotten along. He had this basic theory in the '50s, which I thought was an important development, but he never really thought of it so much as a theoretical framework for applied analysis. I felt he should have been very excited by the empirical work starting in the early '90s that came from some of the convergence implications of his model. Yet, he never seemed to embrace it. I talked to him about it once, but I did not get very far.

More recently, I have worked on other topics, such as religion and political economy, which fit in with my research on economic growth.[6] In 2005, I also started a project on rare economic disaster events, which are often financial-type crises, such as the Great Depression, but also relate to wars. This is a continuing area of my research, much of it joint with a graduate student, José Ursúa, who is on the job market this year. We – particularly José – have constructed a major panel dataset covering up to 42 countries going back before 1914. The work relates to Angus Maddison's contributions on long-term national accounts, but I think we have made a major advance on Maddison.[7]

The other research I am currently pursuing involves empirical assessments of fiscal-stimulus packages. Specifically, I am estimating effects of government purchases and tax rates on real GDP; sometimes the effects are described as spending and tax multipliers.[8] I began with the United States but am now applying the analysis to other countries. I am also looking, in work joint with Price Fishback, at the experience in the 1930s New Deal period in the United States. We are examining the responses across the US states to (exogenous) variations in grants received from the federal government. Overall, I am frankly surprised with my recent work, because I think it is higher quality than I thought I would be doing at this stage of my career.

Do you think it is important to have broad research interests?

I think most people are probably better off with a narrow focus. It may be exciting moving from one area to the other, but it can also have a big cost. Having to learn new literatures can be a major impediment, and very often you have to make a significant investment in new data. For example, in my work on rare disasters, I had to learn a lot of literature related to finance, and the data are certainly different. But at the same time, I view economics as something that you can apply in many places, without having to relearn the basics of the subject.

Do you think there is any difference in the types of work done by researchers at different stages of their careers based on tenure concerns, publication requirements or other pressures? Should there be a difference?

You do not find too many people beyond a certain age who are making major contributions in economics. A good number of top economists give up being active researchers. For example, Bob Solow made a couple of brilliant contributions when he was young, but he did not follow up with important research. Maybe that is optimal, because most people are not capable of producing high-quality frontier research throughout their life-span.

IDEA GENERATION

Where do you get your research ideas?

I have never been able to answer that question, but I would say that a lot of it is idiosyncratic. Take my research on rare disasters that I began in 2005. I remember specifically Marty Weitzman giving a seminar at Harvard on tail events, which he has applied to environmental issues as well as macro-economic disasters. When he was talking, I was thinking that we could use this framework to explain some of the major asset pricing puzzles like the equity premium. Because this was a field that was not familiar to me, I looked at what had been done previously, including John Campbell's survey paper, which led me to Tom Rietz's paper from the late '80s.[9] Rietz's work was a comment on Mehra and Prescott's equity premium puzzle paper from 1985.[10] Rietz argued that the low-probability chance of a disaster, such as the Great Depression, could explain the observed equity premium. Unfortu-nately, Mehra and Prescott seemed to convince people in a rejoinder that Rietz's work was not a great insight, but when I learned about it almost 20 years later, I felt it made a lot of sense. And so I thought about how one could formalize the idea – this notion led to a series of theoretical and empirical papers related to rare disasters, a project that is still ongoing.

At what point does an idea become a project that you devote resources to?

I end up throwing away most things that I start working on. That is one reason that I am reluctant to have co-authors, because then it is harder to discard a project.

IDEA EXECUTION

What makes a good theoretical paper?

A good theoretical paper has an important theoretical insight and potential applications, in terms of further theory as well as empirics.

Can you give an example?

Lucas's initial paper on rational expectations in macroeconomics provided a great theoretical insight about the confusion between monetary and real shocks, but also led to applied work, because it produced some empirical patterns that looked like expectations-augmented Phillips Curves.[11] In fact, it inspired a whole new field.

Paul Romer's two early papers on endogenous technological change were very important contributions.[12] I have been disappointed with the subsequent course of Paul's career, because that was great work, and I was looking for more, but it did not come.

My Ricardian equivalence paper also fits in with this discussion.[13] It was a simple, important concept that was central to macroeconomics; it changed the way people thought about fiscal deficits and public debt, even if they did not embrace the paper's specific results. And Olivier Blanchard's 1985 paper in the *JPE* extended my work to bring in finite horizon effects, and people have used that framework for other things.[14] I remember discussing the paper at a conference. I started out by saying, "I hesitate to say this, and I do not want to compromise my reputation, but I think this is a really good paper." Olivier was very pleased [*laughs*].

What makes a good empirical paper?

It is on an important question, it comes up with some clear findings, and it provides a vehicle for additional testing and ideas about the relationships.

Can you give an example?

Milton Friedman's book on permanent income is one of the most important empirical studies.[15] He deals with a topic that people have thought a lot about in terms of consumption and saving behavior, and he shows how some simple theoretical insights have a great deal of explanatory power.

Phillip Cagan's 1950s study on hyperinflation is another important empirical paper.[16] He uses effectively an exciting set of new data to understand money demand and the determinants of inflation.

My most-cited paper, which is from the *QJE* in 1991, is on a very important topic: Why do some countries grow faster and therefore have higher standards of living in the long run? This paper uses a simple conceptual idea (essentially the Solow growth model) applied to data across countries and over time. Many people hate the paper and question the robustness of the results, but it has had a lot of influence.[17]

When you hit a brick wall on a project, do you continue to work on the problem or do you take a break and work on something else?

I would not usually describe it as a 'brick wall'. For example, I am working on a study with my wife, Rachel, on how the Catholic Church chooses saints in terms of numbers and geographical distribution.[18] We have the idea that the Church chooses saints to make its Catholic population more enthusiastic, and that it cares more about that when it has to compete with other groups, particularly evangelicals. We started putting together the data, which go back to the 1500s, about five or six years ago. But since then, we have put the project aside on several occasions and not worked on it. That is not because we hit a 'brick wall'; it is just that we were doing other things. We will eventually complete this project!

What has been the biggest change during your career in how researchers in your fields conduct research?

The field has become more technical in terms of the mathematical apparatus and there have been major developments in computer power. For example, I am currently working on a project (with Emi Nakamura, Jón Steinsson, and José Ursúa) that tries to assess whether macroeconomic disasters have permanent or only temporary effects.[19] That work is very intensive in terms of numerical analysis, and I could not have done it ten years ago.

THE WRITING PROCESS

Which aspect of the writing process do you find most difficult?

I do not have a lot of trouble with writing. I am pretty good at it.

What steps have you taken during your career to improve the quality of your writing?

In terms of popular writing, one has to be careful with jargon and concepts that are too difficult. In the US, more than the UK, for example, you really have to bring things down to a moron level. Sometimes I question whether this makes sense. Why should it be that important issues of economic policy can be analyzed effectively in ways that are understandable to journalists, or politicians, or other persons who lack economic expertise?

COLLABORATION

When you work with co-authors, how do you decide whom to work with?

The dominant form of my co-authorship has been with current and former students. As already mentioned, I am doing work right now with José Ursúa on rare disasters. Earlier in my career, I worked a lot with Xavier Sala-i-Martin, who was my first PhD student at Harvard. He was doing his thesis on growth and convergence, particularly across the US states. We co-authored a number of articles that came out of that work, and we also wrote a book, *Economic Growth*, which has been successful.[20] Sala-i-Martin was a hard worker and had many ideas.

Did you enjoy writing the book with him?

The first edition was a positive experience. It was exciting putting the theoretical and empirical work on growth into a form that was accessible to graduate students. But the second edition was more tedious. It was mostly a matter of improving on what we already had, so there was little innovation. And Xavier was too much into FC Barcelona (the famous soccer team) at the time.

Are you comfortable with your students being on the job market with a co-authored paper?

It has become much more common now to have co-authored work on the job market, and I think it can work. A few years ago, Mike Golosov took a diversified approach when he was on the market. Sometimes, he talked about his best paper, which was co-authored with Bob Lucas.[21] It was clear that Mike had contributed more than 50 per cent to that paper, and he got credit for it, but he was worried about the issue, and I think that is why at other times he presented one of his own papers. Of course, he is a brilliant economist, and sometimes students have more difficulty in presenting joint work on the job market.

What are the main challenges associated with collaborative work and how do you overcome them?

A few years ago, I did a couple of papers with Alberto Alesina on common currencies.[22] We both viewed ourselves as idea people, and that did not work that well when there were two of us. More generally, the hardest thing in collaborative research is telling a co-author that I am no longer going to work on a project because I have decided it is not that promising.

RESEARCH ASSISTANCE AND FUNDING

How do you use undergraduate and graduate research assistants?

In my recent research on fiscal effects, I worked with a brilliant undergraduate here at Harvard, Charles Redlick. I took the intellectual lead, but he played a big role in a very effective partnership. He did things readily on his own, particularly in terms of putting together the long-term US macro time-series data, so that we could estimate spending multipliers and tax effects. In fact, he is a full co-author on that paper, which will be published in the *QJE* in February.[23]

I have had a similar type of interaction with my graduate student, José Ursúa, who I have been working with for five years. I will hate to see him go. His work on assembling the national accounts data for the rare disasters research has been truly amazing.

How important is funding for getting your work done?

It's of some importance, but I cannot remember a time when I thought, "Oh, if only I could get another $10,000, that would make a key difference to my research."

SEMINAR PARTICIPATION AND NETWORKING

What are the benefits to attending a seminar that is closely related to your work versus one that is not closely related?

Harvard has so many seminars that it is difficult to attend a large share. I go mostly to the regular macro seminar plus the macro lunch, where graduate students present their work. Those lunch seminars are excellent. The students get a lot of constructive suggestions on how to go forward with their dissertations, and it also promotes an excellent interplay among the faculty, better than that in the regular seminars. On Tuesday, for example, I went to a seminar by Danny Shoag, who is on the job market, and he presented a clever paper on estimating spending multipliers across the US states, using recent data. I got a lot out of that seminar.

How important is professional networking to success in research?

It is not something that I have relied on in my career. My wife is always telling me that I do not network enough, but I think she means with people at Harvard.

To what extent is the absence of departmental colleagues working in one's research area a major disadvantage?

Having colleagues who work in your research fields is a big deal. It certainly shows up all the time in seminars.

COMMUNICATION OF RESEARCH

How do you find the right balance between communicating your research at an early stage versus the close-to-finished stage?

I tend to err on the side of distributing my research, including any data that I have collected, at an early stage.

What are the unique challenges to giving a seminar and how do you overcome them?

I remember the job market seminar I gave at Columbia in the late '60s. I was in the third year of my PhD. I did not have a thesis advisor, but I had completed most of the research on my own. There was nobody among the faculty at Harvard doing macroeconomics and I think that was better than having somebody mediocre as an advisor. The vacuum forces you to figure things out. Anyway, even though I did not formally go on the job market, I managed to get interviews at three places: Brown, Northwestern, and Columbia. The talk at Columbia sticks in my mind. My thesis was about hyperinflation and, at a certain point in the seminar, somebody from the audience began to complain about the econometrics. It was Raj Chetty's father! He was really criticizing me and, before I could say anything, Gary Becker gets up and starts arguing back and forth with him. Eventually, Gary ended up being triumphant. I thought to myself, "This is great. Seminars are easy. A brilliant guy from the audience will do all the arguing for you." But it has never happened to me again [*laughs*].

PUBLICATION

Do you think that the current structure of the publication process in economics facilitates or impedes scientific understanding and knowledge production?

There have been some puzzling developments. The top journals have become more dominant over time, even though there has been a large increase in the number of field journals. And you would have thought that the number of articles published in the top journals would have gone up commensurately with the size of the profession, but it has not. In fact, the number moved downward in the case of the *JPE*, which is now a dysfunctional journal. I edited the *JPE* with George Stigler back in the '70s and '80s, and I think it was the best journal up to a certain point in the '80s. But since then, it has been terribly managed. If you submit a paper there, you are lucky if you hear back in 15 months, and often you just receive something that makes no sense. I do not send anything to the *JPE* these days. You have to be a masochist to put yourself into that ridiculous arena.

I feel bad about the *JPE*. I worked very hard on it when I was an editor. I think one of the problems today is that it has too many co-editors, which means it is difficult to give each one a real stake in the journal, particularly when they also turn over so often.

Meanwhile, the *QJE* has been on the way up. My colleague, Larry Katz, has been mostly responsible for its success. He is compulsive about getting things done quickly and efficiently. When you work with him, you have to do the same, otherwise you feel really guilty. And so we are very productive. You typically do not have to wait more than 70 days to get a first response, and we usually provide valuable feedback in the form of referee reports, which improve the quality of the paper.

A couple of years ago, Lars Hansen from Chicago was put in charge of a committee to figure out what to do about the *JPE*. He was asking for advice, and I said that we were thinking of making a takeover bid because we seem to be able to manage journals better. I said we would run it as an efficient separate enterprise, not a merger, but he did not take us up on the offer [*laughs*].

How would you best describe your approach to dealing with a 'revise and resubmit' request from a journal? How about an outright rejection?

Sometimes when I get a rejection, which certainly happens often enough, I think the referees have nothing useful to say and I just ignore it and send it somewhere else. But other times, there can be good grounds for criticism. For example, in one of my recent papers, I can see what the basic problem is, and I have not solved it yet. I had to lower my standard in terms of where that particular paper is likely to be published.

'Revise and resubmits' are usually fairly straightforward, and I always address productive comments.

What has been your best and worst experience during the publication process?

My worst experience has been with papers that I submitted to the *JPE* that have just sat there forever without any answer and ultimately got rejected without any particular rationale. That has happened more than once.

I might guess at Bob Lucas's worst experience. His 1972 paper that introduced the idea of rational expectations in macroeconomics was originally submitted to the *AER*. The editor at the time was George Borts, who was my colleague at Brown in the '70s. Borts rejected the paper because it was too mathematical. Bob wrote back accusing him of running *Newsweek* magazine. Borts once said to me, "What would you have done?" I told him, "I would have accepted that paper immediately. I think you were crazy."

My best experience would probably relate to the work Herschel Grossman and I did on Keynesian macroeconomics in the early '70s. We had submitted it to the *AER*, and I remember Borts calling us into his office to explain how we should revise the paper. He ended up accepting it and, for a long time, that was my most-cited paper.[24]

REFEREEING AND EDITING

Do you have any advice for a young scholar on being a referee?

I often send papers to people who have not been asked to referee in the past. PhD students or young assistant professors will be honored and excited. They will spend a tremendous amount of time doing the reports and will be very conscientious. They tend to be up on the fresh, new ideas and often they provide not only constructive comments, but also find flaws in the work. Senior people are usually lousy referees. They tend not to take things seriously and will not be careful enough. But there are a few hundred referees that we use at the *QJE*, and you get an idea over time about which people are willing and good referees.

When I was an editor of the *JPE*, I introduced the business of paying the referees, which I think was the first time it had been done in economics. At the time – 30 years ago – it was $50. I had to open a bank account so I could write checks from the *JPE*. Continental Illinois Bank was the bank that was then the most connected to the university, and they said, "Oh, we know all about the *JPE*. We'd be happy to open an account, but you need something that proves that you own the journal." So, I opened an account instead at a local bank. Once I had that account, I was able to open a Fidelity account for the *JPE* and that was the one we actually used. It had the restriction that you could not deposit checks that were smaller than $50, so that was why we set the paper submission fee at $50 [*laughs*]. At one point, we received a check for $50,000 that was payable to the *JPE*. George Stigler told me, "You could go down to the courthouse and change your name to the *Journal of Political Economy* for $200. Then you can cash this check for yourself." George was a very funny guy.

Do you have any advice for a young scholar on being an editor?

I was a junior faculty member at Chicago when I was editing the *JPE* with George Stigler. I ended up with a lot of trouble, particularly when I rejected some papers from my colleagues. It did not work out very well in that respect. But it has been exciting editing the *QJE*, because it is one of the top journals. I do not think I would want to do the work for a second-tier journal. It would be much less rewarding. Olivier Blanchard took up the position of being the editor of the *AEJ Macro*. He thought he could make it into a top-tier journal for macroeconomics but I did not think so. He was doing all right, but people were not sending papers there as a first choice. And so he became disappointed and stopped doing it. I do not know what it takes to make a top journal, but whatever it is, it persists for a long time and it is very hard to enter the business of being a top journal.

TIME MANAGEMENT

How do you divide up your working day, both in terms of quantity and timing of different kinds of work?

It varies. I try to do the routine work on the *QJE* every other day, but the main work comes when I have to seriously consider an article for publication and I have to read it carefully. Sometimes I am working actively on one of my own research projects and I will want to devote a lot of time to it. Some parts of the year, I will be teaching and that makes a big difference to my day. And, of course, my job also requires me to travel, but I try not to do that too much, because it takes a great deal of time and energy.

How do you balance multiple research projects?

It is a problem when there are too many things going on at once and I cannot be heavily involved in the details of a project. That means I am not on top of the work.

How do you balance your personal and professional lives?

[*Laughs*]. My wife says I should do more things besides being an economist. Maybe that is true. Gary Becker always told me he had a lot of trouble when reporters asked him about his hobbies, because he thought economics was his hobby as well as his vocation. And so he would make things up like, "I play tennis." Sometimes I think I should be spending more time with things that are not economics, but then I get over it.

REFLECTIONS AND THE FUTURE OF ECONOMICS

What are the biggest challenges facing your research fields?

The key challenges in macroeconomics are related to unusual, but large, adverse events, such as the recent financial crisis and, in particular, the policies that might deal with them.

What are the strengths and weaknesses of your own research?

I am able to apply a common way of reasoning to a lot of different problems, which can be either macro or micro. That is a plus for me. I said earlier that it is better for most people to be specialized, but that is not the way I function most effectively. And I am also able to combine theory with empirical applications. I might benefit from having more mathematics in my work, so perhaps that is a weakness.

In the end, do you think the profession has helped to bring out and shape your research for the best?

I have a lot of uneasiness about my status within the profession. I do much better if you look at things that are objective, particularly citation patterns, compared to 'popularity contests', such as awards and prizes. This reality is annoying, but it spurs me on to do more work rather than less.

Do you have any professional regrets?

Sometimes I think about the difference it might have made if I had gone to graduate school at MIT rather than Harvard. But then I realize I was probably better off not going to MIT, which clearly had a much better department at the time, because I would have been too influenced by the professors there.

What are your professional ambitions?

I am pretty content with myself in terms of what I have produced over a long period. It has already gone beyond my expectations. I hope to be able to continue producing frontier-type research. Gary Becker is the best role model in that respect.

How would you describe the state of economics today? Are you optimistic about its future?

For many key economic problems, like dealing with potential depressions and financial fragility, economics is all there is. It is not the case that some other field is going to do better. Despite some views to the contrary, the recent financial crisis did not reduce the demand for economics; it increased it, even though at the same time, there was a lot of attack on economists for not having predicted the events, or at least knowing what to do once they happened. The fact is that economics is a counter-cyclical profession.

NOTES

1. See, for example, Barro, R.J. and H.I. Grossman (1971), 'A General Disequilibrium Model of Income and Employment', *American Economic Review*, Vol. 61, No. 1 (March), pp. 82–93.
2. See, for example, Barro, R.J. (1976), 'Rational Expectations and the Role of Monetary Policy', *Journal of Monetary Economics*, Vol. 2, No. 1(January), pp. 1–32; Barro, R.J. and A.M. Santomero (1976), 'Output and Employment in a Macro Model with Discrete Transaction Costs', *Journal of Monetary Economics*, Vol. 2, No. 3 (July), pp. 297–310; Barro, R.J. (1976), 'Indexation in a Rational Expectations Model', *Journal of Economic Theory*, Vol. 13, No. 2 (October), pp. 229–244.
3. See, for example, Barro, R.J. (1974), 'Are Government Bonds Net Wealth?', *Journal of Political Economy*, Vol. 82, No. 6 (November), pp. 1095–1117.
4. See, for example, Barro, R.J. (1977), 'Unanticipated Money Growth and Unemployment in the United States', *American Economic Review*, Vol. 67, No. 2 (March), pp. 101–115; Barro, R.J. (1978), 'Unanticipated Money, Output, and the Price Level in the United States', *Journal of Political Economy*, Vol. 86, No. 4 (August), pp. 549–580.
5. See, for example, Barro, R.J. (1991), 'Economic Growth in a Cross Section of Countries', *Quarterly Journal of Economics*, Vol. 106, No. 2 (May), pp. 407–443.
6. See, for example, Barro, R.J. (1996), 'Democracy and Growth', *Journal of Economic Growth*, Vol. 1, No. 1 (March), pp. 1–27; McCleary, R.M. and R.J. Barro (2006), 'Religion and Economy', *Journal of Economic Perspectives*, Vol. 20, No. 2 (Spring), pp. 49–72.
7. See, for example, Barro, R.J. and J.F. Ursúa (2008), 'Consumption Disasters in the Twentieth Century', *American Economic Review*, Papers and Proceedings, Vol. 98, No. 2 (May), pp. 58–63; Barro, R.J. and J.F. Ursúa (2008), 'Macroeconomic Crises since 1870', *Brookings Papers on Economic Activity*, Economic Studies Program, The Brookings Institution, Vol. 39, No. 1 (Spring), pp. 255–350.
8. See, for example, Barro, R.J. and C.J. Redlick (2011), 'Macroeconomic Effects From Government Purchases and Taxes', *Quarterly Journal of Economics*, Vol. 126, No. 1 (February), pp. 51–102.
9. Campbell, J.Y. (2000), 'Asset Pricing at the Millennium', *Journal of Finance*, Vol. 55, No. 4 (August), pp. 1515–1567; Rietz, T.A. (1988), 'The Equity Risk Premium: A Solution', *Journal of Monetary Economics*, Vol. 22, No.1 (July), pp. 117–131.
10. Mehra, R. and E.C. Prescott (1985), 'The Equity Premium: A Puzzle', *Journal of Monetary Economics*, Vol. 15, No. 2 (March), pp. 145–161.

11. Lucas, Jr, R.E. (1972), 'Expectations and the Neutrality of Money', *Journal of Economic Theory*, Vol. 4, No. 2 (April), pp. 103–124.
12. Romer, P.M. (1986), 'Increasing Returns and Long-Run Growth', *Journal of Political Economy*, Vol. 94, No. 5 (October), pp. 1002–1037; Romer, P.M. (1990), 'Endogenous Technological Change', *Journal of Political Economy*, Vol. 98, No. 5 (October), pp. S71–S102.
13. See article in Note 3.
14. Blanchard, O.J. (1985), 'Debt, Deficits, and Finite Horizons', *Journal of Political Economy*, Vol. 93, No. 2 (April), pp. 223–247.
15. Milton Friedman (1957), *A Theory of the Consumption Function*, National Bureau of Economic Research.
16. Cagan, P.G. (1956), 'The Monetary Dynamics of Hyperinflation', in Milton Friedman (ed.), *Studies in the Quantity Theory of Money*, Chicago: University of Chicago Press, pp. 25–117.
17. See article in Note 5.
18. Barro, R.J. and R.M. McCleary (2011), 'Saints Marching In, 1590 – 2009', *NBER Working Papers* 16769, National Bureau of Economic Research.
19. Nakamura E., Steinsson, J., Barro, R.J. and J. Ursúa (2010), 'Crises and Recoveries in an Empirical Model of Consumption Disasters', *NBER Working Papers* 15920, National Bureau of Economic Research.
20. See, for example, Barro, R.J. and X. Sala-i-Martin (1992), 'Convergence', *Journal of Political Economy*, Vol. 100, No. 2 (April), pp. 223–251; Barro, R.J. and X. Sala-i-Martin (1992), 'Regional Growth and Migration: A Japan–United States Comparison', *Journal of the Japanese and International Economies*, Vol. 6, No. 4 (December), pp. 312–346; Barro, R.J. and X. Sala-i-Martin (1992), 'Public Finance in Models of Economic Growth', *Review of Economic Studies*, Vol. 59, No. 4 (October), pp. 645–661; Robert J. Barro and Xavier Sala-i-Martin (2004), *Economic Growth* (MIT Press, second edition).
21. Golosov, M. and R.E. Lucas, Jr (2007), 'Menu Costs and Phillips Curves', *Journal of Political Economy*, Vol. 115, No. 2 (April), pp. 171–199.
22. Alesina, A. and R.J. Barro (2000), 'Dollarization', *American Economic Review*, Papers and Proceedings, Vol. 91, No. 2 (May), pp. 381–385; Alesina, A. and R.J. Barro (2002), 'Currency Unions', *Quarterly Journal of Economics*, Vol. 117, No. 2 (May), pp. 409–430.
23. See article in Note 8.
24. See article in Note 1.

Richard Blundell
(University College, London)

Richard Blundell was born in Shoreham, England in 1952 and graduated with a BSc in economics and statistics from the University of Bristol in 1973 before obtaining an MSc in econometrics and mathematical economics from the London School of Economics in 1975. Between 1975 and 1984, he was a Lecturer in Econometrics at the University of Manchester before moving to University College, London, where he currently serves as the David Ricardo Chair of Political Economy. Since 1986, he has been Research Director of the Institute for Fiscal Studies, where he is also Director of the ESRC Centre for the Microeconomic Analysis of Public Policy.

Professor Blundell's research interests are microeconometrics, labor supply, savings and consumption, household behavior, taxation, and public economics. His most-cited articles in chronological order include 'An Exogeneity Test for a Simultaneous Equation Tobit Model with an Application to Labor Supply', *Econometrica* (1986), co-authored with Richard Smith, 'Quadratic Engel Curves and Consumer Demand', *Review of Economics and Statistics* (1997), co-authored with James Banks and Arthur Lewbel, 'Initial Conditions and Moment Restrictions in Dynamic Panel Data Models', *Journal of Econometrics* (1998), co-authored with Stephen

Bond, 'Market Share, Market Value and Innovation in a Panel of British Manufacturing Firms', *Review of Economic Studies* (1999), co-authored with Rachel Griffiths and John Van Reenen, and 'Evaluation Methods for Non-Experimental Data', *Fiscal Studies* (2000), co-authored with Monica Costa Dias. His books include *Unemployment, Search and Labour Supply* (Cambridge University Press, 1986), co-edited with Ian Walker, and *The Measurement of Household Welfare* (Cambridge University Press, 1994), co-edited with Ian Preston and Ian Walker. Most recently, he was a co-author of the *Mirrlees Review: Tax by Design* (Oxford University Press, 2011).

Professor Blundell was awarded the Yrjö Jahnsson Prize (1995), given every two years to the best young economist in Europe aged under 45, for his work in microeconometrics and the analysis of labor supply, welfare reform, and consumer behavior. In 2000, he was awarded the Econometric Society's Frisch Medal for the paper 'Estimating Labor Supply Responses using Tax Reforms'. In 2008, he was the fourth recipient of the Jean-Jacques Laffont Prize, given to an international high-level economist whose research combines both the theoretical and applied aspects of economics. In 2006, he was awarded the CBE (Commander of the Order of the British Empire) in Her Majesty Queen Elizabeth II's New Year's Honours List for "services to Economics and Social Science."

Professor Blundell was elected as a Fellow of the Econometric Society in 1991, a Fellow of the British Academy in 1996, and an Honorary Member of the American Academy of Arts and Sciences in 2002. He was awarded an honorary doctorate by the University of St. Gallen, Switzerland in 2003 and by the University of Bergen, Norway and the University of Mannheim, Germany in 2011.

Professor Blundell was Co-Editor of *Econometrica* from 1997 to 2001 and Co-Editor of the *Journal of Econometrics* from 1992 to 1997.

I interviewed Richard Blundell in his office in the Department of Economics of the College of Arts and Sciences, New York University, where he was a visitor. It was mid-morning of Friday, 11 March 2011.

BACKGROUND INFORMATION

What was your attraction to economics?

I began my undergraduate studies as an electrical engineer, but then started to think about solving problems of importance to society, which led me to transfer to economics.

As a student, which professors were most influential or inspirational?

There were two people who stand out when I was doing my master's in econometrics at the London School of Economics. One was Denis Sargan. He was the pre-eminent econometrician at that time in the UK. Why is he important? He showed the precision and clarity of econometrics, and made you think that it was an attractive area to study. But probably the most influential person was Terence Gorman, who was more of a mathematical economist. He convinced me that economic theory could be a useful way of thinking about the world.

Why did you decide to pursue an academic career?

I liked research and I thought that I might like teaching. I already had a bit of a research agenda because I was interested in microeconometrics and household behavior. At that time in Europe, economic theory was dominated by general equilibrium theory and econometrics by macroeconometric modeling, neither of which I was particularly skilled at or wanted to follow. And so I thought I could probably cut out something fresh in the microeconometrics and individual behavior area.

To what extent did not writing a PhD thesis affect your transition into a highly successful researcher?

The option was there to do a PhD, but so too was the opportunity to move straight into a lectureship, which I did at the age of 23. What was the advantage? As a lecturer, I could do what I wanted to do.

I wouldn't advise anyone these days to go into an academic career without a PhD, and I was part of the last cohort that did it in a successful way. On the other hand, there's nothing special about a PhD. In the end, you need to come up with some genuine, original ideas and figure out whether they're going to work or not. A PhD could be one way of doing that, but I don't see it as essential as some people might think [*laughs*].

As a researcher, which colleagues have been most influential or inspirational?

In microeconometrics, there are three names that stand out: Dan McFadden, Jim Heckman, and Chuck Manski. They created the very exciting early agenda in that field and continue to be active in the most admirable way. In theory, there is Ken Binmore, who came back to join me at UCL to build the theory group. That was a remarkable association. Finally, Terence Gorman who joined as a visiting professor in the early days of UCL. But those five people have had a huge influence on many people, not just me.

GENERAL THOUGHTS ON RESEARCH

There is an increasing emphasis in many economics departments on applied research. Is this true at UCL?

I came into UCL when it had gone through a pretty rough period, especially for the oldest economics department in England. It had a very small group of people, but the advantage was that we could build something different and special. Hopefully, we did that and achieved something quite special. My general view is that you have to mix applied work with theory and econometrics. If they work well together, then it can be a brilliant outcome.

How would you describe the dialogue between theory and empirics in economics?

It is difficult for me to figure out how you can do economics successfully without both of them.

How would you characterize your own research agenda and how has it changed through time?

It hasn't changed by a huge amount. I have always been fascinated with trying to understand microeconomic behavior. But the way in which my research interacts with macro behavior and policy is probably more profound than I first thought.

Do you think it is important to have broad research interests?

I suspect it is, if you can do it. And I prefer it if people have a broader perspective because they're usually more interesting to interact with. But sometimes digging in a narrow field can bring some pretty good rewards. It can be especially worthwhile at the outset of a career. It's a matter of being original and influential.

Do you think there is a difference in the life of a researcher in Europe versus the US? Has this changed through time?

Apart from the poverty? [*Laughs*]. I think economics may be one of these grand areas in which the term 'small world' is a good characterization. Obviously, there are different policy issues and perspectives, but the research agenda is remarkably similar. And I doubt if that has changed very much. Europe and the US have always been linked in economics. If you look at the highfalutin journals, the editors and the papers have flipped between Europe and the US. It's certainly true that the mass of high-powered work is done in the US, and it is difficult to be a European researcher without acknowledging that fact and also spending time visiting the US. But in the UK, for example, there is some very fine economics research going on and some of that research is leading the field.

IDEA GENERATION

Where do you get your research ideas?

I don't think there's one place. Some ideas come out of the blue. You've been to a seminar, you've talked to people, and then you're sitting around at home listening to music, playing guitar, or maybe on a holiday beach, and suddenly a good idea appears. Applied ideas often come straight out of a policy issue; you hit on a way of thinking about how people behave in respect to a particular policy. And methodological ideas typically come about when you see someone tackling a problem and you spot a way to address it better.

At what point does an idea become a project that you devote resources to?

I think about each one of the things that I've just mentioned for an hour or two, jot down some notes, and then put it to one side. A pen and paper for note taking is essential. If the idea still stands up after a few days, then it's worth thinking about further with colleagues or students. But lots of ideas fall apart after a couple of days – that's the way it goes.

IDEA EXECUTION

What makes a good theoretical paper? Can you give an example?

The theory must distill the salient points about behavior into a model that is fresh and accessible. I would pick James Mirrlees' paper on optimal income taxation.[1] The mathematics is totally beautiful. The beauty is in the clarity of the insight. Terence Gorman had some like this, too. It is not something that you can immediately take to application or policy, but it gives you incredible insight and can be drawn on many times.

What makes a good empirical paper? Can you give an example?

A good empirical paper is one that establishes something quite original in data that enhances our understanding of behavior or allows us to develop some new policy perspective. For example, a paper might tell you something new about how consumers respond to a change in income uncertainty or the importance of asymmetric information in annuity markets. I don't want to get into a methodological debate, but a good empirical economics paper in my mind draws on both theory and data. Among others, Jim Heckman, Martin Browning, Jim Poterba, Dave Card, not to mention my colleagues at UCL – Orazio Attanasio, Guy Laroque, Steve Machin, Costas Meghir, and Jean-Marc Robin – have shown this ability to mix theory and empirics. I could pick on many of their papers as brilliant examples.

When you hit a brick wall on a project, do you continue to work on the problem or do you take a break and work on something else?

I don't give up easily; I see it as a challenge. If you've got something that looks like it will hold up but you hit a brick wall, then that's potentially a good thing because it suggests it's not going to be easy to solve and probably nobody else has been able to figure it out either. Most original work has hit a brick wall at some point. I'll give you an example. When I started out, there wasn't a lot of panel data available for studying life-cycle household decision-making. That was a problem. And so a number of us started thinking about how best to deal with it. After a bit of thought, we realized that you could use certain decisions found in the cross-section data, such as those relating to consumption or savings, to reflect the way in which individuals were viewing the rest of their life-cycle. It's not perfect, and we've learned how to do things even better, but at the time it was something of a surprise and, subsequently, a useful development.

Related to the previous question, when a project isn't going to turn out as hoped, do you scrap it or aim to send the work to a second-tier or field journal?

It's not a good idea to have lots of little things all over the place, some of which are not very great. Of course, there are lots of good field journals, but if something doesn't work out as I had hoped, I will probably decide just to scrap it.

What has been the biggest change during your career in how researchers in your fields conduct research?

If you're in empirical microeconomics, it would have to be data collection and technology. You can certainly point to many of the great ideas in microeconometric papers that were done long before easy access to big datasets and computational techniques, but nonetheless, being able to sit down and analyze the many new datasets on very interesting sub-populations is very important. It brings precision, and it has also motivated many of the more robust approaches to econometrics. For example, when you think about trying to model behavior, it is now much more reasonable to model the way in which the quantiles of the distribution evolve rather than simply modeling the mean.

THE WRITING PROCESS

Which aspect of the writing process do you find most difficult?

I don't like writing, and I'm not very good at it. I think it's partly a skill that some people have and others don't. One of the key reasons for the existence of the Institute for Fiscal Studies is to try to bring together people with different skills. The set of work that comes out of the Institute is often written up for wider digestion in policy circles. It mixes rigorous economics research with policy insights. This often involves working with skillful, but less academic, economists who are good at getting ideas across. I think that's really worthwhile. In other words, some of the papers that I write for the top journals are not easily digestible [*laughs*].

What steps have you taken during your career to improve the quality of your writing?

I just keep working on it. I like working in teams, and that's where you also learn how to put over an idea. If you can communicate it successfully to colleagues, then that creates a way of writing it up.

How do you split up the writing tasks among co-authors?

We write everything together.

COLLABORATION

When you work with co-authors, how do you decide whom to work with?

That comes from ideas you're working on. Every day, I try to discuss new ideas with different colleagues, including students and young researchers at the IFS. Most of the time, none of the ideas are going to come to anything, but occasionally they will, and that will turn into a project or a paper. The group of co-authors then follow naturally.

How do you prefer to interact with them (e-mail, phone, or face-to-face)?

I always prefer to work face-to-face with people. So far, we haven't found a good way of replicating the whiteboard interaction – arguing and working things out on the board is very difficult to beat. I can't think of anything that I've written that hasn't had that as its main foundation. But technology is changing rapidly and Skype is clearly changing old habits.

Of course, there are some famous cases of co-authors who never met each other. In mathematics, there was G.H. Hardy and John Littlewood. They even lived in the same town – Cambridge – but just sent things by post [*laughs*].

What are the biggest challenges associated with collaborative work and how do you overcome them?

Any work you do in this field is probably going to take at least a couple of years to come to fruition. And so the challenge is making the collaboration work in a way that's enjoyable.

I like working with people. I wouldn't like to work on my own. I've never written a key paper without collaboration. I'm quite proud of that, although many people wouldn't be [*laughs*].

RESEARCH ASSISTANCE AND FUNDING

How do you use undergraduate and graduate research assistants?

Interestingly, one philosophy we have at the Institute is that we don't have research assistants. If you work with a graduate student or a young researcher, then they either come in as a co-author or you don't use them at all. That has some constraints, but I've found it to be a good rule because you're only going to pick people who you really want to work with and who you think will be effective collaborators.

How important is funding for getting your work done?

It has been very important to have a very good external and independent funding stream at UCL and the Institute. The Research Council in the UK (ESRC) has been invaluable in this respect. The work is largely empirical and so you require money for both people and resources.

Do you have any advice for a young scholar on the funding process?

The first thing I would say is that it's much easier than you think to get funding. If you already have an original idea, then there's a very good chance that you can get funding from somewhere, and so you should keep plugging away at it.

Having some funding is great because it gives you independence; you can buy your own data, spend your own time, and work with your own collaborators, all of which are important.

SEMINAR PARTICIPATION AND NETWORKING

What are the benefits to attending a seminar that is closely related to your work versus one that is not closely related?

I enjoy going to seminars and, on the whole, find them valuable. I rather like the idea of attending at least one a week in a field that is not related directly to mine, such as theory, macro, or development. There are almost too many seminars at UCL, but that's true at any good place, and I don't know how to get over it [*laughs*]. I find a good rule is not to go to more than two seminars a day!

How important is professional networking to success in research?

It's important. One piece of advice that every young researcher who comes to UCL receives is that you have to get your work out there, which means giving seminars. Both in North America and Europe. If you want to succeed, you have to take that step. That's the way to get your research noticed and also to find out how original it really is.

COMMUNICATION OF RESEARCH

How do you find the right balance between communicating your research at an early stage versus the close-to-finished stage?

I think it's a good plan to take an idea on the road well before it's finished. And it's fun.

What are the unique challenges to giving a seminar and how do you overcome them?

Connecting to the audience. I'm not too bad at it. You certainly have to be aware of who the audience is, and what their background is, so that you can get them to relate to what you're doing. People who don't bother to figure out who is in the audience, and what aspects of the research might be worth emphasizing and/or explaining more, tend to come unstuck in seminars. And so I think it is key to put some work into how you're going to address the audience, and get them involved, before the presentation.

PUBLICATION

How do you decide upon the appropriate journal to send your research to?

It's not so difficult when you've been doing this for a while to know where to send a paper. For young people, it's difficult to judge, and it does matter. But I always just say that you should try for the top because if it gets into, say, *Econometrica* or the *American Economic Review*, it will be treated very seriously and typically widely cited.

How would you best describe your approach to dealing with a 'revise and resubmit' request from a journal? How about an outright rejection?

A quick drink [*laughs*]. You tend to think that everybody else gets an easy ride, but that's certainly not the case. Most people do get outright rejections, and they don't always like them. And economists are pretty mean to each other. 'Revise and resubmits' can look very tough, but I take the points raised step by step. That's the only way to do it.

Do you think that the current structure of the publication process in economics facilitates or impedes scientific understanding and knowledge production?

The problem with publication, not just in economics, is that it only tells you about the successes, not the failures. So if you're trying to do research, you don't learn a lot from published work or you only learn a selected view of it. Of course, to do good work, you've got to figure out the paths not to go down, as well as the ones to follow. And that's why you need to be in an active research environment. If you're brilliant, you can probably work on your own, but for most people, it is crucial to figure out from others what does and doesn't work.

The big missing journal is the one about ideas that failed. Interestingly, there isn't a discipline that has such a journal. It might not sound particularly attractive, but I think it's a glaring omission. Wisdom is about knowing what works and what doesn't work.

What has been your best and worst experience during the publication process?

One thing I've learned is that when you think you've written your best-ever paper that will fly into a journal … it doesn't happen. A couple of years ago, I had a paper that was rejected pretty much everywhere before it got in the *AER*.[2] It was related to something that I had published previously in the *QJE*, but they didn't like it and neither did the *JPE*. I thought it was a really good idea and would go straight in. Now it is quite heavily cited. Most great papers were rejected several times and there's nothing wrong with that. You should read that nice little book called *Rejected*.[3]

Just for good balance, I'll tell you about another paper that went into the *AER*. It was on the retirement-savings puzzle.[4] This is the idea that, as people retire, they appear to cut their consumption. Of course, there's good reason for why this might happen, but there's also the possibility that they didn't figure out that they needed to save enough, and so they drop their consumption in a non-rational way. We wrote that up and it went straight into the *AER* – the quickest thing ever! But I would say the two papers that I've just mentioned are of equal standing, which just goes to show that you can never predict what's going to fly and what isn't. Perhaps the process is more random than we like to admit [*laughs*].

REFEREEING AND EDITING

Do you have any advice for a young scholar on being a referee?

Don't do too much of it, but do some of it. As a young scholar, it's good to become an editor or join an editorial board. In fact, it can be a very good signal, especially if you are not in one of the top ten departments. Typically, the only way you're going to be asked is by doing a little bit of refereeing. And if you get asked to referee for the top journals, do it.

Do you have any advice for a young scholar on being an editor?

I think everybody should try, if you get a chance, at least if you have tenure. You can have some influence on the profession. Most good journals move their editors around quite quickly – in fact, that's almost the way in which I judge whether a journal is a success or not. And so there are lots of opportunities. It is quite time-consuming, but it's a good thing to do, once you've got tenure.

I enjoyed being an editor. I got to read many papers and interacted with many people. The downside is that people don't like being rejected, and they can take it more personally than you would like. Some people never forgive you, and that's a shame. But, in a sense, you can see why. I was a co-editor at *Econometrica* and the majority of papers there are being submitted after careful consideration – typically the author is selecting the best paper he or she has written in the last two or three years. They will be really, really disheartened by a rejection. And so you have to do it carefully and make it as reasonable as possible. It's not an easy task [*laughs*].

TIME MANAGEMENT

How do you divide up your working day, both in terms of quantity and timing of different kinds of work?

The advantage of collaboration is that you can spend some of your day interacting with people and doing real research. I tend to do research at night, but collaborations happen during the day. It would be sad if you went through a day without discussing your ideas with others because that's why we're in this business. Never let administrative tasks get in the way of good research.

How do you balance multiple research projects?

I do have lots of projects because I run a research program which involves many people. It is a balancing act. But I like to get things out for publication quite quickly, and that's usually the way to set deadlines. No procrastination if possible [*laughs*].

How do you balance your work at UCL and the IFS?

Formally, it's half and half. I'm the Research Director at the IFS, but there's also a big research center there, which is funded by the Economic and Social Research Council of the UK. I have to spend a lot of time running and refinancing that. But it is joint work between the IFS and UCL since all PhD students involved at the IFS are registered at UCL. I'm supervising a lot of them! And many of the people who work at the IFS are also professors or younger colleagues at UCL. It's not quite as differentiated as you might think.

How about the balance between your personal and professional lives?

No sleep [*laughs*].

REFLECTIONS AND THE FUTURE OF ECONOMICS

What have been the most important findings and contributions in your research fields during your career?

There have been many improvements and contributions in econometrics, particularly in dynamics and in nonparametric approaches of microeconometrics. In terms of consumer theory, household models have proved to be a very fun area; thinking about household decision-making, and its interaction with the labor market, by developing the classical models into collective and non-cooperative bargaining ones.

Getting models to be consistent with expectations and dynamics has been the key difficulty. We still don't understand fully how people plan for the future, although it's so important when writing down models and doing policy analysis. But we're learning more and more, and finding ways of dealing with it. The other challenge is making sure we're getting the decision-making right, and being open to revising our models to reflect new things that we learn about behavior.

You were awarded the CBE in the Queen's New Year's Honours List for "services to Economics and Social Science." What has been your biggest contribution to economics?

That's a good question. I guess people would probably point to two. One is that I'd like to think that I've had some impact on the microeconometric modeling of individual and household behavior, and the implications for policy whether it be taxation, welfare design, or redistribution. And for some reason or another, I've managed to be reasonably good at directing research and policy analysis at the IFS, which I've worked on for nearly 25 years.

What are the weaknesses of your research?

There are plenty [*laughs*]. One thing that happens is you get rather good at selling the strengths of your work. This is why I think it's very important to have peers who are willing to challenge you, which has certainly been the case at UCL! If you end up at the top of a hierarchy, then you're not going to recognize your weaknesses because they're very easy to cover up. And one big weakness, which I've been guilty of from time to time, is drawing conclusions that are not founded on any substantive science. A good colleague is one who will tell you that in a pretty blunt way [*laughs*].

In the end, has the economics profession helped to bring out and shape your research for the best?

There are some people who have helped, and some people who haven't. But to think what it would have been without the profession is not an easy one to answer [*laughs*].

Do you have any professional regrets?

Anybody who took up economics 30 years ago has just been incredibly lucky. It's a discipline that's flourished, it's interesting and, amazingly, they pay us quite well to do it. And so it's difficult to have professional regrets. I do like having good colleagues and losing them is always hard. But it is also inevitable because economics is a very mobile subject area.

What are your professional ambitions?

I'm happy with the way things are working. But sometimes I do worry about the profession. It can be more self-destructive than it need be. We probably don't learn enough from the debates, and there are a lot of negative things that come out of some interactions among economists. My ambition has always been to create a very lively group with all the debates going on, but within a constructive environment. To some extent, that has happened, but we can do better.

How would you describe the state of economics today? Are you optimistic about its future?

Again, we're just lucky. We go through a crisis where many things that we thought were true turn out to be less secure, but economics becomes even more popular, and more fun to do.

You see trends happening where you get very worried about where it's going; it's not particularly scientific or it's not dealing with the big picture. But you also see things turning around.

I'm pretty optimistic. By the way, I think you have to be. If you're not, then you're probably not going to hang around because it takes so long to get success in this profession.

NOTES

1. Mirrlees, J.A. (1971), 'An Exploration in the Theory of Optimal Income Taxation', *Review of Economic Studies*, Vol. 38, No. 114 (April), pp. 175–208.
2. Blundell, R., Pistaferri, L. and I. Preston (2008), 'Consumption Inequality and Partial Insurance', *American Economic Review*, Vol. 98, No. 5 (December), pp. 1887–1921.
3. George B. Shepherd (ed.) (1994), *Rejected: Leading Economists Ponder the Publication Process*, Thornton Horton & Daughters.
4. Banks, J., Blundell, R. and S. Tanner (1998), 'Is There a Retirement-Savings Puzzle?', *American Economic Review*, Vol. 88, No. 4 (September), pp. 769–788.

Colin F. Camerer
(California Institute of
Technology)

Colin Camerer was born in Philadelphia, Pennsylvania in 1959 and graduated with a BA in quantitative studies from Johns Hopkins University in
1977 before obtaining an MBA in finance and a PhD in decision theory
from the University of Chicago in 1979 and 1981 respectively. Professor
Camerer has taught at the Kellogg Graduate School of Management at
Northwestern University, 1981–1983, the Wharton School at the University
of Pennsylvania, 1983–1991, the Graduate School of Business at the
University of Chicago, 1991–1994, and the California Institute of Technology, where he currently serves as the Robert Kirby Professor of Behavioral
Economics.

Professor Camerer's research looks primarily at the interface between
cognitive psychology and economics. This work seeks a better understanding of the psychological and neurobiological basis of decision making in
order to determine the validity of models of economic behavior. His
most-cited articles in chronological order include 'The Effects of Financial
Incentives in Experiments: A Review and Capital-Labor Production Framework', *Journal of Risk and Uncertainty* (1999), co-authored with Robin
Hogarth, 'Overconfidence and Excess Entry: An Experimental Approach',
American Economic Review (1999), co-authored with Dan Lovallo, 'In

Search of Homo Economicus: Behavioral Experiments in 15 Small-Scale Societies', *American Economic Review* (2001), co-authored with John Heinrich, Robert Boyd, Samuel Bowles, Ernst Fehr, Herbert Gintis, and Richard McElreath, 'Experience-weighted Attraction Learning in Normal Form Games', *Econometrica* (2001), co-authored with Teck Hua Ho, and 'Neuroeconomics: How Neuroscience Can Inform Economics', *Journal of Economic Literature* (2005), co-authored with George Loewenstein and Dražen Prelec. His books include *Behavioral Game Theory: Experiments on Strategic Interaction* (Princeton University Press, 2003) and *Advances in Behavioral Economics* (Princeton University Press, 2004), co-edited with George Loewenstein and Matthew Rabin.

Professor Camerer was elected as a Fellow of the Econometric Society in 1999 and a Fellow of the American Academy of Arts and Sciences in 2003.

I interviewed Colin Camerer in his office in the Division of the Humanities and Social Sciences at the California Institute of Technology, Pasadena. It was mid-afternoon of Monday, 16 August 2010.

BACKGROUND INFORMATION

What was your attraction to behavioral economics?

I went to graduate school in the mid-'70s at the University of Chicago, where I was confronted with an orthodox, highly rational choice view of economics. But it had one of the few business schools whose approach to psychology formed the early foundations of behavioral economics. This brewing alternative argued that people are neither perfectly rational nor completely stupid, but there may be limits to rationality that are systematic and can be modeled formally. And so it seemed evident to me that it was just a matter of time before the rational choice model would be extended and softened, and that new parameters would come in to form a better picture of human nature. I should also add that I am probably not a dogmatic enough person to be a serious traditional economist [*laughs*].

As a student, which professors were most influential or inspirational?

In graduate school, Hillel Einhorn and Robin Hogarth were my thesis advisors, and they were a study in contrast. Hillel was a very candid New Yorker who had studied industrial psychology, and Robin was a Scottish former accountant [*laughs*]. It was amazing they could write any papers together. I would hand one of them a draft of my thesis, and Hilly would take out all the commas and prepositions, and then Robin would put them back in. It was like a ping-pong match! But they did something in their own work, which I really admire and have often tried to do, which is to think very hard about an important topic and try to find something innovative to say about it. They were relentless. They would meet every day for coffee to update each other on what they had thought since the day before.

Another person who is quite the opposite, but from whom I learned a great deal, is Gene Fama, the finance professor. He left an impression for a number of reasons. One was that in college, I had taken an independent study course from his book *Foundations of Finance*, which had just come out. I worked in the college bookstore and remember literally unpacking the book, and the new-book smell of it. (Proust has his madeleine memory, while I, sadly, have a finance book). It was exciting to feel like you were in the first generation of people reading that book and learning from it. Fama always struck me as somebody who was not as mathematically brilliant and deep, as, say, Fischer Black, Steve Ross, and others in finance, but he had good ideas, was very tenacious and collected a bunch of data himself. He also knew a million empirical facts. It is true that I now fundamentally disagree with him about most topics, but you don't have to embrace somebody's religion to admire how they do their science.

Why did you decide to pursue an academic career?

One summer when I was in graduate school, I worked for JP Morgan Company as a summer intern. It was intellectually interesting working as an analyst intern, but I had to get up early and wear a tie [*laughs*]. And I had a sense that, as a business school professor, you could have the best of both worlds: work hard on the things you're interested in, and once tenured, have a lifetime deal to do whatever you like.

As a researcher, which colleagues have been most influential or inspirational?

One person was Ken McCrimmon. My first job out of graduate school was at Northwestern in 1981, and it was very unusual. It was in the business school there and I was teaching business strategy, which I didn't know very much about. We treated it as a combination of industrial organization economics, game theory, and managerial psychology. Ken was very supportive, but also tough.

At the time, the MEDS department (Managerial Economics and Decision Sciences) at Northwestern was also an unbelievable ground zero of game theory. Paul Milgrom was there, and so too was Bengt Holmstrom and Roger Myerson. Those guys were having fun, but they were also very principled and deep in their thinking. I remember sitting in on Paul Milgrom's class on industrial organization theory that was studying a paper by George Stigler on information economics.[1] By today's standards, it would be rejected as a first-year graduate student paper because it didn't have any math, was very naïve about information, and (of course) did not mention behavioral economics. The students were very vicious about it, saying, "I can't believe this got published, and the guy won a Nobel Prize." But Paul pointed out that was actually good. If your paper is so influential that 100 papers come after it that make the original one look anemic, that is known as progress [*laughs*].

And so Paul and Bengt and a number of other people had a lot of wisdom about what they were doing and they also got me very intrigued by game theory. It seemed like it was in need of the psychology of limits of rationality, along with some role for emotions. That was inviting.

GENERAL THOUGHTS ON RESEARCH

How would you describe the research setting at Caltech?

Caltech is very special. The mission statement, as I think of it, is to do work that is innovative, technically difficult, and interdisciplinary, with either an immediate or eventual eye to engineering and application. And so when I am thinking about, say, what the brain is doing when someone is bargaining, I don't have a mind-boggling machine to sell, but the idea that there is something to be engineered and a problem to be solved further down the road informs how I think about it.

Caltech is also very tiny. There are about 25 people in Social Science. On that scale, you either have a Noah's Ark model where you try to have two people of each area of social science, but that is very difficult because it is so fragile, or you pick two or three areas that you think you can stand out in and just leave the others aside. And so we don't do macroeconomics at all, except where it intersects with economic history. Mostly, we do micro theory, experimental economics, and neuroeconomics, and we have some presence in anthropology.

How would you describe the dialogue between theory and empirics in economics?

That's an interesting question. I think there has been inertia in accepting fundamental change in theory that has probably held economics back, particularly at the level of graduate education. My favorite example is prospect theory, which is the most widely cited empirical paper in economics published since 1970.[2] This landmark piece of work is still not routinely taught to first-year graduate students, whereas something that Daniel Bernoulli thought about 300 years ago (expected utility theory) is considered very important. Of course, there has been dramatic progress in something like game theory, which now stands alongside standard economic treatments, but even that was very slow to be adopted. The main ideas began in the 1940s and 1950s, and when I was at Chicago in 1977 it was hardly taught at all (only one class on 'the core' of non-cooperative games).

Some economists argue that experimental economics informs theory rather than applied or empirical problems. What is your view?

I don't agree with that at all. There are a number of strands in which experimentation has influenced design and application. For example, in environmental economics, economists have been doing experiments for decades to try to measure contingent valuations for non-traded goods. And more recently, in auction theory, experiments have been used to test the robustness of different types of auctions. It is very much like if you build an airplane wing and it breaks in the wind tunnel, you don't build the airplane. It doesn't guarantee that you will make the best airplane, but it will eliminate a lot of bad ideas cheaply.

How would you characterize your own research agenda and how has it changed through time?

I am interested in getting the right model of human nature into economics, particularly adding concepts from psychology and neuroscience, but also ones from sociology and anthropology. And related to this is the fact that I have always been very interested in innovative techniques. For example, in order to explore psychology and rational choice, it is very helpful to measure what people are looking at on a computer screen. If they are not looking at something, it follows that they can't be obeying a theory that requires them to have that information. And so we did some early experiments starting in the late '80s in game theory using that eye-tracking technique. Later, around 2003, we began to look at activity in the brain and measure all kinds of things.

Do you think it is important to have broad research interests?

I think it is important for the profession as a whole to have people who are like bees, pollinating ideas from here and there, but also to have specialists who are good at taking a suggestion that somebody else imported from, say, psychology and then doing the hard work of formalizing it.

How about the importance of broad tools?

In neuroscience, we have had a fairly lively discussion about the natural division of labor in the sciences. One view is there are theorists who just do theory, and there are empiricists who just test theory, and if there is some useful gain of exchange or complementarity, then that will arise from the process of asking questions at seminars and by reading each other's papers. But often it happens best when it is inside one brain. For example, Herb Simon was very influential in a general way in behavioral economics. He thought about an algorithm as being something that computers and brains both do. He was not the first person to think like that, but if it had not been for those ideas coexisting in him, it might have taken 20 more years for the view that the brain is a computing mechanism to get into cognitive psychology. And so if you had tremendous specialization within the economics profession, and no floating people who are bringing ideas back and forth and using both techniques, it could get pretty stale, and there would be a lot of missed opportunities.

IDEA GENERATION

Where do you get your research ideas?

Most of them are opportunistic in the sense that there is a combination of a technique and an open question in economics where progress needs to be made. Those are the ones that I enjoy the most. For example, the impetus for our eye-tracking experiments was the fact that many ideas in game theory relating to how equilibrium might be reached, or how players might be reasoning, could be thought of as formal restrictions on what you need to look at in order to evaluate strategy. It seemed to me that if you had a theory that says people look at certain things and then make certain choices, then you could not efficiently make progress without *measuring* both what they look at and what they choose.

In terms of neuroeconomics, I met a few neuroscientists who were very interested in simple ideas in economics, like preference theory. Does the brain have neural activity that you could measure and map onto a number scale that would look like utility? To an economist, it almost sounds ridiculous, because utility does not have to be in the brain. But it *might* be in the brain, and *where* in the brain it is being computed, and *how* computation develops in a person's life-cycle could be very interesting. That was an example of a recipe where there was a technology and a field that could contribute to understanding the biological underpinnings of economic choice, and that no one else was doing. And Caltech is a place where we can do such things.

At what point does an idea become a project that you devote resources to?

Many ideas die during the walk from the Faculty Club to here. They don't survive the post-lunch conversation in which I have received that glazed-eye look from someone, or the polite response of, "Well, I wish I had more time to work on that one with you."

IDEA EXECUTION

What makes a good theoretical paper?

I don't have a particular taste for highbrow theory because it has not contributed too much, except in some case where it sharpens the thought process of graduate students and helps to raise the bar on the quality of so-called applied theory. And so to me, the best theory paper is not the one that has the most dramatic math in it, but instead generates the most surprising, non-obvious insight from simple assumptions. This is, to me, the style associated with early Chicago (Becker) and the MIT approach. And, after reading it, if I can't think how to do an experiment or test it with field data, then it has failed as a theory paper because I don't know what it is a theory of. That doesn't mean that theorists have to design an experiment or make it super easy, but if you can't somehow see what the empirical insight might be eventually, then it is not that useful as economics.

Can you give an example?

I will give a positive example rather than a negative one. In one project, we used a tool of Roger Myerson's on Poisson Games.[3] Myerson is in a special, rarified league. He seems to have a magician's touch, particularly going back to his work on the revelation principle, which opened up a huge vista into bargaining theory. First of all, I will mention how we used Poisson Games, and then return to why we thought it was so beautiful.

We were interested in a lottery held in Sweden in which people choose a number from 1 to 100,000, and the lowest number that is unique wins a prize. Everyone wants to pick a low number, but if you pick, say, 1, and a bunch of other people pick 1, you don't win. It turns out that 53,000 people played this lottery every day in Sweden, and it seems impossible to compute the Nash equilibrium in pure strategies. But if you assume that the number of players has a Poisson distribution – it isn't the same number of people playing every day – then Myerson's theory of Poisson Games shows you how to compute the equilibrium. I thought it was very clever because in game theory if you go from a fixed number of players to an unknown number, things typically become impossibly complicated (like in auctions, where you can look around the room and know the number of bidders or log on to a website and not know). Here it is the opposite: a fixed number is impossible computationally. But the Poisson distribution is easy, and it is because of an amazing shortcut called environmental equivalence.

The intuition is as follows. After we got the Swedish data, we ran some experiments, where we recruited 50 people and told them the number of people who were going to play each time. The average would be 27, and we said that if you are "live", you got to play. The Poisson distribution has the property that if you are told you are live this time, on the one hand, you think, "Gee, I'm going to play, which means I should think of myself as competing against 26 others. But it also means that since I got picked, the total number is probably pretty high this time, so it could be more than 26 others." And it turns out that those two effects exactly cancel out only for Poisson distributions, which makes a shortcut so you can compute the equilibrium for these games. I don't know how Myerson thought this up [*laughs*]. But it is a very beautiful and mathematically elegant theory paper, which is also a tool to help you think about large-scale systems (he developed it to study voting in large populations).

As an aside, I happened to be giving a talk in Chicago a few years ago, and he had just been working on this topic. We were talking about the Poisson distribution, as I had used it to characterize the number of steps of reasoning people may be doing in thinking about games. And I remember being with him in his office, and he was so excited about Poisson distributions. He was drawing them, and he would instantly rattle off about ten facts about Poisson distributions that I had never known about their structure and what happened in certain ways. His enthusiasm and mastery was charming; it was not something dry and technical. He was in love with those Poisson distributions [*laughs*].

What makes a good empirical paper?

The results should be convincing and not obvious. It is almost like, in reading the paper, your mind goes from, "I don't really quite believe this," to, "Yeah, of course."

Can you give an example?

A paper that I like a lot looks at the relationship between colonialism, malaria, and economic growth, and it is written by Daron Acemoğlu, Simon Johnson, and Jim Robinson.[4] The idea in growth economics is that those former colonies of European countries that fully adopted the country's institutions, such as rule of law, seem to flourish. For example, Singapore is doing great, but Burma isn't. And so the authors go back and say, "Why is it that some places adopted those institutions but others didn't?" The argument is that it related to disease. In places where the Europeans could not settle, because of tropical diseases, they were more likely to establish extractive institutions, which remained after independence and hampered economic growth. On the other hand, in places where they could settle, they tended to establish development-oriented institutions, which have contributed to persistent economic growth.

It is a very tricky paper because the data quality on disease is poor, and it is almost a preposterously simplified hypothesis. But I found it very interesting because it was daring, and showed you how something that seemingly is quite non-economic, like disease, might lie right at the heart of this very classic new institutional story about rule of law and trust.

What makes a good experimental paper?

First, what makes a boring experimental paper? A paper is boring if it is too obvious what the result will be. For example, it is easy to think of a game where people don't converge rapidly to Nash equilibrium. And so a good experimental paper should have fruitfulness. This will mean that after reading it, you immediately want to go run another experiment, not because the first one has a flaw in it, but because it raises some new questions. Or at the end of the seminar, everyone is talking about the paper and you can literally hear the buzz of excitement.

Can you give an example?

I will indulge and talk about one of mine [*laughs*]. It is a co-authored paper that was mostly done by Mónica Capra and Charles Noussair.[5] A few years ago, we became interested in economic growth, and Charles, a former PhD student at Caltech, had written a couple of papers on extremely simple growth models with a threshold technological externality. The idea is that agents in experiments have capital, like corn, which they can eat or save. If enough agents pile up enough capital, there is a threshold that takes off, like a technological discovery, and then marginal productivity becomes much higher. Formally, it is a very simple coordination game. If the agents could all agree to save and build up enough capital, they would get across this technology threshold and become super rich. And when we work out the math, it turns out there are two equilibria. There is a poverty trap where marginal productivity is pretty low, so nobody bothers to save, and you never go above the threshold, and then there is a good equilibrium in which you go above the threshold and marginal productivity is super high.

In our paper, we were interested in whether there was an empirical set of conditions to take us from one equilibrium to the other. And so we tried a bunch of different elements, and it was also one of a small number of papers in experimental economics to allow agents to communicate free form. It turns out that if there is no communication and no political leadership – you can't elect somebody to impose a policy – then you don't get out of the poverty trap. On the other hand, if you have a leadership policy, in which somebody collects your capital, holds it, and makes sure everyone communicates with one another, then you always get out of the poverty trap.

Communication language has been under-studied in economics, but experimentally, it is important for helping groups of people in small-scale experiments solve problems. I am proud of that paper because we introduced a fairly broad paradigm to study the interaction of political and economic factors in a poverty trap setting. And it was the opening step in the experimental economic growth agenda. Unfortunately, we had one rejection at the *AER* on the grounds that we can't learn about growth economics in the lab, which I think is absolutely completely wrong-headed and it is certain to be disproved someday when people get the money and energy to do really complex experiments. We tried to get money for more but couldn't get even modest grant money from the NSF. Anyway, after the *AER*, the paper went right to the second journal which handled it well, and especially appreciated the novelty.

When you hit a brick wall on a project, do you continue to work on the problem or do you take a break and work on something else?

I hate to start things and not finish them, but I also know a lot about the sunk cost fallacy [*laughs*]. Usually, I will put a project aside and think we will revisit it in a couple of weeks and see if it is really worth returning to, knowing that it will definitely not be the case. I have basically broken up with the project [*laughs*]. But it eases the pain of realizing we made a mistake and that we should just abandon it, which is hard but important to do.

I hope this does not sound too smug, but I don't think we hit too many brick walls, partly because much of the work is hedged in the sense that a viable, say, rational choice explanation or an equilibrium may occur, and if it does not, it is probably because something else happens. And as long as we have a statistically conclusive enough result, we can publish it.

Do you scrap many projects?

Almost everything we do in neuroeconomics involves a scale of three to eight co-authors, and in experiments there are at least two or three. And once students are involved, I feel like we have to finish it for their sake. It is very important for them to see the process through from beginning to end. I hate to not finish and not publish, once we get past collecting pilot data, and it has only happened a few times.

What has been the biggest change during your career in how researchers in your fields conduct research?

Within behavioral economics, there has been a rise in middlebrow applied theory and also, more recently, in deeper decision theory. If you go back and read, say, Dick Thaler's early papers, you will see they are written in a literary, pre-math style. You can easily imagine the formalism he had in mind, and often there is some notation, but it is just ideas – great ideas! Economists like David Laibson, Matthew Rabin, and Botond Kőszegi have come along since and formalized the elements of psychology and carefully checked the logic. That has been very good.

A parallel occurrence is the rise in analysis of field data by people like Stefano DellaVigna and others who are thinking about time inconsistency and limits on attention. That is not a dramatic revolution, but it is percolating along, articles are getting published, and there are tons of interesting topics to work on.

Let me add something about neuroeconomics. One thing that is interesting is that behavioral economics received a small push from cognitive psychology, particularly from Daniel Kahneman and Amos Tversky, as well as Paul Slovic and Baruch Fischhoff. But it was a narrow segment of psychology – judgment and decision-making – and we did not get much direct help from those studying, say, attention or emotion. And so since then, behavioral economics has had to take off by itself. But neuroeconomics has been much more collaborative. For example, I have written many more papers with people who are neuroscientists than with psychologists. That rapid kind of collaboration is very unusual in economics, and it has been shocking how well it can work. Of course, it does not always work, but the fact that it ever works is amazing [*laughs*]. And for that reason, I don't think it is crucial that neuroeconomics gets much of a foothold in economics departments.

THE WRITING PROCESS

What steps have you taken during your career to improve the quality of your writing?

In 2004, we published a paper in the *QJE* about steps of reasoning.[6] Ed Glaeser, who is a wonderful editor, forced us to hire a technical editor to write the first four or five pages much more engagingly. I was not going to argue with Ed about how to write a good paper, since he is both an outstanding communicator and was the boss at that point. I thought it was like when someone says you need to go to the gym and you realize after you went and got in shape, as painful as it was, that they were right. And so we hired a woman who writes for applied math journals. She spent hours and hours on the first few pages trying to get the tone just right. That was a very helpful experience to see her slaving over a few crucial paragraphs.

When I wrote a book about game theory (*Behavioral Game Theory: Experiments on Strategic Interaction*), the editor also told me to spend half my time on the first chapter. He said that many people will only read that one. Of course, I was disappointed [*laughs*]. I said, "What do you mean?" He replied, "Look, you should be happy they read one chapter. That's better than zero. And given that a lot of people will stop on that one chapter, try to make it self-contained. Preview your ideas in there and be catchy." I think Ed had the same thing in mind: people decide whether to keep reading after the first few pages and so, as an author, you should work very hard at the beginning of an article or book.

In neuroscience, we spend hours debating the title because titles are often a self-contained abstract. For example, the title might be something like 'Amygdala Damage Erases Loss Aversion.' You may not believe it without reading the paper, but at least you know what the claim of the paper is! My view is that if you don't know how to title it, then you don't really understand your paper. Part of the reason for the title being important is that the papers are short – around 4000 words. For a journal such as *Science*, you have a brief window of space to write for a hugely varied audience of very smart people who don't know much jargon. And so you wind up negotiating over this compact expression of what you think is in your paper. By the way, this is a missed opportunity in economics. The titles are often terribly vague!

COLLABORATION

When you work with co-authors, how do you decide whom to work with?

First I ask: Are they going to do the work? Recently, I have not taken on too many brand new co-authors whom I didn't know. For most of the empirical projects, there will be a junior student who will be the first author typically and who has the most at stake. And so we try to find a combination of the student who can do the work, but also build up some new skills in the process.

When I work with a senior person, it is somebody whom I want to learn from, and I hope they feel the same way. It is like being in a romantic relationship where both of you think, "Wow! I am so lucky to be with this person. Why are they spending time with me?" And so, in my work, I want to be able to say, "I am really going to learn from this famous neuroscientist. It is amazing that he returned my e-mail, and we are doing this together." And it would be nice if they had a similar appreciation for me.

Is geographical proximity ever an important consideration when choosing a co-author?

It depends. I was in Israel traveling this summer, and I had a Skype call about chimpanzee experiments with somebody back at Caltech and a guy in Japan! But when I was at the Wharton School in Philadelphia, I had a co-author, Keith Weigelt, who was in New York. We would each take the train back and forth, hang out and have fun, and also get a lot of work done. But when he moved to Wharton and we were in the same school, we hardly got any work done at all! The synchronization had disappeared. We went from saying, "Okay, we're here for a couple of days. Let's revise the paper" to "We should get together next week ... " Fifty-two weeks went by pretty quickly! And so a lack of geography proximity can sometimes be an advantage because it means that if someone makes a visit, you have to be focused on getting things done with them.

How do you prefer to interact with them (e-mail, phone, or face-to-face)?

When we are getting started on a project, we will have chalkboard conversations. But there are a lot of substitutes. For example, a computer science colleague and I have just started thinking about something for a possible grant proposal. We spent about half an hour on his board, and then he took a picture of the work and e-mailed it to me!

What are the main challenges associated with collaborative work and how do you overcome them?

There are two problems: someone not doing enough or someone doing too much. The way I handle it is to have an extremely candid up-front discussion, using some of the language of economics, like residual decision rights. I will say, "You'll be the first author and I'll be the last one, but you may be demoted if I judge you to be free-riding." Students are often shocked that we have this discussion. They often say, "Why don't we just see how it goes, and then we'll decide?" But I always tell them if we do have a problem, it will be much harder to deal with then than now. It's like a prenuptial agreement.

Sometimes a dispute will arise. For example, I have had cases where students felt their work should be rewarded by having their name on a paper. I try to err on the side of inclusion, and I tell them not to be scared to have a discussion with me about it, but occasionally I have had to say, "I don't think you've contributed as much as you thought. I am not going to put your name on this. I'll try to make it up to you in this other project."

By the way, all of this also means that we have to think very carefully when writing the first draft of a paper. By that stage, you feel like you have made a commitment to keep someone's name on it.

RESEARCH ASSISTANCE AND FUNDING

How do you use undergraduate and graduate research assistants?

I try to delegate as much as possible to them. I treat the undergraduates like graduate students and the graduate students like young assistant professors.

How important is funding for getting your work done?

It is pretty crucial. If I had almost no money, I would just stop and write a book or develop a course that I have been thinking about.

Sometimes we use the funding process as test marketing of an idea. For example, when I was trying to get money to do large-scale political economy experiments on growth, it was evident from the fact that we failed that there probably was not even an audience in the journals either. I sent in one proposal, and then a revision, expecting it to get rejected but just to hear what people would say in print as reasons for rejection.

I should add that there are a number of cognitive and neuroscientific tools that are not too costly at the margin. For example, the eye tracker that we use costs $30,000, but it lasts a long time, and so the marginal cost is effectively zero. Primates do have high marginal costs because they need to be housed and taken care of. The fMRI (Functional Magnetic Resonance Imaging) machine is mostly a big fixed cost because it is always on and you need physicists and staff people to maintain it and help on techniques.

Do you have any advice for a young scholar on the funding process?

Be aggressive. If you want to meet Paul Milgrom and he is giving a talk at a conference, go up afterwards and introduce yourself. He won't bite. Give your papers to people. I remember I once sent a paper to Amos Tversky, a titanic figure in psychology, but he never replied. Later I ran into him at a conference, and he said, "I really liked your paper." When I told him that I did not think he had even got it, he replied, "Oh, no, you should always send people your papers. The worst that can happen is they think you're being a little pushy and so forth, but often they'll look at it and it goes in their memory bank or they hand it to a student who's interested in that topic." I think it is the same with funding. If you feel like you need senior authors to help get some money, e-mail them.

There are some other common amateur mistakes in getting grants. One is to not read the RFP (request for proposals) carefully. At the NSF, for example, they care about 'intellectual merit' and 'broader impact'. You have to use those *exact* words in the proposal. The second is that you typically have to show pilot data or partial progress in order to clarify what you are going to do, and show that you can do it. Unfortunately, it means you need some seed money somehow to do enough work to get the grant to do the rest. The third mistake is that because the grants have deadlines, usually people rush at the last minute and don't proofread. If it is a multi-person project, you can tell that two different people wrote two sections, for example, and then you think, "If they can't even converge on the proposal itself, are they really going to collaborate well?" No. Now in our group we usually show the senior graduate students and post-docs the proposals at all the stages so they at least get a glimpse.

SEMINAR PARTICIPATION AND NETWORKING

What are the benefits to attending a seminar that is closely related to your work versus one that is not closely related?

I always learn much more from a neuroscience seminar, which is not as closely related as economics. I find it quite painful to go to many economics talks these days. The 90-minute seminar based on one paper is an outmoded institution that is designed mainly to help improve someone's paper rather than inform the audience about a general research topic. If I am interested in your paper, I can download it from, say, SSRN, and if you want feedback, there is a refereeing process that guarantees you will receive plenty of opinion about your work.

How important is professional networking to success in research?

It is pretty important. But I do think that academia is meritocratic. For example, Ray Battalio was a famous experimental economist who hated to fly. I met him only once over a 30-year period. But it did not hold back his fame, because he wrote many great papers. Perhaps when someone went through a mental Rolodex of the top economists in topic X, no pictures of him at conferences popped up in that imaginative process and that kept him from getting picked to do honorary things or serve on editorial boards. But nowadays, you can have a presence on the Web and never have to go to a conference.

COMMUNICATION OF RESEARCH

How do you find the right balance between communicating your research at an early stage versus the close-to-finished stage?

In the past, I would present work too early sometimes, because I like to think with my mouth. But in the neuroscience world, people keep their cards much closer to their chest. It avoids feuds about uncertain paternity of ideas. For example, when we started doing imaging around 2003, I made a list of the ten big ideas that we should work on. If I heard somebody talking about one of those ideas in a seminar, I would move it up the queue or think, "Oh yeah, I meant to get back to that one. This guy has just given me an idea of how to do it." Then the person whose idea influenced me might think I stole it. There is no way to negotiate the proper credit, plus self-serving bias can cause a lot of heartache. That person thinks he deserves credit for having conveyed the idea such that it improved your paper. But you say, "Well, you did, but I had those notes from five years ago where I had a similar idea." And so the two of you walk away feeling that your combined contribution to the project was 180 per cent [*laughs*].

All of this means that we are now a little more demure about talking about our ideas. And we also have to modulate it. When I visit colleagues, I will sometimes tell them that this is something that we are working on, and so don't steal it. I will say it jokingly, but they understand that if I later find out that they are doing something related to our work, I will have the right to be mad at them.

At the same time, sometimes presenting not-finished work is a blessing. A couple of years ago, I was giving a talk on neuroeconomics at NYU. It was an overview of the field, but I also presented some of our brand new work. One of the editors of *Science* was there, and he came up at the end and said, "I really liked that last paper on public goods. Have you submitted it? If not, we might be interested." After I told him that it was half-done, I ran back to see one of the students who was also working on it. "Hurry up," I said, "Gilbert Chin wants this paper in *Science*!" It still took quite a while, because it was difficult computationally, but it was eventually published there.[7] Clearly, that initial feedback was absolutely crucial, and is one positive case where talking prematurely about some exciting work made all the difference. That is also a positive testimony to how journals like *Science* work so well. Their full-time editors have time to roam around at conferences and they put a big exploration bonus premium on novel ideas, and they are really smart since they have to know a little about a huge range of science. In economics, it is virtually the opposite.

What are the unique challenges to giving a seminar and how do you overcome them?

I once gave a talk at the Board of Trustees at Caltech, and the president of the university, David Baltimore, gave me some advice. He said the first third should be interesting to everyone, including spouses of board members, the middle third should be aimed at those with more technical know-how, and the final third should just be for those who know the most. And he also told me that sometimes you have to use jargon. "As a biologist," he said, "I'm not going to make up a new word for DNA." And so if you are talking about price elasticity, that is a useful word for people to know, but you have to walk through it so that they understand it. The hardest part of a seminar, particularly for new PhDs, is stepping back and getting ideas across in plain language.

PUBLICATION

How do you decide upon the appropriate journal to send your research to?

We spend a lot of time thinking about that from the very beginning. First, is this an economics paper or a neuroscience one? Once we have figured that out, we decide on the title of the paper and the journal to send it to. For example, if it is economics, I know that the *QJE* likes clever papers that make use of interesting datasets. But, of course, you don't want to become too attached to a particular journal because if the project is not working out, we are back to the sunk cost problem.

Some day, I will write something aimed at a popular audience but that is much harder work, quite different than writing for journal readers.

How would you best describe your approach to dealing with a 'revise and resubmit' request from a journal? How about an outright rejection?

We are respectful of a referee's time in the sense that we have the view that, just as the customer is always right, the referee is always right. And so, with very few exceptions, if we get rejected at one journal, we will revise it a little bit for the next one based on the reports. I think that is a prudent thing to do. First, you may get the same referees again. It really bugs referees to get the same exact paper to review for a different journal, and see that the authors have completely ignored their first review. And second, if three referees are all saying that your paper is too long, the chances are that three more referees will say the same thing.

Also, I don't like to fight with editors. In fact, I hate it, and editors do, too. And there are many other journals that you can try. For example, in neuroscience, *Nature* and *Science* are the main ones, but below those there are a bunch of good ones, like the *Journal of Neuroscience*.

Do you think that the current structure of the publication process in economics facilitates or impedes scientific understanding and knowledge production?

I am dissatisfied with aspects of it. The neuroscience model clearly works much better. If you installed a number of its features in economics, perhaps that would help. One is that the journal editors are professional editors rather than academics. They are very smart people with PhDs, who have a lot of free time because they are not on committees or teaching, go to conferences constantly, so they know a tremendous amount, and don't have conflicts of interest. They reject papers by Nobel Laureates all the time. The second thing relates to paper length. Because the neuro papers are short, you have no excuse to not review it in two or three weeks. And it also means that the reviewing process will not end up with a dramatically changed paper in terms of length and scope. And finally there are two types of journals: ones like *Science* and *Journal of Neuroscience* that contain short, substantive contributions, and others like *Trends in Cognitive Science* and *Trends in Neuroscience* that feature review articles. I like the idea of economics trying to separate more journals into this two-style system. There is a new *Annual Reviews in Economics* series which is off to a great start.

Another problem is that the journals seem to be unwilling to experiment with changes that could be easily reversed if they don't work. For example, there is a new series called *Frontiers* that is only online publication and works very efficiently. One thing that they do is say who the referees were if the paper is published. This means that if accepting a paper is later judged to be something of a mistake, you know what referees are responsible. It also disbands reviewing clubs in which a small number of like-minded colleagues or even friends accept one another's papers and reject all others (or some milder form of favoritism, perhaps even unconscious). If there was such a club, you could then see that Mr A accepted Ms B's paper and vice versa. When I talked to a couple of people about this, they all said "It won't work." It works in *Frontiers*! How do we know it wouldn't work in economics? It might scare off some referees who are sloppy and afraid to praise a paper that might be flawed, but they should not be refereeing anyway – you *want* to scare them off!

What has been your best and worst experience during the publication process?

The worst experience was an experimental paper on dynamic models of savings and consumption that we submitted to the *JPE*. The editor wrote back six months later and said, "We economists don't think that macro models can be tested with individual experiments." We economists?! I am a Fellow of the Econometric Society [*laughs*]. It was clear that the person thought I was a psychologist who had somehow wandered into economics by mistake. Also, it was evident from its title that the paper was an experiment about savings, so the editor was entitled to his or her opinion but should have rejected the paper right away rather than dragging it out six months. I think the *JPE* at that time was also going through a period when they were rejecting a lot of experimental papers, but, ironically, they published a monkey experiment paper around that same time! We then sent our paper to the *QJE*, who liked it, so that was a happy ending.[8]

My best experience was also with the *JPE*. The paper was a field experiment in which we went to a racetrack and made a big bet. First, it was $500, followed by $1000, and then we would cancel it in the last couple of minutes to see if the markets could be moved. It was so much fun to do, and the punch line of the paper was that the markets were pretty resilient. I was aware that it needed a much deeper theoretical structure to help understand the empirics, but the institutional setting was so complex. Every minute, the crowd was finding out how much money had been bet on eight different horses. To write down a model of that process would just be horrendously complicated and is definitely not what I am good at. I was living in fear that the *JPE* would think the paper made an interesting observation, but was incomplete without an accompanying theory. To my surprise, they were merciful! I give great credit to the editor, Lars Hansen, who accepted it with minimal revision.[9]

TIME MANAGEMENT

How do you divide up your working day, both in terms of quantity and timing of different kinds of work?

It is deadline driven, unfortunately. I am also a workaholic, so I am constantly checking my e-mail and managing the lab group members. If you are working with people who are self-motivated and independent, I want to always feel like I am taking advantage of them, but that they don't think so [*laughs*].

In the neuroscience model, you are obliged to answer rapidly to things. For example, a former student of mine, who is now at Baylor, has just sent a revised paper to me, and I told her I would look at it within 24 hours. If it means that I have to go to bed an hour late, that is too bad.

How do you balance multiple research projects?

When something comes back that can be revised briskly, that will go to the top of the queue. But these days, I try not to get involved with brand new projects unless I have a very clear vision about them.

How do you balance your research and non-research activities?

We have a very lean administrative structure in Social Science and Humanities: one division chair and someone who supervises internal faculty issues, including teaching and hiring. And the culture is pretty healthy in the sense that almost everybody wants to finish meetings as soon as possible and get back to their office to do research. The main non-research thing we spend a lot of time on is hiring new faculty. The discussions we have at those meetings are really about our culture and vision for ourselves so they are prolonged and useful. Also, we are small so we cannot afford to make a hiring mistake (with tenure). We have a lot of really wise experienced people in that room when we debate hiring. People also generally rise past their own tastes and don't just choose people like themselves, which is really important. That is the number one disease which makes departments decline.

How do you balance your personal and professional lives?

I have a four-and-a-half-year-old son, so he is the new major developmental psychology project [*laughs*]. I try to spend a lot of time with him. He is interesting, and travels pretty well [*laughs*]. We have been to three or four conferences with him, and then spent an extra couple of days hanging out. That is another nice thing about academic life.

REFLECTIONS AND THE FUTURE OF ECONOMICS

What are the biggest challenges facing your research fields?

There are two big challenges facing neuroeconomics. Doug Bernheim has written a paper in which he argues that if we can understand how the brain works, then we should be able to make fresh, interesting predictions about the relationship between traditionally observable variables, such as prices, and behavior.[10] But, in law, they say never ask a witness a question in the courtroom unless you know the answer. And so I will announce my commitment to that challenge once I am almost done with it [*laughs*].

The second challenge relates to welfare. If the choices that people make don't reveal their legitimate true preferences, because of mistakes or temporary insanity or addiction, then what is the right welfare measure? I must admit that I have stayed away from that one, because I think it is just hard. But if you are willing to admit that there are mistakes at all, which private markets or public regulation might be able to recognize and remedy, then it is likely that some link could be found between mistakes and abnormal or limited brain activity.

At what point in the future do you see IBM or a central bank hiring a neuroeconomist for consulting work?

I can see some applications happening very rapidly, say, within five or ten years. But I have a feeling that it will not necessarily be firms telling a neuroeconomist to "build a machine that will make us money." Instead, it might well be non-profit organizations that are more adventurous about, for example, trying to measure consumer satisfaction.

What are the strengths and weaknesses of your own research?

My weakness is definitely theory. I wish I had spent more time at the beginning of my career learning how to master it. My strengths are that I know a little about a lot of things, and I am a good judge of character in terms of potential collaborators. Early on, I made one or two mistakes. I formed friendships with people whom I thought I could also write papers with. But I quickly realized that does not always work, and that you can't afford to spend time on professional relationships that are not helping you learn and publish.

In the end, do you think the profession has helped to bring out and shape your research for the best?

Despite the profession's best efforts, it has worked out okay for me [*laughs*]. I am lucky to have chosen, and been accepted by, institutions that were pretty adventurous, particularly here at Caltech, but also earlier in my career at the Wharton Business School, where I was in a group called Decision Sciences, which was a very eclectic mixture of people doing psychology and operations research.

Do you have any professional regrets?

One regret is that I did not participate in behavioral finance, which is something that I was very interested in at graduate school. I remember Bob Shiller telling me that when he first spoke to people about market psychology, they would look at him as if he were talking about ESP. Back then, it was a very tough field, because people were focused on only a small number of questions, and the data were not plentiful, but I should have persisted with it.

I went back to the University of Chicago as a faculty member for two years. I regret missing some of the intensity of economists thinking about very practical questions, as well as being around a lot of people, all of whom are smart and communicative. But I hated the winter, and I did not like MBA teaching [*laughs*]. Also, I had a feeling that the frontier in behavioral economics would be more related to the technical side of things and that something like neuroeconomics would emerge. Caltech is an ideal place to do that and now we have an unbelievably great group.

What are your professional ambitions?

I don't have many unscratched itches about something exciting to do. But I would like to write an intense monograph of *Neuroscience for Economists*. That could be influential.

How would you describe the state of economics today? Are you optimistic about its future?

I think economics is unique. What we are especially good at is formalism and using the logic of general equilibrium to understand unintended consequences. Statistically, we are the best social science at inferring causality from correlation and making solid inferences about very difficult questions from data. That is not the case in a whole bunch of other social and biological sciences. But the bad news is that economists, until recently, have been slow to accept computing as an insightful tool for analysis and been unwilling to collect our own data on anything we want to measure. Thankfully, that is beginning to change in practice, though not in core curricula. However, it is still true that in all the economics PhD programs I know of, there are no required courses all PhD students must take in how to produce data. That means students must know a lot about theory to get degrees in economics, but they can get degrees without having any clue about the broad range of ways (including surveys, how governments collect data, experiments) in which theories are actually tested.

The profession is also stodgy and slow to innovate, compared to most other sciences, in how it is organized and run professionally. The way the job market for new PhDs works, use of technology and websites, the nature of professional seminars, slow acknowledgement of the rise of the service and information economy, and the ever-slower, frustrating editorial process, are all behind the times on some dimensions. Even worse, there is no mechanism or daring to experiment with big changes. Other fields are creating new online journals and trying out all sorts of mechanisms in lieu of traditional peer review. I think that economists are so well trained at spotting possible design flaws that it paralyzes them with fear when deciding whether to try out candidate design changes in managing their own profession.

I am extremely optimistic about neuroeconomics. Even if economists voted like a union to exclude it from economics departments, that would be fine. It will flourish someplace else, in neuroscience groups, professional schools that are more adventurous about new methods than economics departments, or at unusual places like Caltech.

NOTES

1. Stigler, G.J. (1961), 'The Economics of Information', *Journal of Political Economy*, Vol. 69, No. 3 (June), pp. 213–225.
2. Kahneman, D. and A. Tversky (1979), 'Prospect Theory: An Analysis of Decision under Risk', *Econometrica*, Vol. 47, No. 2 (March), pp. 263–292.
3. Myerson, R.B. (2000), 'Large Poisson Games', *Journal of Economic Theory*, Vol. 94, No.1 (September), pp. 7–45.
4. Acemoğlu, D., Johnson S. and J.R. Robinson (2001), 'The Colonial Origins of Comparative Development: An Empirical Investigation', *American Economic Review*, Vol. 91, No. 5 (December), pp. 1369–1401.
5. Capra, C.M., Tanaka, T., Camerer, C.F., Feiler, L., Sovero, V. and C.N. Noussair (2009), 'The Impact of Simple Institutions in Experimental Economics with Poverty Traps', *Economic Journal*, Vol. 119, No. 539 (July), pp. 977–1009.
6. Camerer, C.F., Ho, T.H. and J. Chong (2004), 'A Cognitive Hierarchy Model of Thinking in Games', *Quarterly Journal of Economics*, Vol. 119, No. 3 (August), pp. 861–898.
7. Krajbich, I.M., Camerer, C.F., Ledyard, J.O. and A. Rangel (2009), 'Using Neural Measures of Economic Value to Solve the Public Goods Free-Rider Problem', *Science*, Vol. 326, No. 5952 (October), pp. 596–599.
8. Brown, A.L., Chua, Z.E. and C.F. Camerer (2009), 'Learning and Visceral Temptation in Dynamic Saving Experiments', *Quarterly Journal of Economics*, Vol. 124, No.1 (February), pp. 197–231.
9. Camerer, C.F. (1998), 'Can Asset Markets Be Manipulated? A Field Experiment with Racetrack Betting', *Journal of Political Economy*, Vol. 106, No. 3 (June), pp. 457–482.
10. Bernheim, B.D. (2009), 'On the Potential of Neuroeconomics: A Critical (but Hopeful) Appraisal', *American Economic Journal: Microeconomics*, Vol. 1, No. 2 (August), pp. 1–41.

David Card
(University of
California, Berkeley)

David Card was born in Guelph, Canada in 1956 and graduated with a BA in economics from Queen's University, Kingston in 1978 before obtaining a PhD in economics from Princeton University in 1983. He has taught at the Graduate School of Business, University of Chicago, 1982–1983, Princeton University, where he was a Professor of Economics between 1987 and 1997, and the University of California, Berkeley, where he currently serves as the Class of 1950 Professor of Economics.

Professor Card's research interests include welfare reform, immigration, the effects of the Medicaid program in the US, pension incentives and retirement, labor supply, education, minimum wages, strikes and collective bargaining, evaluation of social programs, unemployment, and wage rigidity. His most-cited articles in chronological order include 'On the Covariance Structure of Earnings and Hours Changes', *Econometrica* (1989), co-authored with John Abowd, 'The Impact of the Mariel Boatlift on the Miami Labor Market', *Industrial and Labor Relations Review* (1990), 'Does School Quality Matter? Returns to Education and the Characteristics of Public Schools in the United States', *Journal of Political Economy* (1992), co-authored with Alan Krueger, 'Estimating the Return to Schooling: Progress on Some Persistent Econometric Problems', *Econometrica*

(2001), and 'Skill-Biased Technological Change and Rising Wage Inequality: Some Problems and Puzzles', *Journal of Labor Economics* (2002), co-authored with John DiNardo. His books include *Myth and Measurement: The New Economics of the Minimum Wage* (Princeton University Press, 1995), co-authored with Alan Krueger, *Handbook of Labor Economics* (Elsevier, 1999), co-edited with Orley Ashenfelter, and *Poverty, the Distribution of Income, and Public Policy* (Russell Sage Foundation, 2006), co-edited with Alan Auerbach and John Quigley.

Professor Card's academic awards include the John Bates Clark Medal (1995) and the IZA Prize in Labor Economics (2006), the leading award for labor economists. Among his honors, Card was elected as a Fellow of the Econometric Society in 1992 and a Fellow of the American Academy of Arts and Sciences in 1998. He was Co-Editor of the *American Economic Review* from 2002 to 2005 and Co-Editor of *Econometrica* from 1993 to 1997.

I interviewed David Card in his office in the Department of Economics at the University of California, Berkeley. It was early-afternoon of Thursday, 19 August 2010.

BACKGROUND INFORMATION

What was your attraction to economics?

Originally, I was a science undergraduate. But my girlfriend through college was taking an economics class, and she was having some trouble with the textbook's chapter on elasticities of demand [*laughs*]. I started reading it and thought it was quite informative. I grew up on a farm and there's a puzzle in the agricultural businesses: Why is a good year for farmers really a bad year? It's basically because the elasticity of demand is less than one. And so reading about that was quite enlightening and I went through half the textbook over the next few days. Given that I was also probably not going to be the greatest physicist of all time, I decided to switch to economics.

As a student, which professors were most influential or inspirational?

Because I got into economics so late, I had to take the classes that didn't have any prerequisites. And so I ended up taking classes in labor economics and in income distribution from two relatively young guys, Michael Abbott and Charles Beach. They had just finished their PhDs at Princeton, and I got interested in the set of topics that they worked on. Both of them were advised by Orley Ashenfelter, who, ultimately, recruited me to Princeton and became my thesis advisor.

Why did you decide to pursue an academic career?

I like to wake up late in the morning [*laughs*].

As a researcher, which colleagues have been most influential or inspirational?

Orley Ashenfelter. My first job was at the Graduate School of Business at Chicago and then, luckily for me, Orley had a job offer at MIT, and he wanted to hire some young assistant professors in labor economics at Princeton. He convinced them to hire me back there. We are still friends. In fact, he's visiting here right now. I've been very strongly influenced by him.

I've had many other colleagues and graduate students whom I've worked with and learned a lot from. The first person I worked with closely was a guy at Chicago called John Abowd, who's now at Cornell. When I went to graduate school, I didn't really know that much about statistics. I had a certain level of training, but it wasn't particularly deep. John had more of a background in statistics, and we got working on a project that was fairly successful in the end, and I learned a huge amount from working with him on it.

GENERAL THOUGHTS ON RESEARCH

There is an increasing emphasis in many economics departments on applied research. Is this true at Berkeley?

In the '70s, Berkeley was a very theoretical department and its reputation was built up on that. But various things have happened over the course of the last 30 years, and it's now probably more known as an applied place even though we still have a number of very strong theorists, and are always trying to get more.

It's different at other places. I was at Princeton for a very long time, and it had always had a very theoretical economics department. It became better known as being applied in the late '80s and early '90s with the loss of some top theorists, but at this point it's probably theoretical again. Departments do come and go.

What is the value of pure versus applied research in economics?

The value of a well-done, pure piece of theoretical research is more long-lasting. If you figure out something like Samuelson did in his *Foundations* book, or like Arrow and Debreu did in the '50s, those things influence the way people even *think* about problems for many, many years. Because the economy is a moving target, I believe it's hard for much of what we do as empiricists to have the same influence. On the other hand, the ability to write an important, deep, and fundamental contribution in theoretical economics is pretty small. Maybe there'll be some breakthroughs, and people will come up with new ways to think about problems, but right now I think it's easier to do something on the applied side.

How would you describe the dialogue between theory and empirics in economics?

There's quite a wide divergence of opinion on how those two should be blended. There are those who think that most research should be more theoretical and that applied work should be relegated to the government or researchers outside university, and others who believe that almost all theoretical work is, at this point, not particularly useful. Those are pretty extreme positions. In my own department, all opinions are valued and we don't have any big fights.

But we are in a period when there isn't a new thing in theory, like in the late '80s when there was incredible excitement about reformulating macroeconomics, along with a resurgence of interest in game theory. When I was at Princeton, Hugo Sonnenschein was turning out two or three PhD students a year for almost a decade and they went on to revolutionize game theory. There isn't anything like that right now, and I think that makes it difficult both for students and for researchers. What are we supposed to be doing? Hopefully, something will come along and rejuvenate things.

How would you characterize your own research agenda and how has it changed through time?

Well, it's possible that I don't have a research agenda [*laughs*]. I work on problems that are interesting at the time and ones that I think I can make some progress in answering. But most problems in economics, especially in labor economics and applied micro, have been around for a very long time, like how to infer something about consumer preferences or the way in which markets work. The difficulty is more in getting either a dataset or a method to try and present a new answer to that question. For example, I've been getting interested again in working on the old problem of unemployment, now that there's a lot of it [*laughs*]. Looking at unemployment is much better than it was in the '80s because of improvements in the data and so it's possible that some new insights will emerge.

Do you think it is important to have broad research interests?

I'm not sure there's a single answer to that question. I think each person has to figure out what suits their own interest. One issue for some people, as they get a little bit older, is that the thing that carried them through tenure and promotions, and quite a few good papers, gets mined out and then they have to think about how to adapt it or move on.

Is having a broad set of tools more important?

You can learn new tools. There are a lot of new tools, like dynamic programming, that have been refined, developed, and made more feasible by computing. The basic structure of dynamic programming was understood in the '60s and '70s, but since then people have figured out how to implement estimation schemes when you assume that agents are following dynamic programs with uncertainty and some information processes and so on. I think that's a pretty exciting area of work. But it's not something I learned at graduate school; I've had to pick it up and follow along.

Versions of econometric methodology have changed. When I was a graduate student, maximum likelihood and linear regressions were the state of the art. And often the maximum likelihood methods would be combined with very parametric models of the way in which people behave, but now we are doing research that is much less parametric and much more flexible. That's another example of where you have to pay attention to what's going on in the literature and figure out whether you can use this new method to look at a problem that's been bugging you for 20 years.

Do you think there is any difference in the types of work done by researchers at different stages of their careers based on tenure concerns, publication requirements or other pressures? Should there be a difference?

I think that the pressure on young people today isn't much worse than when I was an assistant professor. But the standard for tenure now is very strongly emphasized when you are first appointed and then reappointed mid-career.

Everyone talks about whether or not you have your five or six papers in the top journals. It is true that there are more and more people all around the world trying to become professional economists than there were in the '70s and '80s, and they're all aiming to get their papers published in the *QJE* and *AER*, so it is extremely competitive. And what this means is that young people today have to be very careful about not undertaking a project that doesn't yield something with relatively high probability in a year or two. On the other hand, it's still the case that most of the innovative new work is coming from junior faculty, so it's hard to say that that's really hurt anything too much. Maybe advisors are helping people pose questions and get started a little more.

In terms of whether there should be a difference, a former colleague of mine embarked on a project in his early 40s that involved collaboration with a bunch of people who weren't economists. A number of my other colleagues said, "That's outside of economics. Why is he doing that?" But I thought, "That's exactly what you're supposed to do when you're tenured." And so there are quite diverse opinions on this issue. But I do think that there isn't only one way to succeed in a career as a researcher. You just need to find your own thing at each point in time; something that you want to do and that you're good at.

IDEA GENERATION

Where do you get your research ideas?

[*Long pause*]. I don't really know. Sometimes there are questions that have been hanging out there in the world for a very long time. And I see myself as having a list of those questions at the back of my head and someone then creates a new dataset or a new theoretical model that makes me rethink them. A good example would be the huge debate about whether health insurance makes people healthier. The difficulty is the research design for tackling that issue: rich or better educated people have more health insurance, and, of course, they're healthier. But a couple of years ago, I started thinking about the Medicare program, which provides very generous, universal health insurance to all Americans once they hit 65 years old. I've been combining my thinking about that system with the regression discontinuity method, which has been very widely adopted in economics in the last decade. As you see more applications of a method, you end up saying, "Oh, I can think of another problem for it." That's what I've done.

At what point does an idea become a project that you devote resources to?

I always say that most projects are at their peak in the third hour of the discussion with your co-author, because it's only going to be downhill from there [*laughs*]. The modeling won't be as clean, the data won't be as good, and the results won't be as decisive. But once I have the project's beginning and end in my head, I can usually sit down and do it.

IDEA EXECUTION

What makes a good theoretical paper?

My feeling is that the better theoretical papers are extremely simple. Although there might be some elegant math someplace, it isn't usually rammed down your throat when you read the paper. And the authors may have stripped away quite a few institutional features and made some crude assumptions, which arguably means that the thing they're working on doesn't ever totally apply to anything, but it will give an insight into a wide range of problems. I do tend to prefer more abstract theoretical modeling.

Can you give an example?

A paper that I've always liked is Hurwicz and Uzawa's 'On the integrability of demand functions.'[1] [*Laughs*]. It's very heavy duty, but it's basically saying, "Okay, this is a problem in solving a differential equation. Let's find out what conditions under which that differential equation can be solved, and let's just blast it." That's what Samuelson set out to do in *Foundations*, but he didn't quite nail it. It's pretty interesting how a relatively straightforwardly posed question could take so long to answer.

What makes a good empirical paper?

There are many kinds of empirical papers. The first kind attempt detective work – they're trying to figure out why something is the way it is. They are useful and I like them. A nice example that I saw looked at the effect of the civil rights law that desegregated hospitals on the drop in infant mortality among African-American children in the '60s. It showed that if you look at black/white infant mortality, it has a constant pattern, then there's a big gain in the '60s and not so much after that. The paper was written by a couple of my former PhD students, and it is the best forensic piece of work I can think of. Unfortunately, it's never been published, because the students got into an argument with each other.

Another kind of hypothesis-testing paper is when somebody conjectures that something is true. For example, one of my best-cited papers is a very simple one on the Mariel boatlift.[2] I was trying to see the effect of over 100,000 people coming very quickly to Miami early in 1980. I got the idea from an undergraduate student at Princeton, who had grown up in Miami and talked to me about the boatlift. He then moved on and got a job, but I thought it was worth pursuing. And so all I did was just collect up the data and compare Miami to a bunch of other cities pre- and post-boatlift. The paper is not published in a great journal, but it gets a lot of cites because it's very straightforward.

A third kind of paper that I like a lot is when somebody poses a theoretical model of a behavioral channel, like demand or a reaction to a phenomenon, and then somebody else tries to figure out a way to find a setting where that is identifiable from all the noise in the system, and estimates how important that behavior is. A classic example would be attempting to estimate demand functions. The problem is that you very rarely get exogenous changes in prices. Actually, you don't often have any variation in prices across people, which makes it a mess. And so I really appreciate those kinds of papers, and I would say that's what people are trying to do today in IO more than in labor.

You are an economist who has reported one or two controversial findings in his papers. When you find a result that you realize is likely to be contro-versial, how does this affect how you write the paper?

You have to be aware that, in most people's minds, theory tests the data. That's just a true fact that I learned from John Abowd when I went to Chicago. And so if you present a finding that is contrary to a theoretical result that someone holds dear and near to their heart, the best you can expect is that they'll say, "Well, you gave it a good shot, but you got unlucky – your errors were such that you didn't get the right finding." They can't find anything that you did wrong, but they're not going to tell you, "This overturns my way of thinking about the world." In my opinion, no one's view in economics is overturned by any single paper, or even any collection of papers. And so the best you can do is what I would call 'professional work'. This means no errors and no obvious omissions. In a lot of papers, it's surprising how many times somebody has made an error that could be quite fundamental, or has missed something, or just didn't spend enough time trying to figure out what was really going on. If you have a controversial finding, the first thing everyone's going to assume is that you did one of those things. I'm the same! When somebody presents a result that I think doesn't make a lot of sense, I assume there's a very good chance they screwed it up [*laughs*]. You must realize that a bunch of very smart people, who have very strong incentives, are going to pore over your results and try and figure out what you did wrong. And if they can find something, that'll be a note or a comment in a journal, which will be extremely embarrassing for you, and they'll be the heroes of the day. So I don't want to publish a controversial result and have it be *possibly* the case that somebody could spend less than, say, three years on the project and find an error [*laughs*]. And I make sure that I've reported enough of a range of my results so that no one can poke around and tell me, "You say the coefficient is 3, but here's a specification showing that it's 0.1." A final thing is you shouldn't be too confident that your controversial result implies anything general. All you can report is, "In this particular circumstance, what we found is … " Don't say that your results are anything other than what they are.

When you hit a brick wall on a project, do you continue to work on the problem or do you take a break and work on something else?

In applied work, a brick wall can arise if you start working on a project with the idea that some proposition from a model you had in your head, but never wrote out, was true, and then you look at it more carefully and realize the empirical design is much less informative about that theory than you thought. For example, for almost ten years, I was working on a very complicated welfare experiment being conducted in Canada. Women who had been on welfare for a while were being offered a short-term incentive to go back to work. I was not involved with the design of the project, but I was called in once it was in the field. And so I got together with a friend of mine, who was a specialist in dynamic empirical modeling, to take a look at the experiment. I said, "There's something wrong with the way we're thinking about the problem." And then one day I realized that it needed to be put into a search theory framework. Once I posed it that way, the whole thing made a lot of sense and it was a very successful project for us; the paper got published and people liked the interpretation.[3] What was most amazing was that all the time we'd been working on the project, we'd been thinking about it incorrectly. It was an inherently dynamic incentive that was offered, and we were looking at it from a static point of view. That was an example of a breakthrough; of necessity being the mother of invention [*laughs*].

When a project isn't going to turn out as hoped, do you scrap it or aim to send the work to a second-tier or field journal?

I usually send it to a second-tier journal. I've got lots of papers in those journals. Sometimes you start a project and you know that even if it's outstanding and well done, it's going to go to a specialist journal like the *Journal of Labor Economics*. Other times, you start a project with high hopes, but it turns out to be less decisive, and so it has to move down the food chain. That's just the nature of the business.

What has been the biggest change during your career in how researchers in your fields conduct research?

When I started, most projects would have a pretty explicit theoretical front-end, and sometimes the best ones would then map that directly into the empirical approach using, say, maximum likelihood. That was like my thesis. But then some time in the '80s, it became less and less important to have this well worked-out theoretical framework. In some cases, people were focusing on extremely straightforward questions with much more emphasis on how credible and carefully identified were the empirical results. You might call it the research design revolution. But in the last ten years, there's been a backlash, and for almost all of my PhD students, I really emphasize the importance of having a well-posed theoretical model.

The other thing that has changed is that when I was doing my PhD, Princeton was the very best place for empirical labor economics. It was a producing a steady stream of people, and maybe once in a while somebody would come out of MIT or Harvard. Now there are seven or eight places that are turning out pretty decent empirical labor economists. But the field itself is not very big, and it has also diffused. In fact, most PhD advisors will tell you they haven't trained a true labor economist in 20 years [*laughs*].

THE WRITING PROCESS

Which aspect of the writing process do you find most difficult?

Writing the introduction. If I have to, I can write a 25-page paper overnight, but I won't be happy with the introduction. I never like it and I always change it. I don't know why; it's just my problem.

What steps have you taken during your career to improve the quality of your writing?

I've worked with co-authors who are better or more facile writers, and I've tried to imitate them.

Who proofreads your writing?

Just me and my co-authors. I don't take it to an editor. A few years ago, I wrote a book with Alan Krueger on minimum wages.[4] Alan was working in the government when we were completing it, so I had to do the whole final draft. And I worked with an editor. Editors can fix awkward writing or repetition and suggest more interesting adverbs and adjectives, but what they can't do is fix the entire tone of an article, and that's probably the thing that's hardest to imitate. A really good writer of an empirical labor economics article writes in a 'stripped down' way, where the technical details are suppressed or put aside. A sociologist or a beginning graduate student in economics should be able to read almost all of it.

COLLABORATION

When you work with co-authors, how do you decide whom to work with?

Most of the time, I work with people whom I know fairly well. At this point, they tend to be younger people, but I don't work with my graduate students very often. Some advisors do, but I don't think it does the students any good. They need ownership of their own projects.

Is geographical proximity ever an important consideration?

I actually like working with people who are not in the same time zone [*laughs*]. If you're in a hurry, you can get a lot done. For example, if you're working with somebody in Europe, you can work a combined 24 hours a day. And I work late at night, so if my co-author is on the East coast, that can work out pretty well too.

What are the biggest challenges associated with collaborative work and how do you overcome them?

I've probably written around 50 co-authored papers. Only once have I had to quit working on a project with a co-author because he and I didn't see eye-to-eye. If you're going to work with me, most people know that I have certain preferences and feel very strongly about certain things. Sloppy mistakes drive me nuts! And I hate crappy computer code. I'll hear people talk about working with a co-author and the results keep changing. If that happened to me, I would shoot the co-author [*laughs*]. I can't deal with moving targets. If I think that the person is not somebody who's going to nail it, then I do the empirical work myself. The guy whom I mentioned earlier had very strong priors about what the results would be. Every time we'd do the results, I felt he was molding them into this prior rather than looking at them and saying, "Well, there are some things that are working this way and others that are not. Maybe there's something else going on." He was too rigid; he wanted to estimate this one equation to get this one coefficient and that was going to be the paper. That's not how I write my papers.

RESEARCH ASSISTANCE AND FUNDING

How do you use undergraduate and graduate research assistants?

The problem is that training graduate students to be research assistants in empirical work is really painful and slow. Undergraduates are better. People tend not to understand that most of what we have to do as researchers is just crap work. Yesterday, for example, I spent the whole day in the library going through historical volumes. It's very hard to get graduate students to do something like that, or collect data, code it carefully, and then put it in a spreadsheet. They don't pay attention, or put in the hours, unless they're a co-author on the project. But an undergraduate thinks it's fun. In fact, I've just hired a guy whom I ran into at a small college. He's in-between finishing his undergraduate degree and starting graduate school. He'll work for me for a year.

How important is funding for getting your work done?

Hugely important. These days, to do anything empirically, you need to have access to specialized data. Yesterday, a graduate student told me he wanted to do a project on heart attack patients. That data will cost around $9000.

To the extent that you're doing anything remotely interesting computationally or theoretically, you constantly need to upgrade your computers as well.

You also need the time to work on a particular project and not something else, which usually requires some kind of funding. And so I spend a huge amount of my time trying to write grants.

Do you have any advice for a young scholar on the funding process?

Boy, I wish I were better at it. I've had lots of projects that I thought were really promising but took three revisions to get to funding stage or never even got funded. I served on the NIH panel for many years, and I'm part of a 'college of reviewers'. I think the reviewing process is like the refereeing process – it's getting crazy. You send something to the NIH and it's a bunch of people sitting around saying, "Oh, I don't like that equation." They never step back and ask whether it is generally good or bad or whether the person has a sound track record or not. They want to control the whole damn thing.

SEMINAR PARTICIPATION AND NETWORKING

What are the benefits to attending a seminar that is closely related to your work versus one that is not closely related?

If you can successfully identify them, it's probably better to go to the ones that are not closely related to your work, because that's where you're going to get the best new ideas. But I often think you can do well by just reading the paper. I like to go through papers in the *AER* or *QJE* by people whom I've heard are doing interesting work. That's useful.

How important is professional networking to success in research?

It's important. The first reason is that you have a better sense of what questions are being asked in a particular area. And the second reason is you can also figure out the current topics and angles in that same area. For example, if you could write a paper right now looking at the effect of asymmetric information on somebody's behavior, it'll be publishable. I don't know why, but that topic's in the air. Of course, once in a while, somebody writes a path-breaking paper that just says, "Okay, forget all that – let's work on this instead." While that is incredibly useful, it is also really hard to do.

How does the researcher without extensive networks succeed?

I think they have to look at the work that is being done by the assistant professors at the top ten schools. That will give them a sense of what are the current, interesting topics.

COMMUNICATION OF RESEARCH

How do you find the right balance between communicating your research at an early stage versus the close-to-finished stage?

That's an interesting question. I think what people do nowadays is they get the project done, show it to a few friends, present it to a few selected audiences, try and figure out how to revise the paper as strongly as they can, and then submit it. Because of the competition to get into the top journals, there's a premium to novelty, combined with the fact that no one ever reads a paper twice. In the past, I've submitted a paper that's been completely trashed by the referees, thought about it a lot more, and then revised it into a much better one. The problem is by that stage it's already been rejected by the initial referees and everybody says, "Oh, we saw that paper. It's a piece of junk." You've got one shot with a top journal and you've got to try to make it go there. Otherwise, it will sink like a stone [*laughs*].

What are the unique challenges to giving a seminar and how do you overcome them?

John Abowd once explained to me that every talk is a job talk, and so you should think about every seminar that way. It's yours to lose. I do find it amazing how people don't prepare enough in terms of pacing themselves during a seminar. It's really important that you don't get up there and bullshit your way through the first few slides for 45 minutes and waste the audience's time. I've been in a situation more than once where a department is thinking about making an offer to a senior person, who then gives a talk that kills it. From a Bayesian perspective, a seminar should not provide any new information, but it seems to be inevitable that it does. I think it's partly because we view someone as like a reformed alcoholic, who at any moment could fall off the wagon and become irrelevant. I don't think many 45 or 50 year-olds are aware of how people are very concerned that you are no longer what you used to be [*laughs*].

PUBLICATION

How would you best describe your approach to dealing with a 'revise and resubmit' request from a journal? How about an outright rejection?

Most of my papers get rejected at least one or two times. Usually, it's very annoying, but don't belabor it too much. You'll always hear, "Try it at a different journal," but in my experience, that doesn't help. If it's not going to make it at the *QJE*, then it's not going to make it at the *AER* either. Younger people tend to look at the referee report and pretend, or think to themselves, that there's something in there that's saying why their paper didn't make it, but oftentimes that's not really why. The reason was because it's not quite interesting enough, or not quite decisive enough, or not quite fitting in with the scheme of how things are going in the field, or it doesn't seem plausible even though it looks superficially okay, or the research design is maybe decent but not super strong.

The 'revise and resubmit' is the most important stage of the project. It's your job to address every single thing that's raised by the referee and nail it. If you speak to Larry Katz, who's been editing at the *QJE* for more than ten years, he'll tell you that that's the kind of paper that gets in. Somebody takes the comments seriously, follows the advice, tries to nail down the loose ends, and even fesses up if there's a problem by saying, "There's one thing we can't figure out. But we're going to rewrite the paper to acknowledge it." When I was editing the *AER* in the mid-'90s, I also noticed that that's how the successful guys would respond. Those who were less well trained would send back only a few pages of comments and the referees would then be alienated, which meant the end of the paper. I learned a lesson.

Do you think that the current structure of the publication process in economics facilitates or impedes scientific understanding and knowledge production?

Can I take the Fifth on that? [*Laughs*]. I guess it's like what people said about democracy: it's not a very good system, but it's better than the alternatives.

What has been your best and worst experience during the publication process?

One time, years ago, I wrote a paper with a guy about the interpretation of strikes in the 1880s. We sent it to the *QJE*, even though it wasn't quite good enough, got it back and came up with a much better way to pose the problem. The *QJE* still didn't like it, and so we submitted it to the *Journal of Labor Economics*, where it was accepted as is.[5] That was my best-ever experience. Most of the time, it's nothing like that. Sometimes the editors, for example at the *AER*, will say, "We've got to fill up the last 25 pages of the journal, and we'll let you send it in as a shorter paper." That's a bitter disappointment, and certainly leaves a bad taste in your mouth, because you've just won the booby prize.

I try not to aim my papers too high. I wrote a paper a while ago with some colleagues, and they really wanted to send it to a top journal. I knew it had no chance, but I couldn't talk them out of it. We sent it in and it got promptly canned! Normally, I win the argument and say there's no point in submitting this paper to a top journal; it's just not going to work. I think if you send a well-executed and well-written paper to a second-level journal, that's something they will like. They get lots of papers that are interesting but screwed up, and so with your paper the editor will say, "Oh my God, here's one I don't have to worry about too much." That's helpful.

REFEREEING AND EDITING

Do you have any advice for a young scholar on being a referee?

Editors appreciate good referee reports. You can tell when somebody has understood the paper, spent time with it, digested it and put into a form. There are cases when you can see that a paper is way better because of a particular referee. It's probably useful to accept a refereeing job just for that reason. It can also be good experience if you're able to abstract back to your own work. But sometimes, you'll say, "I could see how to fix that paper. Why can't I see how to fix mine?" [*Laughs*].

Do you have any advice for a young scholar on being an editor?

One thing is that you're only making enemies. People hold it against you for a very long time that you rejected their paper. And so you don't want to be getting into that position unless you're capable of handling that level of negativity. You have to reject some of your friends' papers, former students' papers, and older, well-respected people's papers. You have to cajole referees to send reports, and you'll be disappointed that people say that they're going to do things and then they don't. I've never been a department chair, but I think it would be very similar: you'll be largely disappointed with your colleagues, and you end up feeling like you only bring bad news [*laughs*]. It's true that you do bring some good news as an editor, but when you tell somebody you've accepted their paper, it's not like they send back an effusive note saying, "Of course, you accepted my paper. It was the greatest genius contribution since Milton Friedman!" You only get the blowback, as I used to call it, which can mean that when you reject a paper, you'll get an e-mail from the author later that same day saying the most amazingly negative things.

Most people think that editors have an agenda or a predisposition to like certain kinds of papers or certain people. And so if their paper gets rejected, their first reaction is that you're not being fair. And the second reaction is that the judgment was made on completely incorrect grounds, like something was argued to be a weakness in the paper, but it's not true. I learned from Orley when he was the head editor at the *AER*. If somebody complained, he would say, "Okay, give me a list of a couple of people, and I'll choose one of them off your list and one off another list, and we'll send out your paper for refereeing again." The *AER* had a process to let people calm down, but these days 95 per cent of papers are rejected at the top journals and so there's not much positivity.

I do have a funny story. At the time when I was editing the *AER*, we refereed every single paper; there were no desk rejects. My wife was my assistant. She has a PhD in music, but even she could tell that at least half the papers were not going to make it, but we would still send them out to referees. One paper came in that was about the artificial economy in a computer game where people buy avatars, which are scantily dressed women. At the end of the article, there were a couple of pages of pictures of the avatars. I needed somebody to referee the paper, and so I sent it to a very serious Mormon who I'd known for many years. He said, "You only gave this to me because of the scantily clad women at the end." But I had also read the paper and I told the author that we couldn't publish it. About two weeks later, I got a call from National Public Radio. The reporter said, "We're doing a story on artificial worlds and avatars … why did you reject that paper?" I started laughing. I said to my wife, "You're not going to believe what's going on here!" I told the reporter I couldn't discuss the reasons why it got rejected, but I might have at least mentioned the last couple of pages of the paper [*laughs*].

TIME MANAGEMENT

How do you divide up your working day, both in terms of quantity and timing of different kinds of work?

My wife and I don't have any children, so I spend a much longer time working than most people probably do: a minimum 60 hours a week. But I waste more time at work than most! There have been articles published on why Americans don't take vacation and Europeans do, and I think it's partly because we tend to get 'on the job' leisure. Ideally, I come in at around 10:30, go home for dinner around 7:00, and then come back and work until midnight in the office. At weekends, I work at our house in Sonoma.

How do you balance multiple research projects?

I'm no good at that. I always do one thing at a time. I prefer to get really into one project, have it all in my head, remember exactly what I'm doing, and then finish it and move on. I hate multitasking.

How about the balance between your research and non-research activities?

I have a lot of PhD students, so I probably spend more than a day a week on them. I teach one undergraduate class. It's a mathematical version of intermediate micro theory. I've taught it for many years and it's very straightforward. But I hate teaching graduate classes, because it's so much work. For my labor economics course, I spend many hours the night before preparing every lecture. I've never gotten to the stage where it's easy, and I find it very stressful.

How do you balance your personal and professional lives?

I probably don't spend enough time in my personal life, because we don't have children. But it's okay. My wife used to teach at Columbia when I was at Princeton, so we could only spend weekends together. Now that she's retired, I count on her to do a lot of stuff around the house. And so relative to what most people would put up with, I'm way over the boundary [*laughs*].

REFLECTIONS AND THE FUTURE OF ECONOMICS

What have been the most important findings and contributions in your research fields during your career?

At the beginning of my career, one important set of findings showed that labor supply elasticities are relatively modest. Many, many people, especially macroeconomists, continue to reject that hypothesis, but my reading of the latest round of research, which is mostly being done by public finance economists, suggests it's still true. In fact, I think if you were to take the point estimates from what we thought we knew in 1985 and look at what's coming out today, you would say that we were right all along.

In the 1990s, a huge amount of research started to work on education. In the early part of that decade, Alan Krueger and I wrote a paper that tried to estimate the effect of quality of education on earnings.[6] That topic had been talked about in the 1960s, and I think our paper was one of the first to bring it back to the table. Now, it's a huge issue, and the findings have implied that it's pretty hard to change the quality of education. My interpretation is that there aren't any obvious free lunches. Everyone says, "Good teachers matter." Yes, but we haven't figured out a way to get good teachers and keep them. Do we have to pay them more? All we do know is that there is an effect of school quality and it is like any other investment we can make. For example, there was a big controversy up until the '80s about whether going to school more increased your earnings or whether it was just you went to school more because you were more able. That's a topic in Gary Becker's book, *Human Capital*, from the early '60s. And then starting in '89 or '90, there was a whole band of research being done on the issue, mostly by students and colleagues at Princeton. I contributed a couple of small things around the edges, and I think that work has shown that, in fact, if you take a typical person who's going to drop out at twelfth grade and push them another year, it's not going to be, perhaps surprisingly, a worthless investment. That's another important finding.

What are the biggest challenges facing your research fields?

In labor economics, a major problem right now is that the newest lines of work are using more complicated administrative data where you can follow individuals over time as they change employers and you can match them with their employer. That kind of data is not available in the United States, so the research frontier in labor economics is moving offshore very quickly. I've written a few papers using data from Austria and Italy, and many of my students have written papers using data from Germany, Sweden, and Norway. When I started my career, the entire labor economics field was centered in the United States. If we don't do something soon, that's going to be lost.

What are the strengths and weaknesses of your own research?

I tend not to write a series of papers on the same thing over and over and over again, which means my research doesn't have a synthetic view. And people might say my papers are also quite negative, because I often find that such and such program or policy doesn't work. But I don't think there are many mistakes in my papers relative to the average. And my topics and approaches are pretty diverse, too.

In the end, do you think the profession has helped to bring out and shape your research for the best?

Sometimes when I get a referee report, I think not [*laughs*]. But I would say I've managed to be successful despite some of my own limitations, and so I certainly don't feel like I can complain relative to lots of other people who have worked hard and maybe not been as successful.

Do you have any professional regrets?

I'm probably going to spend the last ten years of my career in a public university, when public universities are going down the shithole [*laughs*]. I suspect that will turn out to be the most difficult thing that would have happened to me. The future for public universities is pretty tough, and we're going to struggle here for a long, long time in trying to maintain quality. Whether we'll succeed is very unclear because it's increasingly difficult in the United States. It's amazing that we have public education here, let alone public higher education – people are not very public-oriented in this country. You're an immigrant like me. You must feel that to some extent, too.

What are your professional ambitions?

Retire as soon as possible. I don't want to be one of those guys who hang on forever and everybody makes fun of. You see them at the faculty club with crumbs on their beard [*laughs*]. I think you should do your thing and get out.

How would you describe the state of economics today? Are you optimistic about its future?

Relative to the rest of academia, we've done extremely well over the last 30 years. I hope we maintain being able to attract incredibly bright kids into our PhD programs, because that's the number one thing. If you talk to somebody in sociology, for instance, a big concern they have is that the quality of students entering the PhD programs today is not the same as it was in the '40s, '50s, and '60s. We rely on getting future Robert Solows into our programs; really brilliant people who can see things a new way and once in a while change them.

Every field should be judged by its 28 year-olds and 30 year-olds. But I don't know that in economics we're doing a great job of nurturing them in quite the right direction. If they're all working on Wall Street, that's tragic, because they're just stealing money from each other. If they're talented and interested in doing something that is positive and engaging, it is our job as professors to help them as much as possible … and for old guys like me to get out of their way [*laughs*].

NOTES

1. Leonid Hurwicz and Hirofumi Uzawa (1971), 'On the Integrability of Demand Functions', in John S. Chipman, Leonid Hurwicz, Marcel K. Richter, and Hugo F. Sonnenschein (eds), *Preferences, Utility and Demand*, New York: Harcourt Brace Jovanovich, Chapter 6.
2. Card, D. (1990), 'The Impact of the Mariel Boatlift on the Miami Labor Market', *Industrial and Labor Relations Review*, Vol. 43, No. 2 (January), pp. 245–257.
3. D. Card and D.R. Hyslop (2005), 'Estimating the Effect of a Time-Limited Earnings Subsidy for Welfare-Leavers', *Econometrica*, Vol. 73, No. 6 (November), pp. 1723–1770.

4. David Card and Alan B. Krueger (1995), *Myth and Measurement: The New Economics of the Minimum Wage*, Princeton University Press.
5. Card, D. and C.A. Olson (1995), 'Bargaining Power, Strike Durations and Wage Outcomes: An Analysis of Strikes in the 1880s', *Journal of Labor Economics*, Vol. 13, No. 1 (January), pp. 32–61.
6. Card, D. and A.B. Krueger (1992), 'Does School Quality Matter? Returns to Education and the Characteristics of Public Schools in the United States', *Journal of Political Economy*, Vol. 100, No. 1 (February), pp. 1–40.

Raj Chetty
(Harvard University)

Raj Chetty was born in New Delhi, India in 1979 and obtained a BA in economics from Harvard College in 2000 before obtaining a PhD in economics from Harvard University in 2003. Between 2003 and 2008, he taught economics at the University of California, Berkeley, where he received tenure at the age of 27. He then moved to Harvard University in 2009 as Professor of Economics and, at the age of 29, became one of the youngest people to achieve tenure in the history of the Department of Economics at Harvard.

Professor Chetty's research focuses on theoretical and empirical issues relating to taxation, unemployment, risk preferences, and social insurance. His most-cited papers in chronological order include 'Dividend Taxes and Corporate Behavior: Evidence from the 2003 Dividend Tax Cut', *Quarterly Journal of Economics* (2005), co-authored with Emmanuel Saez, 'A New Method of Estimating Risk Aversion', *American Economic Review* (2006), 'Consumption Commitments and Risk Preferences', *Quarterly Journal of Economics* (2007), co-authored with Adam Szeidl, 'Cash-on-Hand and Competing Models of Intertemporal Behavior: New Evidence from the Labor Market', *Quarterly Journal of Economics* (2007), co-authored with David Card and Andrea Weber, and 'Salience and Taxation: Theory and

Evidence', *American Economic Review* (2009), co-authored with Adam Looney and Kory Kroft.

Professor Chetty received the American Young Economist award in 2008 and the CESIfo Distinguished Research Affiliate Award in the same year. He is the Co-Director of the Public Economics Program at the National Bureau of Economic Research and is Editor of the *Journal of Public Economics*.

I interviewed Raj Chetty in his office in the Department of Economics at Harvard University. It was mid-afternoon of Thursday, 23 September 2010.

BACKGROUND INFORMATION

Why did you decide to pursue an academic career in economics?

When I was in high school, I was very interested in science and thought that I might become a bio-medical engineer, but then I realized that I didn't like working so much with my hands and preferred more conceptual work. My Dad is an economist and so I knew a little about economics and its potentially great importance for the world.[1] I took a class on the subject as a freshman at Harvard with a professor named Andrew Metrick, who is one of the best teachers I've ever seen. I was really captivated by the material and then, starting in my sophomore year as an undergraduate, I did the PhD sequence in economics.

Why the academic career? From a young age, I was interested in doing research because my parents and both of my sisters are researchers. I wanted to answer questions that I thought would have a big impact on people's lives and that's specifically why I'm interested in public economics, which is very much about applying economic thinking and ideas to policies to improve the world.

As a student, were there any other professors at Harvard apart from Andrew Metrick who were particularly influential or inspirational?

Early on, Marty Feldstein played a huge role in my career. I started working as a research assistant for him two months after I showed up at Harvard as a 17-year-old. And since then, I have continued working with Marty. He was my undergraduate thesis advisor and one of my PhD thesis advisors.

As a researcher, are there any colleagues apart from Martin Feldstein who have been particularly influential or inspirational?

David Card at Berkeley is a phenomenal scholar. I try to emulate his work. He truly views economics as a science more than anyone else in the profession. His approach is very rigorous. He doesn't come with any ex-ante biases; he just states what the data says. I think that is very inspiring and very influential.

And then, also at Berkeley, there is Emmanuel Saez, who just won the Clark Medal. We are constant collaborators, and that makes a huge difference.

It's important to have mentors at different stages. There are people like Feldstein and Card who you look to as the kind of guys you want to be like in the long run. And then there are people closer to your age like Emmanuel.

GENERAL THOUGHTS ON RESEARCH

What is the value of pure versus applied research in economics?

Both have a very important role. A lot of the applied research that people do now is based on the pure research that was done, say, 10 or 20 years ago. For example, the theories that were developed in game theory or mechanism design – the pure theoretical fields of economics – have now permeated the more applied fields of economics and are very important in policy discussions today.

How would you describe the dialogue between theory and empirics in economics?

I am very interested in that issue because public economics is really about combining those two parts of the field. Often we start out with a model of how some part of the economy works and then we ask what the optimal policy is. But what I tell my students is that theory doesn't tell you enough. The traditional theory of taxes in its purest form, for instance, just tells you that optimal tax rates are between 0 and 100 per cent. A policymaker wants to hear something better than that! And so the modern evolution of the field – and the focus of my research – has been about how we can make more precise statements about policy, which has involved combining theory and data.

Has your research agenda changed at all during your short career?

I have gotten more interested in behavioral economics over time. Your thinking evolves as you see data and problems, and you consider what features seem to be important. I'm more interested in the social aspects of behavior. Often we focus on economic incentives and changes in prices as being the key determinants of behavior, but my sense is that in many contexts, it's actually social incentives that matter quite a bit; you are concerned about what other people think of you in addition to just the dollar and cents aspects.

And then in terms of topics, one naturally shifts over time. Most recently, I have started working on topics related to education, whereas in the past, I was more focused on tax and social insurance welfare policies. All of those things are policy-related, but in different domains.

Do you think it is important to have broad research interests?

I think it makes you a more creative economist if you can draw ideas from many different fields, but there is value in expertise. My approach has been, for two or three years, to focus on one set of topics and write a series of papers that address some of the important issues, and then move on to another area.

Tools are also very important, although you don't want to be totally tool-driven because that approach leads to research that is not as creative.

Do you think there is any difference in the types of work done by researchers at different stages of their careers based on tenure concerns, publication requirements or other pressures? Should there be a difference?

My sense is that people tend to do more abstract work earlier in their career and more applied work later. And from a tenure perspective, people tend to do riskier work after they have tenure, which I think is the great benefit of having tenure. I am engaged in projects that could easily take a couple of years to pan out. They are complicated experiments. I would say that, out of five projects, one of them is surely not going to work. But you want to give people tenure so they can produce the highest-risk, highest-reward projects.

IDEA GENERATION

Where do you get your research ideas?

I don't get my best ideas by sitting at my desk, reading papers and thinking, "What can do I better?" It's more about being aware of what the literature says and what the questions are, and then going out into the world and thinking, "What is it about the real world that we are missing in standard economic models?" For example, a standard assumption we make is that everybody pays attention to all the incentives that we face; we always take taxes into account and we always think about the implications of our behavior for government policies. I was once in the grocery store and was thinking about the fact that when you buy something here in the US, the price that you pay at the check-out is more than that quoted on the shelf. The implicit assumption in economics is that everybody is thinking about the tax-inclusive price of that product when we are deciding whether or not to buy it. But is that actually true? It seems plausible that people focus on the price on the shelf. And the reason I thought that might be the case was that a lot of the prices that are quoted are just below an integer, like $5.99 or $9.99. The tax-inclusive prices are already above the integer and so intuitively it makes you think that people are not focusing on the tax-inclusive prices, which could have important implications for tax policy. And so that led to a paper conducting an experiment of posting tax-inclusive price tags for a thousand products in a grocery store and seeing whether that affects demand patterns and then developing a theory of why it does and what that means for tax policy.[2]

At what point does an idea become a project that you devote resources to?

After thinking about an idea, I'll often look up what other people have done on the topic, talk it over with some colleagues, and then do some preliminary work to see if I might have a strategy to tackle the problem in a compelling way. And then if I feel it meets the bar for interest and I can do a good job, I'll devote time and resources to it.

IDEA EXECUTION

What makes a good theoretical paper?

A good theoretical paper in economics is one that casts light on a new mechanism or intuition in a way that is elegant – it's not overly complicated – and rigorous – it's general and doesn't depend upon strong assumptions.

Can you give an example?

A canonical example of an incredibly influential theoretical paper would be the one by George Akerlof on the market for 'lemons', demonstrating with simple models how asymmetric information has dramatic implications for many economic problems.[3]

What makes a good empirical paper?

A good empirical paper is one that meets the scientific bar for good evidence. First, it's not a paper that is highly sensitive to a lot of assumptions that were made in the empirical analysis. Second, it's a paper that is very transparent, where you can see that such and such policy or experiment had a clear effect. And third, it's a paper that tackles a fundamental question, or provides evidence on a theory that is very influential. For example, is adverse selection an important problem in practice? What can we do about it? What policies have impacts in dealing with the problem of adverse selection?

Can you give an example?

There are so many empirical papers that I think are really important. I would say a lot of the work that David Card has done broadly on how various policies such as minimum wage policies, Medicaid policies, and unemployment benefits affect behavior and welfare are all examples of well-executed and high-quality empirical papers.[4] I also think they will stand the test of time. At some level with theory, conditional on your assumptions and the correct math, there is no disputing whether your work will stand the test of time or not. In empirics, something can often look like a good result, but some factor wasn't taken into account. And so a good empirical paper is one where after 20 years of follow-up work, it is still considered to be right.

When you hit a brick wall on a project, do you continue to work on the problem or do you take a break and work on something else?

I like to focus on the problem and find a way around the brick wall. I don't give up. I think if you have too much of a tendency to switch to a different project, it's too easy to effectively give up. There is a lot of return to just struggling with something. Your best papers are often not ones where you can immediately see all the ways round the road blocks; you had to struggle for a month to figure something out.

Can you give an example?

Yes, I have a set of papers showing that unemployment benefits have less of an efficiency cost for the economy than prior theories had suggested.[5] But I struggled with trying to formulate a framework to make that point clear. And it's also related to some work that I have done on risk aversion. I had an idea on how you could estimate risk aversion from income and substitution elasticities. But there is a technical issue of how to deal with complementarity in the utility function. It took several weeks to figure out how to address that. Eventually I did, and I think that insight has played a role in a number of my papers. In fact, if I had not solved that problem, those papers could not have been published. That's an example of not giving up.

Related to the previous question, when a project isn't going to turn out as hoped, do you scrap it or aim to send the work to a second-tier or field journal?

At this stage, I would scrap it because the returns in the profession are completely convex in the sense that the big hits have a huge payoff and ten small hits don't have nearly as big payoff as one big hit.

You can't get too attached to your projects. It's important not to give up, but it's also important to be able to judge at a certain point that a project is going to hit too many obstacles, and you're not going to invest more time in it.

THE WRITING PROCESS

Which aspect of the writing process do you find most difficult?

Starting from the blank page. But once I have a plan in mind, I don't find it that hard. It's just a matter of putting down your results in a clear way.

What steps have you taken during your career to improve the quality of your writing?

Getting lots of comments from people, and going through numerous versions of each paper.

Who proofreads your writing?

I always have a team of research assistants who proofread my papers very carefully.

How do you split up the writing tasks among co-authors?

In most of the projects I've been involved with, I play the role of bringing everything together and trying to give the paper a single tone and a single vision. It's hard to have three or four people each writing a different section, because the paper will be disjointed.

COLLABORATION

When you work with co-authors, how do you decide whom to work with?

That's a good question. I think a lot of it is chance; whom you end up being around. But then there are certain people whom you just click with. I have written a series of papers with Emmanuel Saez.[6] We have a style that works well together. We trust each other's judgment a great deal. It's very important when you are working with a co-author that you don't feel like you need to replicate everything that he or she does. That's very inefficient. And so with Emmanuel and a number of my other co-authors, I feel very confident in the work they're doing and, likewise, I think they feel confident in the work I'm doing. And it's also about sharing a common perspective about what problems are important and what approach to take.

How do you prefer to interact with them (e-mail, phone, or face-to-face)?

Around 75–80 per cent of the time, it is four different people doing work in four different places, and communicating by e-mail and phone.

How has your working relationship with Emmanuel Saez changed since you moved from Berkeley to Harvard?

We talk on the phone every day and exchange multiple e-mails every day. I think that collaboration started really well because we were in the same place. And because we developed such a strong collaboration before I left Berkeley, it's been very easy to maintain it.

What are the main challenges associated with collaborative work and how do you overcome them?

It's always tricky to keep everybody motivated and involved. Inevitably, somebody feels like they are left out of the loop and then they end up contributing less. It's hard when that arises. And so we try to lay out each person's responsibilities up front and try to stick to that.

RESEARCH ASSISTANCE AND FUNDING

How do you use undergraduate and graduate research assistants?

If I have derived a result in a special case and I think that theoretical result holds more generally, but perhaps there are some technical complications, then I might assign a graduate student a very specific problem to solve. Then I'll look over what they've done.

In empirical projects, a graduate student will often be involved in the data set-up work. When we want to analyze the effect of, say, early childhood education on long-term outcomes, they will construct a dataset that contains information on both the kindergarten classroom and the adult outcomes, and that work will take several months.

With undergraduate research assistants, I assign more narrow tasks like doing literature reviews and proofreading.

How important is funding for getting your work done?

It's important for hiring research assistants and getting data.

Do you have any advice for a young scholar on the funding process?

It's important to apply for NSF grants early on. One of the tricks to getting funded is you have to talk about the work you have done rather than the work you plan to do. I think a lot of people make the mistake of doing it the other way around.

SEMINAR PARTICIPATION AND NETWORKING

What are the benefits to attending a seminar that is closely related to your work versus one that is not closely related?

The seminars that are closely related to your work are important because you need to know what is going on in your field and what other people think about it. The seminars that are further away are informative for potentially new ideas. A lot of those ideas are at a subconscious level or at a broad methodological level in terms of how someone tackled a problem. Maybe you can approach your problem in a similar way. That's how I learn from seminars.

How important is professional networking to success in research?

It's somewhat important, but what draws me to academia is that it is a merit-driven profession. It's true that once you have achieved a certain status, it's easier to get things published, you have more resources at your disposal, and you have better students. But, at the end of the day, all of that is earned by merit. And so, as a young faculty member, if I were to choose between spending an extra day working on a paper versus an extra day spent working on networking, I would spend the day working on the paper because I think it has a higher return. And it will lead to the networking that is important.

To what extent is the absence of departmental colleagues working in one's research area a major disadvantage?

It's somewhat of a disadvantage, but it's not insurmountable. We live in such a connected environment these days. I'll often talk to people at many other universities about their papers. One just needs to reach out.

COMMUNICATION OF RESEARCH

How do you find the right balance between communicating your research at an early stage versus the close-to-finished stage?

I talk informally to colleagues at an early stage. If I give a presentation, it's pretty polished because I think every time you present, you are making a big impression on people. And so I'm not one who likes to give unpolished presentations at other places with the intention of getting feedback. I don't feel comfortable doing that.

What are the unique challenges to giving a seminar and how do you overcome them?

Giving a seminar is a different set of skills to doing research. Making that transition from, "Here's how I came up with my results ... " to "Here's the best way to explain my results to someone else ... " is a tough one. I think a lot of people tend to tell you their course of thinking and not restructure the entire material in a way that is most conducive to conveying it to a different audience. It's all about overcoming that challenge.

PUBLICATION

How do you decide upon the appropriate journal to send your research to?

I aim to send my work to the top economics journals to try to reach economists broadly.

How would you best describe your approach to dealing with a 'revise and resubmit' request from a journal? How about an outright rejection?

I try to get onto 'revise and resubmits' immediately. I deal with every comment that is raised very thoroughly, and I write a very detailed response. I do what it takes to get a publication in a top journal rather than sacrifice and go to a lower journal.

With a rejection, I would try another top journal if I still thought the paper had a shot. I would only go to the lower journals if I had tried a couple of times and it didn't look like it was going to work out.

Do you think that the current structure of the publication process in economics facilitates or impedes scientific understanding and knowledge production?

There are some huge delays in the top journals. That's problematic, but most of the time, people get their information about the latest research from working papers, not from published papers. That reduces the cost. And so I see publications more as a trophy; it is a signal of the value and merit of the paper and less about knowledge dissemination.

REFEREEING AND EDITING

As Editor of the Journal of Public Economics, *do you have any advice for a young scholar on being a good referee?*

Referee reports should be targeted at the core substance of the paper. As an editor, I often get referee reports where young people are eager to impress and write five pages. That's useful, but it's really nice to see reports that hit at the two key points. That skill of reading a complex 50-page paper and being able to distill it into a couple of its core ideas is not only critical for good refereeing, but also for writing good papers.

TIME MANAGEMENT

How do you divide up your working day, both in terms of quantity and timing of different kinds of work?

I just set aside blocks of time to be able to work on papers.

How do you balance multiple research projects?

I am a sequential type of guy; I don't jump back and forth between papers. I will get a paper to the point where I have submitted it, or completed the revisions, or sent it to a co-author, and then I will switch to the next paper. I like to get really deep into one paper. It has to be the only thing on my mind. The reason I do that is because the times when I have the best ideas on those papers are not when I'm sitting at my desk executing the paper, but rather when I'm taking a shower or exercising.

How do you balance your personal and professional lives?

My wife is also an academic and we try to co-ordinate around each other's schedules. But I also like the academic lifestyle. I will often work, go home and play tennis and then work again in the evening. I don't have a sharp boundary where I have to leave the office at 6 pm. That's not how I work.

REFLECTIONS AND THE FUTURE OF ECONOMICS

What have been the most important findings and contributions in your research fields during your career?

I feel that some of the papers that Emmanuel has written on optimal taxation have been some of the most influential in public economics in the past ten years.[7] His research has tremendous relevance for lots of different types of problems and is very practical. More broadly, a great deal of influential work has been done in slightly different areas in labor economics and in development economics; more method-oriented work like development of regression discontinuity-type research designs, which are currently very influential in empirical economics.

What are the biggest challenges facing your research fields?

I think behavioral economics poses one of the greatest challenges. You want to design optimal public policy, but the whole premise behind our theories to design policy is the assumption that people optimize perfectly. And we don't really know what to do when people don't optimize perfectly. We shouldn't be paternalistic and say that the government knows better about what's good for us, because the government doesn't know what we should be maximizing. What do people want? How do we get at that? Those are some core, almost philosophical questions. While they are not public economics themselves, they bear so heavily on the conclusions one would draw that it's hard to avoid them.

What are the strengths and weaknesses of your own research?

If I were to pick a strength, it would be in trying to connect theory with the data in a transparent way. But that in itself leads to a weakness – the theoretical models that I work with are not as rich and don't account for as many features of the world as you might like. But I feel like I sacrifice that from a practical perspective to be able to say something in the data.

In the end, has the profession helped to shape and bring out your research for the best?

I have benefited tremendously from the profession in terms of colleagues here at Harvard, at Berkeley, and at many other universities. I really enjoy being part of the profession. Although economists emphasize self-interest, I think the group of economics researchers is extremely generous in terms of time and in promoting other people's work.

Do you have any professional regrets?

Sometimes I wish I had learned more about psychology when I was in college. I was very oriented towards learning economics, mathematics, and statistics, and ignoring other social sciences. But as I feel like I understand the world better – and how much we don't understand about the world – I think there are insights from the other social sciences that could matter a lot. I have thought about taking a graduate psychology class because there's something to be learned from just seeing the way psychologists – or sociologists for that matter – might teach this material. I would like to do that in the long run.

Another person who is a great role model for me is George Akerlof. What always impressed me about George was that he would take a class every year, even after aged 60. And when he retired from Berkeley, his plan was to apply to law school even after he had won the Nobel Prize. I like that idea of trying to constantly learn from different fields.

What are your professional ambitions?

My ambition is to have a big impact on economics research and also on policy; to do research that is relevant for improving social welfare, but also make a contribution to knowledge at a more pure level. We've talked earlier about examples of people who are doing that, and it would be great to follow the same path.

What are the advantages and disadvantages of being tenured at such a young age?

The advantages are that you have a great deal of resources and freedom to spend your most energetic years working on big projects. The disadvantage is that it comes with a tremendous amount of expectation. I feel like I owe it to the people who have invested in me, and to people more generally, to deliver. I'm very conscious of that. Yes, academia is about merit and so people have more respect for you for having achieved at a young age because they know how hard it is, but you are also a target in the sense that they want to see whether you are doing well.

People often ask me, "What motivates you to work really hard even after getting tenure?" Part of our goal as professors is to make a difference to the world. And I think if I were to just take it easy and not do anything at this point, it would not be fair because there has been a tremendous amount invested in people like me and there is an obligation to return that to society.

How would you describe the state of economics today? Are you optimistic about its future?

We're at a very exciting point because economists are starting to incorporate insights from many other fields. It's like the evolution in some of the other sciences that were very theoretical and then became much more empirical. I think economics is going to become much more scientific and much more relevant in many, many areas. There are a huge number of problems that economists will tackle, which will improve the world in many important ways. I really believe that.

NOTES

1. Raj Chetty's father is V.K. Chetty, a health economist at Boston University and Boston Medical Center. He is formerly a professor of economics at Columbia University and the Indian Statistical Institute, New Delhi, India.
2. Chetty, R., Looney, A. and K. Kroft (2009), 'Salience and Taxation: Theory and Evidence', *American Economic Review*, Vol. 99, No. 4 (September), pp. 1145–77.
3. Akerlof, G.A. (1970), 'The Market for "Lemons": Quality Uncertainty and the Market Mechanism', *Quarterly Journal of Economics*, Vol. 84, No. 3 (August), pp. 488–500.
4. See, for example, Card, D. and A.B. Krueger (1994), 'Minimum Wages and Employment: A Case of the Fast Food Industry in New Jersey and Pennsylvania', *American Economic Review*, Vol. 8, No. 4 (September), pp. 772–793; Card, D. and P.B. Levine (2000), 'Extended Benefits and the Duration of UI Spells: Evidence from the New Jersey Extended Benefit Program', *Journal of Public Economics*, Vol. 78. No. 1–2 (October),

pp. 107–138; Card, D. and L.D. Shore-Sheppard (2004), 'Using Discontinuity Eligibility Rules to Identify the Effects of the Federal Medicaid Expansions on Low-Income Children', *Review of Economics and Statistics*, Vol. 86, No. 3 (November), pp. 752–766.

5. Chetty, R. (2006), 'A General Formula for the Optimal Level of Social Insurance', *Journal of Public Economics*, Vol. 90, No. 10–11 (November), pp. 1879–1901; Chetty, R. and A. Looney (2006), 'Consumption Smoothing and the Welfare Consequences of Social Insurance in Developing Countries', *Journal of Public Economics*, Vol. 90, No. 12 (December), pp. 2351–2356; Chetty, R. (2008), 'Moral Hazard vs. Liquidity and Optimal Unemployment Insurance', *Journal of Political Economy*, Vol. 116, No. 2 (April), pp. 173–234; Chetty, R. and E. Saez (2010), 'Optimal Taxation and Social Insurance with Endogenous Private Insurance', *American Economic Journal: Economic Policy*, Vol. 2, No. 2 (May), pp. 85–114.

6. Chetty, R. and E. Saez (2005), 'Dividend Taxes and Corporate Behavior: Evidence from the 2003 Dividend Tax Cut', *Quarterly Journal of Economics*, Vol. 120, No. 3 (August), pp. 791–833; Chetty, R. and E. Saez (2006), 'The Effects of the 2003 Dividend Tax Cut on Corporate Behavior: Interpreting the Evidence', *American Economic Review*, Papers and Proceedings, Vol. 96, No. 2 (May), pp. 124–129; Chetty, R. and E. Saez (2010), 'Dividend and Corporate Taxation in an Agency Model of the Firm', *American Economic Journal: Economic Policy*, Vol. 2, No. 3 (August), pp. 1–31.

7. See, for example, Saez, E. (2001), 'Using Elasticities to Derive Optimal Income Tax Rates', *Review of Economic Studies*, Vol. 68, No. 1 (January), pp. 205–229; Saez, E. (2002), 'The Desirability of Commodity Taxation under Non-linear Income Taxation and Heterogeneous Tastes', *Journal of Public Economics*, Vol. 83, No. 2 (February), pp. 217–230; Saez, E. (2002), 'Optimal Income Transfer Programs: Intensive Versus Extensive Labor Supply Responses', *Quarterly Journal of Economics*, Vol. 117, No. 3 (August), pp. 1039–1073; Saez, E. (2004), 'Direct or Indirect Tax Instruments for Redistribution: Short-run versus Long-run', *Journal of Public Economics*, Vol. 88, Nos 3–4 (March), pp. 503–518; Saez, E. (2004), 'The Optimal Treatment of Tax Expenditures', *Journal of Public Economics*, Vol. 88, No. 12 (December), pp. 2567–2684.

Janet Currie
(Princeton University)

Janet Currie was born in Ontario, Canada in 1960 and graduated with a BA and an MA in economics from the University of Toronto in 1982 and 1983 respectively before obtaining a PhD in economics from Princeton University in 1988. Professor Currie has taught at the University of California, Los Angeles, 1988–1991 and 1993–2006, the Massachusetts Institute of Technology, 1991–1993, Columbia University, 2006–2011, and is currently serving as the Henry Putman Professor of Economics and Public Affairs at Princeton University and the Director of Princeton's Center for Health and Well Being.

Professor Currie's research focuses on the health and well-being of children. Her most-cited articles in chronological order include 'Does Head Start Make a Difference?', *American Economic Review* (1995), co-authored with Duncan Thomas, 'Saving Babies: The Efficacy and Cost of Recent Changes in the Medicaid Eligibility of Pregnant Women', *Journal of Political Economy* (1996), co-authored with Jonathan Gruber, 'Health Insurance Eligibility, Utilization of Medical Care, and Child Health', *Quarterly Journal of Economics* (1996), co-authored with Jonathan Gruber, 'Socioeconomic Status and Child Health: Why is the Relationship Stronger for Older Children?', *American Economic Review* (2003), co-authored with

Mark Stabile, and 'Child Mental Health and Human Capital Accumulation: The Case of ADHD', *Journal of Health Economics* (2006), co-authored with Mark Stabile. Her books include *Welfare and the Well-Being of Children* (Harwood Academic Publishers, Chur Switzerland, 1995), and *The Invisible Safety Net: Protecting Poor Children and Families* (Princeton University Press, 2006).

Professor Currie is a Fellow of the Society of Labor Economists, an Affiliate of the University of Michigan's National Poverty Center, and an Affiliate of IZA in Bonn. She is the Editor of the *Journal of Economic Literature* and is on the editorial board of the *Quarterly Journal of Economics*. She has also served several other journals in an editorial capacity, including the *Journal of Health Economics*, the *Journal of Labor Economics*, and the *Journal of Public Economics,* and served on the advisory board of the National Children's Study.

I interviewed Janet Currie in her office in the Department of Economics at Columbia University where, at the time of interview, she was the Sami Mnaymneh Professor of Economics. It was late-afternoon of Wednesday, 16 June 2010.

BACKGROUND INFORMATION

What was your attraction to economics?

I liked the combination of intellectual rigor and broad subject matter. In my first year of university, I did a broad sequence of courses, and it was the one that I liked the best.

As a student, which professors were most influential or inspirational?

As an undergraduate, one of the professors who was most impressive to me was Donald Dewees, who came every day with a current newspaper article and introduced whatever he wanted to speak of with this article. He was able to take whatever the topic at hand was – and this was just a principles class – and show that it was relevant to the news of the day. That was impressive.

Why did you decide to pursue an academic career?

I think I have an academic temperament. I'm always interested in why things are the way they are, which is the fundamental epistemological academic question.

As a researcher, which colleagues have been most influential or inspirational?

I've been fortunate to have a lot of really good mentors. My advisors in graduate school, Orley Ashenfelter and David Card, were superb. David, in particular, must have read my thesis a million times and always had interesting comments. He was just so accessible and so available to his students; he's always been a role model for me in terms of how you should deal with your graduate students.

When I got my first job at UCLA, my senior colleague there was Finis Welch, who's a very different sort of person. I remember very well my job talk. I got about two seconds into it and he said, "Why should anyone care about unions when unions are dying?" [*Laughs*]. That was actually a really good question for me to think about, so it was the tough love approach. But he is also a good mentor in his way. He had very high expectations, and he let you know what they were.

When I went to MIT, Jim Poterba was a wonderful mentor in terms of reading my papers and commenting on them, and also pointing me in the right direction. So those are some people that stand out.

GENERAL THOUGHTS ON RESEARCH

There is an increasing emphasis in many economics departments on applied research. Is this true at Columbia? What is the value of pure versus applied research in economics?

I think a lot of people would see the department at Columbia as being more on the applied side these days in the sense we have a lot of theorists, but they're more applied theorists and not so much, say, pure 'math econ' types. That being said, I also try to reject the division between pure and applied research. I think all research is motivated by questions from the real world to some extent. Even some purely mathematical research into patterns is rooted in the real world because those patterns arise in nature. Maybe too much is made of this distinction between pure and applied.

How would you describe the dialogue between theory and empirics in economics?

People like to frame work in terms of theory or empirics, but you can't do anything without both. You can't measure something, which is the fundamental part of empirical work, unless you have some reason for measuring that thing rather than something else. If you ask an empiricist, "Why are you looking at this?", they have an idea: "Because if you do this, the following will happen … " That's a theory. And similarly, people don't come up with theories in a vacuum; they come up with them because there is something empirical that they want to explain. If you ask a theorist, "Why are you doing this model?", they'll often say, "Because when I went to the store, I observed that there were three different prices for the same good and I thought, 'Oh, that's odd.'" To me, theory and empirics are two sides of the same coin.

How would you characterize your own research agenda and how has it changed through time?

My research has changed a lot through time in that I started off working on collective bargaining questions.[1] After a while, I got tired of that and thought, "I want to work on something else that I think is of fundamental importance." And so I started the work that I've been doing ever since on things that affect children, such as public programs. I began that research by looking at cash transfers, and then decided that the theory wasn't very well developed in the sense that I didn't really know what the cash transfers were supposed to be affecting, so it was very hard to look for a result.[2] Whereas with an in-kind transfer program, you had a much better idea about what it was supposed to do. For example, if you're giving somebody food, presumably that's because you expect that it will have some effect on their diet, or you give them medical care because you want them to be healthier; there's a much clearer empirical question in terms of what you ought to be looking for. That led to my work on health insurance, and then at a certain point I realized that the trouble with working on that topic is that, while it's important, most kids are basically healthy until something happens to them.[3] In other words, whether or not they have health insurance is not determining if they have this health shock that creates a bad health condition. That's determined by other things. And so I would characterize my recent research as trying to identify those other things that are affecting child health.[4]

Do you think it is important to have broad research interests?

If you ask most scholars, they probably would tell you that they had broad research interests. I can't imagine too many people saying, "Oh, yeah, I'm really narrow." [*Laughs*]. Breadth is in the eye of the beholder to some extent. I think everybody has reasons for studying what they're studying, and they do so because they believe that it has some importance for some question.

Do you think there is any difference in the types of work done by researchers at different stages in their careers based on tenure concerns, publication requirements or other pressures? Should there be a difference?

There are naturally going to be many differences just because when people come out of graduate school, they typically know a lot about very few things. As they go through their careers, their research is probably going to become less technical and less focused on a very particular question just because they get exposed to a broader set of issues.

Somebody who's going to be a successful researcher will be doing what they're doing because they think it's important and not so much because they think it will sell in a particular journal. The people who tell you, "I'm doing this because I think the editor will like it and it'll get published in this journal," are often wrong [*laughs*]. That's a very poor way to develop a research strategy in my opinion.

IDEA GENERATION

Where do you get your research ideas?

That's a really good question. Everybody would like to know where ideas come from. I often get ideas at conferences when I hear people talking about what they think is important and an unknown question. Sometimes somebody will say, "We don't know anything about this," and I'll think, "Oh, I could say something about that." So that's one source.

Reading the newspaper is very useful, in the kind of work that I do, to get a sense of what are the issues, what's going on in the world, and what are the sorts of things you might be able to measure.

Sometimes I get ideas from the process of preparing for teaching. Again, if you're trying to teach somebody about an area, I might think, "Oh, I never really noticed that before, but there's an obvious gap in this literature." The responses of students can be interesting too in terms of things that they think are important or that they get excited about. That's one way to get a sense of what other academics might think are interesting questions.

At what point does an idea become a project that you devote resources to?

I tend to work with a lot of students, but I almost always spend some time looking around myself and asking, "Can I do anything about this idea? Are there any data that could be used? Are there any other papers on this?" If it looks like there might be something there, I very often give a summer job to a student that involves looking at a dataset, doing some means, and looking up references. At the end of a summer, I might get an idea from the student's work about whether it seems like there's anything worth pursuing. If there is, then I will spend more of my own time trying to develop the idea.

IDEA EXECUTION

What makes a good theoretical paper?

In my opinion, a good theoretical paper is one that makes you see some aspect of the world in a different way. The theoretical papers that have had an influence on me are those that make you understand that some result that is the opposite of what you thought would be the case is, in fact, plausible.

Can you give an example?

One theoretical paper that I like is by David Card. It's called 'Estimating the Return to Schooling: Progress on Some Persistent Econometric Problems', and was published in *Econometrica* in 2001.[5] He wants to understand why instrumental variable estimates of the return to schooling are often higher than ordinary least squares estimates. He comes up with a theory of the return to schooling that emphasizes not only differences in ability but also differences in the ability to afford education. If you have heterogeneity in both of those things, he shows that it is possible to obtain fairly linear returns to education, which is what is observed. And so the nice thing about that paper is that it starts with an empirical puzzle and then sheds some light on it to help you think about the data in a new way.

What makes a good empirical paper?

A good empirical paper is one that convinces you of its argument. Many of the best empirical papers are in the nature of a collage of different approaches. Somebody will have a clear question and a range of different ways to try and answer that question. They will make the argument that all these different ways of answering the question point to the same answer. Then you read the paper and feel convinced that, "Well, yes, what they're saying is true." Hopefully, it's something important that you actually care about as well.

Can you give an example?

I like an empirical paper called 'Are Emily and Greg More Employable than Lakisha and Jamal?' which was published in the *AER* in 2004.[6] It is an audit study that took a bunch of resumes, randomly assigned names to them, and then looked at how many people get called back for job interviews. What's really nice about the paper is that they then try and understand why the people with black names get fewer call backs for interviews. And there are many potential reasons. For example, it may be that a black name is a signal of something else about you; you live in a lousy part of town or you have less education. And so they try varying those things as well. If you have a high-quality resume, is it less likely that the black name will be costly to you? They don't find any evidence that that's the case. The authors make a very big effort to think of all the theories that might explain their results, other than just sheer discrimination, and they test those theories.

When you hit a brick wall on a project, do you continue to work on the problem or do you take a break from it and work on something else?

I usually take a break for at least a while. I find that if you put the project on the backburner, sometimes an idea will occur to you about how to go in a different direction.

What is the typical kind of brick wall that you tend to hit?

In my case, I would say that a problem that occurs not infrequently is when you're doing some sort of data analysis, and you have a clear idea about what it's supposed to look like, and then it doesn't look like that [*laughs*]. That usually causes me to scratch my head and think, "Okay, what's wrong either with my theory – maybe I'm missing some important aspect of the problem – in which case I should revise it, or what's wrong with my data or my program in which case I should fix it?" There are many things that could be wrong.

Related to the previous question, when it appears that a project isn't going to turn out as hoped, do you scrap the project or aim to send the work to a second-tier or field journal?

I haven't scrapped very many projects. I don't write papers and say, "This is going to be an *AER* paper." Whenever you start off, if the project's worth doing at all, you hope that it's going to turn out really well and go to a top-tier journal. Sometimes it does and sometimes it doesn't. But I don't abandon a project because it's not as exciting as I hoped. I usually try and finish things [*laughs*].

What has been the biggest change during your career in how researchers in your fields conduct research?

The biggest change is how much easier it's become to analyze data, and how much more sophisticated people are about analyzing data. Now it's routine to look at datasets – such as Social Security records or something like that – where you just have millions of observations. When people want to do something very complicated with the standard errors, they can do it very easily, whereas when I started out, it would have been very time-consuming to do the same thing.

THE WRITING PROCESS

Which aspect of the writing process do you find most difficult?

I like writing. I don't really find any aspect of it very difficult. I especially like writing the first draft of a paper. To me, that's the most artistic part of the process.

What steps have you taken during your career to improve the quality of your writing?

I think becoming more patient. Just being willing to rewrite things, put them away for a while, try and look at them with fresh eyes before sending it out as a working paper is the main thing.

What I find works the best in terms of improving writing is to have a very clear conception in your mind before you write anything. In my best papers, when I sat down to write, I knew exactly how it was going to go and could just write it from start to finish. Then it turns out the best in terms of having a clear message and a very smooth writing style. They tend also to be shorter that way.

Who proofreads your writing?

I often ask my students to proofread things. I don't make a lot of grammatical errors, but I ask them to read things for understanding and underline parts that confuse them. That can be very helpful in improving writing.

How do you split up the writing tasks among co-authors?

That depends a lot. Sometimes we split it up by the section of the paper, and then we'll take turns giving it a 'once over'. But I do the writing in a lot of my papers just because I enjoy it, and it works reasonably well that way.

COLLABORATION

When you work with co-authors, how do you decide whom to work with?

I work with almost anybody [*laughs*]. I think the key thing is whether the sum will be greater than the parts. There are a lot of different things that people can bring to a paper. I've written a lot of papers with students, with colleagues, and with people that I don't actually even know all that well – maybe somebody I met at a conference, where we talked about an idea and realized that there was something to be done. Most of my collaborations have produced at least one paper, so I can't complain.

Is geographical proximity ever a consideration in choosing a co-author?

That's another thing that's changed. It's much easier now to keep in touch with people over long distances. But I think it's still the case that most papers seem to require proximity to get off the ground. For most of my papers, I've been overlapping with the person from at least the beginning of the project. But once the paper is initiated, it's easy to keep it going by e-mail or phone or meeting occasionally at conferences.

To what extent does the stage of a project influence the type of interaction that you have?

E-mail isn't all that efficient to start off with. If you have a lot of ideas to transfer or you're trying to narrow something down, I find that it's better to talk on the phone or face-to-face if possible. But by the end of the project, almost anything can be done over e-mail; it's not really necessary to talk all that much.

What are the main challenges associated with collaborative work and how do you overcome them?

Most work in economics is collaborative these days, so somehow we've managed to collectively overcome whatever challenges there are [*laughs*]. Obviously, people don't always see eye-to-eye about everything, but I find that it is generally easier to work on a paper with someone than by myself just because it's good to have at least one other perspective on the problem.

RESEARCH ASSISTANCE AND FUNDING

How do you use undergraduate and graduate research assistants?

Usually, I use undergraduates to survey literature or collect data. Unfortunately, they don't tend to have the skills to do a lot of data analysis. I have graduate students doing many different things. Much of it is data processing of one sort or another, but I do try and have them do some of the analysis as well since it's not very interesting to just be wrestling with some dataset for weeks at a time. I try to meet with most of them at least once a week. They show me what they've been doing, and I make suggestions about what they should do.

How important is funding for getting your work done?

If I had no funding at all, I would still get some work done; I would just get less work done or get it done more slowly because I wouldn't be able to hire as many students and so on. But the general thrust of my research would probably be quite similar. So it's not like in, say, medicine or some bench sciences where if you didn't have any funding, you wouldn't have a lab, and therefore you wouldn't be able to do anything.

Do you have any advice for a young scholar on the research funding process?

I think the best thing for people to do is to get a hold of a successful application, because what I have found is that often funders either don't fund exactly what they said they were interested in funding, or the successful proposal doesn't really have to have the format that they're telling you. Then try and copy the successful application in terms of the format and style and so on.

SEMINAR PARTICIPATION AND NETWORKING

What are the benefits to attending a seminar that is closely related to your work versus one that is not closely related?

Seminars are like conferences in that they're idiosyncratic; sometimes you get an idea as a result of what somebody's saying, and sometimes you don't [*laughs*]. Assuming that I'm not going to be going to too many seminars on topics that are completely unrelated to anything that I've ever done, I don't think it is necessarily the case that something that's on a very closely related topic is more likely to generate ideas than something that's a little bit further away.

How important is professional networking to success in research?

It's very important. There's so much information being produced and distributed that people really do tend to favor sources that they're familiar with. If an editor or referee knows you, they're just going to give your work that ten seconds more of attention than if they've never heard of you.

How does the researcher without extensive networks succeed?

There are many ways for people to acquire networks. I tell my students that when they go to a conference, they should have in mind something they want to accomplish, like meeting certain people. They should set some goals and make sure that they achieve at least some of those goals for those kinds of opportunities to interact with people. They can send their papers as well. Realistically, they shouldn't expect that people are going to drop everything and read their papers. But if they send a little cover note that's very short and says, "I've sent this paper that you might be interested in," they might remember that you sent them a paper and eventually get around to reading it if it's related to their topic of research.

Applying for funding is actually a good way to get yourself noticed because the people who are on the review panels then are exposed to your research. When I went to MIT as an assistant professor, for example, I found out that Jim Poterba knew who I was because I had applied for NSF funding and he was on the review panel. And so that was sort of an 'in' which I hadn't really thought about at the time that I applied.

Generally being a good citizen, like refereeing in a responsible way when you're asked to and being a discussant for conferences, is a good way to do it.

Another thing that I think is quite important for junior people is if they can invite people to give seminars at their institution. In some places, it may be the case that the senior person controls all the seminar slots. But the senior person doesn't really want to go for dinner with a speaker every week and do all the work that's associated with running those things. And so if a junior person went and asked, "Can I invite 'so and so' and host them?" I would think, most of the time, whoever's in charge would be agreeable to that. If you invite somebody to come and give a talk, chances are they'll invite you back at some point. That's also a good way to develop a network.

To what extent is the absence of departmental colleagues working in one's research area a major disadvantage?

I think it is a disadvantage. It's nice to have a critical mass of people who are interested in what you're doing in many different ways. In terms of seminars, you'll end up with more people coming through who are doing work that you're interested in. In terms of students, it's very helpful in training students if you have a bunch of people who have related interests. And just in terms of asking about things, having people around who might know something about data or estimation problems is very useful.

COMMUNICATION OF RESEARCH

How do you find the right balance between communicating your research at an early stage versus the close-to-finished stage?

What I would say is that, over my career anyway, I've just learned to be more patient and not to circulate the first draft of my papers and post them on my website and so on. Who wants to have a mistake in their first draft and then have to retract it once it's been fixed? There's little advantage in posting things at a very preliminary stage, and a lot of advantage to circulating work that's of high quality and well finished. It's also a good idea to present a paper and get some reactions to it at least a few times before you send it off to a journal.

What are the unique challenges to giving a seminar and how do you overcome them?

The main challenge of giving a seminar is deciding what to present. There's often a trade-off. You may wish to present something that's very preliminary because you want to get feedback on it, but on the other hand, it may not be all that good if it's really preliminary. And so the competing interest is that you would like to show yourself in the best light, and present the most polished work. That can be a bit of a quandary sometimes.

I used to find presentations very stressful. But now that I've given so many of them, I don't really find them stressful at all anymore. It's just a matter of practice.

PUBLICATION

How do you decide upon the appropriate journal to send your research to?

That's a hard thing to determine, and I guess is based on experience and also on other types of considerations. If I already have a paper sitting at a journal, then it's probably not a very good idea to send another paper to the same journal. And so I look around somewhere else and see who the editors are and think about what sorts of things they would likely find interesting.

How would you best describe your approach to dealing with a 'revise and resubmit' request from a journal? How about an outright rejection?

Well, there's not really much you can do about a rejection [*laughs*]. The interesting thing about 'revise and resubmits' is that I think most people find them very annoying, even when they're relatively positive. You read it over the first time, and you generally just feel annoyed because they want you to do 'this and that', and you don't think 'this and that' is all that important, or you would have done it to begin with. And so what I try and do with a 'revise and resubmit' is, I read it over, I get annoyed, I put it away for a while until I feel less annoyed and able to deal with it [*laughs*]. Then you just try and be as responsive as you can and get it back to the journal. I think it's very important to get it back in a reasonable amount of time because it imposes a much higher cost on the editor and the referees if you send it back after such a long time that they've forgotten everything that was in the paper. Whereas if you send it back within a couple of months and they remember the paper, they can see whether you've responded adequately or not, and it's just going to require much less work on their part.

Do you think the current structure of the publication process in economics facilitates or impedes scientific understanding and knowledge production?

My personal opinion is there are a lot of things wrong with the economics publishing paradigm. One problem is the tendency for there to be so many 'revise and resubmits' for a paper before it finally gets published. Most of the 'revise and resubmits' don't add very much; either the paper has an interesting finding or it doesn't. Sticking in ten more robustness checks is not really going to add very much to the sum of scientific knowledge, but it does slow down the publication process, it makes papers longer, and it makes them more complicated. Those things make it less likely that papers are going to have an impact.

Delays at all stages of the publication process in economics are a problem. It takes a very long time sometimes to get any referees' reports and for the editors to make a decision. Then once a decision is reached and the paper is forthcoming, it can take years for it to actually appear in print. In a world that's used to the *New England Journal of Medicine* model where the press is alerted that on 'such and such' a day a paper will appear that shows 'such and such', I think it really puts economics papers at a disadvantage. You can say to a journalist, "I have this paper that's forthcoming." They say, "Oh, when will it appear?" You say, "Well, I don't know. Maybe in two years, maybe in three years." The journalist then hangs up. I think that economists could do a lot more to make their work available in a timely way without really compromising its quality.

REFEREEING AND EDITING

How do you decide upon whether or not to accept a refereeing job? What are the benefits to refereeing?

The benefit of being a referee, particularly if people send you things in your own field, is keeping current with what is out there. Given the long lags in publication that we were talking about, sometimes it's the only way to really know what people are doing. That can be a big benefit.

In terms of what I decide to referee, since I have had quite a lot of editorial responsibilities over the years, I do try to cut back a little bit on the amount of refereeing that I do for random journals. But generally, if somebody sends me something that's exactly in my area, I will do it because I want to read the paper anyway.

How has your approach to refereeing changed through time?

People probably agonize more over everything when they're younger. At this point, I've refereed hundreds of papers, so I can tell pretty quickly if it's a good or bad paper. That determines how much time I spend on it. If it's a bad one, there's not much point spending a lot of time, although you might try and say something helpful to the authors. If it's a good one, or an important paper, then it's worth spending more time.

How do you decide upon whether or not to accept an editing position? What are the benefits to being an editor?

That's a good question. I think most people take editorial positions because of the prestige that's associated with them, or maybe with a view to trying to shape what's in the journal a little bit. But it's not so easy to shape what's in the journal because that depends on what you get coming through the pipeline.

So how do you decide on editorial appointments? Again, that would depend on the type of journal and how related it was to the work that you were doing. Most people, when they're asked to do something like be an editor at the *AER* actually accept. If they're asked to be an editor of a lower ranked journal, then there might be more costs and benefits associated with that.

TIME MANAGEMENT

How do you divide up your working day, both in terms of quantity and timing of different kinds of work?

Another good question. For me, it's not so much how I divide up the day but more how I divide up the days of the week, because what I like to do if I'm working on a research project is clear at least some time to think about that project without being interrupted. Ideally, if I have a paper in my mind, with all the tables done, I would like to have a week where I didn't have anything to do except sit down and write that paper. Now that doesn't happen very often. But still, you'd like to have a day where you can not worry about anything else but just that one thing. On the other hand, you have days when you have to catch up on all of the administrative tasks. I might spend a whole day dealing with e-mail and get that out of the way, so that I can go back and spend time on a project without having all these nagging things going on.

How do you balance multiple research projects?

That turns out not to be so difficult because projects get bogged down at different stages. For example, right now, I have a project where I have a research assistant who's gone off to Trenton to try and get some data. She's probably going to be in Trenton for a while, and there's not much I can do about it except monitor her progress from time to time [*laughs*]. I just sit down and think, "Okay, here are all the possible projects. Which one can I actually achieve something on, and which ones need to be nudged along in different ways?"

What is the optimal number of projects that you could be working on at any given time?

That's probably a lot fewer than the number that I actually have going [*laughs*]. It's probably something like three or four.

How many are you typically working on?

Maybe ten. Some of my projects are taking way too long. They get sidetracked, and I just don't have time to work on them. It's inefficient to think about something, and then put it aside for so long that you've forgotten everything about it.

How do you find the right balance between research and non-research activities?

That's a problem for people as they become more senior; they get asked to do more and more things. You could easily spend all your time doing those things and not do any research. Every senior person probably struggles with it because you do have a comparative advantage after a while in doing administration – you just know more about it than a lot of other people. But, as I say, it can eat up all your time, and so you have to decide what the highest-value uses of your time are, and then say "no" to other things.

How about the balance between your personal and professional lives?

One handy trick is just to mark off things on your calendar. For example, if I have to go to a parent–teacher interview at my son's school and somebody asks me to do something at that period of time, I can just say, "I have an appointment." I don't have to tell them what it is. I think it's important to block out time on your calendar to do those kinds of personal things and then honor that time in the same way that you would honor other types of professional commitments.

REFLECTIONS AND THE FUTURE OF ECONOMICS

What have been the most important findings and contributions in your research fields during your career?

One of the fields that I am associated with is a new one: the economics of family and children. The largest overall finding and contribution there is that things that happen to people very early in childhood, even pre-natally, seem to have very long-lasting effects on their human capital. And so the view that everything starts in school has been discredited.

What are the biggest challenges facing your research fields?

There are two challenges, and they tie back nicely to our discussion about theory and empirics. One is lack of data. Ideally, you would like data that was pretty detailed and followed people from pre-natal up to age 25. And you would like lots of that kind of data for many different cohorts. The second problem is that even if you had such data, what would you do with it? [*Laughs*]. You would need to have some theory and structure on the problem to be able to make any headway.

What are the strengths and weaknesses of your own research?

Most people would say that my work is creative – it's gone into new areas that were not previously explored by economists and that helps you to have an influence. They would also say that I wasn't afraid to tackle a very big data collection process or to try and get data on things where, on the face of it, it wasn't very promising to expect to find any. Those would be viewed as strengths. In terms of weaknesses, people probably would say that my work would be better if it were a little more theoretically inclined.

Do you have any professional regrets?

No, I don't think so. I feel very lucky. I've had a great career so far, and things have worked out very well. Many people have been exceptionally nice to me, and so I can't really complain.

What are your professional ambitions?

That's also a tough one for me to answer because things are going very well at the moment. I'm honored to have been elected Vice President of the AEA, I'm giving the Ely Lecture, and I've just accepted a job at Princeton. And so I feel like I've achieved a lot of my ambitions, and now I have to think about what my ambitions are going to be for the next 20 years.

One thing I think I haven't done very well at necessarily is communicating my research to non-academics. I've done okay with, say, other social scientists, but I don't think I've had as much impact as I could have on the debate about what to do to help poor children. That's something that I need to work on and think about how best to do.

I've written a couple of books.[7] I would like to try that again. That's an interesting process because it's so different than writing academic articles. You have much more freedom to say what you want in a book. You negotiate a topic with the publisher, and then chances are they're going to publish your book. Then the problem is whether anybody is going to buy your book and read it. That's a different problem from whether you are going to be able to publish your paper in the *AER*.

My second book was a lot better than my first one. Maybe my third book will be better, even though I haven't started that yet [*laughs*]. I would like to write a book that had a broader impact beyond academic economists.

How would you describe the state of economics today? Are you optimistic about its future?

I'm incredibly optimistic about economics. Economists have done exceedingly well over my professional career, and there doesn't seem to be any sign that they're not going to continue to do very well. There are good reasons for that: we teach people things that are very useful, and that's why they want to learn them.

Economists have shown that they have a set of tools that can be applied to many social problems that are outside the traditional realm of economics. The scope of economics has become broader and broader. I don't see that going away either. Certainly relative to other social sciences, economics is in a very good position, and there's no reason not to expect that we're going to continue to take over things that were traditionally the province of other areas like political science or sociology or even psychology.

NOTES

1. See, for example, Neelin, J., Sonnenschein, H. and M. Spiegel (1988), 'A Further Test of Noncooperative Bargaining Theory: Comment', *American Economic Review*, Vol. 78, No. 4 (September), pp. 824–836; Currie, J. (1989), 'Who Uses Interest Arbitration? The Case of British Columbia's Teachers, 1947–1981', *Industrial and Labor Relations Review*, Vol. 42, No. 3 (April), pp. 363–379; Ashenfelter, O. and J. Currie (1990), 'Negotiator Behavior and the Occurrence of Disputes', *American Economic Review*, Papers and Proceedings, Vol. 80, No. 2 (May), pp. 416–420; Currie, J. and S. McConnell (1991), 'Collective Bargaining in the Public Sector: The Effect of Legal Structure on Dispute Costs and Wages', *American Economic Review*, Vol. 81, No. 4 (September), pp. 693–718.
2. See, for example, Currie, J. and N. Cole (1993), 'Welfare and Child Health: The Link between AFDC Participation and Birth Weight', *American Economic Review*, Vol. 83, No. 4 (September), pp. 971–985.
3. See, for example, Currie, J. (1995), 'Socio-Economic Status and Child Health: Does Public Health Insurance Narrow the Gap?', *Scandinavian Journal of Economics*, Vol. 97, No. 4 (December), pp. 603–620; Currie, J. and D. Thomas (1995), 'Medical Care for Children: Public Insurance, Private Insurance, and Racial Differences in Utilization', *Journal of Human Resources*, Vol. 30, No. 1 (Winter), pp. 135–162.
4. See, for example, Currie, J. and M. Neidell (2005), 'Air Pollution and Infant Health: What Can We Learn from California's Recent Experience', *Quarterly Journal of Economics*, Vol. 120, No. 3 (August), pp. 1003–1030; Currie, J., Neidell, M. and J.F. Schmieder (2009), 'Air Pollution and Infant Health: Lessons from New Jersey', *Journal of Health Economics*, Vol. 28, No. 3 (May), pp. 688–703; Currie, J. and J.F. Schmieder (2009), 'Fetal Exposures to Toxic Releases and Infant Health', *American Economic Review*, Papers and Proceedings, Vol. 99, No. 2 (May), pp. 177–183; Currie, J. and R. Walker (2011), 'Traffic Congestion and Infant Health: Evidence from E-ZPass', *American Economic Journal: Applied Economics*, Vol. 3, No. 1 (January), pp. 65–90.
5. Card, D (2001), 'Estimating the Return to Schooling: Progress on Some Persistent Econometric Problems', *Econometrica*, Vol. 69, No. 5 (September), pp. 1127–1160.
6. Bertrand, M. and S. Mullainathan (2004), 'Are Emily and Greg More Employable Than Lakisha and Jamal? A Field Experiment on Labor Market Discrimination', *American Economic Review*, Vol. 94, No. 4 (September), pp. 991–1013.
7. Janet Currie (1995), *Welfare and the Well-Being of Children*, Harwood Academic Publishers, Chur Switzerland; Janet Currie (2006), *The Invisible Safety Net: Protecting Poor Children and Families*, Princeton University Press.

Partha Dasgupta (University of Cambridge)

Sir Partha Dasgupta was born in Dhaka (at that time in India) in 1942 and graduated with a BSc in physics from the University of Delhi in 1962 before obtaining both a BA in mathematics and a PhD in economics from the University of Cambridge in 1965 and 1968 respectively. He taught at the London School of Economics between 1971 and 1984 and then moved to the University of Cambridge in 1985 as Professor of Economics. Between 1989 and 1992, he was on leave from the University of Cambridge and served as Professor of Economics, Professor of Philosophy, and Director of the Program in Ethics in Society at Stanford University. He is currently Frank Ramsey Emeritus Professor of Economics at Cambridge, Fellow of St John's College, Cambridge, and Professorial Research Fellow at the Sustainable Consumption Institute, University of Manchester.

Professor Dasgupta's research interests include welfare and development economics, the economics of technological change, population, environmental and resource economics, the theory of games, and the economics of undernutrition. His most-cited articles in chronological order include 'Notes on the Measurement of Inequality', *Journal of Economic Theory* (1973), co-authored with Amartya Sen and David Starrett, 'The Optimal Depletion of Exhaustible Resources', *Review of Economic Studies* (1974), co-authored with Geoffrey Heal, 'Industrial Structure and The Nature of Innovative Activity', *Economic Journal* (1980), co-authored with Joseph Stiglitz, 'The Existence of Equilibrium in Discontinuous Economic Games, I: Theory', *Review of Economic Studies* (1986), co-authored with Eric Maskin, and 'Inequality as a Determinant of Malnutrition and Unemployment: Theory', *Economic Journal* (1986), co-authored with Debraj Ray. His books include *The Control of Resources* (Harvard University Press, 1982), *An Inquiry into Well-Being and Destitution* (Clarendon Press, 1993), *Human Well-Being and the Natural Environment* (Oxford University Press, 2001; revised version, 2004), and *Economics: A Very Short Introduction* (Oxford University Press, 2007).

Professor Dasgupta was elected as a Fellow of the Econometric Society in 1975, a Fellow of the British Academy in 1989, a Member of the Pontifical Academy of Social Sciences in 1997, a Member of the Third World Academy of Sciences in 2001, and a Fellow of the Royal Society in 2004. He is a Foreign Honorary Member of the American Academy of Arts and Sciences (1991), a Foreign Member of the Royal Swedish Academy of Sciences (1991), a Foreign Associate of the US National Academy of Sciences (2001), and a Foreign Member of the American Philosophical Society (2005). He was named Knight Bachelor by Her Majesty Queen Elizabeth II in her Birthday Honours List in 2002 for "services to economics."

I interviewed Sir Partha Dasgupta at his hotel in Montreal, Canada, where he was attending the World Congress of the Associations of Environmental and Resource Economists. It was early-afternoon of Friday, 2 July 2010.

BACKGROUND INFORMATION

You hold bachelor's degrees in physics and mathematics. How did you end up with a PhD in economics?

I was intending to be a high-energy, particle physicist, but two things made me abandon that ambition. One was that the subject was going through what seemed to me to be an uninspiring patch in the mid-'60s, although that probably reflected my own intellectual shortcomings more than the state of the subject. The other reason was that the Vietnam War was on and, like many other students, I was bothered by it. My friends among the mathematicians at Cambridge weren't interested in the War. A philosopher friend insisted he didn't have enough information to have a view about it. I found that the only people in college with whom I could have informative discussions on the War and its probable causes were economists, particularly Marxists, who provided me one interpretation, and political scientists, who insisted on another class of interpretations. That was very educational for me.

In my own college at Cambridge, Jim Mirrlees (now Sir James Mirrlees, Nobel Laureate) had done math as a first degree and a PhD in economics. I got to know him through a discussion group we both belonged to, and he encouraged me to shift to economics. And that's what I did, in 1965.

As a student, which professors were most influential or inspirational?

The greatest influence was unquestionably my father, who was however never formally my teacher. He was a professor of economics and a profound educationist. He was also a terrific father. Our home was always filled with visitors: his students, colleagues, and friends. Also, between the ages of 13 and 15, I went to a school (now known as Rajghat Besant School, Varanasi) that was phenomenally good. I came under the spell of several remarkable teachers there. About three months ago, I visited the campus with my wife. We spent a week there. It was an unforgettable experience for us both.

I don't believe there was anybody at university in Delhi who inspired me. But as a PhD student at Cambridge, Jim Mirrlees was a big influence. He had enormous technical abilities and I could tell he asked deep questions.

Why did you decide to pursue an academic career?

That was the influence of my father. I assumed I would be an academic because that's the only life I had known at close quarters. Our home was regularly filled with visitors, who were often distinguished academics. They were invariably kind to me, asked me questions and shared their ideas, even when I was very young. It was but natural that I would be attracted to a life of the mind. And I was. But when I moved to economics I wasn't setting out to change the world or help the poor, or anything so noble. All I wanted to do was to obtain a PhD and become an academic. I belong to a caste in Bengal, India, that nurtures professionals, especially doctors and teachers. My outlook must have been narrow, it never occurred to me to work in the private sector, say for a business firm. If I had joined the private sector, my parents' friends would have merely inferred that I wasn't a serious person, most certainly not a good student [*laughs*].

In the mid- to late-1960s, at least in the UK, students of mathematics who had converted to economics (there weren't that many) were viewed with suspicion. Did we have the 'horse sense' that was necessary for economics, senior economists would ask. For some years after I obtained my PhD, I was unsuccessful in obtaining a tenure-track post. Two of the chapters in my thesis were published in the *Review of Economic Studies* almost immediately, so they must have been reasonable pieces of work.[1] But they were technical papers. As I had little formal training in economics, I was also diffident, and that may have showed. About the time I completed my PhD, that was 1968, I obtained a research fellowship at Cambridge, spent a year at Carnegie Mellon University as a visiting assistant professor, followed by a year as a visiting fellow at the Delhi School of Economics. Then, in the summer of '71, three years down the road, I was appointed to a lectureship at the LSE; but that was after five candidates who had been placed above me had declined the lectureship! If you ask my wife she will tell you that for a long while after we were married she was worried whether I would ever get a job that would enable us to settle down.

As a researcher, which colleagues have been most influential or inspirational?

At the time I joined the LSE, it had a phenomenal economics department. (It still does). Bauer, Gorman, Hahn, Johnson, Morishima, Sargan, and Sen are a formidable list of names, by any standard. (Hahn had left for Cambridge, but visited for a day every two weeks). None of them was particularly interested in my research interests, though. Maybe that was because I didn't have any particular interests in those days. Intellectually, I was still quite rootless. But my senior colleagues were supportive of the young. I was left alone to get on with my work, which, however, wasn't much. I think being left alone was good for my development; it meant I didn't get depressed that I wasn't producing papers by the week. I was influenced more by my contemporaries, especially Joseph Stiglitz, whom I met way back in '65 when I had just moved to economics. He was inspiring even then, brimming with ideas. The contrast with me was all the more sharp because I rarely *had* an idea. I owe Stiglitz an un-repayable debt because he made me feel as though I was contributing to our joint work, even while I was unsure what I was bringing to the proverbial table. Geoff Heal was another contemporary whose work and engagement I found exciting. We collaborated all through the 1970s in developing the economics of exhaustible resources.

Among my senior colleagues at the LSE, I saw much of Amartya Sen, from whom I learnt how one might interpret economic development. He had style and a flair for polemics. I read pretty much everything he wrote at that time. In recent years, our visions of what economics should be about have diverged somewhat. That may be why we haven't seen much of each other. As far as I can judge, he feels development economics should get closer to moral philosophy and has influenced international agencies and charities to adopt that position, whereas I am convinced the subject's greatest weakness lies in that it's not informed by the natural sciences, especially ecology. I don't think the failure of official development economics to successfully address extreme poverty and demographic distress in the poorest countries has had anything to do with not knowing what poverty or justice mean, rather it seems to me the answer lies in the fact that professionals have neglected to uncover the pathways that determine the poverty-population-environment nexus. If you read Sen's famous 1999 book, *Development as Freedom* and his recent book, *The Idea of Justice*, and my 1993 book, *An Inquiry into Well-Being and Destitution* and my 2001 book, *Human Well-Being and the Natural Environment*, you will see what I mean. For example, in his book on justice, Sen makes it his central point (or so it has been read by reviewers in UK newspapers and literary magazines) to criticize Rawls's theory of justice on grounds that the theory characterizes the just society, the attainment of which presupposes a well-ordered society; whereas a useful theory should be able to provide a moral ranking of unjust societies too, even dysfunctional societies. I don't know whether Sen's charge against Rawls will be found by experts to stick, what I do know is that his view of what theories of justice should offer is bread and butter in modern welfare economics. The idea of a social welfare function, now over 70 years old, does precisely that. It ranks all alternatives; it doesn't merely identify what's judged by the theory of justice to be the best. Theories of the Second Best, constructed by James Meade in 1955, are an illustration of what I mean. But even the usage of the term 'second best' carries with it the thought that the society under study is nearly just. So it struck me some years ago that what needed doing was to apply the idea of a social welfare function to rework welfare economics and develop a unified theory of policy evaluation that covers not only Utopia (the ideally ordered society) and Agathotopia (Meade's name for a Good Enough society), but also Kakotopia (the name I gave to dysfunctional societies). In my 2001 book I just mentioned, I did that, and it required of me to study a number of socio-ecological pathways that sustain dysfunctional societies. It seems to me that's where the hard work lies, unearthing further pathways that are bound to be site-specific and time-specific. But I found no reference to that applied-theoretic work in Sen's book on justice. But at the time I speak of, the 1970s at the LSE, I didn't know much about development economics, certainly I didn't know then the way I would subsequently come to frame and study the state of affairs called poverty.

By the mid-1970s, I had worked on several fields. One reason I moved fields then and have continued to do so is that I haven't had a proper training in economics. Working on a field has been my way of getting acquainted with it. For example, when I started working on industrial organization and technological change with Stiglitz (that was in 1975 or thereabouts), I had little prior knowledge of the subject. Ignorance may have been a help, though. As I didn't know the literature, I wasn't minded to make an advance on someone else's work. Stiglitz and I simply chatted about what might drive an entrepreneur to innovate. Once we had arrived at a formulation, I was sufficiently intrigued to read Schumpeter and Scherer, who were very much worth reading of course; but it was as well I hadn't read them before. Their style was very different from the one Stiglitz and I adopted in our attempt to understand the character of technological competition.

Ignorance has helped my work over and over again. For example, even after completing the first paper Geoff Heal and I wrote together, on the optimal depletion of exhaustible resources, I didn't know of Hotelling's now-famous paper of 1931.[2] In this instance even my co-author didn't know it. We learnt of that paper from Robert Solow. My guess is that if we'd read the paper before starting our work, we would have modeled the problem as an extension of Hotelling's work, which was entirely Marshallian, partial equilibrium. Heal and I knew some capital and growth theory, so we found it natural to embed the exhaustible resource in a larger economy. I like to think our paper helped frame the contemporary literature on sustainable development.

GENERAL THOUGHTS ON RESEARCH

There is an increasing emphasis in many economics departments on applied research. Is this true at Cambridge?

Yes and I am all for it. I certainly tried to bring more applied people into my department in Cambridge when I was Chairman. I felt we were particularly weak there, especially in applied microeconometrics. Traditionally, the Faculty of Economics at Cambridge has been of a highly theoretical bent.

One reason is that, at least since World War II, there was a separate department called the Department of Applied Economics (DAE), which had been established owing to Keynes' urgings, essentially to advise him on the kind of numerical figures he needed for his own work. I can only think Cambridge was a most patriarchal society [*laughs*]. The DAE built its reputation on its first Director Richard Stone's innovative work on consumption and the social accounting framework that's needed to describe an economy's doings. It may be that because the DAE was in the same building as the Faculty of Economics, appointments in the economics department, which did most of the lecturing, were mainly in economic theory. When I was a student, the great names were Joan Robinson, Nicholas Kaldor, and Piero Sraffa, who were all theorists. It makes me blush even to think of what Robinson, Kaldor, and Sraffa thought applied economics amounts to. They really were hard-line Mandarins. I think Austin Robinson was the only applied economist of note in the Faculty when I was doing my PhD. James Meade was also in the Faculty, and he straddled both theory and empirical policy with enormous distinction, but the politics in the place at that time was so virulent that he remained an outsider even while occupying the Professorship of Political Economy.

As you know, applied economics (by which I mean applied microeconomics) has grown by leaps and bounds in the last 30 to 40 years, but our department is not yet a balanced one. We are pretty strong in microeconomic theory, not so strong in applied microeconomics. Macroeconomics remains a mystery to me. Meanwhile, the DAE has closed. The quality of its research had deteriorated. Like most other think-tanks, it survived on soft money, which meant it had to chase research programs that others were interested in. That doesn't do much for the university it inhabits. That's not to say there aren't outstanding research centers built on soft money. The Institute for Fiscal Studies is excellent, but that's in London.

What is the value of pure versus applied research in economics?

Both are valuable. I'm not a believer in 'relevant' theory, though. It's hard to tell in advance when, if ever, good theory will turn out to be useful in practical, policy terms. Take the case of Frank Ramsey's 1928 paper.[3] Ramsey asked how much of an economy's national income should be saved. It was a highly mathematical, esoteric piece of work. For a long while, the paper languished, probably because the world entered a depression and nobody was interested in the long run. But after World War II, people became interested in the long-term development of nations, such as India, and Ramsey's was the obvious theoretical tool for one class of questions, concerning the optimal magnitude and composition of investment activity over time. So Ramsey's question and the way he framed it became useful even to economists with a huge interest in policy, such as Jan Tinbergen. At the time I was working on my PhD, my teachers such as Joan Robinson used to think Ramsey's paper was about how many angels are able to dance on the head of a pin. Recently, the paper has made another return in the economics of climate change. It contains the only machinery available for thinking about the long-term trade-offs.

My father once said that if you see a piece of theory that looks directly applicable, you should be suspicious. I think he meant that if the theory is so designed that the gap between its formulation and application is small, there should be a suspicion the theory may have been doctored to suit the answer desired by its authors or their patrons. The advantage of maintaining a certain distance between theory and policy is that it encourages the author to seek deep answers, not shallow ones. I'm not saying all theoretical papers should be like that, but it's the more esoteric type of theoretical work that gets criticized for its lack of 'relevance'. My father provided a sophisticated defense of pure theory.

How would you describe your own research agenda and how has it changed over time?

Most of my work has been on what is often called 'applied theory'. No one is the best judge of their own work, but I believe much of my work has sprung from the ground up, motivated by some phenomenon out there that demands an investigation. Of course, being a theorist by temperament and training, I pretty soon lift the phenomenon up many miles, so that it may even become unrecognizable by the time I am done with it, but I like to think it's still likely to be useful to someone concerned with the phenomenon.

Do you think it is important to have broad research interests?

It's a matter of personal taste, nothing more. Gerard Debreu is a good example of someone who did foundational work, but never took interest in anything other than a narrow set of very abstract problems. And Wassily Leontief appeared to me to be rather dull (input-output tables, not much else), but I only met him when he was quite old. Debreu is one extreme. At the other end is Kenneth Arrow, who is interested in a huge number of problems and can explain why we should be interested in them. And of course, he has written fundamental papers on pretty much any subject he has touched. In 1975, I came across, quite by chance, his short book *The Limits of Organization,* and it transformed my work. I had known Arrow's work on social choice, general equilibrium, technical progress, health, and economic externalities, of course, but as I read that little book of his, I could feel that at last I knew what basic research in the social sciences amounts to and how to go about it. Among economic theorists of my generation, Joe Stiglitz has the widest reach in terms of research interests. He is simply phenomenal.

Do you think there is any difference in the types of work done by researchers at different stages of their careers based on tenure concerns, publication requirements or other pressures? Should there be a difference?

The answer to the first part of the question is "yes". The American PhD program is very much like an apprenticeship, which England is now mimicking. Students tend to take their supervisors' research lead. This means that at an early stage, you are shaped by someone else's style of research. And there is no question that, intellectually, we are history-dependent. Our capital stock is created by the time we're 27 or 28, and it takes quite some time to overcome it and break out on one's own.

The answer to the second part of the question is also "yes". Many years ago, Robert Solow put it nicely. If I remember him correctly, he said the really hard problems in the social sciences relate to policy. That however looks easy, which is why even taxi drivers with no training in economics spout on it. Solow said the technical stuff is relatively easy, although seemingly very difficult. He also said he liked young economists to get their fingers burnt in the technical stuff and wouldn't trust someone with the policy stuff if he or she hadn't undergone the technical test.

IDEA GENERATION

Where do you get your research ideas?

By observation, I guess. On one occasion in the early '80s, when passing through Calcutta on my way to visit my parents in Santiniketan, I noticed that the baby of a mother beggar on the sidewalk was being molested by flies. I thought, "That's odd. Why isn't the baby swatting the flies?" Then it dawned on me that the baby was conserving energy. That eventually triggered my joint work with Debraj Ray on malnutrition and the capacity to work. Of course, he had been thinking along similar lines before we met at Stanford, which is how we came to collaborate, but it was a casual observation that led me to seek a theory that would cover what I had observed. When Ray and I discovered we had been thinking along similar lines, we closed the deal, so to speak, and produced our analysis.

If you travel by train in West Bengal, you will notice that every village has a pond, supplying water for drinking, washing, and cultivating root crops. On several such journeys, I observed that villagers have built their homes very close to one another around their pond. Why? One answer is that you have more land for cultivation if you crowd the huts. It occurred to me that another possible answer was that closeness would enable people to observe each other's behavior easily. We know of the old adage that in the third world there's no privacy. But maybe you don't enjoy privacy because life there is built on social norms. There are few private property rights to those commons, so presumably communities have had to devise norms of behavior. And norms of behavior involve sanctions for misbehavior. But how do you know somebody has misbehaved? You have to observe it. Those problems led me to the then nascent literature on social capital, and I tried to understand the concept in terms of modern resource allocation theory.

At what point does an idea become a project that you devote resources to?

I've never had a project in the sense most people mean by a project. I've never applied for a research grant. My guess is that you have to have a fairly well-defined notion of what you want to accomplish when you apply for a grant. But mostly I've not even been able to frame the question I was tackling until locating the answer. So, by the time I might have been in a position to apply for a grant, I'd completed the paper and moved on to a new set of problems, ones that I would be unable to articulate. Of course, I have enjoyed grants indirectly. For several years, Joe Stiglitz included me in his grant applications, but it was he who had an idea of where we would be heading.

My research practices are very old-fashioned. I do all the ancillary work that's needed to be done in preparing a paper: reading other people's work, referencing, checking citations, proofreading, the whole works. Even now I don't Google for references; I go to the library and browse. The latter is a pleasure in itself. In the course of browsing, I frequently find very interesting things to read, material I didn't know existed. My book, *An Inquiry into Well-Being and Destitution*, has about 65 pages of references. Believe me, I read, or at the very least glanced at, each of the items mentioned, all in libraries. For certain chapters, I used to walk to the library of Addenbrooke's Hospital (our University hospital), quite a distance from the University Library, because that's where I could browse the literature on clinical under-nutrition. In describing my long-standing work habit, I am neither apologizing nor bragging. It's how I have always worked. I have always felt chasing material is part of my job.

IDEA EXECUTION

What makes a good theoretical paper?

It should have a surprise.

What makes a good empirical paper?

Good applied work doesn't necessarily have to have a surprise because you may be engaged in repeating a previous investigation in a different geographical location. That can be extremely valuable work. You may discover subtle differences from the findings of previous investigators, and that might suggest that the phenomenon is site-specific, a frequent characteristic of phenomena in the social sciences and challenging to the theorist. Often it may be that you are investigating the same phenomenon others have examined, but you are deploying better tools, and so on. For example, the theoretical models Kenneth Arrow, Karl-Goran Mäler, and I have been developing over the past few years show that wealth changes rather than movements in GDP per capita are the true indicators of the progress and regress of nations.[4] But then, what is wealth? It must be the value of all capital assets of an economy. Does that include natural capital? Of course it does. So, if a national income accountant claims that the savings ratio in Brazil is nearly 15 per cent, we should respond by insisting that the statistic doesn't take into account the forests that are being razed there. That's depreciation and should be deducted from savings. If accountants buy the argument, they would repeat the exercise by deducting forest depletion. The research wouldn't be novel in the conventional sense, but it would be illuminating and useful.

When you hit a brick wall on a paper, do you continue to work on the problem or do you take a break from it and work on something else?

I take a break and then, *usually*, serendipitously, I get an answer. Eric Maskin and I once worked on a paper that took us ten years to complete. It was on the existence of equilibrium in games in which payoff functions are discontinuities.[5] It was very esoteric stuff in game theory (not the sort you would bore your partner with), but Maskin and I thought it was important to determine whether such games possess Nash equilibria (in mixed strategies). Pretty quickly, we managed to prove an existence theorem, but it was only for symmetric games, meaning that players were assumed to be identical. Now, we could have tried to publish that result, in fact all the then existing theoretical models with discontinuous payoff functions were symmetrical, which is a perfectly sensible modeling strategy to adopt when trying to capture something else about the phenomena out there in the world; but Maskin and I chose not to submit our result for publication. And the reason we didn't is that we knew we hadn't dug deep enough, we still didn't understand the underlying structure of the problem. So, we sat on the problem for some more time. Then, in one set of interchanges we found a simple trick that enabled us to prove the result in its generality.

Related to the previous question, when it appears that a project isn't going to turn out as hoped, do you scrap it or aim to send the paper to a second-tier or field journal?

I have been enormously lucky. I've rarely been involved in a paper that hasn't eventually been published. There have of course been occasions when a submission didn't get accepted, but I always interpreted rejection to mean I hadn't drafted the work well. That meant working on the problem some more and improving the exposition. But I don't think I have entirely abandoned any work. And I've also had amazing luck with editors. Over 40 years, I have found journal editors almost always to be fair and encouraging. Journal editors generally get a bad press, so there was one occasion I can't help recalling, to illustrate how shrewd and fair-minded editors can be.

In the mid-1980s, my friend Debraj Ray and I developed a timeless general equilibrium model in a world where nutrition affects productivity, a project I mentioned earlier. There were some interesting technical problems that the model threw up (having to do with non-convexities in nutrition-to-productivity transformation possibilities), and it showed, among other things, how and why equilibrium allocations can violate horizontal equity, in the sense that very similar people end up with vastly different utility levels. Arrow–Debreu equilibria, as you know, satisfy the principle of horizontal equity. Ray and I showed that in a rich world, the principle would be maintained, but not in a poor world. And we identified several other properties of the model, each of which spoke to the world we believed we knew in India. So we felt we had understood something of importance about the nature of poverty; and we submitted the paper to the *Economic Journal*. In return we got a referee's report that was eight pages long in A4, single spaced paper, offering as many reasons as you care to number as to why the paper should be rejected. The referee basically had sat down and asked how many reasons he could think of for not liking the paper. Ray and I could tell the referee was technically proficient, but we could also tell that he had little imagination and suffered from an inability to discover general truths from non-standard models. Now you would think the editor, who was the economic historian, Charles Feinstein, would have written to me to ask why I had wasted his time submitting such a shoddy piece of work. But he didn't. He smelt something not right in the report, the referee had gone for over-kill, so he wrote to say that, obviously, he couldn't accept the paper as it was drafted, but that he would publish it if Ray and I re-wrote it, having dealt with all the reasons the referee had collated for recommending rejection. Ray and I did that, and the paper was published in two install-ments.[6] I don't know if many people have read the paper, but it has been the basis on which I have tried to understand poverty traps.

What has been the biggest change during your career in how researchers in your fields conduct research?

People are a lot tenser now about research than they were in my time. I can see that amongst young colleagues. Life for the researcher is harder today. There is far greater competition. Moreover, family life has changed beyond recognition. And remember, economics remains a male profession. In UK economics departments, women average around 10 per cent of senior appointments. Responsibilities at home among males have changed enor-mously and that adds to the pressure. I like to think I was a good father and husband, but the division of labor between my wife and I, one that we reached without thinking, would be unthinkable today.

THE WRITING PROCESS

Which aspect of the writing process do you find most difficult?

I used to find writing difficult, but having gained experience over the years I find it much easier now. The word processor has of course helped. I frequently take the lead in writing a first draft when working in collaboration, largely because I enjoy composing papers. In the process of drafting, based on notes, I at last begin to understand the point of the paper we have been working on [*laughs*].

COLLABORATION

When you work with co-authors, how do you decide whom to work with?

If you look at my CV, you will find an enormous amount of collaborative work. Swapping ideas is always good and it also encourages friendship. Conferences are terrific breeding grounds for collaborative research and my guess is that some personal relationships do then develop. But in my case, the causal chain has been the reverse. Almost always, the collaboration starts over a conversation with a friend, maybe over a drink, an idea comes up, and then we work on it together. Joe (Stiglitz), Eric (Maskin), Karl-Goran (Mäler) and Geoff (Heal) were friends first; collaboration came later. In the case of Ken Arrow, collaboration began many years after we first met, but that's because I used to be terrified of him. It was no fault of his, but for a long time I found conversations with him an agony. It slowly dawned on me that the problem was with me, that Arrow believes everyone is as deep and quick as he. That's the only intellectual error I have ever known him to make, but once I realized he wouldn't notice my intellectual shortcomings, I found it possible to collaborate with him! It's been not only a privilege, but a wholly pleasurable experience.

How do you prefer to interact with your co-authors (e-mail, phone, or face-to-face)?

With Mäler, it's been face-to-face discussions, but that's because we have met frequently over the years in connection with the teaching programmes he and I helped to initiate in South Asia and sub-Saharan Africa. With Maskin, too, it's never on the phone or by e-mail, it's always been face-to-face; but that's because over the years he and his wife Gayle have made it a point to stay in touch with us, as have my wife Carol and I with them. Maskin and I have a discussion and then we do our writing separately. We're about to write a paper on a problem where we don't know which of two models we ought to use to illustrate the point we want to make. He has one, I have another. But we will write down both models and then decide which best makes the points we want to make.

With Stiglitz, it used to be walks in Oxford or Princeton or while he cooked supper. He would talk nineteen to the dozen, throwing out one model after another to capture a phenomenon we agreed was worth understanding. With Ken Arrow, it's been a meeting or two where we have discussed a problem, followed by e-mail exchanges on how best to model the phenomenon, or as in a five-way paper we have just completed (with Larry Goulder, Kevin Mumford, and Kirsten Oleson), most of the discussions were held over conference calls.[7]

SEMINAR PARTICIPATION AND NETWORKING

How important is professional networking to success in research?

It's very important. It was very important even in times long gone. Isolation is never a good thing. I remember talking to Fred Hoyle, the great astrophysicist, who courted notoriety. As we all know, he held on to the steady state theory of the universe. He never gave up on it, partly I believe because he chose to be isolated. I am told by friends who know, that his best papers were early collaborative efforts, like his work on how heavy elements are cooked up in the stars. But when I met him, it must have been ten years ago, he lived out of reach from university campuses. On the occasion we sat next to each other at dinner at St John's College, I asked him if he didn't feel isolated. And he replied, "Oh, no, that's the advantage – I don't get contaminated by other people's ideas." I thought it was sad that such a powerful mind could be so wrong.

To what extent is the absence of departmental colleagues working in one's research area a major disadvantage?

I don't think it's a major disadvantage. As I mentioned earlier, at the LSE, I was isolated in terms of the work I was doing, but I always had access to the great minds there. Conversations with powerful minds, even if they don't work on the problems you work on, is always helpful. It keeps you alert and prevents you from becoming sloppy. They set the standard, if you see what I mean. For example, in Frank Hahn's presence one could never say anything remotely imprecise; he would tell you in a booming voice that you had slackened your intellectual muscles, maybe even that you had been educated beyond your natural limits. And who wants to be told that in public? Moreover, even though my colleagues at the LSE, and later at Stanford, didn't work on my problems, they were world experts in their fields of expertise. I could, and did, pick their brains for what to read. When I was at Stanford in 1989–91, working on my book on *Well-Being and Destitution*, it's not that any of my colleagues had much interest in the subject, but I could always collar them on the corridor for a quick tutorial on some technical matter I hadn't understood, or when I needed a reference to a paper that would explain something I wanted to understand. My colleagues saved me hours of work by telling me what to read and explaining something I had not understood.

COMMUNICATION OF RESEARCH

How do you find the right balance between communicating your research at an early stage versus the close-to-finished stage?

It has to be a pretty finished paper before I put it up on my website. If you have that option, you should exploit it. In the past, you had to rely on being part of a discussion paper series that was then mailed to a restricted number of people. Being able to retrieve other people's writings easily today is an enormous boon.

What are the unique challenges to giving a seminar and how do you overcome them?

I haven't been worried about seminars. I think I'm fairly articulate; in any case, I like teaching, and I'm generally not shy to talk about my own work. Of course, there have been occasions when a seminar has gone badly; but that's generally been because I wasn't particularly proud of the quality of the paper I was presenting. If you don't find your own work exciting, your audience will know that pretty quickly, which is when you start wondering when the seminar will end.

Do you have any advice for a young scholar on giving a seminar?

Be excited about your paper. Of course, the problem is somewhat the other way in America, where there is abundant self-confidence. And so the advice I would give to young scholars there is, don't overrate yourself. Very often, I hear seminars where the presenter thinks he (it's still usually a 'he') has solved the world's greatest problem; worse, he often seems to be selling a product. Overconfidence in the quality of your own work can distort your notion of what is genuinely important work. I'm not saying you should be humble, but it's one thing to be self-confident and at ease with yourself, it's another to think that you are the greatest. Just read a page or two of Arrow and you will realize you are not.

PUBLICATION

How do you decide upon the appropriate journal to send your work to?

At my age, I write quite a number of papers that are invited ones. You write in a style appropriate for the occasion. But on the whole, I have tended to send my research papers to journals where the reader is more likely to be interested in what I am doing. It's a marriage; there is a natural place for most articles.

Do you think that the current structure of the publication process in economics facilitates or impedes scientific understanding and knowledge production?

Today, there is an obsession with the top five journals and I think it's absolutely dreadful. It's stalling progress. I feel so bad for young scholars because they are convinced they have to submit their work to *Econometrica* or to the *American Economic Review*, where there is more than 95 per cent chance it will be rejected; that too after two years. It can then be that after three years into your first job, you still haven't got a publication. At the end of the day, it's the quality of the paper that matters rather than where it has been published. The problem is, people, especially those who are on appointments and tenure committees, don't appear to have confidence in judging a paper for its quality. So they look for quality by the journal in which it was published.

The practice has so annoyed me, it's now arrived in Cambridge, that some years ago I ran an experiment to judge how top the top five journals are. As you know, over the years there has been a big increase in the number of economics anthologies. The publisher Edward Elgar has produced more than 100 anthologies, on various themes in economics. What they do is to print about 500 copies and sell them at a very high price to libraries. They are clever to commission well-known people as editors. Those anthologies are very useful to university libraries in poor countries. They can't afford books or journals, but at a stretch they can afford anthologies, which give students and scholars the opportunity to read the classics in their field. For teaching purposes in a third-world country, they are invaluable.

What I did was to peruse a dozen Edward Elgar anthologies. After all, if experts have edited anthologies, they could be relied upon to know what's stood the test of time. My very cursory research suggested that the major journals in economics are overrated. Most of the papers in those anthologies were published in journals other than the top five. The point it seems to me is a simple one. The top five journals publish excellent articles on currently fashionable topics. The signaling effect of ability is certainly strong. But papers that may have lasting value, or are novel, get crowded out by good but standard-quality papers on hot topics. I suspect some of today's best papers are appearing in second-tier journals. It would be interesting if someone were to do a more thorough study of anthologies than I was able to do.

How would you best describe your approach to dealing with a 'revise and resubmit' request from a journal? How about an outright rejection?

I've never had a quarrel with an editor. There have of course been instances where my submission has been rejected and where I could have written a letter showing that the referee was perhaps illiterate; worse, prejudiced. But I never felt the need to do that. What I took away from a rejection was that I (or I and my co-author) had not drafted the paper well. Usually, I have re-drafted a rejected paper and published it elsewhere, sometimes in a better journal.

In 1996, you helped to establish the journal, Environment and Development Economics. *Part of its purpose is to provide an opportunity for scholars in developing countries to publish their findings in an international journal. Do you think there should be more examples of journals like this?*

Yes, of course. But if the journal is going to be any good, submissions must go through the same screening process that other journals insist on. You mustn't introduce affirmative action. How do you achieve that? You need to ensure that three things happen. First, the editor mustn't necessarily chuck a paper in the way he or she would have if it were a standard journal. If there is a semblance of an idea in the submission, the editor needs to be sympathetic and should ask referees not only to referee, but also to act as mentors. Secondly, you have to build up a body of academics who are willing to be those mentors. And third, you need funds to enable authors to spend time with one of their mentors so as to be able to complete their paper for publication.

That's how it's been working at the interface of the journal, *Environment and Development Economics* and the South Asian Network for Development and Environmental Economics (SANDEE). SANDEE has in its roster such outstanding economists as Enamul Haque, Subhrendu Pattanayak, Priya Shyamsundar, E.S. Somanathan, and Jeff Vincent. They give a lot of their time to teaching and training young scholars from Bangladesh, India, Pakistan, Nepal, and Sri Lanka. Karl-Goran Mäler and I have also been engaged in that work, as we had been involved in obtaining the funds for starting SANDEE. Collectively, we have been hugely successful. Journal articles (in *Environment and Development Economics*; even the *Proceedings of the National Academy of Sciences*) and collections of articles on selected themes have been published by scholars who entered the international academic community first by attending SANDEE teaching and training workshops. It's the most exciting venture I have ever been involved in.

But building capacity in poor regions takes patience, time, and a great deal of good will. And it requires a collegiate atmosphere. SANDEE's director, Priya Shyamsundar, is an outstanding environmental economist in her own right, but is also simply out of this world as a leader, mentor, and administrator. Mäler and I are in awe of her. We do whatever she asks us to do, whenever.

Perhaps the most striking example of success is the case of a woman economist, Saudamini Das, who came from an out-of-the-way place in the intellectually unpromising state of Orissa. She had a bit of economics training, had raised a family, and then sought to understand the role of mangroves, which are an important form of natural capital in hurricane-ridden Orissa. She attended a SANDEE teaching and research workshop, was successful in obtaining a grant from SANDEE (we are talking of at most $12,000, so this is research on the cheap) and eventually produced a joint paper with her mentor at SANDEE, Jeff Vincent, who is one of the best minds in environmental and resource economics. The paper was published last year in the *Proceedings of the National Academy of Sciences*.[8] This is research that came from the heart, to put it one way. Das knew that mangroves protect coastal villagers. Every NGO or international organization I know will agree that mangroves are an important form of natural capital. But how important are they? Do we have any quantitative feel for how much of a buffering capacity they offer to shorelines? Das and Vincent used data on the effect of the Indonesian Tsunami on coastal villages to show us how to estimate the social worth of mangroves. Theirs is a very important paper.

BOOK WRITING

You have written numerous books. Do you enjoy the process?

Yes, I enjoy the art of writing, and books enable me to understand the subject on which I had been working. As I told you earlier, all of my understanding is incremental; I've never had a eureka moment. Articles are of necessity narrow in focus. If you want to understand a complex phenomenon, you want to break it up into small bits and publish articles on those small bits. Putting them together in the form of a book enables you to put those bits together, explore the way they feed one other. When I've finished writing a book, I know a lot more about the subject. Writing books has been a way I have tried to educate myself. Economists are writing more books now than they did 40 years ago. That's good news.

Tell me about writing A Very Short Introduction to Economics.

That was a curious experience. It took me eight years to complete it, but not for reasons you might think. I signed the contract with Oxford University Press in 1998 or '99, but I didn't know how to write it. I asked several people for advice on how to squeeze economics into 160 small pages, but the advice I received didn't match my temperament. So I sat on the book for several years. The delay was so great that I got into trouble with the department at Oxford University Press responsible for the VSI series. They had huge expectations for the series, it had become very successful; they were aiming for more than 200 titles, but seven years had gone by and they were still missing the economics title. Meanwhile, as I didn't know how I was going to frame economics for the book, I did what comes naturally to me: go into denial and continue working on other things.

Then out of the blue, sometime in 2005, Tim Gowers, a distinguished mathematician at Cambridge (he is a Fields Medalist), asked me to write a chapter on Mathematics and Economic Reasoning for the *Princeton Companion to Mathematics* he was editing. Naturally, I was flattered; I didn't even dream of saying "no." However, I was required to pack my chapter into 15 printed pages of admittedly a large size book. That concentrated my mind. I thought, "How do I give the flavor to a mathematician of what our subject is about in 15 pages?" Once I cracked that problem, I knew it would be the model I'd use for *Economics: VSI*. If you read it, you will see that it reflects all the prejudices and convictions I have laid bare before you the last two hours.

REFEREEING AND EDITING

What are the benefits to refereeing?

You learn something new, but I've been a bad referee all my life. I think it's because of my lack of training in economics. I've been learning 'on the hoof', so I don't have that much of a command over the literature at any moment to be able to be a good referee. I am likely to say, "This is not a very interesting paper because it's rather obvious." Somebody else might say, "But it's not published anywhere in the literature." And I'm then likely to say, "Well, maybe it's just as well it's not in the published literature because it's so obvious." I feel nervous refereeing.

You have never been an editor of a journal. Is that for the same reason?

I think my colleagues realized that I wasn't a very reliable referee as well. I'm not disciplined enough to say on Mondays and Tuesdays, I will work on the journal, and on Wednesdays, I will get back to research. My research life contaminates everything else, even when I was Chairman of my department at Cambridge. I was a diligent chairman and I had a very, very clear vision of where I wanted to see my department go. I was raised in an academic household, so I was fully prepared to be Chair in my department at Cambridge. That meant I didn't agonize over decisions. Consequently, I continued to publish during my tenure. I see the world through a particular lens, and that's a bad thing for an editor; an editor is supposed to be an Olympian [*laughs*].

TIME MANAGEMENT

How do you divide up your working day, both in terms of quantity and timing of different kinds of work? And how do you balance your personal and professional lives?

I had some very, very lucky breaks in terms of my genes; I can concentrate no matter how noisy is the environment. And I don't need to be comfortable when at work. For example, I've never had a study at home. I've very often worked on a problem or drafted a paper, sitting at the dining table with small children running round, even one of them sitting on my lap. If my wife were here, she would tell you there's never been a time at home when our children were told to be quiet because "father is working." They were always running around or sitting on my lap when I was working. My family life never interfered with my research and my research certainly never interfered with my family life. Even today, when I'm washing up, I might be thinking about a problem while my wife and our family friends are sitting at the dining table, chatting.

My office door is always open, people are drifting in and out, and I can switch on and off. I'm not bragging about it; it's a fact. But I am rather grateful that my genes allow me to do that. We're a very close family, and if any of my children write to me about anything, it's unthinkable that I would not respond immediately; it doesn't matter what I'm doing. My wife often asks, "What do you do at the office? Do you ever work?" She asks because she can't imagine how I could be at academic work and would nevertheless be able to set everything aside the moment an e-mail arrives from one of our children. That doesn't mean I am efficient with other matters; I'm not. If it's an invitation to a conference, that will go in the hold bin, because the e-mail is impersonal.

Do you also find it easy to balance multiple research papers?

Yes, because I've got this wide-ranging, interconnected body of research. Everything is tied up with everything else, or so it seems to me to be so in the social world.

Do you have a sense of the optimal number of papers that you could be working on at any one time?

No. I've never been able to plan my research and don't suppose it would have been a good thing if I had. In the first 20 years of my academic life, my publications appeared in bunches. In the early '80s, I published quite a number of papers, but then there was a fallow period. On the work on technological competition that I did with Joe (Stiglitz), we produced seven to eight papers out of one massive manuscript we had created for ourselves. But that manuscript took a couple of years. We then produced a string of papers out of that.[9] I am from a fortunate generation in the UK. I got tenure pretty quickly and easily. It didn't bother me when I was publishing nothing, even before receiving tenure.

REFLECTIONS AND THE FUTURE OF ECONOMICS

What have been the most important findings and contributions in your research fields during your career?

The economics of asymmetric information is one big one. There are two strands to that literature: mechanism design when the agents are asymmetrically informed, and analysis of markets under asymmetric information. But usually when economists are asked to explain asymmetric information, they take examples from the latter. I'll do the same here.

It's not that people didn't know that information was asymmetrically distributed – of course, they did – but as there was no canonical formulation, the profession was waiting for the right language in which to talk 'information'. Just to give you an idea of how difficult the matter was, in the 1960s a number of very fine economists thought the way into the economics of information would require first of all a measure of information (for example, the Shannon measure). But that didn't seem to lead anywhere: the social world requires a different treatment from the world of communication. Kenneth Arrow was the first to realize, at least in a published form, that we should bypass that obsession and model an economy in which different people knew different things. To my mind, his 1963 paper on health economics and the medical profession is the real origin of the economics of asymmetric information.[10] If you read it, you will find it had everything, but for algebra, that was in Akerlof's famous 'lemons' paper (in Arrow read 'quacks' for Akerlof's 'lemons').[11] But it went beyond the lemons example by offering an explanation for why the market for medical practitioners never collapsed. Arrow suggested that medical associations monitor quality and that you need institutions to control quality. At a time when most economists viewed such associations as creating cartels, Arrow's analysis must have been a revelation.

The person who carried out the bulk of the next stage of work on asymmetric information in markets is Joe Stiglitz. Stiglitz relentlessly pursued the problem, basically by re-constructing price theory. It's interesting that no single paper of his on the subject nailed things down, it's only when you put them together (studying markets for credit, insurance, labor, capital), that you begin to make connection to an enormous number of features of the world which were beyond the reach of economic analysis until then. Of course, Stiglitz was essentially studying the same model, but after having given a different name to the market being modeled. It was very Stiglitzian [*laughs*]. But it was necessary he did it that way. He was trying to produce a canonical model; and he succeeded.

What are the biggest challenges facing your research fields?

It's best to respond by noting it's not just *my* research field, but the biggest challenge in economics.

Bringing Nature into economics will prove to be the biggest challenge, largely because whenever Nature is mentioned, the hard-boiled economist says "externalities" and suppresses a yawn. Economics has established bad cultural practices. The profession doesn't reward someone who may be doing vital work estimating those yawn-generating externalities in, say, a situation where forests in the uplands of a watershed are being cut down and damaging farmers downstream. The profession rewards empirical work in socially acceptable fields, such as education, health, labor, insurance, and various industries producing private goods. But when it comes to natural capital, they give it a thumbs-down. It's very hard for empirical environmental and resource economists to get jobs in leading economics departments. The natural sciences are far more sophisticated in their appreciation of good applied work. In the case of upstream deforestation, the economist has to obtain data from scratch because the government doesn't publish data on the subject; he or she has to collaborate with hydrologists, soil scientists, and agronomists if they are to estimate the 'externalities'. If there has been a recurrent theme in my own work, it's been the attempt to introduce Nature (natural capital) into economics in a seamless way; in many ways to re-construct economics. Sustainable development is a buzz word among intellectuals. But that doesn't make it a bogus word. Until economists take Nature seriously, we will not know how current policy will affect future people. We have to understand humanity's relationship with Nature at different levels of economic development. In order to do that, we need to make contact with neighboring disciplines. The profession isn't prepared to do that as yet.

If we want to understand, say, poverty in the Third World, we need to engage with anthropologists and ecologists, because they have gained insights from years of experience. I have found engaging with them very, very fruitful. If we want to understand rural life, we need to engage with geographers too, because they have developed tools about the landscape. It's taken me years to appreciate how deeply interconnected our social systems are with the natural system, and how we have also isolated ourselves from Nature via the market. We need to be constantly aware of the unintended consequences of that isolation.

We've got to really engage with a whole group of different, but related disciplines. We're not doing enough of that at the moment, and we don't have the willingness; our entire training process and subsequent career go against it. I can't help thinking that we economists are missing the most significant problems of our time, or for that matter of anybody's time, by avoiding them.

In the end, do you think the economics profession has helped to bring out and shape your research for the best?

I think so. I have been very lucky and the profession has been good to me; but in an unusual way. Judging by citations, or rather the lack of them, most of my solo work has gone unnoticed, but by the remarks my colleagues make, I have the sense they approve of the titles of my publications. Recently, I had to prepare introductions for a pair of volumes of my collected papers that Oxford University Press will be publishing, so it made me reflect on what others were doing when I worked on a particular set of problems and why I chose to work on them and how I framed the problems and why. I guess such reflective moments are a sign of getting old! In drafting the introductions, it came to me that I have a non-standard way of framing social problems. For example, I have written extensively on the poverty–population–environment interface. But it hasn't had the slightest impact on development economists or on environmental and resource economists. And the papers on population and fertility behavior have gone unnoted by economic demographers. It may be that I am remorseless in trying to link seemingly disparate features of daily life, and because we economists are trained to consider them only piece by piece, one at a time, my analyses probably appear alien to my colleagues. For example, if I'm studying the way rural people use natural resources (for example, disappearing forests), I can't resist modeling such other human activities in the world of the poor as reproduction. The problem for me is that the typical environmental economist is unfamiliar with the word 'poverty', the development economist won't know how to spell 'environment', and the economic demographer thinks fertility depends entirely on the value of time. So I face a problem. What continues to surprise me though is that this intellectual distance I feel that separates me from my colleagues hasn't made me an outsider: I have enjoyed more than my fair share of honors.

One advantage of framing problems in a quirky fashion, it's not a conscious decision of course, is that I've been able to get on with my thinking without having to compete with others. You will notice from my CV that I have many papers on the same subject. One reason I have done this is that when working on my own I have rarely arrived at an understanding of the phenomenon I was studying in one paper; it's been almost always incremental. Discovery for me has usually meant a growing realization, rarely a revelation. I have been able to indulge in that slow process because I was aware I wouldn't be beaten to the post by somebody else – nobody else would be working on my problems, most certainly no one would have framed the problems in the way I do! So, I have had a very, very lucky life. Colleagues seem to approve my work, even though mostly they don't read any of it [*laughs*].

How did you feel about being awarded a knighthood for "services to economics"? What has been your biggest contribution to economics?

I was totally surprised on receiving the letter from the Prime Minister's Office, in May 2002. I was surprised because I had never consulted for governments, in fact I didn't know any government officials. The recommendation must have come from the UK's Economic and Social Research Council. When I showed her the letter, my wife took some time to digest the question I was asked, namely whether I would accept a knighthood. The question didn't arise. I was very pleased with that recognition, it seemed to me to be an affirmation of my research, but it has had no effect on my life.

An Inquiry into Well-being and Destitution (1993) is unquestionably the work with which I am most satisfied. Working toward it made me understand the social world in a way I couldn't have by reading anything else. I wrote it over a four-year period, start to finish, and it knocked me out. Unconsciously, I wanted to change the way economics is understood, but of course I wasn't about to write a methodological work, I focused on well-being and destitution as my object of study with which to re-write economics. I was writing the book as a letter (a very long letter!) to my father, who I knew was going to die soon. The book wasn't finished when he died, so I wrote a memoir for him as an introduction to the book. *Economics: A Very Short Introduction* (2007) resembles that earlier work, but it's a whole lot briefer.

Do you have any professional regrets?

I don't think so, largely because I've never taken my professional life that seriously, qua professional life. That explains a good deal of my answers to your previous questions. Research for me has never really been research; it's been an engagement with life. And my work has never been compartmentalized from the rest of my life. Of course, if you ask my wife, she will say, "There were periods when he was impossible to live with; when I would talk to him in those moments, it was clear he wasn't listening." But that's inevitable; any person who's engaged in research, no matter how compartmentalized he or she is, will have moments when they're slightly disconnected.

I've never had a big agenda and I've never wanted to change the world. It's been self-indulgence all the way; I've wanted to understand the social world, and the way economists handled it wasn't good enough for me, which is why I was led to geographers, anthropologists, nutritionists, ecologists, and development biologists. And I've had enormous help from some of the greatest minds in those disciplines, scientists like Paul Ehrlich, Jack Goody, and John Waterlow. Whenever I have written, seeking guidance, sometimes to scholars whom I had never met, they have responded handsomely. And of course, I have had enormous help from my professional colleagues. My co-authors in particular have taught me a great deal.

I also don't think I've made a wrong move in terms of employment. In 1977, when I was at the LSE, I turned down a very fine offer from Princeton, mainly because I was hoping to become a Professor at the LSE, where my father had done his PhD and my father-in-law had been a Professor. I should say it wasn't competition with my elders, it was a matter of seeing through an intergenerational agreement, if you see what I mean; carrying the proverbial torch. For a couple of years, I regretted not moving to Princeton. I also wanted to live in a campus environment, and London doesn't provide that. On the other hand, London was exciting, and my wife and I enjoyed an active social life. But, when in 1984 Cambridge approached me with the offer of a chair, both my wife and I knew we were going to accept it. She had grown up in Cambridge and I had been a student. That was an easy decision.

What are your professional ambitions?

It goes without saying I did want to become a professor. Once I became one, at the LSE in 1978, that ambition was fulfilled. From then on, what was important for me, professionally that is, is that I continue to explore the social world.

OUP is publishing my collected papers in the autumn. About ten years ago, I turned down the offer, saying I didn't see the purpose. I thought that those who did it did it either as a vanity project or because they felt that their creative period had come to an end. (I was dead wrong, of course). But then two years ago, I had to undergo major surgery for cancer. I was given two weeks' notice and was told there was about a four per cent risk of fatality at the operating table, not to mention that there could be further problems. When I learned that, I thought, "Well, if I'm dead, then it's dead (the volume)." But another (worse for me, personally) possibility was that I would survive but the experience would dampen my curiosity about life and the social world round me. If that were to happen, I thought editing my collected papers would be no bad thing. So I informed OUP that I was willing. They sent me a contract immediately. However, within two weeks of the operation, even though I could hardly do anything physical, I found myself reading a textbook on Earth Science. While lying in the hospital, a day following my operation, I had realized I knew little formal about the mathematics underlying plate tectonics. Recognition that I had reverted to being a student cheered me up no end. However, I began to regret that I signed that contract! But a deal is a deal, and I have done part of my job producing the two volumes. As I said, I was quite wrong earlier. I enjoyed collecting the articles and writing the introductions.

How would you describe the state of economics today? Are you optimistic about its future?

At one level, economics is in a very good state today. The last 30–40 years has seen extremely fruitful progress in both theoretical and applied work. Before then, the applied–theory divide was enormous. Theorists knew little about what applied people did, and applied economists couldn't understand the point in theory. Today, most theorists know something about the applied work to which their theory relates, and applied economics has changed beyond belief because of the development of advanced econometric techniques.

But there is a huge downside to the state of affairs. Good people usually do good research, but they don't necessarily work on the most important problems. And economists can misread the social and natural world so badly that even good people end up doing flippant research. The profession even rewards such work. I have already alluded to the fact that our profession is dismissive of really hard, empirical work on environmental externalities. Let me elaborate on it. Take the enormous literature that has been built up over the past two decades and more on endogenous growth. I find most of it wholly unreal. Here is the present world, heading for a population of more than nine billion by the middle of the century, everyone wanting to enjoy the lifestyle of, if not Dubai's Sheiks, but certainly the average income of a resident in a high middle-income country. But the environmental requirements of such a state of affairs would require three to four Earths. We economists don't even begin to appreciate that fact. We simply postulate technological progress and think that Nature's constraints can always be overcome through education and research. How have we come to such a pass? We have after all only about 250 years of experience of what we now call the modern world, which seems a moment in 11,000 years of human 'history'. Economists as a profession don't want to think about population and it doesn't want to take Nature seriously. I can only conclude that we have detached ourselves from the world. None of that would matter if we economists weren't enormously influential. But we are. The language we use seeps into the journalistic and political world. Economic growth, wealth, markets, and technological progress are expressions we have fashioned. We help others to go into denial about possible adverse futures of human societies, because we are smart enough and articulate enough to say knowledge and ingenuity will solve all problems. Periodically, we write to say that "Malthus was a false prophet" (a quote from a recent issue of *The Economist*). And it's the economics profession that identified 'externalities'. Put all the terms I have just mentioned together and you get a contradiction in the economist's favored model of the long run. That's not just ironic, it's tragic.

NOTES

1. Dasgupta, P. (1969), 'Optimal Growth when Capital is Non-Transferable', *Review of Economic Studies*, Vol. 36, No. 1 (January), pp. 77–88; Dasgupta, P. (1969), 'On the Concept of Optimum Population', *Review of Economic Studies*, Vol. 36, No. 3 (July), pp. 295–318.
2. Dasgupta, P. and G. Heal (1974), 'The Optimal Depletion of Exhaustible Resources', *Review of Economic Studies*, Vol. 41, Symposium on the Economics of Exhaustible Resources, pp. 3–28; Hotelling, H. (1931), 'The Economics of Exhaustible Resources', *Journal of Political Economy*, Vol. 39, No. 2 (April), pp. 137–175.
3. Ramsey F.P. (1928), 'A Mathematical Theory of Saving', *Economic Journal*, Vol. 38, No. 152 (December), pp. 543–559.
4. See, for example, Arrow, K.J., Dasgupta, P. and K.-G. Mäler (2003), 'Evaluating Projects and Assessing Sustainable Development in Imperfect Economies', *Environmental and Resource Economics*, Vol. 26, No. 4 (December), pp. 647–685.
5. Dasgupta, P. and E.S. Maskin (1986), 'The Existence of Equilibrium in Discontinuous Economic Games, I: Theory', *Review of Economic Studies*, Vol. 53, No. 1 (January), pp. 1–26; Dasgupta, P. and E.S. Maskin (1986), 'The Existence of Equilibrium in Discontinuous Economic Games, II: Applications', *Review of Economic Studies*, Vol. 53, No. 1 (January), pp. 27–41.
6. Dasgupta, P. and D. Ray (1987), 'Inequality as a Determinant of Malnutrition and Unemployment: Policy', *Economic Journal*, Vol. 97, No. 385 (March), pp. 177–188; Dasgupta, P. and D. Ray (1986), 'Inequality as a Determinant of Malnutrition and Unemployment: Theory', *Economic Journal*, Vol. 96, No. 384 (December), pp. 1011–1034.
7. Arrow, K.J., Dasgupta, P., Goulder, L.H.,, Mumford, K.J. and K. Oleson (2010), 'Sustainability and the Measurement of Wealth', *NBER Working Papers* 16599, National Bureau of Economic Research.
8. Das, S. and J.R. Vincent (2009), 'Mangroves Protected Villages and Reduced Death Toll during Indian Super Cyclone', *Proceedings of National Academy of Sciences*, Vol. 106, No. 18 (May), pp. 7357–7360.
9. Dasgupta, P. and J.E. Stiglitz (1980), 'Industrial Structure and the Nature of Innovative Activity', *Economic Journal*, Vol. 90, No. 358 (June), pp. 266–293; Dasgupta, P. and J.E. Stiglitz (1980), 'Uncertainty, Industrial Structure and the Speed of R&D', *Bell Journal of Economics*, Vol. 11, No. 1 (Spring), pp. 1–28; Dasgupta, P. and J.E. Stiglitz (1981), 'Market Structure and Resource Depletion: A Contribution to the Theory of Intertemporal Monopolistic Competition', *Journal of Economic Theory*, Vol. 28, No. 1 (October), pp. 128–164; Dasgupta, P. and J.E. Stiglitz (1981), 'Market Structure and Resource Extraction under Uncertainty', *Scandinavian Journal of Economics*, Vol. 83, No. 1, pp. 128–164; Dasgupta, P. and J.E. Stiglitz (1981), 'Entry, Innovation, Exit: Towards a Dynamic Theory of Oligopolistic Industrial Structure', *European Economic Review*, Vol. 15, No. 1, pp. 137–58; Dasgupta, P., Gilbert, R.J. and J.E. Stiglitz (1982), 'Invention and Innovation under Alternative Market Structures: The Case of Natural Resources', *Review of Economic Studies*, Vol. 49, No. 4 (October), pp. 567–82; Dasgupta, P., Gilbert, R.J. and J.E. Stiglitz (1983), 'Strategic Considerations in Invention and Innovation: The Case of Natural Resources', *Econometrica*, Vol. 51, No. 5 (September), pp. 1439–1448.
10. Arrow, K.J. (1963), 'Uncertainty and the Welfare Economics of Medical Care', *American Economic Review*, Vol. 53, No. 5 (December), pp. 941–973.
11. Akerlof, G.A. (1970), 'The Market for "Lemons": Quality Uncertainty and the Market Mechanism', *Quarterly Journal of Economics*, Vol. 84, No. 3 (August), pp. 488–500.

Jordi Galí
(CREI, UPF and
Barcelona GSE)

Jordi Galí was born in Barcelona, Spain in 1961 and graduated with a Llicenciat en Ciències Empresarials and a Master in International Management from the Escuela Superior de Administración y Dirección de Empresas (ESADE), Barcelona in 1985 before obtaining a PhD in economics from the Massachusetts Institute of Technology in 1989. He taught economics at the Graduate School of Business, Columbia University between 1989 and 1993 before accepting a tenured position at New York University in 1994 where he was promoted to Professor of Economics in 1999. He currently holds four academic positions: Director and Senior Researcher, Centre de Recerca en Economia Internacional (since 1999 and 2001 respectively), Professor of Economics, Universitat Pompeu Fabra (since 2001), and Research Professor of Economics, Barcelona Graduate School of Business (since 2009).

Professor Galí's research focuses on the causes of business cycles and on optimal monetary policy, and he is regarded as one of the main figures in New Keynesian macroeconomics. His most-cited articles in chronological order include 'How Well Does the IS–LM Model Fit Postwar Data?', *Quarterly Journal of Economics* (1992), 'The Science of Monetary Policy: A New Keynesian Perspective', *Journal of Economic Literature* (1999), co-authored with Richard Clarida and Mark Gertler, 'European Inflation Dynamics', *European Economic Review* (2001), co-authored with Mark Gertler and David López-Salido, 'Optimal Monetary Policy in Open versus Closed Economies: An Integrated Approach', *American Economic Review* (2001), co-authored with Richard Clarida and Mark Gertler, and 'Monetary Policy and Exchange Rate Volatility in a Small Open Economy', *Review of Economic Studies* (2005), co-authored with Tommaso Monacelli. He is also the author of *Monetary Policy, Inflation and the Business Cycle: An Introduction to the New Keynesian Framework* (Princeton University Press, 2008).

Professor Galí received the Yrjö Jahnsson Award from the European Economic Association in 2005, and was elected as a Fellow of the Econometric Society in 2004. His current editorial duties include being Associate Editor of the *International Journal of Central Banking* (since 2005), *Journal of Economic Perspectives* (since 2005), and *American Economic Journal – Macroeconomics* (since 2007).

I interviewed Jordi Galí at his hotel in Cambridge, Massachusetts, where he was attending the NBER Summer Institute conference. It was early-evening of Wednesday, 14 July 2010.

BACKGROUND INFORMATION

What was your attraction to economics?

What drew me to economics is hard to say. It was a bit by fluke. I didn't know what to study in college. In Europe, we specialize very early on, so I had to choose a field. I didn't have any strong preferences, but I went to a business school called ESADE in Barcelona, and that's where I discovered economics. I thought it was really interesting. It was also a time in Europe, but particularly in Spain, when inflation and unemployment were both very high. The unemployment rate in Spain got close to 25 per cent, and that problem was at the center of policy discussions. I thought that economics could solve it, and that led me to graduate school at MIT.

As a student, which professors were most influential or inspirational?

If I have to name one, it would be my advisor, Olivier Blanchard, at MIT, and then all the people there from whom I took courses related to macroeconomics, including Stan Fischer, the late Rudi Dornbusch, and Julio Rotemberg. Also, Danny Quah was doing macroeconometrics at that time, and introducing serious methods that have become widely adopted by macroeconomists. And Bob Solow, who was still teaching in the macro sequence, was also very influential.

But I would say that working as a research assistant for Olivier Blanchard and Stan Fischer on their book, *Lectures on Macroeconomics*, which was published by MIT Press in 1989, was probably one of the most rewarding and influential experiences. I had to go over all the chapters, so I really had to immerse myself in the material of the book, and make suggestions and possible changes. The book may be a bit outdated now in some respects, but its spirit still permeates a lot of modern business cycle theory and modern macroeconomics.

Why did you decide to pursue an academic career?

What were the alternatives? I like the freedom that academia gives you, but that's something that I have discovered *ex post*. I don't come from a family with anyone in academia. At the same time, it's demanding and challenging. I like it. Even if I had not been an economist, I think I would want to be a professor in another field.

As a researcher, which colleagues have been most influential or inspirational?

Most of my co-authors have been very influential, but if I have to name one, it would be Mark Gertler, whom I met when I went to NYU. He's the one who got me interested in monetary policy and monetary theory. Together with Rich Clarida, who was also very influential, we worked on four or five papers in one year. In a sense, I shifted fields within macro as a result of that, and ten years later or more, I do work that is still strongly influenced by that line of research.

Someone who I haven't worked with directly as a co-author, but who has been very influential because of the work he's done, is Mike Woodford. Even when I was starting as a researcher, and I hardly knew him at that time, his papers were always very influential. I like his research style very much.

GENERAL THOUGHTS ON RESEARCH

There is an increasing emphasis in many economics departments on applied research. Is this true at CREI?

Yes. I work at a relatively small institution, so I would say, compared to the rest of the profession, we may have some theoretical bias as an institution, but this may have to do with the fact that the law of large numbers doesn't apply. But I clearly see the trend that you mention towards more applied research. In macro, for instance, it's very hard these days to publish a paper, or to present a paper at a seminar, that is purely theoretical. It has to have some empirical support. That was not true in the past. You had purely theoretical papers and some applied papers, and sometimes the connection was very weak between those doing the empirics and those doing the theory. Now it's blended. It's clear that theory just for the sake of it gets little attention, unless you come up with some revolutionary concept. But that happens very seldom.

What is the value of pure versus applied research in economics?

Both presumably should be valuable to society to the extent that they deal with real-world problems. If they don't deal with real-world problems, then I won't defend them. But you can have good, theoretical research that points to some hypothetical mechanisms that could explain some interesting and important real-world phenomena, and so then it's up to empirical researchers to validate the existence of those mechanisms and their importance.

How would you describe the dialogue between theory and empirics in economics?

It's hard for me to think of empirical research that is not subject to some discipline that is provided by the theory. And theoretical work is useless unless you subject it to the discipline of the data. So, theory and empirics go hand-in-hand in my view, and this is becoming more and more prevalent.

How would you characterize your own research agenda and how has it changed through time?

I've always been very interested in business cycles and economic fluctuations as a phenomenon. To me, it's still really puzzling that economies fluctuate as much as they do, and I've always wanted to understand that.

When I was in graduate school, the so-called real business cycle school of thought was very influential and viewed those fluctuations as being not necessarily undesirable or inefficient. They were interpreted as the optimal responses to shocks that were hitting the economy. In a sense, all my research since those days has sought to challenge that hypothesis and to try to understand what kind of imperfections in markets could lead to the fluctuations that we observe, and could make them undesirable so that there is room for policy to attenuate the losses or the costs that are generated. So, originally, most of my research was done in the context of real models, and I was emphasizing the role of imperfect competition, and also thinking of economic fluctuations as the result of what we call sunspot fluctuations, which is essentially multiple equilibria. More recently, especially after my work with Mark Gertler and Rich Clarida, I have devoted more attention to monetary models, and have focused on the role that rigidities in prices and wages may play in making those fluctuations either unnecessarily large or undesirable from many respects, and in providing a role for the government to dampen those fluctuations.

Do you think it is important to have broad research interests?

Yes, but I think that's becoming more and more difficult. There's a force that pushes you towards specialization as the only way to remain close to the frontier. Some people manage to do that without specializing, and I can only feel strong envy for them.

As a consumer of research, I try to maintain that broad perspective and to keep track of what people do, even in areas outside macro, but I don't even attempt to make novel contributions to those areas as a researcher.

Do you think having a broad set of tools is more important?

Yes, I would say so. Having a broad set of tools can be useful both for empirical work and theoretical work, but it's more useful in the sense of allowing you to remain in touch with frontier research in a specific area.

Do you think there is any difference in the types of work done by researchers at different stages of their careers based on tenure concerns, publication requirements or other pressures? Should there be a difference?

I can certainly see there is a difference. When you start out, you need to make a big splash. You certainly want to try to publish in top journals, especially if you're in a top institution, otherwise there's no way you will draw much attention in the profession, and you may not be promoted. So, I think there's a bias, and it's good because you have people who are taking risks and exploring in order to write papers, some of which will be highly influential. That's how the profession makes progress.

And then different people pursue different avenues. Some people keep working on extensions of what they did when they were starting out as assistant professors. Others, once they get tenure, are happy to explore perhaps even other fields. But it's true that the papers that get more cited are the ones that are written at the early stage of people's careers. That's what I see as a general rule. Sometimes, I think it's similar to what you see in music. Look at some rock bands. They keep coming up with new albums, but the really good ones were put together at the beginning of their careers. Of course, there's a selection bias; if they hadn't come up with good work early on in their careers, they would probably have given up and we wouldn't know about them. The same is true in economics.

What are the main differences between working as a researcher in Europe versus the US?

It depends on where you work. But one thing I can say is that, in economics, there are certainly many more places in the US where it's relatively easy to pursue an academic career and keep doing research at the frontier. In Europe, there are some places where you can do roughly the same, so you don't feel at a disadvantage, but there are fewer places; I would say no more than ten. And in macro, my area, there are probably six or seven that would be comparable to good places in the US. So, if you don't happen to be in one of those places, then I think it's harder to keep in touch with what is being done at the frontier, and to remain connected with the top researchers. But the same is true if you were in the US at some small college lost in the middle of the woods; it's not so much about Europe. I feel very fortunate in this respect, because when I've worked in the US and in Europe, I've been in institutions that are very much part of the circuit (an elite group of economists).

IDEA GENERATION

Where do you get your research ideas?

That's hard to say. I have this feeling, which is hard to prove or verify, that I get most of my research ideas while I sleep, and some of them are still in my mind when I wake up. I don't try to work while I sleep, but the brain keeps functioning.

I know for sure that most of my ideas come very early in the morning, when I shower or have breakfast. That's a time when I feel very alert. But this is for ideas that involve small thinking; tricks that you could use to model one thing or another, or an alternative way to do some empirical tests.

When it comes to the big ideas that somehow shape your whole career, those have been with me all the time, and the fact that they remain in my mind is what keeps me working on them. I mentioned some of them to you early on, like the extent to which imperfections in different markets may be at the root of economic fluctuations, and whether or not government should do something about them. I cannot get those off my mind.

At what point does an idea become a project that you devote resources to?

Maybe you test it with your colleagues and see how they react. Then, you can elaborate a bit, do some toy modeling, or some very simple, rough empirical work to see if there's some promise. Then, you present that in an internal seminar at your institution. In any of those stages, there's a possibility of just discarding the whole thing if you see that it doesn't fly. But if it passes those stages, you try to write the paper, and that's when you make a commitment to devoting some serious time and resources.

IDEA EXECUTION

What makes a good theoretical paper?

It's one which brings to life some new mechanism that people had not thought about before. It's not necessarily one that makes use of a model that you can take to the data immediately. It could be a toy model that is useful to point to that particular mechanism, or possibly to a counterintuitive result.

Can you give an example?

The work of Greg Mankiw, and George Akerlof and Janet Yellen from the mid-'80s pointing out that small menu costs (the cost of adjusting prices) can have large first-order welfare consequences for society.[1] I remember reading those papers when I was a student. They were purely theoretical papers using very simple models, but they were very powerful and extremely influential. Their points are now part of our baggage; they are embedded in any of the monetary models with nominal rigidities that we use.

What makes a good empirical paper?

One would be a paper that points to an empirical observation or phenomenon or relation that no one had come across before, that is somewhat surprising, and that cannot be explained easily with current models. That's what I would call an inspirational paper, because it's likely to trigger a lot of research trying to account for this, either in the context of existing models or with new models.

And then you have papers that are narrower, but can still be very influential, because they try to test a very strong tradition of a particular class of models. In those, typically the empirical work comes after the theory, whereas in the ones that I mentioned earlier, the empirical work inspires or motivates the theory that follows.

Can you give an example?

I view Bob Hall's work on the permanent income hypothesis as a very clean example of the second type of papers that I mentioned.[2] It was very influential in terms of the econometric approach to testing a theory.

For the first kind of papers, I'll mention a paper of mine, which is my favorite, from the *AER* in 1999.[3] It provides evidence suggesting that positive technology shocks have a negative impact on employment in the short run. Why did I find that result interesting? Because, if you believe it, it implies that technology shocks cannot be a dominant source of economic fluctuations. In the data, we observe a very strong, positive co-movement between employment and output over the business cycle, but my empirical findings suggest that in response to technology shocks, output and employment move in opposite directions. And there are other papers that have provided supporting evidence along the same lines.

I view my paper as a potentially useful one because it makes the reader update his or her priors about the validity of a certain class of models, not necessarily a specific model. It's very easy to reject a specific model, whereas evaluating a family of models, which share certain predictions, is more useful in helping us make progress in macro.

When you hit a brick wall on a project, do you continue to work on the problem or do you take a break and work on something else?

I have to say I usually don't run into brick walls, not because of my technical skills, but precisely because I'm fully aware of my limitations. I don't engage in projects that are likely to hit brick walls. I like simplicity, and I value it. I also have the feeling that simple ideas and simple projects that are novel get more attention than others that are extremely complicated.

Earlier in my career, especially when I was a graduate student, perhaps I was more into trying to show my technical skills, and so I hit lots of brick walls and dumped projects. But now I dump projects because I end up thinking they are not worth my time, or the time of potential readers; they don't make an important point, or they don't deal with an important issue. It's a question of substance.

What has been the biggest change during your career in how researchers in your fields conduct research?

People have become much more open-minded in macro. When I was a graduate student, and in my early years as a researcher, there was a huge gap in terms of the language and tools that people were using in the Midwest versus the East coast in the US. It's amazing how the two have converged over time. So, there's been widespread adoption of stochastic dynamic general equilibrium models, but also models in which we embed all kinds of imperfections. And in monetary economics, which is mostly what I work on these days, we've seen a huge change in emphasis from trying to understand the effects of a one-time monetary policy shock to the impact of monetary policy rules.

THE WRITING PROCESS

Which aspect of the writing process do you find most difficult?

Writing the first few sentences. I tend to postpone writing the introduction because it's a bit scary; it can shape very much what the paper will become or how you will sell it.

I do write very slowly, and I don't find it particularly enjoyable. I appreciate papers that are well written, so I try to write in a clear fashion. But it does take a long time, and it's painful.

What steps have you taken during your career to improve the quality of your writing?

I haven't made a deliberate effort. When I get referee reports, they tend to say that the paper is very clearly written, and probably that's because I spend a lot of time polishing the writing, and trying to make sure that it can be understood, even by someone who's not an insider on that particular topic.

Who proofreads your writing?

When I have a first draft of a paper, I give it to a couple of research assistants, largely so that they can look for inconsistencies or mistakes or omissions.

How do you split up the writing tasks among co-authors?

The way it works best, in my opinion, is that someone takes the lead in writing a very rough first draft, and then, once that is done, you take turns. If you work with a co-author in the US then it's ideal, because someone is working on the paper around the clock. You go to bed, and someone else takes over. Here's an advantage of transatlantic co-operation!

COLLABORATION

When you work with co-authors, how do you decide whom to work with?

That's very hard and completely unpredictable. Sometimes, a project may be just an extension of work that you have done previously with a person. But when you initiate a project with someone whom you haven't worked with before, that typically involves bringing together research that had been pursued separately by the two authors in the past, and realizing that there may be some gains in combining the two ideas or two assumptions or two approaches. That's a natural co-operation.

I'm a bit reluctant to write with my own graduate students, because I don't think it's a good idea to go on the job market with a paper that was co-authored with your supervisor. And it's also diverting my student's attention from his own research, which is the one that should land him a job. The same applies, to some extent, to working with one's junior colleagues.

How do you prefer to interact with them (e-mail, phone, or face-to-face)?

I like face-to-face at an early stage of the project, and then e-mail is fine. The good thing about e-mail is that it gives you time to think before you respond.

What are the main challenges associated with collaborative work and how do you overcome them?

When I disagree with a co-author on whether to include or not a certain section, or on whether a certain result or perspective should be emphasized more or less. How those differences are overcome is not independent of what my co-author's answer to the same question would be! I tend to be pretty flexible (I think!)

RESEARCH ASSISTANCE AND FUNDING

How do you use undergraduate and graduate research assistants?

I don't think I've ever used an undergraduate student as a research assistant. I use graduate students for proofreading, as I said earlier, and also for programming. I like to do my own programming, both for empirical research and theoretical simulations, but I also want someone else to try to replicate my results independently. If they can't, then I may send them my codes and they can find all the mistakes.

I don't rely heavily on my research students, because I do like to see the sausage machine. But if someone can replicate my work, then that's comforting.

How important is funding for getting your work done?

It helps me finance research assistants more than anything else. I do empirical work, so I buy some datasets occasionally, and I try to keep all my software updated, so funding is good for all that. But the kind of work that I do uses mainstream, standard data, so the datasets are not particularly expensive. And, as I said earlier, I don't do very sophisticated technical work, so I don't require lots of research assistant time.

Do you have any advice for a young scholar on the funding process?

I think that research funding is somewhat biased towards people who are well established. So my advice would be to try to become a well-established researcher as soon as possible, and then things will be easier for you. But this is easier said than done!

SEMINAR PARTICIPATION AND NETWORKING

What are the benefits to attending a seminar that is closely related to your work versus one that is not closely related?

Both are useful. In the first case, I will certainly understand more, and I may be able to be more critical about the details in the paper. And the second case keeps me posted as to what people are doing in other areas. That's important. I most likely wouldn't have read the paper, and so when someone makes a nice presentation of some interesting work, I find that a very satisfactory and pleasant experience as a consumer.

How important is professional networking to success in research?

That's a good question. I think it's important, at least to get started, to draw people's attention to what you are doing. Believe it or not, I think it is more important now than in the past when the dominant form of research dissemination was through physical journals that landed on well-established researchers' desks.

How does the researcher without extensive networks succeed?

The truth is that there may be networks that operate at different levels. But what I think is really important starting out is whether your institution is part of the circuit or not. Also, your senior colleagues are supposed to offer support at an early stage of your career to help you build those networks. I've seen very bright people on many occasions becoming discouraged because their work isn't getting the attention it deserves. That's why I think going to a good institution is so important.

To what extent is the absence of departmental colleagues working in one's research area a major disadvantage?

I particularly value being surrounded by researchers who are working in macro, but not necessarily in my specific research area. I don't want to be talking all the time about the area in which I work, but at the same time, I want to have a good number of macroeconomists around me as colleagues so that we can have a lively seminar series and organize good conferences.

COMMUNICATION OF RESEARCH

How do you find the right balance between communicating your research at an early stage versus the close-to-finished stage?

In terms of communication outside the immediate boundaries of my institution, the first thing I will do is post a paper on my website. But I won't do that until I've presented it in an internal seminar, and perhaps even in one or two other institutions.

What are the unique challenges to giving a seminar and how do you overcome them?

Usually, when I give a seminar, I have already tested the basic idea among my colleagues and I feel on relatively safe ground. So, I don't view a seminar as a challenge, but as a way of getting feedback to help me with the paper or even to think of possible extensions.

PUBLICATION

How do you decide upon the appropriate journal to send your research to?

If it's a paper that contains a novel idea, I will send it to a top journal, but if it's a paper that's just an extension of earlier work, I will send it to a more specialized journal. I also look at the editors. If I know them, I will try to imagine whether they will be minimally sympathetic to the paper, and then it's usually a process of ruling out journals.

How would you best describe your approach to dealing with a 'revise and resubmit' request from a journal? How about an outright rejection?

With pain in both cases. Each of us thinks that the rejections are unfair on many occasions, and that the revisions are quite often unnecessary, and divert you from the more creative aspect of the research process.

Do you think that the current structure of the publication process in economics facilitates or impedes scientific understanding and knowledge production?

We definitely want a filter and some quality standards. That's very important, especially for young researchers, and I think it works well, overall. If we adopt a social perspective, it's clear that the paper is getting proofed during the publication process. But in economics, referees and editors are too interventionist. They want the papers to end up looking as if they had written them. A consequence is that researchers spend too much time with revisions.

What has been your best and worst experience during the publication process?

I haven't had any terrible experiences, but I've had some interesting ones. I remember sending a paper to the *European Economic Review*, and by some bureaucratic mistake, it was handled by two editors simultaneously, which meant that I got two independent editorial decisions. Each decision was accompanied by two referee reports, which invited me to resubmit the paper, but they were asking for revisions along very different lines. Eventually, I was told to focus on one of the editors, and the paper got published.

One of the chapters of my PhD dissertation was also very hard to publish, and I was an assistant professor at Columbia Business School at the time. I had maybe three or four rejections from reasonable journals, and I decided, "Look, I'm getting tired of this." So, I went to the library of the business school to look for a journal to publish my work. I found a journal whose name I won't reveal, which was published from Italy. I read in the instructions for submissions that they were asking for a CV. I was so desperate at the time that I said, "Well, these guys may decide to publish my paper on the grounds that I already have several publications in very good journals." In the end, I didn't submit it there, but, at the time, it seemed like my last resort was to send it to a journal that would accept it on the basis of my CV [*laughs*].

Do you have a good experience to share?

I'm afraid not [*laughs*].

REFEREEING AND EDITING

How do you decide upon whether or not to accept a refereeing job?

I have a very simple rule: Is this a paper that I would want to read anyway? If the answer is "yes", I'll accept a refereeing request independently of the journal.

What are the benefits to refereeing?

The benefits are the same as those from reading a paper. If a paper deals with a topic that you're interested in, and it has a minimum quality, then it may help you in your own research. But if it's on a topic that you don't care about, it's better not to referee it. If it's a disaster, you can write a very quick and easy referee report.

How has your approach to refereeing changed through time?

I don't think it has changed much. I try to be somewhat open-minded in the sense that I can see how people may have different approaches from the one I would have taken, and I try to respect that and be constructive.

How do you decide upon whether or not to accept an editing position?

That involves a lot of work. I was Co-Editor of the *European Economic Review*, and then of the *Journal of the European Economic Association*. I did it because I felt some kind of commitment to the European Economic Association. But I'm not doing it now, and I will think twice before accepting another position.

What are the benefits to editing?

If you are very efficient at handling manuscripts, you can certainly be very influential in your area by publishing papers that you think are important and, thus, deserve attention. All of us, to a lesser or greater degree, try to leave a mark, and that's one way to do it.

TIME MANAGEMENT

How do you divide up your working day, both in terms of quantity and timing of different kinds of work?

That's something that has evolved over time, but I have converged to a situation in which I try to allocate the first four hours of the day – 8:00 am to noon – to research. I like to start early. I know that for the first hour at least, I'm the only one around, and so no one will knock on my door [*laughs*]. After that, it's a free-for-all; I could be writing a referee report, preparing a discussion of a paper, dealing with administrative work, drafting a grant proposal, talking to a junior colleague about his work, attending seminars, or just taking a nap.

How do you balance multiple research projects?

That's hard. I may have many research projects open at any point in time, but I cannot handle working actively on several projects at one time. I try to work on one – finish a revision and put it aside – and then take the next one.

How do you balance your personal and professional lives?

Again, this also has evolved over time due to family requirements, but now when I go home, I try to disconnect completely from work. I don't bring anything home except in special circumstances, and I have to admit I try not to work at all on the weekends. But there are things that are important, like trying to keep in touch with what goes on in the real world. So, I devote a good amount of time every day to reading the newspaper, like the *Financial Times*, or occasionally I just browse one of the monthly bulletins of the ECB or the latest *World Economic Outlook*. But it is light reading.

Your mind doesn't stop, but you need some discipline. I have young kids and I want to be able to have time for them. I cannot work more than ten hours a day, so if I work from 8:00 in the morning to 6:00 in the evening and then go home, that's fine. I wouldn't be much more productive if I stayed in the office, so I find it's perfect to disconnect and have dinner at home with the family.

To me, the most disruptive thing for my personal life is travel, especially if your spouse is also a professional because a lot of co-ordination needs to be done. But I think my wife and I have handled it well at home.

Hopefully, academics have more flexibility. After all, we decide whether or not to accept an invitation to a seminar or a conference, and we don't have bosses that tell us, "You should go there." But some people have spouses who are economists, and they even work in the same institution, have offices next door to each other, work in the same field, and co-author papers. Don't ask me how they handle that.

REFLECTIONS AND THE FUTURE OF ECONOMICS

What are the biggest challenges facing your research fields?

In macro, there is no way to be able to understand perfectly the issues that are of interest. The phenomena are extremely complex. So, I think we have to be humble and open-minded, and accept that we can learn from all of the alternative approaches. It won't be easy to integrate them all in a single framework, but we should be able to live with that.

What are the strengths and weaknesses of your own research?

Weaknesses are much easier. As I said earlier, I like the creative aspect of research, so that may lead to a certain laziness in trying to tighten all the loose ends in a given paper. I feel some kind of a desire to move on to think about new ideas. I have to admit that is a weakness, but I can't help it.

Strengths? Something that I have inherited from my advisor, Olivier Blanchard, is that I have tried to stay away from 'technical fireworks': doing something just to display some cool idea or skills. I try to stick to things that I view as important or relevant.

In the end, do you think the profession has helped to bring out and shape your research for the best?

I think there's a trade-off. The way the profession is organized is good because it keeps you alert and tense, and working hard to come up with new things, as opposed to relaxing. It's competitive. The not-so-good part of it, which hasn't necessarily affected me negatively, is that if you're not working in an area of research that is hot at some point in time, you may be ignored. One consequence is herd behavior; suddenly, most people start working in these few areas. One may have a very good idea, but because it does not have an immediate application to those hot areas, one may not explore it further. I don't think that's good.

But I'm not complaining. I've been lucky because the areas that I was interested in at each point in time, and that I really wanted to work on, were ones that people were paying attention to. They were all central issues in macro; not marginal or exotic.

Do you have any professional regrets?

I read somewhere that Keynes was asked a similar question during his last days. To which he answered, "My only regret is not having drunk more champagne." Maybe I have written too many papers. I might have put less emphasis on quantity. There are some papers that I have written that the world could have lived without for sure. And I could have been mountain-biking instead ... or drinking champagne [*laughs*].

What are your professional ambitions?

I think of myself as someone who has been ambitious in his professional life, and I'm happy in the sense that I have accomplished my goals. The one thing that makes me really happy is that I still enjoy doing research, and I remain quite productive. I write papers that I don't view as being of less quality than papers that I wrote ten or fifteen years ago. I'm very satisfied with that, and if I ever have the feeling that the work that I write gets much less attention, I will be happy to remain on the sidelines. I will keep enjoying reading the good work that is being done because I enjoy economics.

How would you describe the state of economics today? Are you optimistic about its future?

Contrary to what seems to be the general perception, even among some of my colleagues, economics is more relevant than ever because the financial crisis that we have experienced has reminded us that there are many things that we still need to understand and improve. Just a few years ago, I was more pessimistic from that point of view, especially being someone who has devoted much of his research to questions related to economic fluctuations.

It was like being a medical researcher who specializes in some innocuous illness, like a minor cough. But, suddenly, issues related to macro stability are very much at the center, not only of economics, but of what matters to the world. And any advances we can make will contribute to making the world a better place. That is the ultimate goal any economist should have in mind.

NOTES

1. N.G. Mankiw (1985), 'Small Menu Costs and Large Business Cycles: A Macroeconomic Model of Monopoly', *Quarterly Journal of Economics*, Vol. 100, No. 2 (May), pp. 529–537; G.A. Akerlof and J.L. Yellen (1985), 'A Near-Rational Model of the Business Cycle with Wage and Price Inertia', *Quarterly Journal of Economics*, September, Vol. 100, No. 5 (Supp.), pp. 823–838.
2. Hall, R.E. (1978), 'Stochastic Implications of the Life-Cycle Permanent Income Hypothesis: Theory and Evidence', *Journal of Political Economy*, Vol. 86, No. 6 (December), pp. 971–987.
3. J. Galí (1999), 'Technology, Employment, and the Business Cycle: Do Technology Shocks Explain Aggregate Fluctuations?', *American Economic Review*, Vol. 89, No. 1 (March), pp. 249–271.

Douglas A. Irwin
(Dartmouth College)

Douglas Irwin was born in Lansing, Michigan in 1962 and graduated with a BA in political science from the University of New Hampshire in 1984 before obtaining both an MA and a PhD in economics from Columbia University in 1985 and 1988 respectively. Between 1986 and 1987, he was a Junior Staff Economist at the Council of Economic Advisers and then spent three years as an Economist at the Board of Governors of the Federal Reserve System. Between 1991 and 1997, he was an Assistant Professor of Business Economics at the Graduate School of Business, University of Chicago before moving to Dartmouth College where he currently serves as the Robert E. Maxwell '23 Professor of Arts and Sciences.

Professor Irwin's research focuses on US trade policy, past and present. His most-cited articles in chronological order include 'Learning-by-Doing Spillovers in the Semiconductor Industry', *Journal of Political Economy* (1994), co-authored with Peter Klenow, 'Trade Blocs, Currency Blocs, and the Reorientation of World Trade in the 1930s', *Journal of International Economics* (1995), co-authored with Barry Eichengreen, 'The United States in a New Global Economy? A Century's Perspective', *American Economic Review*, Papers and Proceedings (1996), 'Changes in US Tariffs: The Role of Import Prices and Commercial Policies', *American Economic*

Review (1998), and 'Does Trade Raise Income? Evidence from the Twentieth Century', *Journal of International Economics* (2002), co-authored with Marko Terviö. His books include *Managed Trade: The Case Against Import Targets* (AEI Press, 1994), *Against the Tide: An Intellectual History of Free Trade* (Princeton University Press, 1996), *The Genesis of the GATT* (Cambridge University Press, 2008), co-authored with Petros Mavroidis and Alan Sykes, *Free Trade Under Fire* (Princeton University Press, third edition, 2009), *Peddling Protectionism: Smoot-Hawley and the Great Depression* (Princeton University Press, 2011), and *Trade Policy Disaster: Lessons from the 1930s* (MIT Press, 2011).

Professor Irwin is a Research Associate of the National Bureau of Economic Research and is on the Board of Advisers of the Center for Trade Policy Studies, Cato Institute. His editorial positions include being on the Editorial Board of the *Journal of Economic History* and *Explorations in Economic History*.

I interviewed Douglas Irwin at the National Bureau of Economic Research, Cambridge, Massachusetts. It was late-afternoon of Tuesday, 13 July 2010.

BACKGROUND INFORMATION

What was your attraction to economics and to economic history, in particular?

I've always been interested in the social sciences. As an undergraduate, I was originally drawn into political science, but after about two years of doing that, I began to realize economics is a broader and richer way of thinking about society. It's a more integrated, systematic way of thinking about different elements of how people interact, and encompasses political science, sociology, and history. Economists can speak about political issues with a lot of knowledge and intelligence, but it is much more difficult for political scientists to speak about economic issues with the same authority because they don't have the same tools and they lack an explicit framework.

I have an interest in economic history because I've always been curious about how we got to where we are today. What were the precursors to what we see today? I don't want to take a policy or institution as a given; I want to understand where it came from. And so that naturally leads one back in time to think about the origins of things.

As a student, which professors were most influential or inspirational?

One professor who was very important was my father. He was a professor of economics. I never took a course with him, but growing up we used to talk about economics quite a bit around the dinner table. That made me much more sympathetic and knowledgeable about what economics had to offer.

As an undergraduate, there was one inspirational political scientist at the University of New Hampshire, Bernard Gordon, who tried to bridge the gap between economics and politics. And he was also a very tough teacher with very high standards, so you had to earn his respect. He was very compelling on many dimensions.

In graduate school, I knew I wanted to work on international trade issues, and there were three figures at Columbia who were important: Jagdish Bhagwati, Ronald Findlay, and Donald Dewey. Bhagwati and Findlay taught a year-long course on international trade, and it was just tremendous. Both of them are excellent instructors, and they really gave you great insights into international trade theory and policy. They're also open to history, and thinking broadly about the subject, not just narrowly in terms of models. Dewey also encouraged my interest in exploring one's field through the lens of history.

Why did you decide to pursue an academic career?

I was attracted to academia partly because my father was an academic and so I knew what I would be getting myself into. But just as important is the fact that I've always been very curious about things. And there's no better way of continuing to feed that curiosity throughout one's life than to become an academic because then you're given license to continually discover and learn anew.

Also, I've always loved libraries. To me, a library holds an infinite amount of material of potential interest. You could never grow bored in a library. As a student, I knew I always wanted to be tied in with those resources. And so academia gives you the freedom to play all day in the library.

As a researcher, which colleagues have been most influential or inspirational?

In terms of people I've worked with or other people I've admired, Barry Eichengreen would be high on the list because he has paved the way for scholars who are interested in international economics and economic history. And he does it so well, both the analysis and the writing and the drawing of lessons for today, that he's been a guiding light. And I would also include Jeff Williamson at Harvard. He's also an economic historian interested in international and cross-country issues. His approach and style have been very instructive to me.

And when I was an assistant professor at Chicago, there were a number of colleagues whom I interacted with a lot and wrote some papers with. Randy Kroszner and Peter Klenow were my two most important collaborators.

And, of course, Jagdish Bhagwati and Ronald Findlay have been inspirational throughout my career.

GENERAL THOUGHTS ON RESEARCH

There is an increasing emphasis in many economics departments on applied research. Is this true at Dartmouth?

Our department has always had that emphasis, largely because it has always been (until recently) a relatively small department that does not have a PhD program. So, a few decades ago it was decided to specialize in a few applied fields rather than having one person represent every field in economics. By having a cluster of faculty, we could have many colleagues working on similar topics and be able to sustain a seminar series. This has proven to be a great success. We've grown to nearly 30 faculty members, but still don't have and don't want a PhD program, but we're all applied. That's what makes us a unique and a fun department to be in, because you can talk to all your colleagues. We're all working with data and asking empirical questions, many of which have a policy angle to them. It makes recruiting much easier because if you are working on applied issues you are guaranteed to have colleagues in your field, whether it be labor, international, health, development, or what have you.

What is the value of pure versus applied research in economics?

I do have a bias towards applied, policy-oriented, empirical research, so there's a lot of theory that is not so useful for someone like me. But I wouldn't denigrate the value of pure theory at all, because that work may have a payoff that's not immediately recognized.

How would you describe the dialogue between theory and empirics in economics?

Theory informs empirical questions and the choice of approach. Even if an applied paper does not formally 'test' a theory, it still has to be informed by theory so you have some guidance as to what might be expected or how an issue should be presented.

How would you characterize your own research agenda and how has it changed through time?

I've always been interested in international trade policy, particularly its history. Early in my career, I was working on various topics on history and trade with no real focus. But my research path changed when I received a call from Michael Bordo of Rutgers in 1996. He was organizing an NBER conference on the Great Depression, and he asked if I would be interested in doing a paper on US trade policy during the period, which I hadn't really looked at too much. I thought it would be an easy paper to write because all I would have to do is look at the work that's been done, summarize it, and add my own twist. It was a conference volume paper after all. But what I found is there was almost nothing out there on US trade policy during the Great Depression, at least research that was empirically-oriented and used modern methods. So, I had to write about three or four background papers (that turned into journal publications) just to write the conference paper.[1] For example, there was almost nothing on the famous Smoot-Hawley tariff of 1930, despite the fact that it is discussed all the time.

At any rate, all of this got me on the path of looking at US trade policy and how it's evolved through time. I've gone back in time from the Depression to the colonial era, and I've gone forward and looked at some later periods.[2] It's given me a research direction and focus that I never would have anticipated prior to his call.

Do you think it is important to have broad research interests?

I think there's an advantage to studying one area in depth and working with it for some time. But I certainly think that it is important to have broad and important questions in mind when doing so.

Do you think there is any difference in the types of work done by researchers at different stages of their careers based on tenure concerns, publication requirements or other pressures? Should there be a difference?

There is a difference. One's dissertation usually involves an incredible amount of work on one topic, but as an assistant professor seeking tenure, you cannot devote several years to understanding a new issue and getting a dataset together when the payoff is highly uncertain. You have to shift quickly from the graduate school mode to one where you have to be faster in terms of churning out working papers and getting publications. And then once you have tenure, you don't have to flit as much from paper to paper and can concentrate on longer-term projects.

I think the process could be changed for the better by having a longer tenure clock. Most people come up for review in five or six years, and that's much too short in my view. It is difficult for junior faculty to invest quite as much in any particular project. At the University of Chicago, where I started out as an academic, the tenure clock was ten years. That allows you the time to undertake more speculative and riskier, but potentially higher payoff, projects because if it doesn't work out there's still time to recover and do other things. So, I'm in favor of stretching out the tenure clock, and I think it would lead to higher quality, less rushed work.

IDEA GENERATION

Where do you get your research ideas?

You have to start with a question that has puzzled you. Then I read a lot of journal articles and books to see what has been done on the topic. Anytime you go to the library, or go on the Internet to look for a paper, the paper that you are looking for has references to other papers that merit attention, and the chase is on. The more you read, the more questions you have, and the more you begin to see gaps in the literature and in our knowledge.

At what point does an idea become a project that you devote resources to?

When you see a gap in the literature, there is opportunity. If an important question has not been addressed satisfactorily, and with the right data or approach, then it is worth pursuing. If you find better data or have a better explanation for an issue, you probably have a paper.

IDEA EXECUTION

What makes a good paper in economic history?

I like papers that address an important question very simply or cleanly so that it becomes obvious after the fact that the finding is useful and true. In a paper in the *Scandinavian Journal of Economics* in 1991 ('The Scientific Illusion in Empirical Macroeconomics'), Larry Summers describes what constitutes compelling and path-breaking empirical work and finds it is often informal data analysis with a focus on natural experiments.[3] I agree with him. It's not about doing something technically difficult; it's about identifying things that haven't been seen before.

In terms of economic history more specifically, a 1985 *Journal of Economic History* paper by Barry Eichengreen and Jeff Sachs entitled 'Exchange Rates and Economic Recovery in the 1930s' is extremely simple in its analysis of the data but is very rich in terms of clarifying what was going on during the Great Depression.[4]

When you hit a brick wall on a project, do you continue to work on the problem or do you take a break and work on something else?

If I hit a brick wall, I don't try to knock it down. Sometimes, there is a brick wall because it is difficult to find the data to make a point, but you are not going to get a paper published based on suspicion or intuition. Other times, your question is not well formulated and so you have to read and appraise what other people have done and mull it over. But in both cases, the kernel of an idea may stew in your head for a year or two before it gradually comes together. But forcing it doesn't work for me.

Related to the previous question, when a project isn't going to turn out as hoped, do you scrap it or aim to send the work to a second-tier or field journal?

I certainly will abandon things. And I still have files on things that I may turn back to five or ten years later if I think of a better way of pitching or framing it, or I find an empirical approach that will be useful. But sometimes I've also just accepted that I won't be able to find the data or answer the question quite as well as I had hoped, so I will submit it to a second-tier journal. That can be disappointing, depending on my expectations for the project, but I don't necessarily consider it a failure.

What has been the biggest change during your career in how researchers in your fields conduct research?

I'm not sure economic history has changed all that much, but international trade as a field has become much more empirical. When I was in graduate school, personal computers were just coming out and most people were doing theory. But now there's much greater computing power so that most people are doing some empirical work as well. If you look at the types of papers being presented here at the NBER today, they're almost all empirical, whereas that was not the case 15 or 20 years ago.

I should also add that the Internet has been a huge resource for economic historians, in terms of finding data and getting sources through Google Scholar, old newspapers, and JSTOR. It has saved so much time, and you can find out more quickly about whether a project might pay off.

THE WRITING PROCESS

Which aspect of the writing process do you find most difficult?

I don't think I find any aspect of it difficult, but the later stages of finishing something can be laborious. I must say that I do the research and writing at the same time. As soon as I start a project, I'll be thinking, "What is the abstract going to look like? What is the introduction going to look like? How am I pitching it? What am I going to show? What literature does it relate to?" So, I view the research and writing as very interactive. And I also enjoy the initial writing part. It's an act of creation, like having a block of clay on your pottery spinning wheel and molding it into something.

What steps have you taken during your career to improve the quality of your writing?

I've always emphasized rewriting. I'm always looking over things, even when it's finished and a journal has accepted it. I find things that I'd like to improve and change. Sometimes, that becomes drudgery and you hit diminishing returns, but I still enjoy rewriting because you almost always see improvements. Rarely do you rewrite and it ends up worse than when you began.

Who proofreads your writing?

I've written a few books, and sometimes I've hired a freelance editor to look over them, somebody who is informed but not trained as an economist. I want their view on how it reads and how it would be received by non-economists. For example, I have one book, *Free Trade under Fire*, which I've tried to make accessible to non-economists. Just having someone proofread it and give you advice on how to say things for a lay audience is very useful. But journal articles are more straightforward and the literary quality is not as important!

How do you split up the writing tasks among co-authors?

Usually someone takes a stab at a first draft, and then it just goes back and forth by e-mail.

COLLABORATION

When you work with co-authors, how do you decide whom to work with?

I don't think I've ever started a paper where (a) I didn't know the person or (b) they e-mailed me and something started up. Usually, I've been talking to the person about something, and we've both had sufficient interest to pursue it.

Is geographical proximity ever an important consideration?

I think geography does matter, at least for meeting people to start projects. You need to make sure that you're both on the same page in terms of what you want to do and how you want to do it. After that, I think e-mail can do 90 per cent of it. But I would say that, at some point, you reach a juncture in the research where it's much more efficient to talk about something than to try to type out what you think. Usually, the e-mailing back and forth is about addressing little things, but it's difficult to work out bigger issues that way.

What are the biggest challenges associated with collaborative work and how do you overcome them?

Nothing major comes to mind.

RESEARCH ASSISTANCE AND FUNDING

How do you use research assistants?

Not to a great extent. First of all, Dartmouth is only an undergraduate institution. Undergraduates don't have much training in economics, so you can't rely on them like graduate students to be well versed in econometric techniques and so forth. So, a lot of the work that I have RAs do is just data entry or looking in the library for sources. But even then I'm reluctant sometimes to have a research assistant because I want to make sure the data are put in correctly and also to be familiar with what's in the data sources. Just browsing through things, you can often find new data that you know are important. But you can't communicate that to an RA.

How important is funding for getting your work done?

Not very important because I think I'm driven by satisfying curiosity about a question. I'm also very dependent on libraries, and the Dartmouth library is very good and has a lot of older materials that I can use, and Harvard and other places are very close by. Funding can facilitate a project, in terms of travel and data collection, but is not always essential for a project.

Do you have any advice for a young scholar on the funding process?

A lot of people look just to the NSF in the United States, and that's a very competitive process. The chances of success are pretty low, even for very good projects. So, one has to be diverse in terms of tapping different sources of funds. Think outside the NSF box. Go to private foundations, private institutions, and academic units.

SEMINAR PARTICIPATION AND NETWORKING

What are the benefits to attending a seminar that is closely related to your work versus one that is not closely related?

When you attend seminars outside your area, sometimes you learn about different empirical approaches that can be applied to questions in your own research agenda. There can be some spillover benefits for what you're thinking about and doing. The only downside is it takes a lot of time, and the payoff may be zero in some cases.

The benefits to attending seminars in your area are obvious. You have to know what other people are doing, what their approach is, and what the standards are in the literature. Once again, that's why the NBER fills a very unique, important, and distinctive role.

How important is professional networking to success in research?

It's very important to get people to read your work in this age when time is so valuable and there are so many other things one can do. No one is going to go out of their way to read your work. So, presenting your work to them face-to-face is crucial. You have to be there to tell people about it and to answer questions about it. There is no substitute for this.

How does the researcher without extensive networks succeed?

If you're starting out as a relatively unknown junior person, you have to go to conferences to meet people and present your work. You cannot overlook those opportunities, and soon you will be invited to fly out to give departmental seminars somewhere. That's how you have to build your reputation – through many road trips early in one's career.

To what extent is the absence of departmental colleagues working in one's research area a major disadvantage?

It's a disadvantage because I think a senior colleague can provide an entry to the professional networks that that person has already developed. One would hope that he or she would be looking out for the junior colleagues; mentioning the conferences they should be going to, and talking about their work to other colleagues to get them known.

The only advantage I could see in being the only one in a particular field in a department is that there is some scarcity value. Because of that, they might want to keep you around. But they also may find it difficult to assess your work, and perhaps might not view the field as important. So, it can cut both ways.

COMMUNICATION OF RESEARCH

How do you find the right balance between communicating your research at an early stage versus the close-to-finished stage?

It's important to get preliminary research out to stake your claim to a certain question and to announce to the world that you're working on this issue. But at the same time, you don't want to do it so early that it's going to be dismissed or not be perceived as being well done. You can e-mail preliminary work to trusted colleagues who will understand that it is work in progress and hopefully they will cut you slack and help you improve it. Then you can send it out to a more general audience.

What are the unique challenges to giving a seminar and how do you overcome them?

I'm not sure there are unique challenges, but I do think it's incredibly useful to get feedback from people who are not in your research area. They will ask questions about things that you probably took for granted. And it's one thing to get written feedback from someone who has probably skimmed your paper, but it's another thing when you're up in front of other people presenting it. You can't hide. Weaknesses will be exposed. But it will improve your paper.

If it's a good paper, it is a joy to present. If I'm unsure whether it's a good paper, then I definitely try to approach the seminar with caution and modesty, in the spirit of trying to learn from the audience. How can I make this better? What haven't I thought of? Does this make sense? You have to adjust how you present based on how well prepared you are to defend your work.

PUBLICATION

How do you decide upon the appropriate journal to send your research to?

Every paper is different. It's not as though I send everything to top journals, because I realize right from the outset that a certain question may be very narrow and will have a limited readership, and therefore, should go into a field journal. Other things may also be narrowly pitched, but if there's some unique data or insights that I think might be of interest to a broader audience, it may be worth sending to a top journal.

How would you best describe your approach to dealing with a 'revise and resubmit' request from a journal? How about an outright rejection?

The advice I was given, and inculcated in me as a junior person, was as soon as you get a 'revise and resubmit', act on it immediately, and do everything the referee says to the best of your ability unless it is quite unreasonable. That will improve your chances of success.

There are different types of rejection. One is where there is a fundamental flaw in your work. In that case, you have to re-think things. The other type is where your approach is good, but the question is narrow. That simply means you should send it to a lower-tiered journal.

Do you think that the current structure of the publication process in economics facilitates or impedes scientific understanding and knowledge production?

I've noticed that journals are now aware of the fact that there's a long publication lag, and they're trying to act more quickly. *Economic Inquiry* now has an 'accept or reject' process with no revisions. It asks the referees if the paper is publishable or not, but they don't want to tie up the author in terms of a lengthy revision cycle. That's one way of facilitating things. But sometimes critical referees make good points and they ought to be taken into account, even if that ultimately slows publication.

What has been your best and worst experience during the publication process?

One of the best experiences was a paper that went from conception to final draft within three months, and then was accepted very quickly at a top journal. It was a paper with Peter Klenow on learning-by-doing in the semiconductor industry, and was published by the *Journal of Political Economy*.[5] If only all papers could come together and get published like that …

I'm not sure I've had a worst experience. I guess it's bad when you've had a paper rejected two or three times, and it doesn't land where you think it should.

One odd episode occurred when I sent a paper to a top field journal, where it was rejected, and then for some reason I sent it to a higher-ranked general interest journal, where it was accepted.

BOOK WRITING

You have written several books. Why do you write them?

Mainly because I want to communicate to a broader audience. A journal article is usually narrowly focused and tries to convince the academic reader about one point. That is not the place for tackling broader issues and putting things in perspective, nor does it reach the intelligent non-economist.

How would you describe how the book-writing process is different compared to writing journal articles?

With journal articles, the writing process itself is a small part of what you're doing, and the writing tends to be very efficient. You're setting out the context and the question that you're addressing in terms of the literature. It's almost workman-like writing. While the presentation matters, it is the data analysis that really counts in terms of whether the paper is persuasive or not. You just explain what you have done and why.

Writing a book for a broader audience is a much lengthier process. There, the effort is very much in the writing, as much as in the analysis itself.

Do you enjoy the book-writing process?

Dorothy Parker supposedly said, "I hate writing; I love having written." There is definitely something to that. When you're done with a book, you can take some satisfaction from the work. But a great deal of the writing process itself is laborious. I think most authors would agree with me that you get bored with the book after a while, and just want to be done with it. Starting a project is always much more fun than trying to complete a project.

REFEREEING AND EDITING

How do you decide upon whether or not to accept a refereeing job?

I think it's a professional obligation to referee, and so in most cases I'll do it. If the paper is on a topic that I don't know too much about, however, there is a mismatch and I'll turn down the offer.

What are the benefits to refereeing?

I'm not sure there are many benefits to being a referee. It's time-consuming, and it's not one of the most enjoyable things that one has to do as an academic researcher. But it does require you to look at someone's work very carefully.

How has your approach to refereeing changed through time?

As a junior person, you're more interested in technical details and how conclusions are reached. Now I think I'm more in an *Economic Inquiry* mode: is the paper addressing an interesting issue, and in a reasonable way? I'm not going to nit-pick the author and give them a laundry list of things to do.

How do you decide upon whether or not to accept an editing position?

I've only been editor of one journal, *The World Trade Review*. I took it because I'm interested in the area, and I thought it's something where research should be cultivated and built up.

What are the benefits to editing?

You get to shape a field, you learn who is doing work in the area, and you can encourage younger scholars. But I'd say the cost is it's a lot of time and one could always be doing other things.

TIME MANAGEMENT

How do you divide up your working day, both in terms of quantity and timing of different kinds of work?

Being an academic means there can be a lot of inter-temporal substitution. If there are travel or teaching or family matters that interfere, you just use other portions of the day or week to do one's work. When my kids are in school and they leave the house at 7:30 in the morning, the day is free, and I can allocate it the way I want.

When I get to the office, what I do depends on what's on my plate. Sometimes, the whole day will be administrative chores. Other times, I'll spend the whole day in the library, or I'll do a little bit of reading in the morning and then data collection, regression running, and writing in the afternoon. Every day is different.

How do you balance multiple research projects?

I'm not a great multitasker. I only have one project on the front burner at any one time. I may shift that pot back and bring other things forward, but when I really need to make progress on a paper, and think it through carefully and deeply, it has to be to the exclusion of other projects.

REFLECTIONS AND THE FUTURE OF ECONOMICS

What are the biggest challenges facing your research fields?

The most important challenge for anyone who is trying to bridge history and international trade is making your work relevant to other economists and to the policy community. One example is the recent economic crisis. There's been a lot of worry that protectionism might be spreading around the world, or that it might be a by-product of the crisis. And I think that's where an understanding of the past in terms of how trade policymakers respond to economic shocks can be useful in knowing, predicting, and addressing how policymakers might react today.

What are the strengths and weaknesses of your own research?

The weaknesses are specific to thinking about trade in history. There is not a lot of historical trade data and there are very few country observations. And so everything that you do is going to be more fragile in terms of inference compared to the power and robust effects that you might get from having an abundance of micro data.

In terms of strengths, I think any time you bridge two fields you can take insights from each and create something that wasn't there before. Pure economic historians won't necessarily have the detailed knowledge of a particular field, and pure international economists won't necessarily have the historical background. And so joining the two can be very fruitful. But the challenge for any economist who seeks to build that bridge is to gain credibility with both groups. That requires asking questions that interest both groups and answering the questions with compelling and persuasive evidence.

In the end, do you think the profession has helped to bring out and shape your research for the best?

One thing that has been very useful for me is professional conferences. In particular, I can't overstate the importance of the NBER in terms of my career because it is a place where you can present your work to specialists in your area, receive feedback, network professionally, and gain a reputation, for better or for worse. International trade is a field that does not have many conferences because it is not highly funded, so the NBER has played a tremendous role in being a venue where you can present your work.

Do you have any professional regrets?

Not really, because I've enjoyed most of what I've done and that matters a lot. One regret could be that you invest a lot of time in a project that didn't pay off. But that hasn't happened to me. I've learned something from just about everything I've done.

What are your professional ambitions?

I'd like to finish a major book on the history of US trade policy that I have been working on (with many interruptions) for many years. I think that'll be a capstone to a lot of the work that I've done on individual episodes and periods. I'm fairly confident I will complete it, but it has taken a long time. Still, it's something that I'm looking forward to finishing off.

How would you describe the state of economics today? Are you optimistic about its future?

I'm an optimist by nature. Economics will always be relevant, and there will always be interesting, unanswered questions as economic circumstances change and economies evolve. And I also think the increased movement over the past few decades towards more empirical work on practical issues has been a good one for the economics profession. The recent financial crisis has raised the stock of economic history, in my view. When asked in 2009 what advice he would give to young economists today, the late Paul Samuelson said: "Well, I'd say, and this is probably a change from what I would have said when I was younger: have a very healthy respect for the study of economic history, because that's the raw material out of which any of your conjectures or testings will come. And I think the recent period has illustrated that." For the last century's greatest economic theorist to concede the importance of economic history is a great step forward.

NOTES

1. Irwin, D.A. and R.S. Kroszner (1996), 'Log-rolling and Economic Interests in the Passage of the Smoot-Hawley Tariff', *Carnegie-Rochester Conference Series on Public Policy*, Vol. 45, No. 1 (December), pp. 173–200; Irwin, D.A. (1998), 'The Smoot-Hawley Tariff: A Quantitative Assessment', *Review of Economics and Statistics*, Vol. 80, No. 2 (May), pp. 326–334; Irwin, D.A. (1998), 'Change in US Tariffs: The Role of Import Prices and Commercial Policies', *American Economic Review*, Vol. 88, No. 4 (September), pp. 1015–1026; Irwin, D.A. and R.S. Kroszner (1999), 'Interests, Institutions, and Ideology in Securing Policy Change: The Republican Conversion to Trade Liberalization after Smoot-Hawley', *Journal of Law and Economics*, Vol. 42, No. 2 (October), pp. 643–673.
2. See, for example, Irwin, D.A. (2001), 'Tariffs and Growth in Late Nineteenth Century America', *The World Economy*, Vol. 24, No. 1 (January), pp. 15–30; Irwin, D.A. (2005), 'The Welfare Cost of Autarky: Evidence from the Jeffersonian Trade Embargo, 1807–09', *Review of International Economics*, Vol. 13, No. 4 (September), pp. 631–645; Irwin, D.A. (2010), 'Trade Restrictiveness and Deadweight Losses from US Tariffs', *American Economic Journal: Economic Policy*, Vol. 2, No. 3 (August), pp. 111–133.
3. Summers, L.H. (1991), 'The Scientific Illusion in Empirical Macroeconomics', *Scandinavian Journal of Economics*, Vol. 93, No. 2 (June), Proceedings of a Conference on New Approaches to Empirical Macroeconomics, pp. 129–148.
4. Eichengreen, B.J. and J. Sachs (1985), 'Exchange Rates and Economic Recovery in the 1930s', *Journal of Economic History*, Vol. 45, No. 4 (December), pp. 925–946.
5. Irwin, D.A. and P.J. Klenow (1994), 'Learning-By-Doing Spillovers in the Semiconductor Industry', *Journal of Political Economy*, Vol. 102, No. 6 (December), pp. 1200–1227.

Steven D. Levitt (University of Chicago)

Steven Levitt was born in Boston, Massachusetts in 1967 and graduated with a BA in economics from Harvard University in 1989 before obtaining a PhD in economics from the Massachusetts Institute of Technology in 1994. He was a Junior Fellow at the Harvard Society of Fellows between 1994 and 1997 and then joined the University of Chicago, where he has remained ever since, currently serving as the William B. Ogden Service Professor of Economics and Director of the Becker Center on Chicago Price Theory.

Professor Levitt's research interests include crime, corruption, the criminal justice system, education, business, race, real estate, and sports. His most-cited articles in chronological order include 'The Effect of Prison Population Size on Crime Rates: Evidence from Prison Overcrowding Litigation', *Quarterly Journal of Economics* (1996), 'Using Electoral Cycles in Police Hiring to Estimate the Effect of Police on Crime', *American Economic Review* (1997), 'The Impact of Legalized Abortion on Crime', *Quarterly Journal of Economics* (2001), co-authored with John Donohue, 'Understanding Why Crime Fell in the 1990s: Four Factors that Explain the Decline and Six that Do Not', *Journal of Economic Perspectives* (2004), and 'Understanding the Black-White Test Score Gap in the First Two Years of School', *Review of Economics and Statistics* (2004), co-authored with Roland Fryer. His books include *Freakonomics: A Rogue Economist Explores the Hidden Side of Everything* (William Morrow, 2005) and *SuperFreakonomics: Global Cooling, Patriotic Prostitutes, and Why Suicide Bombers Should Buy Life Insurance* (William Morrow, 2009), both co-authored with Stephen Dubner.

Professor Levitt was elected as a Fellow of the American Academy of Arts and Sciences in 2002 and was awarded the John Bates Clark Medal in 2003. *Time* Magazine named Levitt as one of the "100 People Who Shape Our World" in 2006.

I interviewed Steven Levitt in his office at the Becker Center on Chicago Price Theory at the University of Chicago. It was mid-morning of Monday, 25 July 2011.

BACKGROUND INFORMATION

Why did you decide to pursue an academic career in economics?

I was the worst kind of undergraduate in that I was not intellectual at all. I approached my college years solely with the goal of achieving high grades so that I could get a good job. And I succeeded. But when I got into the real world as a management consultant, I saw how completely devoid it was of thinking, curiosity, and rigor, which spurred a desire to become an academic. I defaulted into pursuing a PhD in economics because it was the only subject that I'd ever been good at.

GENERAL THOUGHTS ON RESEARCH

What is the value of pure versus applied research in economics?

I'm not sure that I see a huge amount of value in either theoretical or applied research. I've always thought that you should be an economist because it's fun. My view is that it's unlikely that any individual will make a research contribution that will change the world in a fundamental way. And I don't even know whether it's right to *think* about your profession in terms of how you'll change the world. The most successful people get enormous consumption value out of being an economist. We love having the freedom to tackle questions that appeal to us, and so I think I'm very selfish in that I do what I like and not so much because it'll make the world a better place.

Within those parameters, I don't therefore make a hierarchy of theoretical versus applied research. The best theoretical work has the largest impact on the profession or the world around us, but most of it has zero impact. And I think applied work, when done well, falls in-between. Ultimately, the research that I prize the most – and that I'd love to be able to do – is at the intersection. The toughest challenge in economics is how to do research that makes a theoretical contribution and has useful applied elements to it. That's the Holy Grail to me.

How would you describe the dialogue between theory and empirics in economics?

In my lifetime as an economist, I don't think there's ever been a very good dialogue between theory and empirics. There are very few people who successfully excel at that intersection, although they do exist; Kevin Murphy, David Card, and Pierre-André Chiappori spring to mind. I have come to believe that work at the intersection of theory and empirics is the ideal. But it's only in an aesthetic sense. I use an analogy to fashion. There is 'high fashion', which is outrageous and you wouldn't be caught dead on the street in it. And there is 'ready-to-wear' fashion. The work at the intersection of theory and empirics is the 'high fashion' of economics, which is exceptionally hard to do. And so most of us, myself included, engage in 'ready-to-wear' economics. I take some data, analyze it, and then reach a conclusion. And the theorists prove a theorem that's maybe not very important, but it extends our knowledge. Yet, as I've gotten older, I've realized that the real fun is to be found in that 'high fashion' category; trying to do research that seems 'un-pull-off-able'.

Do you think it is important to have broad research interests?

No. What I think is important is to be yourself, figure out what you're good at, and what you enjoy. If there's one single thing that predicts success in our profession – and something that I've observed when I interview young prospects – it is passion for what you do. If being an economist is a job, you'll never be good at it. The best economists are those who don't go to sleep at night because they want to find the answer to a question or those who, when asked about their hobbies, act puzzled and say, "Why would I want to have a hobby when I'm an economist?" I managed to brainwash myself into that mindset when I was younger. One of the reasons why I was so productive was because I loved what I was doing; there was simply nothing I wanted to do more than answer economic questions.

How has your research agenda changed through time?

Certainly my agenda has changed in terms of the kinds of questions that I answer. *Freakonomics* is to blame in large part. When I wrote that book, we didn't expect anyone to read it, but people did, it sold a lot of copies, and changed my opportunity set dramatically. What I realized was that the things outside of academics were more fun for me. And so given a broader set of choices, I devote less time to research, and the research that I actually do is now very different because, for instance, I have access to company data that allows me to answer questions that I wouldn't have been able to do as an anonymous academic.

But maybe a better answer to your question is that I've never had a research agenda. Honestly, I have been driven by completely selfish motives of what's interesting to me. And what happened to be interesting to me at any given point in time was always in flux. For instance, I started out asking political economy questions. But I never liked politics. I realized after I'd written six or seven papers that I just wasn't interested in the subject. The only reason I was writing them was because I knew I could get them published.[1] But then I started writing papers on crime, which were much more intrinsically interesting to me.[2] Why in the world would I spend my time writing papers just so I can get them published when there's something much more fun to do? That was a fundamental change. And so since then, I have had two rules when I consider a paper. Number one: is this a fun paper to write? Number two: is there any 'economics' in the paper? Initially, I approached economics from what I'd call an identification perspective; if I could differentiate correlation from causality, then I would feel like that was a good paper. But when I came here, I really got won over by the Chicago world view that there should be something more, namely that being an applied statistician was not sufficient for an economist; you should also try to engage with economic theory. And so in the last decade, while it may not be always apparent looking at my papers what my definition of economics is or how an individual paper fits in, I've always had that criterion in mind.

IDEA GENERATION

Where do you get your research ideas?

Mostly I get my research ideas just from wandering around. I'm rarely motivated by the literature. I'm not proud to say this, but I just have never been very interested in other people's research. At heart, I'm not really an economist, or certainly not a very good economist in the sense that I think good economists care deeply about the economic body of knowledge. I never have; I've always just wanted to do my own thing. And I've always seen being part of the economics community more as a tax than a benefit. I'm anti-social, and my ideal activity within the profession would be to sit in my room alone trying to figure out the answers to questions. And so most of my research ideas have come out of simple observations in my own life, or out of questions that I wanted to answer. Rarely have I tackled big questions; it's almost always been small ones. My view is that it's better to answer a little question well than to answer a big question poorly. For instance, for a long time, I've been very interested in corruption and cheating. And I'd love to say something profound about corruption on a global scale. But instead I keep my eyes open for other cases. And so when I read a one paragraph newspaper article in *The Washington Post* about how a sumo wrestler had accused other sumo wrestlers of cheating, that triggered me to think that, while I'm never going to figure out why corruption is rampant in India, maybe if I got the data I could answer the question of whether they're cheating in sumo wrestling.[3] Economists call these opportunities 'natural experiments', but I think a better term for it is 'accidental experiments'. You have a chance to carve out a little piece of the world and answer it well.

At what point does an idea become a project that you devote resources to?

I've always had a pretty low threshold for starting projects, but I'm draconian in terms of ending them. When I have an idea for a paper, the first thing I usually ask myself, which I talked about earlier, is whether it will be fun and interesting to me. If it can't pass that threshold, then I stop right there. The second thing I ask is whether there is any possible state of the world where this paper will turn out to have a chance of being published in a top journal. If the answer is no – and you often just have a feeling – then I sometimes do the project anyway purely for consumption value. But I'm really going to have to enjoy it to want to do it, because I feel better about attacking projects when I feel like there's some chance somebody else will be interested in it.

One thing that I cannot emphasize enough when I talk to graduate students is what I call 'failing quickly' or a 'fast first cut'. I want to know within a day of looking at data whether or not the project will succeed. I think a real skill in our profession is how to find simple ways that tell you whether a project will fail with near certainty. And so I collect broad data that can rule out my hypothesis or not as quickly as possible. If I had to put numbers on it, I would guess that no more than one in ten of the projects I start lead to academic papers. And most of the failing nine I kill within days of investing any resources in it. That is something I think I do much more effectively than the typical economist. I often see graduate students investing three months or six months or nine months cleaning data without any idea whether the project will succeed or not, when it's pretty clear that if they'd tackled it the appropriate way they could have seen failure was certain right from the beginning. If you're somebody like me, who tends not to write big seminal papers but rather succeeds by writing a lot of little papers that answer questions, you just don't have the luxury of burning several months of your time on a project that will go nowhere.

IDEA EXECUTION

What makes a good theoretical paper? Can you give an example?

The best papers, whether they're theoretical or empirical, are ones that have a number of traits. First, the conclusions are often unexpected *ex ante*, but obvious *ex post*. Those are hard papers to write because you have to convince your audience that they didn't know the answer beforehand. On a couple of occasions, I have started a seminar by asking people what the answer is to the question. Then I'll work through the paper and show an answer that is obvious *ex post*. Many people will tell me that they already knew it, but I remind them that they gave the wrong answer at the beginning of the seminar. It can be immensely frustrating.

A second characteristic of the best papers is that they are very convincing. I don't mean simply that the proofs are right; it just feels like the author has the right model of the world.

A third characteristic is that they are interesting. What's surprising in our profession is that people often agree on what's interesting, even with the diversity of tastes and preferences.

Finally, the best papers have excellent storytelling. Storytelling is a dirty word in our profession because we like to masquerade as scientists, and pretend that we're talking only in facts. But so much of what we do is storytelling. That is true of most science; it's about helping people to understand through good examples and well-written probes.

An old paper that has some of these elements is the Coase Theorem.[4] The result shocked people, and they had a very hard time coming around to the idea that it was right. But once you understand it, it's totally obvious. And relative to most economics papers, it's very much about storytelling.

What are some of my favorite other papers? I like Bresnahan and Reiss's paper from the *JPE* that looks at isolated markets as a means of answering the age-old question of how increases in competition affect mark-ups.[5] It's a beautiful paper that puts theory and data together in a very remarkable way. I don't actually believe the result in the end, but it's a paper that I teach over and over again because it's a classic example of finding a simple insight that jumps out of economic theory and allows you to answer a question that otherwise you would have struggled with forever.

Akerlof's 'lemons' paper and Spence's 'signaling' paper also have a number of the characteristics that I've just talked about.[6] And some of Schelling's work falls into the same category. So too does Axelrod's book on 'tit-for-tat', which contains the finding that a simple strategy empirically was a powerful strategy in the iterated prisoner's dilemma.[7]

I also like *Nudge* by Sunstein and Thaler.[8] It made a simple point that should have been obvious to me, but wasn't. As an economist, I think if you want to change behavior, you alter incentives. But what Sunstein and Thaler say is that it's just easier to trick people than it is to change their incentives; whether it's by changing the order of where the food is in the cafeteria or by putting a bull's-eye at the bottom of the urinal so that we aim better. That doesn't involve teaching people; it's simply a way of taking advantage of the unconscious things we do. That book has had a powerful influence on the way I think about the world. When I wander around and try and figure out the answer to problems that policymakers ask me, my toolkit used to only contain incentives, but now tricks are in there, too. Ultimately, one of the main goals of academic research is to provide other people with toolkits for thinking about the world.

You are an economist who has reported one or two controversial findings in his papers. When you find a result that you realize is likely to be controversial, how does this affect how you write the paper?

To be honest, I often am oblivious to what will be controversial or not. For instance, with my abortion and crime paper, it never occurred to me, number one, that it would be controversial, or number two, that anyone would care.[9] I had done work in the past that I thought was interesting, but nobody cared. I think the only thing that I might do differently on controversial topics is to invest more heavily in anticipating what possible critiques there would be and responding to them ahead of time. That's true as a general principle on every paper that you write, but there's a trade-off because papers are not perfection. There are diminishing marginal returns to investments in papers and as they are more likely to be controversial, you're willing to invest more to ride down that diminishing marginal returns curve.

But I don't mind controversy. I don't publish papers unless I think I have the right answer. And part of thinking you have the right answer is entertaining other possible explanations and either being able to reject them or openly acknowledging the fact that you can't reject them. Over time, as I've thought more and more about how to do research, I've moved away from the model of coming up with a hypothesis and then testing it. That's a false model. We pretend to be scientists, but that's not the way most people operate, and I don't think it's the way they *should* operate. I've much more come to embrace a different model, which is to understand the facts. What are the things that everyone can agree on? And what models of the world are those facts consistent with? Not to choose one favored model and then see whether the facts are consistent with my particular model. But rather to come up with 14 models, of which 11 don't do very well relative to the facts, and to have no idea which of the other three is right because the data aren't sufficient to distinguish between them. It's a very unusual approach to doing research because it often entails putting the results first and the theory second. If I weren't so lazy, I would devote the rest of my academic career to trying to change the profession to carry out research in that manner. I really think it's a fundamentally better way of learning about the world, but no one else seems to agree with me. And so while I fantasize about trying to change the profession, I'm pretty sure that I never will put in the effort to even try to win the battle.

THE WRITING PROCESS

Which part of the writing process do you find most difficult?

I don't like to think about economics as a writing process, because the writing is such a trivial part of the overall exercise. There's a paper creation and paper generation process, of which writing, for me, is often 5 per cent of the activity as a whole. The part that I like the least is everything that follows after you know the answer to a problem, which comes after only about 20 per cent of the work. And so I like the discovery of the answer, not the packaging of the product in a way that will allow it to get recognition. Especially unpleasant for me is responding to critics in the 'revise and resubmit' process. I'll start by saying that although everyone else in the profession complains about how terrible their referees are, I've never had that feeling. I've been uniformly shocked at how insightful referees are on my papers and how much I learn from them. Nonetheless, I absolutely despise the process of revisiting the paper after maybe nine months have elapsed and my interests have moved somewhere else.

Writing a paper is almost purely formulaic. If you know the formula, you just march through the pieces and it's extremely easy. I find that I can write perhaps five pages of text in a few hours because I can only concentrate hard for that long, but that means for a standard paper of 25 pages, I can just sit down for a few hours in the morning for five days and I've written the paper. That's the sense in which I think writing is just a trivial part of the overall process of creating a paper, because I might very well spend six months or a year in total on a project.

What steps have you taken during your career to improve the quality of your writing?

I wouldn't say I'm a great writer, but I've always been audience-focused, which is one of the most important things. Many economists write papers from their own perspective instead of thinking about what the audience needs to hear. One of the clearest cases is when they punish you by taking you through every misstep that they did; they had an idea that was no good and didn't work. But it took six months and they feel horrible at the fact that it won't ever appear in print. And so they put some section in their paper where they write about something that failed. That is the wrong way to think about doing research. If you have bad ideas that don't work, that's your fault and you shouldn't worry about it. It's not important to the reader. The thing that is most artful about writing a paper is figuring out what institutional background to put in it; how to give the reader as much of the background as will be interesting and important for interpreting results, without inundating them with everything that you've had to learn.

I'd say the only thing that I've really done that has made me a better writer has been working with Stephen Dubner, my *Freakonomics* co-author. He's a writer in a way that no academic is a writer. But I think being able to observe the way he writes has spilled off on me a little bit. It's helped me to understand how to tell stories and package information.

But ultimately, you can be an above average economics writer simply by knowing what the formula is for writing papers and following that formula. That is the core of writing for an academic audience. By formula, I mean things like the first paragraph usually says next to nothing and makes grand pronouncements that you don't really believe, but eases the reader into what you're going to do. The second paragraph of the introduction says what the question is that you're trying to answer. The third paragraph says how you're going to answer that question. The fourth paragraph says what the answer is. The fifth paragraph maybe talks about other things that are of interest in the paper. And the sixth paragraph says what the rest of the paper looks like. That's literally how I think about it. When you have such a clear recipe for writing papers, it's just trivial.

COLLABORATION

When you work with co-authors, how do you decide whom to work with?

It's more fun to write papers with co-authors. I often equate writing economics papers with having a fantasy sports team. For instance, when you have a fantasy baseball team, no one else in the world cares at all about what happens to that team. My wife will not tolerate me talking about how my team is doing, but it's more fun to be able to talk about it. And so I've found having a co-owner in fantasy baseball is incredibly valuable because it allows you to get much more consumption value out of it. I think economics is the same. Nobody cares very much about your project unless they're a co-author, and it's a lot more fun to have somebody to talk to about what you're doing. And so one of my main criteria in choosing a co-author is that it must be somebody who will be fun to work with.

I also have a pretty limited set of skills; I'm terrible at econometrics and I can't write down an internally consistent theory if it's at all hard and has more than two actors and two states of the world. And so I often will seek out co-authors who have disparate sets of skills. For instance, I co-authored some papers with Jack Porter, the econometrician, which worked out great.[10] He could do things there was no way in the world I could ever do. And he was fun to do it with.

I also tend to pick co-authors who are around me. A lot of the papers I work on come out of simple conversations where you're wondering about this or that and some idea comes up. And so I've written a bunch of papers with John List and Chad Syverson because they're the guys who I go to lunch with.[11] I think geography matters a lot when it comes to co-authors. It's just sensible and easy to write papers with the people whose offices are next door to yours rather than with those who are across the country.

There are two other things you want in a co-author. One is that it's great to have co-authors who want to work really hard and carry a big part of the load. The second thing is that they need to have enough self-awareness to know the difference between good and bad ideas. The worst co-authors are those who fall in love with their own ideas even when they're no good. The best co-authors have tons of ideas but eventually can sort out the good ideas from the bad ones. It becomes very painful when you're working with a co-author who thinks their ideas are great, but you think they are terrible. One of the best co-authors in that regard is Jim Snyder at MIT. Jim had more ideas than almost anyone else alive. And a lot of those ideas were really bad. When I first started working with him, I thought, "Oh, my God, what are we going to do?" But he always had a perfect filter. At first, he couldn't tell the difference between his absolutely incredible ideas and the ones that were not good at all. But within a day he could, and so he was a fantastic co-author because he added so much insight. You never had to fight with him about whether something made sense or not because he always knew the answer.[12]

RESEARCH ASSISTANCE AND FUNDING

How do you use research assistants?

Unfortunately, data analysis and data cleaning is one of the few parts of the process for creating empirical research that you can subcontract out to research assistants. I say "unfortunately" because it's actually the part of the process I've always loved the most. If I had an infinite amount of time, that's what I'd do all day long; clean data, analyze data, be knee-deep in data. I think part of what's jaded me as an economist is that the part I love the most about our profession is the part I do the least because it's the one aspect that I can rent out to other people. And so I do have a team of RAs. Most of the time, they'll be the ones who get the data, clean the data, and write the data code to get to the answers. I'm heavily involved in thinking about the data and how to analyze it and, to a certain extent, looking over their code and making sure it's right. But the reality is if you have a lot of demands on your time and you want to write more than a few papers a year, I think there's no other way to do it than to heavily involve research assistants.

I've never been very comfortable with having research assistants write parts of the paper or try to conceptualize the problem. And I've never really had research assistants who have been in the idea generation business. I've always felt it would be morally wrong to co-author papers when the ideas came from the research assistants. I think of them as budding economists and ideas are the scarcest thing in our profession. If an established economist co-authors a paper with someone unknown, then the presumption is that the established economist had the idea. And so I've always had the view that if a research assistant has an idea, they should write the paper by themselves.

COMMUNICATION OF RESEARCH

What are the unique challenges to giving a seminar and how do you overcome them?

Often the biggest challenge with seminars is trying to fill 90 minutes productively. In many cases, at least if you write papers like I do, 30 or 40 minutes is plenty to get the idea of the paper across, to show the results, and to give people ample time to digest it. And so I think the challenge of seminars is how to make them interesting. I've never really thought about seminars as being about showing other people you're right. The typical demeanor of a seminar is there's a presenter with an answer who's trying to convince the audience that that answer is correct. That's the wrong way to view a seminar. The ultimate goal should be to convince the audience that you are a smart, honest, creative, and reliable researcher. But often the way to achieve that goal is to fail to convince people that you're right about *this* paper; to admit that there are weaknesses, to admit when faced with good challenges that you might be wrong, or that you'll have to do more research. Seminar-giving is a lot easier when your goal isn't to prove to people that you've got the right answer. And so I'm usually more open-minded as a presenter. I want to show a bunch of facts, I want people to entertain various hypotheses about those facts, and then I want to throw out my favorite hypotheses. But I like a seminar to be more of a dialogue, very much in the Chicago style, than a debate. And the difference between a dialogue and a debate is in a dialogue you follow the ideas and the data wherever they lead, but in a debate you have a preordained position which you defend even when you are being out-argued by your opponent.

Of course, it's easier for me as an established economist to get up in front of an audience and say, "I have these ideas, and maybe they're wrong," and at the end of the day say, "Yeah, I guess you convinced me they're wrong." It's much harder for a young person in the profession to be willing to admit that, but I think it's very powerful. In fact, some of the nicest things people have ever said about me have related to instances where I have been open-minded to criticism and dramatically changed the way I wrote a paper because someone pointed out I was thinking about things the wrong way. One thing that really helps me in that regard is I've never been under the illusion that I'm the smartest guy in the room. The people who struggle the most when giving seminars are those who are convinced they're the smartest person in the room. It leads you to think and act in ways that often lead to bad outcomes. Even if you think you're the smartest person in the room, you're usually wrong about that.

PUBLICATION

How do you decide upon the appropriate journal to send your research to?

I used to worry a lot about where my papers got published. And in that world I would aim high, not worry much about rejection, and work ceaselessly when given the opportunity to 'revise and resubmit', even if I thought it would make the paper worse and even if it was an enormous amount of work. As I've gotten older, I care much less about what journals my papers come out in. And so I've much more gravitated towards publishing my papers in places where I think it will be easy to get them published. For instance, *Economic Inquiry* has got an option where you submit the paper and they either accept it as is or they reject it. I had a paper published there last year under that regime.[13] I think it's a smart way to think about the role of a journal. But there's no question that papers that get published in the top journals are read much more, receive much more exposure, and are much more influential. And so it's certainly worth suffering the pain of likely rejection and putting in effort to get your work published there. But ultimately, I'd say if I'm trying to decide within a set of journals, I think about editors' likes and dislikes, and whether I feel that they'd be open-minded to it.

TIME MANAGEMENT

How do you divide up your working day, both in terms of quantity and timing of different kinds of work?

I don't work very hard anymore. I used to work really hard; just sequester myself and work extremely long and isolated hours. And I loved doing that. Now people bother me all the time. I'm pulled in a million ways. And so I spend most of my time looking at what RAs are doing, talking with co-authors, and then writing when there's something to be written. But somewhere along the way, I got into a nasty trap of starting way too many papers. If I had to honestly tell you how many papers I have in process right now, I fear the answer might be 25 or 30. Even in the best case, if I were to allocate my time equally between those 25 papers, I'd spend a day a month on each of them. And nothing would ever get done. It's a miracle when I actually finish a paper. But I don't really care that much anymore whether I finish my papers. The fun part is starting them and learning the answers. How many papers do John List and I have together where we know the answer, but I can't convince him to write it up and he can't convince me to write it up, and so the paper just lingers there for years? We have a dozen papers like that. But in some sense, part of our utility function is that we both enjoy finding out the answers and much less do we care about telling the world about them.

REFLECTIONS AND THE FUTURE OF ECONOMICS

What are the strengths and weaknesses of your own research?

There are three things I'm good at: taking a pile of data and making sense of it, figuring out unusual ways to answer questions that superficially seem like they'd be hard to answer, and being honest about the strengths and weak-nesses of what I do. What am I bad at? I'm terrible at math. I can take a derivative, but other than that there's not much I can do anymore. I'm terrible at econometrics. I have reasonable intuition for it, but I just don't have a lot of interest or skill at rigorous econometrics. And I know nothing about the literature. I've never liked to read the literature. I wish I were the kind of person who liked to read other people's work. But the good news is that those weaknesses are all easily solved by the right co-author. There are many potential co-authors out there who are good at math, who are good at econometrics, and who like to read other people's work. And so I always try to have one of those people around when I'm writing papers. It's just a nice way to hide my weaknesses.

In the end, do you think the profession has helped to bring out and shape your research for the best?

I would say that what the economics profession has done for me is to provide an incredibly powerful and ever growing set of tools for answering questions. When I'm the only economist in the room, I often leave discussions thinking I'm the smartest person who ever lived. I have brilliant insights that change the nature of the conversation. But whenever there are two economists in the room, I realize that it is very little to do with me and everything to do with the toolkit that economists carry around. We almost always say the same things, and that, to me, is the power of the economics profession.

Do you have any professional regrets?

I would say my only professional regrets are mistakes that I've made. They've always been simple coding errors either that I've done, or the RAs have done that I haven't caught. In most cases, they haven't even mattered that much to the answers. But it's just the worst thing. Number one, it hurts your reputation. Number two, it's an enormous time sink; you have to go back and see that you made the mistake, to apologize for making the mistake, and think about what the implications of the mistake are. When you're high-profile and maybe not liked so well by many members of the profession, mistakes are just so costly.

But I've been so lucky in the choices I've made. I've bumbled through my economics career in a very fortuitous manner. I ended up at MIT when I didn't even really know it was a good school. And then I somehow managed to get in to the Harvard Society of Fellows, which gave me three years to do research unencumbered. That was just an unbelievable opportunity. But the best active decision I made was to come to the Economics Department at the

University of Chicago. Everybody told me it was a bad idea. In fact, Andrei Schleifer at Harvard said that if I were to come here, it just showed I was so stupid that he would never even bother speaking to me again. But I had a sense that if I wanted to be a good economist, my best chance was to come to Chicago and spend time with people like Gary Becker and Kevin Murphy. And it turned out to be absolutely true. For me, Chicago price theory is the window on the world that I need to understand it. Unfortunately, I'm not very good at Chicago price theory, but I'm just good enough that I can use it as the basis for almost everything I do.

Writing *Freakonomics* was a half-thought-out choice, but it was an incredibly good one in terms of what it's allowed me to do. I really thought when I wrote the book that it would be purely a substitute for academic research and that it would lead me in other directions. But what's interesting is that the book has actually turned out in many ways to be a complement to doing real research. It has opened up so many opportunities for interesting data and people come to me with interesting problems. Realistically, my research over the six years since the book came out is far better and far more interesting than it would have been had I never written that book. That is ironic, but a nice unintended consequence of its success.

What are your professional ambitions?

I don't have any professional ambitions. As I mentioned earlier, if I were ambitious, my goal would be to change the way people think about theory and data. Other than that, I just simply want to figure out the answers to my little questions, write them up when I feel inspired, and continue what I've done my whole life, which is to be very self-indulgent when it comes to those questions.

How would you describe the state of economics today? Are you optimistic about its future?

There's a lot of intellectual firepower going into economics today. At the same time, I think the profession has gone off the rails. The fetishistic infatuation with technicality and mathematical difficulty is extremely unhealthy. Ultimately, what stands the test of time is ideas. And yet I don't think our profession is structured in such a way as to reward ideas and to select economists who are likely to have great ideas. To get into graduate school today primarily requires enormous investment in undergraduate mathematics; the kind that is rarely used by practicing economists. I'm not sure I have a great way of selecting who should be an economist or not, but I'm pretty sure that the one we're choosing now is radically distorting the set of people who come and study economics. And so my hunch is that our profession will increasingly move in the direction of emphasis on technical sophistication. And I think that will make us increasingly irrelevant to the real world. The macroeconomists get angry at me when I say this, but I do think that the trends in macroeconomics towards microfoundations and rigor have made macro more and more divorced from the real world.

I think we're likely to go the same direction in microeconomics. Structural analysis, while motivated by admirable goals, which is to come up with parameters that are portable and generalizable, struggles with the reality that when you try to model things in a way that's consistent enough with theory, the problems just get so hard so fast that the believability and the reliability fly out the window. And I've always felt like answering simple questions well is a more useful endeavor than answering hard questions poorly. That biases me towards simple approaches that maybe don't give you exactly the parameter you'd want to answer a big public policy question, but do give you the parameter that actually describes accurately the dataset that you're investigating. And so I would say I'm not so optimistic about the profession. It's not that I want all economists to look like me. If every economist looked like me that would be a complete disaster; there's no question about that. But I do think that it is a much harder challenge today – than it was for me 20 years ago – for young people who want to look at the world in simple ways and who want their careers to be about ideas.

NOTES

1. Levitt, S.D. (1994), 'An Empirical Test of Competing Explanations for the Midterm Gap in the US House', *Economics and Politics*, Vol. 6, No. 1 (March), pp. 25–37; Levitt, S.D. (1994), 'Using Repeat Challenges to Estimate the Effect of Campaign Spending on Election Outcomes in the US House', *Journal of Political Economy*, Vol. 102, No. 4 (August), pp. 777–798; Levitt, S.D. (1995), 'Policy Watch: Congressional Campaign Finance Reform', *Journal of Economic Perspectives*, Vol. 9, No. 1 (Winter), pp. 183–193; Levitt, S.D. and J.M. Snyder, Jr (1995), 'Political Parties and the Distribution of Federal Outlays', *American Journal of Political Science*, Vol. 39, No. 4 (November), pp. 958–980; Levitt, S.D. (1996), 'How Do Senators Vote? Disentangling the Role of Voter Preferences, Party Affiliation, and Senator Ideology', *American Economic Review*, Vol. 86, No. 3 (June), pp. 425–441; Levitt, S.D. and C.D. Wolfram (1997), 'Decomposing the Sources of Incumbency Advantage in the US House', *Legislative Studies Quarterly*, Vol. 22, No. 1 (February), pp. 45–60; Levitt, S.D. and J.M. Snyder, Jr (1997), 'The Impact of Federal Spending on House Election Outcomes', *Journal of Political Economy*, Vol. 105, No. 1 (February), pp. 30–53.

2. His early work on crime included Levitt, S.D. (1996), 'The Effect of Prison Population Size on Crime Rates: Evidence from Prison Overcrowding Litigation', *Quarterly Journal of Economics*, Vol. 111, No. 2 (May), pp. 319–351; Levitt, S.D. (1997), 'Incentive Compatibility Constraints as an Explanation for the Use of Prison Sentences instead of Fines', *International Review of Law and Economics*, Vol. 17, No. 2 (June), pp. 179–192; Levitt, S.D. (1998), 'Juvenile Crime and Punishment', *Journal of Political Economy*, Vol. 106, No. 6 (December), pp. 1156–1185.

3. Duggan, M. and S.D. Levitt (2002), 'Winning Isn't Everything: Corruption in Sumo Wrestling', *American Economic Review*, Vol. 92, No. 5 (December), pp. 1594–1605.

4. Coase, R.H. (1960), 'The Problem of Social Cost', *Journal of Law and Economics*, Vol. 3 (October), pp. 1–44.

5. Bresnahan, T.F. and P.C. Reiss (1991), 'Entry and Competition in Concentrated Markets', *Journal of Political Economy*, Vol. 99, No. 5 (October), pp. 977–1009.

6. Akerlof, G.A. (1970), 'The Market for "Lemons": Quality Uncertainty and the Market Mechanism', *Quarterly Journal of Economics*, Vol. 84, No. 3 (August), pp. 488–500; Spence, A.M. (1973), 'Job Market Signaling', *Quarterly Journal of Economics*, Vol. 87, No. 3 (August), pp. 355–374.

7. Robert Axelrod (1984), *The Evolution of Cooperation*, New York: Basic Books.

8. Richard H. Thaler and Cass R. Sunstein (2008), *Nudge: Improving Decisions about Health, Wealth and Happiness*, Yale University Press.

9. Donohue III, J.J. and S.D. Levitt (2001), 'The Impact of Legalized Abortion on Crime', *Quarterly Journal of Economics*, Vol. 116, No. 2 (May), pp. 379–420.

10. Levitt, S.D. and J. Porter (2001), 'Sample Selection Estimation of Airbag and Seatbelt Effectiveness', *Review of Economics and Statistics*, Vol. 83, No. 4 (November), pp. 603–615; Levitt, S.D. and J. Porter (2001), 'How Dangerous Are Drinking Drivers?', *Journal of Political Economy*, Vol. 106, No. 6 (December), pp. 1198–1237.

11. See, for example, Levitt, S.D. and J.A. List (2007), 'What Do Laboratory Experiments Measuring Social Preferences Reveal About the Real World?', *Journal of Economic Perspectives*, Vol. 21, No. 2 (Spring), pp. 153–174; Levitt, S.D. and J.A. List (2009), 'Field Experiments in Economics: The Past, The Present, and The Future', *European Economic Review*, Vol. 53, No. 1 (January), pp. 1–18; Levitt, S.D. and J.A. List (2011), 'Was There Really a Hawthorne Effect at the Hawthorne Plant? An Analysis of the Original Illumination Experiments', *American Economic Journal: Applied Economics*, Vol. 3, No. 1 (January), pp. 224–238; Levitt, S.D. and C. Syverson (2008), 'Antitrust Implications of Home Seller Outcomes when using Flat-Fee Real Estate Agents', *Brookings-Wharton Papers on Urban Affairs*, pp. 47–93; Levitt, S.D. and C. Syverson (2008), 'Market Distortions when Agents are Better Informed: The Value of Information in Real Estate Transactions', *Review of Economics and Statistics*, Vol. 90, No. 4 (November), pp. 591–611.

12. Levitt, S.D. and J.M. Snyder, Jr (1995), 'Political Parties and the Distribution of Federal Outlays', *American Journal of Political Science*, Vol. 39, No. 4 (November), pp. 958–980; Levitt, S.D. and J.M. Snyder, Jr (1997), 'The Impact of Federal Spending on House Election Outcomes', *Journal of Political Economy*, Vol. 105, No. 1 (February), pp. 30–53.

13. Doyle, J.J. and S.D. Levitt (2010), 'Evaluating the Effectiveness of Child Safety Seats and Seat Belts in Protecting Children from Injury', *Economic Inquiry*, Vol. 48, No. 3 (July), pp. 521–536.

Robert E. Lucas, Jr (University of Chicago)

Robert Lucas was born in Yakima, Washington in 1937 and graduated with both a BA in history and a PhD in economics from the University of Chicago in 1959 and 1964 respectively. Between 1964 and 1975, he taught at the Graduate School of Industrial Administration at Carnegie Mellon University before moving to the University of Chicago, where he has remained ever since, currently serving as the John Dewey Distinguished Service Professor in Economics and the College.

Professor Lucas is widely acknowledged as one of the most influential macroeconomists of the twentieth century. He is perhaps best known for his work on the development of the theory of rational expectations, but he has also made significant contributions to the theory of investment, the theory of endogenous growth, the theory of asset pricing, and the theory of money. In addition, he introduced the 'Lucas critique' of the use of econometric models in policy design. His most-cited articles in chronological order include 'Expectations and the Neutrality of Money', *Journal of Economic Theory* (1972), 'Some International Evidence on Output-Inflation Trade-offs', *American Economic Review* (1973), 'Econometric Policy Evaluation: A Critique', *Carnegie-Rochester Conference Series on Public Policy* (1976), 'Asset Prices in an Exchange Economy', *Econometrica* (1978), and

'On the Mechanics of Economic Development', *Journal of Monetary Economics* (1988). His books include *Studies in Business-Cycle Theory* (MIT Press, 1983), *Recursive Methods in Economic Dynamics* (Harvard University Press, 1989), co-authored with Nancy Stokey and Edward Prescott, and *Lectures on Economic Growth* (Harvard University Press, 2004).

Professor Lucas was elected as a Fellow of the Econometric Society in 1975, a Member of the American Academy of Arts and Sciences in 1980, and a Member of the National Academy of Sciences in 1981. He was awarded the Nobel Prize in Economic Sciences in 1995 "for having developed and applied the hypothesis of rational expectations, and thereby having transformed macroeconomic analysis and deepened our understanding of economic policy."

I interviewed Robert Lucas in his office in the Department of Economics at the University of Chicago. It was early-afternoon of Monday, 25 July 2011.

BACKGROUND INFORMATION

Why did you decide to pursue an academic career in economics?

I was an undergraduate in history at Chicago and was drawn to the historical importance of economic forces. I began graduate work in history at Berkeley and took exciting economic history courses from David Landes and Carlo Cipolla. I realized that I needed to learn some economics, but was shocked to discover that I couldn't read past the first page of many economics books. And so I switched fields to economics and came back to Chicago.

GENERAL THOUGHTS ON RESEARCH

There is an increasing emphasis in many economics departments on applied research. Is this true at Chicago?

Chicago's always been involved in applied research. For example, Paul Douglas did pioneering work on production functions, Henry Schultz looked at demand systems, and Milton Friedman's research was always applied. The idea is that economic theory helps us understand the workings of the world that we observe.

What is the value of pure versus applied research in economics?

They're in it together. I don't know how to approach new evidence, except by trying to ask, "Well, what would I have expected to see based on economic theory? What were the discrepancies, and how can I make it all fit together?" Of course, you can't always do it, but there have been enormous gains in the building, understanding, and analysis of mathematically explicit models, which is at the center of all my work.

How would you describe the dialogue between theory and empirics in economics?

Some of the best theorists don't seem to have any interest in empirical work at all, and some people do valuable empirical work with very little theory. And there are others who mix them together in various ways. I like the mix. I think the empirical research that is most lasting identifies the underlying economic forces that interact to produce whatever we see, whether it be economic growth, depression or panic. In other words, what kind of model could produce that behavior?

How would you characterize your own research agenda and how has it changed through time?

In terms of substance, I've never really had an agenda. I've just accumulated a wish list of unsolved problems. And then when I run across a new paper or some new mathematics or new evidence that opens up new avenues for one of those problems, I'll drop what I'm doing and go for it. In that sense, I behave very opportunistically.

Do you think it is important to have broad research interests?

Economics is a very unified field. We have one body of theory and try to force the whole world into it. It's not like the biological sciences where specialties are so different that they can't even talk to one another. I feel I can work on anything in economics, and I think other people feel the same way. The economists whom I admire, like my Chicago heroes, Milton Friedman and Gary Becker, have worked on a vast range of problems. And people from Friedman's generation, like Kenneth Arrow and Paul Samuelson, have influenced my thinking in a very strong way, as have my own contemporaries, like Tom Sargent and Ed Prescott.

IDEA GENERATION

Where do you get your research ideas?

I like to work on basic problems. They're obvious in economics; things like business cycles, economic growth, and the effects of international trade. Everybody who reads the newspaper knows that they're good problems.

At what point does an idea become a project that you devote resources to?

When some kind of modeling that will be helpful in thinking about it occurs to me.

IDEA EXECUTION

What makes a good theoretical paper? Can you give an example?

There are different kinds. The work of the general equilibrium theorists, Kenneth Arrow, Gerard Debreu, and Lionel McKenzie brought a new level of mathematics into research, and they did it not to deal with specific problems, but just to recast the basic ideas of Smith, Ricardo, Marshall, Walras, and others.[1] It was beautiful work and extremely useful for those doing more applied research. I don't do that kind of work myself, but I apply it every day. I usually try to figure out a model that will illuminate a particular observation or event that I think is important. To pick an example out of the hat, economic development at some point involves a large outflow of people from the traditional agricultural sector into the cities and into the modern world. That says to me, "How does that take place? Why does it take so long?" And so I've done some work on models in the migration process.[2]

I want to get the right answer in my work; it's not a question of creating beauty. I want to make as clear as I can what the structure of the model is; I don't want anything mysterious. One of my friends who was talking about somebody's work said, "If I wrote a book and five years later people were still arguing about what it meant, I'd be ashamed." I agree [*laughs*].

What makes a good empirical paper? Can you give an example?

Milton Friedman's *Theory of the Consumption Function* [*goes to his bookshelf to show the book to me*].[3] I've still got the library copy. Cheapskate! [*Laughs*] That was an incredible book. It's a model of how to do empirical work bringing evidence from very different sources to bear on the same question. He examined time series on consumption behavior and cross-sectional data for different families ... anything he could find. What a powerful way of looking at the world.

When you hit a brick wall on a project, do you continue to work on the problem or do you take a break and work on something else?

I just stop and do something else. Sometimes you wait around for new mathematical tools, and when they come along, they give you a new life to something that you thought about but couldn't quite articulate. But there are plenty of problems that you just don't know how to solve. In my case, it's this business of price stickiness. When we have a monetary contraction of some kind, it plays out as spending reductions and then decreased production and unemployment. The clearest theory we have says that it should play out only as changes in prices or a change in the unit of account. It's true that sometimes it does happen that way. For example, when the euro was introduced, it didn't have any effect on spending in France or Germany; they just figured out the correspondence of how many francs or deutschmarks equaled a euro, and took it from there. But that does not happen in short-term movements within an economy ... something else does. What is that something else? What governs it? That's an unsolved problem. I've worked on it off and on for my whole life and never got the right answer [*laughs*].

What has been the biggest change during your career in how researchers in your fields conduct research?

I'm a very self-centered person, so I don't care about changes in other people's research, unless it helps me do something that I want to do, which of course happens all the time. The work that I do now in economics is influenced by, for example, game theory and time series analysis, which are areas that I didn't know about when I started my career.

THE WRITING PROCESS

You have a reputation within the economics profession for being a beautiful writer. When I interviewed Tom Sargent for this book, he told me that he didn't know whether you worked at it or whether it just comes easily. Can you shed some light on this?

I have been grammatically pretty close to a flawless writer since the 8th grade. Stylistically, I have had to work at it; trying to avoid falling into clichés and jargon that doesn't tell you anything that you didn't already know, and using words that I don't understand. But as I get older, mathematics is more important to me and I trust it more and more. I want to write down a mathematical model that will take me into new territories. If I cheat on the math and get too sloppy, I am already telling it where I want it to take me. By beating it into compliance, I haven't learned anything. And so I like keeping the mathematics tight and explicit. Those rules help me to become a better writer and thinker. I trust them more than anything else.

Have you learned about the art of writing from anybody else?

I wrote a paper called 'Expectations in the Neutrality of Money', which has influenced many people, when I was at Carnegie.[4] When I had it worked out, I was trying lots of different introductions, none of which seemed to click. And then Jimmy Savage, the well-known mathematical statistician, came to give a lecture that I went to. Savage was almost blind – he could barely see the blackboard – but he gave a clear description of the problem he was going to look at; nothing grand at all. It felt like he was just saying, "If this problem interests you, stick around. If it doesn't, go away." I went home after the talk and tried to write my introduction to the paper in the way Savage had given his lecture. It certainly worked for me. What an inspiration that was.

One of my tricks in writing the introduction is for the first two words to be "This paper ... " Not to start out by saying something like, "The 1990s have witnessed ... " Get that "have witnessed" crap out of here [*laughs*]. I also remember Sandy Grossman giving a talk when he was a kid. Sandy's a super-ambitious guy and so he had something grand in mind, but he began simply by saying, "I'm going to talk about the following mathematical structure ... " He set it out in five minutes and then gave us some examples of good economic questions that this structure might help us think about. I thought that was really beautiful: you must help people get into your logic.

What do you think of the standard of writing in economics?

It's not so good. Economics isn't that much fun to read anyway, but the refereeing process these days makes many papers mostly unreadable. They are becoming longer and longer because you have to spend so much time relating what you've done to the research of others and why yours is better than what somebody else did. Well, maybe it isn't better than what somebody else did. But as long as it's competently done and bears on an interesting question, then the damn thing should be published in six weeks. And everything is co-authored now, which also affects the quality of writing.

How do you divide up the writing tasks when you work with co-authors?

It's a problem. I like writing by myself much better because I can present it as, "Here's the way I think about it," without consulting with anyone else. But sometimes you need help and that means different views have to be honored, and different writing styles have to be reconciled. It has to be that way.

When I was working with Esteban Rossi-Hansberg, whose native language is Spanish, I wrote everything. At some point, I realized it would be good for him to write *something*, even though he didn't want to do it. (Since then, he has become very fluent). And when I was working with Andy Atkeson some years ago, he told me at the beginning that he wanted to be the author of the whole paper because he wanted to shape up his writing and develop his own style. It wasn't the way I would have done it, but I respected his wishes and kept my mouth shut. In my heart, of course, I wanted to do it all.

COLLABORATION

When you work with co-authors, how do you decide whom to work with?

I've worked with so many different co-authors during my career. Lately, it's been with people who have been able to take me into new territory. For example, when I visited the research department at the Minneapolis Fed, Mike Golosov was assigned to be my RA. I got him to work on something, but once I saw how good he was, I realized I could raise the ambition level of the project, and asked him to be a co-author.[5] (My work with Esteban started out in the same way). Now I'm working with Ben Moll, who has just started at Princeton after graduating from here. I had asked him to write a referee report on a paper by some French mathematicians who thought they had some ideas that would be useful in economics. Ben and I agreed, but thought we could get a better economic application by doing the economics our way. We discussed this and began working on it ourselves.[6] Again, I had to look at what he could do before I realized, "Hey, if I work with him, there are some questions we can look at that I wouldn't take on by myself. I'll go for it." Those collaborations are opportunities, and they offset the egotism [*laughs*].

How do you prefer to communicate with your co-authors (e-mail, phone, or face-to-face)?

I like to exchange pieces of paper. I'm not that interested in thinking out loud. I'd rather make my dumbest mistakes in private. Of course, you should do some talking. Ed Prescott and I did some of our best joint work when we both had a few beers [*laughs*]. But I can't deal with Skype. One time, I was working with Fernando Alvarez, whose office is next door to mine, and Francisco Buera, who was at Princeton at that point. Fernando's screen was connected up to Princeton but we had to go into my office because there was something on my computer that we needed to look at. Fernando picked up the screen and said, "We'll take Paco." He carried this talking head into my office! It was creepy.

What are the main challenges associated with collaborative work and how do you overcome them?

Writing down the math. There's always a lot of hand waving going on, and then at the end of it, you often think, "This thing is just as unclear now as it was 45 minutes ago." And so you go home, do some quiet thinking on your own, and come back later. But you can't write sentences collectively. That's impossible for me.

RESEARCH ASSISTANCE

How do you use research assistants?

I use them very rarely. I'm just a mediocre programmer by the standards of people who are doing numerical work. I love the fact that you can work out the math on your PC, but at some point it does get beyond me. And so I've hired students to help with that.

SEMINAR PARTICIPATION AND NETWORKING

What are the benefits to attending a seminar that is closely related to your work versus one that is not closely related?

As I said earlier, economics is a unified field, which means there are a wide variety of topics that I want to hear about. When I was at Carnegie, there was maybe one good speaker every week. But when I came to Chicago, there were two seminars a day on everything. How many hours of the week are you going to spend listening to other people describing their work? It's forced me to specialize. I spend about three hours of the week attending seminars in both micro and macro that I think I will find interesting. That's enough.

How important is professional networking to success in research?

Research is networking. Getting ideas, developing them, and talking about them. You can't be an economist by being up in the mountains.

COMMUNICATION OF RESEARCH

How do you find the right balance between communicating your research at an early stage versus the close-to-finished stage?

I write 35–40-page papers. I'm not like Darwin who keeps it all hidden until he's got a 400-page book that's air-tight [*laughs*].

What are the unique challenges to giving a seminar and how do you overcome them?

To me, it's just fun; writing something out and then trying to explain it. And the new technology is beautiful for presenting technical work these days.

I also think there is more agreement relative to when I started out on what it means to solve a problem. And there is shared impatience with people who claim they have something they haven't got. The crowd that I hang out with, which is a pretty big section of economics, will smoke you out. You'll pay a heavy price. I feel really cheated when somebody's got you on the hook for a problem that's well stated, but it turns out that he hasn't got anywhere. I'm mad at him!

What has caused this change during your career?

The mathematical end of theoretical and empirical work has become more professionalized, thanks to people like Arrow, Friedman, and Samuelson.

PUBLICATION

How do you decide upon the appropriate journal to send your research to?

When I started out, I tried to get things published in a journal that people might actually read. I was surprised when I once wrote a little paper for the *AER*'s *Papers and Proceedings* because it got a lot of responses.[7] And so I'd then try to get something in there, or the *JPE* or *Econometrica*, if it was technical. But now I mostly don't give a damn if my work ever gets published. The NBER working paper series is a great, unrefereed outlet for people in my field and many others.

Do you have any advice for a young scholar who receives a 'revise and resubmit' request or an outright rejection?

I still recommend that when you get a rejection, you send it off unrevised to another journal. The feedback you get from referee reports is almost always useless. Nancy (Stokey) and I sent a paper to *Econometrica* and we were told that it had some good examples in it, but the general theory was not needed. And so we sent it to the *Journal of Economic Theory*, and we received a response saying that the general theory was very valuable, but the little examples were not needed [*laughs*].

When young people start out, they take each criticism as if it's coming from God, but it's more likely to be someone who just doesn't understand what you're talking about. You get much better feedback from seminars. If some guy in the audience doesn't understand what you're saying or thinks you're wrong, you can have a real conversation with him and argue back and forth. You learn so much from that process. I really like it.

TIME MANAGEMENT

How do you divide up your working day, both in terms of quantity and timing of different kinds of work?

My wife (Nancy Stokey) gets up at 6:00 am and starts working. I do that now, too. But I no longer have the energy to be able to put in ten hours every day.

I bought out a fraction of my time from the university, so I don't go to any faculty meetings and I only teach one course each year. But my teaching is almost the same as research, because it is an advanced course with topics that I don't know anything about. I've got to learn fast to keep ahead of my students [*laughs*].

How do you balance your personal and professional lives?

Nancy and I try not to talk too much with each other about economics. But I pretty much work all the time on some level. I even wake up in the middle of the night thinking about economics. I wouldn't mind finding something else to do besides work, but I don't seem to have that many talents [*laughs*].

REFLECTIONS AND THE FUTURE OF ECONOMICS

What have been the most important findings and contributions in your research fields during your career?

Insofar as possible, incorporating macroeconomic phenomena into the general neo-classical economics framework. Back in the '50s, Robert Solow wrote about growth theory that way. It was the first paper I'd seen that used differential equations in economics.[8] And then people like David Cass, Karl Shell, Buz Brock, Lenny Mirman, Finn Kydland, Ed Prescott, myself, and many others, broadened the scope of Solow-type models by making them stochastic. Kydland and Prescott pushed it to the point of saying that there is nothing but neo-classical economics in macro phenomena, which had a huge influence on all of us.[9] I'd previously thought that the erratic behavior of an economy was due to some kind of monetary glitch, but that just isn't true; many recessions can be explained by a neo-classical model that is modified for shocks. I don't think the Great Depression or the current recession can be accounted for in this way, but Kydland and

Prescott's contribution was a real transformation of macro, and people are now adopting their general framework for work in monetary economics.

Game theory has given us some tools for thinking about economics at a much higher level. For instance, in economic life, reputation is a huge factor: think of retailing. Game theorists have figured out a way to talk about reputation. It's not that it points to directions that nobody had ever thought of before; it's that it gives us an actual framework for thinking about these effects. That's real progress.

Another strand of contributions is in new datasets. When I was writing my thesis, you had to rely on the US Census. But now if you're thinking about individual decision-making, you've got hard data on thousands of people making thousands of different decisions. And you can ask questions that you wouldn't even dream of asking back in the '60s. I'm on the periphery in benefiting from those developments, but in terms of developing the science, it's been important and exciting.

What has been your greatest contribution to economics?

I was certainly involved in making economic dynamics specific enough to focus on a particular phenomenon. You wouldn't want to describe that as my achievement because many people have been involved. For example, Arrow and Debreu took a static model and reinterpreted it as different goods that are available under different contingencies and different dates. Then you can think of a dynamic economy as one with a vast space of goods. That's very powerful. It's almost not a new theory; it's like they're saying, "Look, we've got this theory sitting right here that we always thought of as static. We can just change the names of the variables, and then we've got a theory of events in an economy with time and uncertainty." But it was a hell of an insight! And applied people like me have picked it up and used it in macro.

How would you evaluate the Rational Expectations revolution?

Totally victorious. It was the best way to look at things. No one even argues about it. The game theorists discovered the same ideas without the jargon. If you're writing down a game, each of the players is responding optimally in full knowledge of the strategies adopted by everybody else, and what they're going to do in the future under various contingencies and so on. You can't just play with those expectations; they have to be tied in with rationality.

When I interviewed Robert Barro for this book, he told me that you are one of the few economists who has continued to do serious research throughout his career. What has kept you motivated?

Lack of imagination [*laughs*]. I've been department chairman, but I don't want to be in charge of anybody. It's a pain in the ass. So, what else am I going to do? I love working on hard problems. Maybe, I should do something grand, and people have tried to talk me into it. For example, I wrote a nice general audience piece for the Minneapolis Fed on the Industrial Revolution, but I wouldn't be able to write a 500-page book at that level.[10] I just prefer technical work, and it's fun to be able to still do it. I'm lucky in that regard.

It's nice of Barro to say that about me. I think he's the best critic of the stimulus package because he's brought some real economics to bear on the issue.

What are the biggest challenges facing your research fields?

Adam Smith and David Ricardo worked out a way of thinking about societies that was pretty well finished by, say, 1820. The progressive element in economics since then only relates to the technical machinery that has been developed. There are people who say that the mathematical and computational methods have gone as far as they can, or even too far. I don't believe that for a minute. The possibilities for formulating and estimating economic models are just getting better and better. It makes you say, "Geez, I can apply that to my problem." And then I do it.

In which direction would you like to see macroeconomics research go?

Everyone thinks they know what macroeconomists should be doing, which is annoying, but at least it means people care. Right now, what should macroeconomists do? We ought to know how to prevent financial crashes, and what kind of legislation to write that would make that happen. We ought to know the lender of last resort policies that the Federal Reserve should have and announce in advance. And we ought to know what to do about the 'too big to fail' problem. Those are real problems that we need to be able to solve. There is a lot of intelligent debate taking place, which has always been the case, but less attention was paid to it than should have been because we somehow slipped into thinking that financial crises weren't going to happen anymore.

What are the strengths and weaknesses of your own research?

I'm not a collector, or even a user, of frontier datasets. But I know how to apply mathematical analysis to problems in economics.

Do you have any professional regrets?

I've had a good research career, but it's easy to think of problems I haven't solved that I wish I had. That's true of anybody, isn't it? So, I guess I don't have any regrets. Maybe, I should regret that I missed out on the birth of artificial intelligence. Herb Simon was a hugely stimulating colleague for me when I was at Carnegie, but I never got involved into the research that he and Allan Newell and others were doing. What was the matter with me? [*Laughs*]. Artificial intelligence does not play much of a role in economic theory or applied economics, but it has had a huge impact more generally. By then, though, I guess I was already fully committed to economics.

What are your professional ambitions?

I'm 73 years old; I'm going to hang in as long as I can [*laughs*]. It's easy to kid yourself, but I'm going to give a talk at the Minnesota summer workshop on Wednesday. I've worked hard on some slides and a pretty cool paper, but I'm nervous about it. That's as it should be. I have to be nervous about how my work is going to be received by smart people whose opinion really matters to me.

How would you describe the state of economics today? Are you optimistic about its future?

I'm very much optimistic. What happened in 2008 wasn't a crisis for economics. We're still the only game in town; the only social science that's still standing from the days of Weber, Pareto, Durkheim, and Boas. Why? We're not politicized, we've got some discipline, and we know how to do competent statistical analysis. And above all, we have a theoretical framework that continues to surprise us by its applicability to new problems, problems that were once thought to be beyond economics.

NOTES

1. See, for example, Arrow, K.J. and G. Debreu (1954), 'Existence of an Equilibrium for a Competitive Economy', *Econometrica*, Vol. 22, No. 3 (July), pp. 265–290; McKenzie, L.W. (1959), 'On the Existence of General Equilibrium for A Competitive Market', *Econometrica*, Vol. 27, No. 1 (January), pp. 54–71; McKenzie, L.W. (1954), 'On Equilibrium in Graham's Model of World Trade and Other Competitive Systems', *Econometrica*, Vol. 22, No. 2 (April), pp. 147–161; McKenzie, L.W. (1981), 'The Classical Theorem on the Existence of Competitive Equilibrium', *Econometrica*, Vol. 49, No. 4 (July), pp. 819–841.
2. See, for example, Lucas, Jr, R.E. (2004), 'Life Earnings and Rural–Urban Migration', *Journal of Political Economy*, Vol. 112, S1 (February), pp. S29–S59.
3. Milton Friedman (1957), *A Theory of the Consumption Function*, National Bureau of Economic Research.
4. Lucas, Jr, R.E. (1972), 'Expectations in the Neutrality of Money', *Journal of Economic Theory*, Vol. 4, No. 2 (April), pp. 103–124.
5. Golosov, M. and R.E. Lucas, Jr (2007), 'Menu Costs and Phillips Curves', *Journal of Political Economy*, Vol. 115, No. 2 (February), pp. 171–199.
6. Lucas, Jr, R.E. and B. Moll (2011), 'Knowledge Growth and the Allocation of Time', University of Minnesota Working Paper.
7. Lucas, Jr, R.E. (1970), 'Capacity, Overtime, and Empirical Production Functions', *American Economic Review*, Papers and Proceedings, Vol. 60, No. 2 (May), pp. 23–27.
8. Solow, R.M. (1956), 'A Contribution to the Theory of Economic Growth', *Quarterly Journal of Economics*, Vol. 70, No. 1 (February), pp. 65–94.
9. See, for example, Kydland, F.E. and E.C. Prescott (1977), 'Rules Rather than Discretion: The Inconsistency of Optimal Plans', *Journal of Political Economy*, Vol. 85, No. 3 (June), pp. 473–492; Kydland, F.E. and E.C. Prescott (1982), 'Time to Build and Aggregate Fluctuations', *Econometrica*, Vol. 50, No. 6 (November), pp. 1345–1370.
10. Lucas, Jr, R.E. (2004), 'The Industrial Revolution: Past and Future', Annual Report (May), Federal Reserve Bank of Minneapolis, pp. 5–20.

Charles F. Manski
(Northwestern University)

Charles F. Manski was born in Boston, Massachusetts in 1948 and graduated with both a BS and a PhD in economics from the Massachusetts Institute of Technology in 1970 and 1973 respectively. Professor Manski has taught at Carnegie Mellon University, 1973–1980, the Hebrew University of Jerusalem, 1979–1983, the University of Wisconsin – Madison, 1983–98, and Northwestern University, where he currently serves as the Board of Trustees Professor of Economics.

Professor Manski's primary research interests are econometrics, judgment and decision, and the analysis of social policy. His most-cited articles in chronological order include 'The Estimation of Choice Probabilities from Choice Based Samples', *Econometrica* (1977), co-authored with Steven Lerman, 'The Structure of Random Utility Models', *Theory and Decision* (1977), 'Identification of Endogenous Social Effects: The Reflection Problem', *Review of Economic Studies* (1993), 'Economic Analysis of Social Interactions', *Journal of Economic Perspectives* (2000), and 'Measuring Expectations', *Econometrica* (2004). His books include *College Choice in America*, co-authored with David Wise (Harvard University Press, 1983), *Analog Estimation Methods in Econometrics* (Chapman and Hall, 1988), *Identification Problems in the Social Sciences* (Harvard

University Press, 1995), *Partial Identification of Probability Distributions* (Springer-Verlag, 2003), *Social Choice with Partial Knowledge of Treatment Response* (Princeton University Press), and *Identification for Prediction and Decision* (Harvard University Press, 2007).

Professor Manski was elected as a Fellow of the Econometric Society in 1984, a Fellow of the American Academy of Arts and Sciences in 1994, and a Member of the National Academy of Sciences in 2009.

I interviewed Charles Manski in his office in the Department of Economics of Arts and Sciences at New York University, where he was a visitor. It was late-afternoon of Tuesday, 14 September 2010.

BACKGROUND INFORMATION

What was your attraction to economics?

I was always interested in how people make decisions. I started out in physics, but that was not intuitive to me, so I switched over to economics.

As a student, which professors were most influential or inspirational?

As a first-year graduate student, I was very lucky that Dan McFadden visited MIT. I was trying to analyze the problem of how people choose where to go to college, using neo-classical consumer theory. But that didn't make any sense since it is oriented towards modeling how many units of something you will buy. When McFadden came through, he was starting his work on discrete choice analysis, and I saw immediately that that's exactly what I needed.

Why did you decide to pursue an academic career?

The only other thing I ever seriously considered was being a professional pilot. I love flying, and I've flown privately, but my eyes weren't good enough to fly professionally. And I did think about going to law school rather than doing a PhD in economics, and I would probably have wound up as a law professor, rather than a practicing lawyer. I guess I always wanted to do research ... other than being a pilot [*laughs*].

As a researcher, which colleagues have been most influential or inspirational?

Dan McFadden. Throughout the '70s, he was incredibly helpful. Our relationship has changed over the years, of course, but we're still close friends.

I arrived at Carnegie Mellon in the fall of 1973. I was an assistant professor in the School of Urban and Public Affairs, where two people were very helpful. One was an urban historian named Joel Tarr. I had to co-teach with him a course on American communities. I knew nothing about the subject, but Joel helped me see beyond economics and the value of quantitative work. He was a good friend and mentor.

Al Blumstein was also in the school. Back in the '70s, he headed the first National Research Council committee that studied the deterrent effect of various punishment. He introduced me to how research affects public policy, so that was helpful.

I moved to Wisconsin in the early '80s. Art Goldberger became a very close friend. I was a full professor by that time, but he spent three or four years reading my papers line by line and making edits the way that an advisor would for a PhD student. He eventually stopped doing that, but I could talk to him about anything. He was just a very wise person, and I miss him quite a bit.

GENERAL THOUGHTS ON RESEARCH

What is the value of pure versus applied research in economics?

I don't like the conventional distinction between pure and applied research. I think they should go together. I have a fairly practical orientation, and I don't see much value in pure research for the sake of it. If that's all there is to it, then economics departments should be financed by universities in the same way as esoteric art history departments. But economics departments are pretty central to most modern universities, and the reason is because they should try to say something about the real world.

Theory should be useful in doing applied work. I've always gone back and forth between econometric theory and applications in my own research, and that's what I like best. But there is an increasing problem in economics of bifurcation between theory and application. There are economists who focus on theory for the sake of it, and would consider their work to be lacking depth if they were able to find an application. That's something you find among pure mathematicians as well.

On the other hand, some economists appear to think that you can do applications without knowing very much theory. The ones that are most troubling to me are the labor economists and public economists at MIT, Harvard, and Princeton, where the paradigm of randomized experimentation has taken hold.

How would you describe the connection between pure and applied work at Northwestern?

I finished being department chair two weeks ago, so I'm freer to talk about this now. What's problematic at Northwestern is that I have colleagues in economic theory, whom I very much respect, but whose work has almost no connection with any application.

How would you describe the dialogue between theory and empirics in economics?

I can describe how it should be. Dan McFadden has always been a great exemplar in this respect. He started his work on discrete choice analysis with basic principles of economics, such as revealed preference, and went very coherently from the theory to the econometric application. Many people would call him an econometric theorist, but he would often say that he was an applied economist, since the theory fed directly into the application, without any leap of faith.

How would you characterize your own research agenda and how has it changed through time?

I've always been motivated by public policy problems. As I mentioned before, my PhD dissertation focused on modeling college choice. That had a very specific application: the federal government of the United States had recently instituted a new scholarship program for undergraduates, and the question was how this would impact enrollments, particularly of lower-income students. To answer that question, I needed to know the kinds of data and theorizing about decision making that might be helpful. And so, early on in my career, methodological issues led me into doing econometric theory. I got some pleasure out of the theory per se, but I always wanted it to be useful for empirical work. That's still true today.

Do you think it is important to have broad research interests?

I think so. I'm constantly bouncing back and forth between specific technical questions and very applied issues. And I'm trying to see things from different perspectives. For example, I've published in sociology and statistical journals, and I've always found it helpful to read psychology. But there is a contrary view that people need to specialize, and I have friends with whom I've disagreed on this very issue. In the end, I've decided that not everyone works the same way as a researcher, and that there isn't just one path to the truth.

Do you think there is any difference in the types of work done by researchers at different stages of their careers based on tenure concerns, publication requirements or other pressures? Should there be a difference?

As I've gotten older, this has increasingly become a sore point with me. Without going into the details, I think I can fairly say that I took lots of risks early on in my own work. One reason is that I've always wanted to be able to look back and be proud of what I did for myself. But in recent years, I have had repeated conversations with assistant professors who tell me, "I would really like to work on this project, but it's too risky. I'm going to wait until after I get tenure because, in the meantime, I must get my papers published in the top five journals." It's true that the major purpose of tenure is to have a license to think broadly. But what I worry about considerably is that when you are risk averse for 12 years – five years at graduate school plus seven years as an assistant professor – it becomes so ingrained that you lose your ability to be creative. I agree that there has to be compromise to some extent, but I think the balance has moved too far towards conservatism for too many young researchers.

IDEA GENERATION

Where do you get your research ideas?

It's a curious process. But there was an extraordinary turning point that I can pinpoint from 1987. Irv Piliavin, a friend from social work at Wisconsin, came to me with a very specific applied problem. He was conducting a longitudinal study of homelessness in the city of Minneapolis, and there was attrition in the sample; he was interviewing people in the winter, but was then unable to find them again in the summer. He knew he had this missing data problem and wanted to know if I had any thoughts on how to handle it. One traditional approach is to assume that the data are missing at random, which solves the identification problem. The other way is to have some kind of a selection model, which is based on very strong assumptions. He said, "I just don't like either of those approaches. I won't believe my empirical conclusions. Is there anything else I can do?" I had known about these missing data problems for many, many years, but I hadn't thought about them seriously in terms of my own work. I told him I'd look at it, and he got me some summer salary from the Poverty Institute of Wisconsin.

At first, I found myself trying to see whether I could build on the literature. But I decided that wouldn't be fruitful, and figured that I needed to go back to first principles. That meant asking, "What if I made no assumptions at all about this missing data process?" And so I wrote down the simplest formulation, which is just the Law of Total Probability (dividing people up into those you can observe and into those you can't). Then I realized that although I couldn't pinpoint the things Irv was trying to learn, I could get a bound on them, and that the width of the bound would depend on how much missing data there was. I saw that there was a very general principle behind the process. It wasn't a case of saying, "What assumptions do I need to get a point estimate?" but, rather, saying from the beginning, "What can I learn from the data?" It may not be enough to get a point estimate, but you can still learn something. And that's what led to my last 20 years of work on what is known as partial identification. I've applied the technique to an enormous variety of problems, including analysis of treatment response and evaluation of public policy programs.

Initially, people hated it. Some very famous economists would tell me, "You can't give bounds. We must have point estimates." When I would ask them why, they would say, "That's just the way it is." But this is where Goldberger, in particular, was very supportive. He encouraged me to keep working on it even though at first it was considered wacky. I'm very happy that he did, because it's grown into what I clearly view as my most important work. And it's a great example of where research came from a very practical question.

At what point does an idea become a project that you devote resources to?

It took me a year to decide to devote a lot of resources to the project that I've just described. And that was for a very curious reason: my early results were ridiculously simple in mathematical terms. I could explain them to a fifth grader. And so initially, I thought, "Gee, I can't write this up as a paper. It's too simple, and people value technical cranking." I had to keep asking myself, "Well, if it's so simple, how come it was missed? Or maybe a thousand people have had this idea and thought that it was not important?" Each morning, I had to persuade myself that just because a simple thing is not in the literature doesn't mean that it's a stupid idea. And once it was published, and people didn't like it, I then had to just keep at it.

In the first ten years that I worked in the area – throughout the '90s – I had the whole field to myself and was able to do an incredible amount of work. It was only in the early 2000s that the broader profession began to catch on and make major contributions. In fact, somebody introduced me recently as, "originally a conventional econometrician, but then an iconoclast." I had to look up the exact definition of iconoclast to see whether I liked it or not, but it was okay [*laughs*].

IDEA EXECUTION

What makes a good theoretical paper? Can you give an example?

Dan McFadden's paper on conditional logit analysis of qualitative choice behavior, for which he won the Nobel Prize, has always been an exemplary theoretical paper.[1] He began with a very broad econometric theory question of how you make inference on decisions from observing choice behavior, but he wanted to have a practical outcome, so he added layers and layers of assumptions to make it tractable for estimation.

In terms of economic theory, a paper written around the same time was Mirrlees' Nobel Prize-winning work on optimal income taxation.[2] Clearly, that's a theoretical paper, but it also has a real problem behind it: the design of income tax schedules. Looking back, there are various things that could be done differently – and it's a difficult paper to read – but he set it out in a very coherent way with great abstractions. A so-called pure theorist would look at Mirrlees' paper and say that it was extraordinarily important to economic theory because, even if they didn't care about tax policy, it represented one of the important beginnings of the mechanism design literature. However, it wasn't something that was just going to stand there as an artistic exercise for theorists. In fact, the IFS in London, where my good friend Richard Blundell is involved, set up a Mirrlees Commission recently. And so 40 years later in the UK, you can see some level of influence of Mirrlees' early work on the formation of tax policy. That's the way it should be.

What makes a good empirical paper? Can you give an example?

It's not as easy to pin down what makes a good empirical contribution. When you see a totally coherent piece of theoretical work, you can say that it is beautiful and elegant. But in empirical research, there are thousands of compromises that you have to make, and it's easy to beat it up on lots of details, and then it's a question of how much common sense there is in the way you do it. Empirical work also tends to accumulate bit by bit, which means it's tougher to identify papers that just lay things open.

But if I had to recommend an empirical paper, it would be one by Adeline Delavande, a former PhD student at Northwestern who, two years ago, published her dissertation work on women's contraceptive behavior. The paper was called, 'Pill, Patch or Shot?' and it's in the *International Economic Review*.[3] Adeline was doing discrete choice analysis of the McFadden type, but this was decision-making under uncertainty. She went out and collected her own data from women around the Chicago area, eliciting, in particular, their expectations about the chances of becoming pregnant if they were to use different forms of contraception. She then inputted that into a discrete choice model and did a beautiful job. This is a paper that you've got to read page by page. There was not just extraordinary care in the analysis, but also extraordinary creativity in being willing to go out and interview people and collect the data, which is something that economists rarely do. It was very risky for a PhD student to do this kind of work as well, so I've always appreciated that aspect of her. When people ask me, "What's the value of collecting expectations data?" or "How would we use expectations data in econometric analysis?" I just say, "Read Adeline's paper. It's a model."

When you hit a brick wall on a project, do you continue to work on the problem or do you take a break and work on something else?

If we knew where research was going, then there wouldn't be anything new to do [*laughs*]. It's about introspection. Sometimes when you hit a brick wall, you've just got to keep pushing because you know it's in there somewhere, and you'll break through. Other times, you decide that it's not going anywhere, and you put it aside.

I've had some papers that I went back to ten years after I'd hit a brick wall and all of a sudden I've had a flash of inspiration. For example, I published a paper in the *Journal of the American Statistical Association* in 1990 on the analysis of intentions data.[4] There had been a long-standing practice of asking people things like, "Do you expect to buy an automobile? Whom do you expect to vote for?" It had always bothered me that you shouldn't be able to give "yes" or "no" answers to these sorts of questions. A forecast is being made and there is uncertainty. The paper that I wrote led me to think that we needed to be eliciting subjective probabilistic responses to the questions. But Dan Nagin and I actually began this work at Carnegie Mellon in the late '70s and then it just stopped. I didn't think about it for a long time, and somehow around 1988, it got back in my head and I started working on it again.

Another example relates to the first paper that I had published back in 1975.[5] It was on maximum score estimation, which was part of my dissertation, and represented a move away from standard parametric modeling, as I was trying to weaken the assumptions of McFadden's conditional logit model. It was a good paper, but I didn't do any further work for some time. And then in 1983 – I can date it exactly – I went back to it because a new piece of research came along. Jim Powell had just done a dissertation on what he called 'censored least absolute deviations estimation'. It was about estimating median regressions rather than mean regressions when you have missing data. I read his work and I remembered that one aspect of my first paper had to do with making median assumptions. I thought, "Hey, there's some connection here," and so I went back to my earlier research. By this point, I knew a lot more mathematics and statistics than at the beginning of my career, and in 1985 I was able to publish a sequel to the original 1975 paper. I titled it, 'Semiparametric Analysis of Discrete Response', and that paper became fairly important in what was then becoming a whole new literature on semiparametric econometric analysis.[6]

What has been the biggest change during your career in how researchers in your fields conduct research?

I think the level of mathematics, and its premium, have gone way up. In the early '70s when I was in graduate school, doing econometrics meant cranking lots of extraordinarily boring linear algebra. And our formal statistical training was very weak. But you could be a great theorist with simple math, like Robert Solow who made enormous contributions. It's true that you need more math to do modern work. In fact, during the mid-'70s, I went on leave to Berkeley and decided that I needed to tool up. Luckily, I didn't have to take exams, but I sat through the first-year PhD courses in the math department in measure theory, functional analysis, and topology, which is very rough. And nowadays, we seem to screen our admissions to

PhD students primarily on math, and accept lots of students who have never had an economics course. That can be very negative because the technique of math gets valued per se, and the economics gets lost.

Sometimes, I call myself a conceptual econometrician rather than a technical one. I've done a great deal of technical work, but I value simple insight, which is not always true for the rest of the profession. I've had a few PhD students whom I thought had extraordinarily good insights in their theses, but they told me, "I can't go on the job market with this paper – it's too simple. I'm not going to be able to show off how much math I know." They had worked on a totally obscure problem and figured out a simple way to view it. I know an econometric theorist who didn't get a job at certain places because they said her paper was too simple. And I know someone else who had two papers, one of which was a conceptual econometric paper that I liked, and the other being a technical paper that I thought was boring. He was advised to go on the market with the technical paper because that's how he was going to get a job.

This issue of the role of math feeds back into the growing estrangement of theory and empirical work. Learning all that math is an enormous investment, and some people are good at it or are willing to make that investment. And there are other economists who find they can go another route by, say, doing randomized experiments where you basically don't need to know any math at all, or even any economics. They put all of their energy, and I say this in a positive way, into trying to be very careful about data collection. And so we now have a situation where we have people who specialize in the math, but don't have the foggiest idea about data collection, and others who are very good at data analysis, but can't read an applied theory paper, never mind a straight theory one, because their math isn't up to it. It's very dangerous for the profession that we have these two groups of people who can't talk with each other.

THE WRITING PROCESS

Which aspect of the writing process do you find most difficult?

Coming up with the title and then writing the introduction [*laughs*]. I can spend a couple of weeks on those things because it's forming your whole orientation towards the work. As well as being absolutely critical, it's also very painful, and one part of the writing process that has probably been difficult for hundreds of years. But the rest of the process has changed extraordinarily because of word processing. I typed my thesis by hand, which meant that you had to keep an enormous amount in your head, write it down in long hand, and then at the very end, put it on the typewriter. Thankfully, that became a lost art when word processors were introduced. Now, I compose my work on the screen in front of me, and I can end up with 500 versions of a paper, because I'm constantly iterating it and molding it. I think it's changed the way that most people work, and it should make the quality of writing higher than in the past. I try to put a lot of care into my writing, both in terms of general organization and line-by-line specific choice of words.

What steps have you taken during your career to improve the quality of your writing?

I am embarrassed by a couple of my early papers. It was the classic graduate student/assistant professor problem of wanting to show how abstract and formal you can be, and making the paper much denser than it needs to be. My writing became far better in the late '80s when I was Director of the Institute for Research on Poverty at Wisconsin, and talking to sociologists, political scientists, and historians. And I was going to Washington and talking with people in the government, occasionally even those in Congress, and I had to learn how to write verbally, which I find much harder than writing mathematically. I also had two editors who went through my work, and I learned from them and became a much better writer. Of course, it was also partly due to maturity, since your ability to do math gets lower with age, but your ability to write coherently should improve with age.

COLLABORATION

When you work with co-authors, how do you decide whom to work with?

The most important thing is you've got to find someone who, temperamentally, you can deal with. I've been fortunate. I don't think I've ever had a case where I really regretted working with someone, although that's not to say that it's always been easy.

Just as an aside, last week, I received some silly questionnaire that someone wanted me to fill out on how you do research. I was bored. I was sitting in the hotel here in New York, so I took 15 minutes and did it. It turned out it came from lab scientists for the National Institutes of Health, where everything is very hierarchal. There's someone who brings in the funding, another person who sets up the experiment, and then someone else who does the data analysis. But that's not how it works in economics. Every collaboration is distinct.

How do you prefer to interact with your co-authors (e-mail, phone, or face-to-face)?

I don't work well face-to-face. I've got to be able to think for, say, an hour, go for a walk, and then come back to it. I don't like the idea of a forced, very intensive situation.

A very important thing is who's going to do the drafting. Usually, I think that I'm a better writer than my co-authors – or maybe it's just that I'm territorial – and so I prefer to do the first draft. On the other hand, there are people whom I trust and they can do the first draft and I can then edit. But there has to be enough shared commonality on that issue, because the first draft is an enormous amount of work and someone can get possessive about it. You can't go in afterwards and say, "Nah, I think we've got to dump this whole thing and start all over again." You have to learn how to work with each other.

RESEARCH ASSISTANCE AND FUNDING

How do you use undergraduate and graduate research assistants?

I never use undergraduates. They would be useless. Often, you need a research assistant to do computational work that you used to be able to do or don't want to do. It could also be something technical. You get better at defining what's an interesting problem, but worse at cranking out proofs. And so you can have a symbiotic relationship with research assistants because they need to know how to do computations and technical work. Of course, you're also paying them.

The most rewarding experiences are when the research assistant puts enough into it such that you say at some point, "Look, you really should be a co-author." Then you become more collegial, and they make their own contributions.

How important is funding for getting your work done?

I don't tend to do work that needs lots of funding. For the small amounts that I need, I'm fortunate that I have an endowed chair and receive a certain amount of money per year, plus NSF or NIH grants that'll pay for the RA's salary. In the cases where funding has mattered, for example, when I've done original data collection on surveys for my measurement of expectations work, it's still been fairly small-scale. I have made a conscious decision to stay away from large-scale empirical projects, because the effort involved in managing them is enormous.

Do you have any advice for a young scholar on the funding process?

The people who need large amounts of money these days are development economists. I've seen this as a department chair. They are doing large field experiments, which is the new wave in that research area, and they spend time overseas in Africa or South Asia. This means that when you make them an offer as an assistant professor, you have to provide packages for them. It's very similar to putting together a lab for a biological scientist. But theorists just need a computer and a pencil!

SEMINAR PARTICIPATION AND NETWORKING

What are the benefits to attending a seminar that is closely related to your work versus one that is not closely related?

You have to go to the ones that are closely related to your work, whether you like it or not. You can pick and choose the ones outside your field, based on whether you think it'll be interesting. Sometimes you'll learn something, and sometimes you won't.

How important is professional networking to success in research?

It's extremely important. Going to the large meetings, like the American Economic Association meeting or the Econometric Society World Congress, is a waste of time. You might network in the sense of meeting people in the hallway and having random conversations, but that's usually not very fruitful. What you need to do is give talks elsewhere, have one-on-one meetings, attend small conferences, and make short visits. I'm sitting here at NYU for a week and, similarly, people come through Northwestern all the time.

Pragmatically, assistant professors have to get their work known. This is part of the system that's essential. I can name cases of assistant professors in my department where, when they've come for midterm review after three years, we've had to say, "It looks like you're doing good work, but you really should go out and talk to more people, because you need to become better known. And maybe you'll get some ideas." We're also social beings. Why write anything up if not to communicate?

To what extent is the absence of departmental colleagues working in one's research area a major disadvantage?

For a senior person, it's not a big deal, because by that time your networks are established worldwide. I go to UCL every March and some of the people who are closest to me are there, like Richard Blundell and Andrew Chesher. If you're junior, and you don't have people in your own field, it's very hard. And when you come up for tenure, who's going to champion you? I have a former student who, until a few months ago, was here at NYU. He was doing very well, but NYU does not have a senior econometrician, and he just decided to move to Cornell with tenure, although NYU was ranked more highly than Cornell among economics departments. For him and what his interests are, it's a good move.

COMMUNICATION OF RESEARCH

How do you find the right balance between communicating your research at an early stage versus the close-to-finished stage?

There's always a trade-off. I may tend to err on the side of communicating a little too early. The reason is you may get excited and want the feedback when it's going to be useful to you.

Some people are very closed. They worry about competition. But as I said earlier, I've been fortunate, because I've usually worked on things that nobody else is doing. And so I'm maybe not as neurotic about people stealing my ideas.

What are the unique challenges to giving a seminar and how do you overcome them?

It's crazy to think that you're going to do proofs in a seminar. No matter how smart you are, it's just impossible to assimilate a hard piece of work in 90 minutes. You've got to get across the main themes and then start working through the details to the extent that's appropriate. A classic problem with seminars is people feeling like they've got to go through *all* the details. I can read the paper for those. And so the hardest part is how to get some intuition for the result without having to go through the paper line by line. You may have been working on this research for months, but even if someone is in your own research area, you can't expect they can come in cold and get to the same point where you are.

I think I do okay at giving seminars. That's also something that gets better with experience.

PUBLICATION

How do you decide upon the appropriate journal to send your research to?

It's a complicated calculus of trying to forecast, substantively, what is the best place and then figuring out who is the editor and whether you are going to get fair referees. It's a horrible process, and it doesn't matter how senior you are. You get really stupid rejection letters, and you must have very thick skin.

I've never had a paper in the *American Economic Review*. I've had ten papers rejected there. I've never had a paper in the *Journal of Political Economy*. And I wouldn't even think of sending a paper to the *Quarterly Journal of Economics*, given their tastes. And so I've got lots of *Econometrica*s and a bunch of ReStuds, but nothing in the generalist journals. They could be right, but maybe it's their loss.

How would you best describe your approach to dealing with a 'revise and resubmit' request from a journal? How about an outright rejection?

What's the difference between a 'revise and resubmit' and a rejection? Almost nothing is accepted in the first round. Sometimes you shrug and say, "It's a judgment call," but other times, you'll say, "These guys are such idiots." And there have been a few occasions when I've protested over the years. Usually, it's just to blow off steam, but I was successful a couple of times.

I once sent a paper to the *Journal of the American Statistical Association* that was then rejected. Initially, I thought that was a mistake, but I received a critical referee report that pointed out something that I had missed. I never learned who the referee was, but I was very thankful, because once I realized he or she was right, I spent a lot more time reworking it with my co-author. We sent it to *Econometrica*, where it was accepted, so that was a very good outcome in the end.

Do you think that the current structure of the publication process in economics facilitates or impedes scientific understanding and knowledge production?

I would say it's impeding those things, except I don't know how to improve it. It tends towards conservatism. Now that everything is electronic, I'd rather see more research coming out than less. Let it see the light of day, and let the research community decide whether it's worth something, rather than suppressing it through the refereeing process.

I write books, which is fairly unusual for an economist, and one good reason for doing that is to avoid referees. I find it an extraordinarily liberating experience. In terms of the generation of ideas, you don't really know where the research is going to take you when you embark on a book, because it's a several-year project rather than a delineated few months. I think the piece of work that I value most in my whole career is the short 1995 book, *Identification Problems in the Social Sciences*, which brought to a head my ideas on partial identification and allowed me to develop them further and get the big themes across. Then I iterated on that in my 2007 book, *Identification for Prediction and Decision*, which was a graduate textbook. It's much more than just a second edition, and the point is I could express myself in it. Senior people should write books more often.

What has been your best and worst experience during the publication process?

Actually, they go together [*laughs*]. I wrote a paper in the early '90s that was originally titled, 'Simultaneity with Downward-sloping Demand'. It related to the classical simultaneous equations in econometrics where you're trying to separate supply and demand with linear model assumptions. That's wonderful work from the '40s and '50s, but I wanted to disentangle it, and so I asked the question, "What can you learn from the assumption that the demand function is downward-sloping without any other assumptions?" It was a beautifully simple paper that I sent to *Econometrica*. David Card was the editor at the time, and he made an absolutely atrocious decision. He said that I should forget all this non-parametric work and instead do linear modeling. He is a complicated guy and he's gone to different extremes at different stages of his career. This was a time when he was totally against structural econometrics, because he had this Princeton background that I alluded to earlier. When he rejected the paper, I was so angry with him. Within a day, I faxed him a very, very nasty response. I had to get it off my chest, even though nothing happened. If David Card were to walk in here today, I would tell him he made a horrible mistake in rejecting that paper.

I sat on it for about two years and got a whole bunch of new results, so that it wasn't the same paper anymore. And then I resubmitted it to *Econometrica*, which, by that time, had a new co-editor, Peter Robinson, the British econometrician. The paper had a new title, 'Monotone Treatment Response', and I told Peter that David Card had rejected a much earlier version, but that this was an entirely new version. I didn't want him to think that I was getting two shots. To his great credit, Peter sent it out to new referees, and the paper was accepted very easily. My good friend, Andrew Chesher, later told me that he was one of the referees, but we didn't know each other at the time. To this day, I still think it's one of the best papers that I've ever written.[7]

TIME MANAGEMENT

How do you divide up your working day, both in terms of quantity and timing of different kinds of work?

I tend to work at home as much as I can, at least in the morning, and then I'll go into the office in the afternoon and deal with the social aspects of seminars and talking with people. I have a wonderful study at home that looks over Lake Michigan, and we also have a second house, a farm in western Wisconsin, where there is nothing in my way when I need big blocks of time. There are too many distractions in the office.

How do you balance multiple research projects?

That's something that comes with experience. A PhD student writing a dissertation is totally single-minded on writing that one piece of work and can't do multiple things. But over time, you learn to go back and forth. And when you hit these brick walls that you talked about before, it helps to have multiple projects.

On the other hand, there are periods when you just need to focus on one thing and have absolutely nothing else intervene. My wife won't like this, but she went off on a cruise with her mother to the Greek Islands a year ago, and I had an idea. I just sat at home and worked flat out for two weeks. I had nothing else on my mind for 24 hours a day.

What was the idea?

It's a piece of public economic theory that is published in a new journal called *Quantitative Economics*. The title of the paper is rather curious: 'When Consensus Choice Dominates Individualism: Jensen's Inequality and Collective Decisions under Uncertainty.'[8] The idea came about as I was thinking about an entirely different area and realized there was a mathematical commonality between the two topics. And I was able to show that, under certain circumstances, a collective decision on provision of private goods Pareto-dominates standard individualistic private decision-making. If I had sent it to the *Journal of Economic Theory*, they would have laughed at it, because it's too simple. But I'm very proud of the paper.

As I say, I got the idea when I was thinking about an entirely different area, which was the old issue in econometrics of aggregating forecasts. James Surowiecki, the *New Yorker* columnist, wrote a book in 2004 called *The Wisdom of Crowds*. He describes walking through some street in Manhattan where people are counting jellybeans. You average their forecast for the jellybeans and they do better than the individual forecast. That turns out to be Jensen's inequality, but the concept dates back to Francis Galton's work in *Nature* back in 1907.[9] The damn thing is just algebra! There's no magic to it at all. I won't take the time now to explain it – you can read the article that came from a beautiful research experience.

How do you balance your research and non-research activities?

Being department chair was particularly hard. I had to be very disciplined, because I knew there were times of the year, particularly in the winter quarter and early spring, when I just could not get anything serious done. And so in the late spring and during the summer, I became extraordinarily jealous of my research time, and that's when I got work done. Looking back over the last three years, I was able to be more productive than I expected, but you still pay a price, because it's a rough job with not much personal reward. I'm glad it's over.

How do you balance your personal and professional lives?

The distinction between 'professional' and 'personal' is not clear for a researcher, because we're basically working all the time. And what's work? To me, grading exams is work. I don't find any pleasure in it at all. And some other administrative aspects are work. But doing research is not work.

Non-academics don't understand this, because they have this 9 to 5 mentality in which you go home and leave your work behind. I am working all the time, but it's not work in the sense that I enjoy it.

REFLECTIONS AND THE FUTURE OF ECONOMICS

What have been the most important findings and contributions in your research fields during your career?

Going back from the beginning, Dan McFadden's extraordinary work on discrete choice analysis was path-breaking, and influenced very heavily the first 10 or 15 years of my career. And so too did the development of nonparametric work in the early '80s, which contained some very simple conceptual ideas that were formalized by statistical theorists. In terms of my own work, it's clear that the research on partial identification is the largest, longest-lasting contribution that I've made.

It's also very easy to forget, because it's not valued sufficiently in the profession, that empirical work requires data. And so the development of large micro datasets has been very important. This began in the late '60s in the United States with the *Panel Study of Income Dynamics* and the *National Longitudinal Survey of Labor Markets*, and has then moved on to the *Health and Retirement Study*. I think a Nobel Prize should have been given to the originators of some of those early datasets.

What are the biggest challenges facing your research fields?

The biggest challenge is to do useful work. Methodological developments should be things that contribute to solving real economic problems, whether they relate to understanding the way the economy works or forming public policy. I'm not looking for some great theoretical breakthrough at this point. It's not like a physicist saying we have to understand the theory of everything, or like a biologist in the '40s and '50s being oriented towards figuring out the genetic code. I don't see anything similar in economics right now, but maybe that's just my lack of imagination.

What are the strengths and weaknesses of your own research?

I'm very hard on myself, and that may be a weakness. I have a reputation as someone who is fairly conservative in drawing conclusions, and so someone who doesn't like my work would call me nihilistic. I don't think that's entirely fair, but it's true that I tend not to stick my neck out and say, "This is the answer." Tomorrow, I have to give a seminar here, which is going to be about those in policy analysis who act as if they know things. I'm constantly saying that we don't.

For example, the deterrent effect of various punishment, particularly the death penalty, is a classic problem. It's critical to forming criminal justice policy, but it's also very hard to study. Back in the early '70s, Isaac Ehrlich stuck his neck out and said in the *American Economic Review* that one execution deters eight murders, which was later cited by the US Supreme Court.[10] Al Blumstein, from the National Research Council, was called in as an adjudicator. I wasn't on the committee, but I went to some of their conferences and had some marginal participation. The NRC concluded that you can't learn anything credible about the deterrent effect of capital punishment. That was an extraordinary statement, and the research area got closed off for the next 20 years. But in the last ten years, there has been a whole spat of new work on the deterrent effect of capital punishment, which has led to the creation of the NRC's Committee on Deterrence and the Death Penalty. I'm on the committee so I have to keep an open mind as to what we'll conclude about the new research. But if you have something as value laden as capital punishment, there's an issue of what the standard of proof should be. That's a very, very hard question.

As another example, Jim Heckman and I have enormously different views on sticking your neck out. He got a Nobel Prize for his work on parametric selection modeling, but I don't believe any of his assumptions. And now his fragile research on early childhood cognitive development is getting a lot of attention because he's pushing it so hard. Steve Levitt does this with his work too. Those guys really hate each other, but they actually share a lot in common.

In the end, do you think the profession has helped to bring out and shape your research for the best?

No. The prevalent view in my mind is I've been against the so-called mainstream in the profession and it's often taken a long time for people to see the value of my work. I feel like I'm respected, but it's begrudged. Some economists do something hot early in their careers and they're immediately rewarded by the profession. That's not the way my career path has gone.

Do you have any professional regrets?

Only one. I finished my PhD in three years, and I hated graduate school. We were spoon fed, told what's the orthodoxy, and I just wanted to get out of there. And so I went on the market much too early, and as a result, had a lot of trouble getting a first job. Twenty-four years old was ridiculously young, and I was too naïve to realize that people wouldn't understand my work on discrete choice analysis. McFadden hadn't even published his first paper on that topic yet! I think if I had waited around another year, I would have got a much better job placement. On the other hand, where I did get a place was a very creative environment and so maybe I was better off being there than a mainstream department.

What are your professional ambitions?

I have this long line of work, starting with the partial identification research, which got transmuted into social planning under ambiguity. That is, how do you make public policy decisions with limited information? I think that is extraordinarily important, because making policy decisions with limited information is what we have to do. I can see one hundred years of work to be done along these lines, but the main thing is to disseminate the ideas that I already have. And so I've signed another contract with Harvard University Press, with whom I've had a long relationship, to publish a book that's tentatively titled *Public Policy in an Uncertain World*. Sometimes I like to personify my audience, and in this case, I want Barack Obama to be able to read it. It's not for the newsstands in the airport; it's for the serious, intelligent, but non-technical, reader who is involved in policymaking.

I hate what goes on in the United States now, where everyone takes out an extreme position, like on macro policy. Either we've got to stimulate the economy or we have to worry about the deficit. No one knows what the right macro model is! I wish people would just face up to the fact that we have to make policy decisions with limited information. If I can somehow get that across so that it influences the way policymaking is done and can just get us out of this ridiculous extreme debating style that this country evolved into … I don't know what the chances of success are, but that's what I want to do.

How would you describe the state of economics today? Are you optimistic about its future?

It's hard for me to be optimistic about anything. Some would say that's part of my nihilistic personality [*laughs*].

NOTES

1. McFadden, Daniel L. (1974), 'Conditional Logit Analysis of Qualitative Choice Behavior', in Paul Zarembka (ed.), *Frontiers in Econometrics*, Academic Press: New York, pp. 105–142.
2. Mirrlees, J.A. (1971), 'An Exploration in the Theory of Optimal Income Taxation', *Review of Economic Studies*, Vol. 38, No. 114 (April), pp. 175–208.
3. Delavande, A. (2008), 'Pill, Patch, or Shot? Subjective Expectations and Birth Control Choice', *International Economic Review*, Vol. 49, No. 3 (August), pp. 999–1042.
4. Manski, C.F. (1990), 'The Use of Intentions Data to Predict Behavior: A Best-Case Analysis', *Journal of the American Statistical Association*, Vol. 85, No. 412 (December), pp. 934–940.
5. Manski, C.F. (1975), 'Maximum Score Estimation of the Stochastic Utility Model of Choice', *Journal of Econometrics*, Vol. 3, No. 3 (August), pp. 205–228.
6. Manski, C.F. (1985), 'Semiparametric Analysis of Discrete Response: Asymptotic Properties of the Maximum Score Estimator', *Journal of Econometrics*, Vol. 27, No. 3 (March), pp. 313–333.
7. Manski, C.F. (1997), 'Monotone Treatment Response', *Econometrica*, Vol. 65, No. 6 (November), pp. 1311–1334.
8. Manski, C.F. (2010), 'When Consensus Choice Dominates Individualism: Jensen's Inequality and Collective Decisions under Uncertainty', *Quantitative Economics*, Vol. 1, No. 1 (July), pp. 187–202.
9. Galton, F. (1907), 'Vox populi', *Nature*, Vol. 75, pp. 450–451.
10. Ehrlich, I. (1975), 'The Deterrent Effect of Capital Punishment: A Question of Life and Death', *American Economic Review*, Vol. 65, No. 3 (June), pp. 397–417.

Eric S. Maskin
(Harvard University)

Eric Maskin was born in New York City in 1950 and graduated with an AB in mathematics from Harvard University in 1972 before obtaining both an AM and a PhD in applied mathematics from Harvard in 1974 and 1976 respectively. Between 1976 and 1977, he was a Research Fellow at Jesus College, Cambridge and then moved to the Massachusetts Institute of Technology, where he taught economics until 1984. Between 1985 and 2000, he was Professor of Economics at Harvard University and then became the Albert O. Hirschman Professor of Social Science at the Institute for Advanced Study, Princeton. In 2012, he returned to Harvard University as Professor of Economics.

Professor Maskin's research interests span diverse areas of economic theory, including game theory, the economics of incentives, contract theory, income inequality, social choice theory, and political economy. His most-cited articles in chronological order include 'Monopoly with Incomplete Information', *RAND Journal of Economics* (1984), co-authored with John Riley, 'The Folk Theorem in Repeated Games with Discounting or with Incomplete Information', *Econometrica* (1986), co-authored with Drew Fudenberg, 'Unforeseen Contingencies and Incomplete Contracts', *Review of Economic Studies* (1999), co-authored with Jean Tirole, 'Credit and

Efficiency in Centralized and Decentralized Economies', *Review of Economic Studies* (1995), co-authored with Mathias Dewatripont, and 'Nash Equilibrium and Welfare Optimality', *Review of Economic Studies* (1999).

Professor Maskin was elected as a Fellow of the Econometric Society in 1981, a Fellow of the American Academy of Arts and Sciences in 1994, a Corresponding Fellow of the British Academy in 2003, and a Member of the National Academy of Sciences in 2008. In 2007, he was awarded the Nobel Prize in Economic Sciences, along with Leonid Hurwicz and Roger Myerson, "for having laid the foundations of mechanism design theory."

I interviewed Eric Maskin in his office at the Institute for Advanced Study, Princeton, New Jersey. It was late-afternoon of Thursday, 22 July 2010.

BACKGROUND INFORMATION

What was your attraction to economics?

I discovered economics when I was in college. I had been studying mathematics, and I took, almost by chance, a course that Kenneth Arrow was teaching on Information Economics, which I didn't know anything about, but sounded interesting. It turned out to be a hodge-podge of lots of different things that Arrow was thinking about at the time, and it was fascinating. It also seemed to suggest a way that I could combine my predilection for rigorous analytic mathematical thinking with problems of real social importance. And so, after that course, I changed direction and ended up having Arrow as my PhD advisor.

How influential was Kenneth Arrow when you were a student?

He was extremely influential. Now, in the classroom he wasn't the most polished lecturer in the world [*laughs*]. He often seemed to be improvising on the spot. And he would speak very quickly and rather elliptically – because he couldn't keep up with his even faster train of thought. Still, his courses were inspirational because he talked about such interesting problems. And since he was clearly wrapped up in these problems, his listeners became wrapped up in them too.

His research too had a profound influence on me. My PhD thesis grew directly out of his work in social choice theory.

Why did you decide to pursue an academic career?

That was something that occurred to me fairly early on. It seemed to be the freest career path possible. What's better than spending your time working on the problems you want to work on? There aren't too many other jobs like that. Teaching turned out to be very enjoyable too, but I didn't know that when I started out [*laughs*].

As a researcher, which colleagues have been most influential or inspirational?

There were many, so let me just mention a few at the beginning of my career. Arrow was the first influence and continues to be inspirational at the age of almost 89. Just after my PhD, I did a post-doc at Cambridge, England, and fell under the spell of Frank Hahn, a highly charismatic figure, who had a big effect on me. At that time, I also got to know Partha Dasgupta – we had marathon conversations about economics and started a collaboration that still continues. In my first faculty job – at MIT – Peter Diamond took me under his wing. In particular, I learned a great deal from working with him on several papers.

GENERAL THOUGHTS ON RESEARCH

How would you describe the research environment at the Institute for Advanced Study at Princeton?

It's excellent. The big difference between the Institute and a regular university is that here you interact with people outside your field every day. At lunch, there's a Social Science table, and so I sit among anthropologists, historians, psychologists, sociologists, and political scientists, besides the economists. The conversations are broader than in an economics department. I'm not sure whether the interdisciplinarity has affected my research agenda all that much, but it's certainly affected the way that I write: I try to motivate my work more than before, to explain to the skeptical non-economist why the issue I'm writing about is interesting.

What is the value of pure versus applied research in economics?

Well, there is no clear-cut distinction between pure and applied research. But, very roughly, in pure research, we're looking for basic principles,

principles that hold across applications. In applied research, the focus is typically more concrete and narrowly focused.

You can think of pure research as the forest, and applied research as the trees. Of course, it's through applied work that basic principles are really tested. If economics consisted only of pure research, people would dismiss it as airy-fairy, and I think that attitude would be appropriate [*laughs*].

When I interviewed Susan Athey at Harvard, she told me that parts of the theory community thought she was 'selling out' or abandoning principles of theory when she did applied work earlier in her career. What is your view?

I'm sorry to hear that she had that experience. As I said, a big attraction of an academic career for me was the freedom to do anything I wanted. And if a theorist wants to do applied work, why not? Of course, there may be a risk of spreading yourself too thin by doing that. But that's for the individual to decide for herself. My own interests have been rather spread out, so maybe I'm being a bit self-defensive here [*laughs*].

How has your research agenda changed over time?

I have always been engaged primarily in theoretical questions, but over time the balance has shifted from abstract projects to those that are more concrete. I've even worked on a few papers that involved some empirical work.[1]

IDEA GENERATION

Where do you get your research ideas?

Sometimes it's from reading other people's work. Maybe they have left something important out or have taken something for granted, or there's an obvious next question to be asked. Other times, it's from reading the newspaper; perhaps some economic event that seems at odds with standard theory. Another important source of ideas is conversation, particularly with long-time collaborators. We'll be working on a particular project, but we'll start talking about something else. And in the course of that conversation, questions will arise that form the seeds for a new project.

At what point does an idea become a project that you devote resources to?

Most ideas don't become projects [*laughs*]. The first hurdle is whether you can construct a formal example – a toy model – of the phenomenon or problem you're interested in. If you can do that, and it still looks interesting – that is, you haven't already answered the question with the example – then you may have a project. So, before I get going on a paper, I usually try to work out an example. If I succeed with that and the problem still engages me, I will probably continue. If not, then it suggests that the problem was either too hard or too vague or too uninteresting to pursue.

IDEA EXECUTION

What makes a good theoretical paper?

A paper that makes you think about an issue in a new way. I'm not saying that all theoretical papers have to be startlingly original, but they ought to be reasonably original. Surprising your reader is a pretty good indication of originality. But even better is when the idea seems so natural that the reader wishes he had thought of it himself. In that case, there really may be something to the paper.

Can you give an example?

There are two papers, making the same point, that immediately come to mind. Long ago, Max Weber made a paradoxical observation about the Protestant work ethic: the Calvinists were both ferociously hard workers and believers in predestination. That's paradoxical because why should people who believe that their fates are already sealed bother to lift a finger? A beautifully simple answer to that question was provided independently by two economists, Roland Bénabou and Jean Tirole, and by two psychologists, Ronit Bodner and Dražen Prelec.[2]

Bénabou-Tirole and Bodner-Prelec suppose that an individual knows that his future is determined. But because he doesn't know what that future is – whether he is going to be saved or not – he will look for signs, for signals about his fate. One positive signal is working hard, because good people work hard, and good people are more apt to be saved. Thus, according to this model, Calvinists work hard because doing so validates the belief that they are good and therefore likely to be saved.

There was an interesting experiment conducted by George Quattrone and Amos Tversky that supports this theory.[3] Two groups of subjects were instructed to keep their hands immersed in cold water for as long as they could stand it. One group – the control group – were given no explanation for the instructions, but the other group were told that the inability to tolerate cold water is correlated with a rare heart disease. It turned out that the group told this story (which, unbeknownst to them, was false) kept their hands in the water for longer. Presumably, they wanted to believe they didn't have the disease and, therefore, validated this belief by their actions.

What makes a good empirical paper?

The challenge in economics is that you are confronted with the data the world gives you rather than the data you would like to have. In particular, real data often have biased samples. But there have been important advances recently in developing tools for dealing with this problem. Good empirical work exploits these tools as far as possible, while bad empirical work ignores the problem altogether.

Can you give an example?

It's controversial, but one example is Steve Levitt's work on the possible link between legalization of abortion and the dramatic fall in the US crime rate.[4] The paper is executed with careful attention to the problems with the data. And, despite this, it is able to establish that a link is plausible, though not completely conclusive.

When you hit a brick wall on a project, do you continue to work on the problem or do you take a break and work on something else?

I generally don't stick with a project forever. At some point, I either abandon it or put it aside temporarily and do something else. But I typically don't work on just one project at any given time. I work on a variety of projects, so that I can switch from one to the other if I run into difficulties. And sometimes, if I come back with fresh energy to a problematic project, I see things that I didn't see before.

Can you give an example of when this has happened?

Yes, there's an example from early in my career. I was trying to characterize the social goals that are implementable in the sense that we can construct mechanisms whose equilibrium outcomes attain these goals. I suspected that there was a link between implementability and a condition called monotonicity, but I couldn't show this in general. So I took a break. When I came back a few months later, I quickly found a way to complete the argument.

When a project isn't going to turn out as hoped, do you scrap it or aim to send the work to a second-tier or field journal?

These days, I'm really no longer interested in doing things just for the sake of getting published. Earlier on in my career, I often felt that I had to show something tangible for my effort. But now if I decide that a project just isn't very interesting, I usually stop.

What has been the biggest change during your career in how researchers in your fields conduct research?

One big change is that a high proportion of work is now collaborative. When I started out, most papers were single-authored. But now the vast majority of papers are multi-authored. On the whole, I think this has been a good change because there are some strong advantages to collaboration. First, it's more sustaining; if you hit a snag, your co-author can help get you through it. You also have a built-in audience; almost anything you say will be fascinating to your collaborator [*laughs*]. Third, you can take incoherent ideas and, through intense back-and-forth discussions, hammer them into semi-coherence. Finally, you can share the burden of writing up the results in a way that readers will find engaging.

THE WRITING PROCESS

Which aspect of the writing process do you find most difficult?

I think the hardest part is putting yourself in the place of the uninitiated reader. You've been thinking about the paper intensely, but your reader hasn't. Somehow you have to imagine how he would see an argument. Does adding more detail make it easier for him to understand or does it overwhelm him? Getting this balance right isn't easy.

What steps have you taken during your career to improve the quality of your writing?

A strategy I've evolved is to present a paper a number of times as a lecture or a seminar before trying to draft it. If you're giving an oral presentation, you will tend to use conversational language, and I think a conversational style is also easier to read. So, when I later actually write the paper, I try to use the language from the seminar.

The questions that people ask in the seminar also help. Of course, sometimes they're about things that hadn't occurred to you, which causes you to make substantive changes. But at the very least, they'll show you which ideas the audience had trouble with and how to get these across more effectively. You'll also see which points do not need to be belabored. And so after you've refined the oral presentation from giving it a few times, you can write up the paper using your PowerPoint slides as a template.

How do you split up the writing tasks among co-authors?

We usually take turns to go through the whole draft.

COLLABORATION

One of the other interviewees in this book is Partha Dasgupta, who is one of your co-authors. He told me that your friendship came before collaboration, rather than the other way around. Is this true of your other co-authors?

Almost all my long-term collaborators are also friends. Sometimes, the friendship evolved simultaneously with the collaboration. And in a couple of cases, as with Partha, we were friends first and then decided to work together (although, as I mentioned earlier, we had had many long discussions about economics before the actual collaboration began).

Is geographical proximity ever a consideration in deciding whom to work with?

A couple of times I wrote papers without ever physically seeing my co-authors, but those were the exception. Usually, collaboration started when we were in the same place and could talk at length about our still not-very-well-formed ideas. Later, when the work was well underway, e-mail and telephone were enough.

RESEARCH ASSISTANCE AND FUNDING

How do you use research assistants?

I use them primarily to vet complicated arguments in my papers and to track down the background and related literature.

How important is funding for getting your work done?

Because my research is largely theoretical, I don't ordinarily need labora-tory equipment or computers, which experimentalists or empirical econo-mists require. And so most of my research projects probably would have been done eventually even without external funding. But my funding from the NSF has been important for two reasons. First, it's helped relieve me from teaching and other non-research work, particularly in the summer. Without that relief, the projects would have taken a lot longer to complete. And second, it has paid for travel to talk with co-authors, which as I've explained is important at the early stage of collaboration.

Do you have any advice for a young scholar on the funding process?

Typically, applying for an NSF or similar grant is not terribly time-consuming. It's only a few days of work and the payoff is many days free to pursue your research at a critical time in your career. So, I strongly advise applying for these grants.

SEMINAR PARTICIPATION AND NETWORKING

What are the benefits to attending a seminar that is closely related to your work versus one that is not closely related?

I attend seminars unrelated to my work mainly as a cheap way of finding out about the topic. It's generally faster getting an oral summary than slogging through the paper itself. But if I'm intrigued by the ideas in a seminar, I'll generally follow up by reading the manuscript.

If the paper is in a field I know well, then I'll go to the talk to hear about details. The great advantage of a seminar is that you can ask questions of the speaker in real time.

How important is professional networking to success in research?

Having access to current work is absolutely crucial. In that sense, things have improved enormously in the last 20 years because it's no longer necessary to hear people's talks live and get onto their mailing lists to follow their unpublished work.

But there is still value, especially for young researchers, to meeting people personally. People who know you at least a little are more likely to read and comment on your work. And so I recommend to students and young faculty that they go to conferences to present their work and talk to people in the hallways. It's a form of self-advertising. Once people have some idea of who you are and what you're up to, they'll be more inclined to look at your work carefully.

To what extent is the absence of departmental colleagues working in one's research area a major disadvantage?

Early in your career, that can be a significant disadvantage for two reasons. First, colleagues in your area are the best source of comments on your work; people with remote research interests or who don't know you well are not as likely to give you useful criticism. Second, colleagues in your field are more likely to talk over new ideas with you and become research collaborators.

COMMUNICATION OF RESEARCH

How do you find the right balance between communicating your research at an early stage versus the close-to-finished stage?

I prefer to give talks fairly early on, but that's not the way that most seminars work. At major departments, seminar series usually consist of papers that are essentially completed. I think that's unfortunate. While it may be easier for the audience to listen to a polished presentation, the speaker himself doesn't benefit as much from comments at that stage. If someone proposes a different way of doing things, you're not as likely to follow the suggestion, because you've already invested so much time and energy in the current approach.

In fact, here at the Institute we have an economics seminar in which only undrafted papers can be presented. The aim is to talk about ideas that are not yet fully worked out, in the hope that this will improve the paper that ultimately emerges.

What are the unique challenges to giving a seminar and how do you overcome them?

A seminar is a performance, and that generates challenges that aren't present in other scholarly activities. You have to figure out a way of grabbing the attention of your listeners … and quickly. With a paper, it's not so important that you do that right away, because people can always skim your paper and jump back and forth. But a seminar has to be presented linearly [*laughs*]. If people are going to follow you all the way to the end, they have to be willing to jump on your bandwagon at the outset. And so part of the art of giving a seminar is motivating people to be interested in it right away.

PUBLICATION

How do you decide upon the appropriate journal to send your research to?

I don't agonize too much about it. I usually try to send a paper to the journal that is going to have the widest readership for the topic that I'm writing on. If it's an extremely technical subject, my readership will necessarily be limited; and I'll put the paper in a theory journal, ideally *Econometrica*. But if I have a paper that can readily be followed by a broad readership, then I'll send it to a general interest journal like the *AER* or the *QJE*.

How would you best describe your approach to dealing with a 'revise and resubmit' request from a journal? How about an outright rejection?

Like everyone else, I don't like rejections, but I've learned to live with them. There have been cases when I thought the editor was wrong. But editors rarely change their mind, and so it's usually not worth putting up a fight. I try to remember the advice I give my students: just because your paper has been rejected doesn't mean that it's no good. Journals make mistakes sometimes. Indeed, some famous, important papers were initially rejected, in part because they were too original, and their novelty wasn't properly appreciated. And so you shouldn't kick yourself over a rejection, painful though it may be. Instead, move on to the next journal.

As for 'revise and resubmits', I try to make a good-faith effort to do what the referees want or at least give them a well-reasoned explanation for why I'm not following their advice [*laughs*]. I usually give them a point-by-point account of each issue they raised. That wasn't standard form when I was just starting out, but I think it's the expected response today.

Do you think that the current structure of the publication process in economics facilitates or impedes scientific understanding and knowledge production?

There is a real problem in economics publishing. Editors choose the 'revise and resubmit' option too often. This slows down publication, which is particularly bad for younger scholars who want to build up a CV. It means authors devote less time to original research. And it eats up an enormous amount of editors' and reviewers' energies.

I edit a journal called *Economics Letters*, where in most cases, we accept or reject a paper on the first round. If a paper is interesting enough and it's correct – though not necessarily beautifully expressed – then it's published. Otherwise, it's rejected.

What has been your best and worst experience during the publication process?

The easiest experiences have been those in which the referees had no major comments. But the most rewarding have been those where referees had substantial constructive criticisms, yet the editor had enough faith in me – and in his own assessment of the paper – to leave it up to me how to react to them. The logic there was that if the paper is good enough to ultimately publish, then the author himself has the best incentive to decide how to use the referees' ideas to maximize the paper's impact.

The worst experiences have been those in which the referee reports push in opposite directions, and the editor insists that the criticisms be addressed. I've also been frustrated on occasion by referees who ask me to write a paper completely different from the one I submitted. I usually prefer the paper I actually did write.

REFEREEING AND EDITING

Do you still referee papers?

Not very often. Usually when I do, it's a paper I was hoping to read anyway. This gives me an excuse to study it carefully. Occasionally, I'll referee a paper I hadn't been planning to read if it gives me a chance to inform myself about a fascinating-sounding topic.

Why did you decide to become Editor of Economics Letters*?*

First of all, *Economics Letters* is a general interest journal, so it's an opportunity for me to educate myself rather easily about all sorts of economics I wouldn't see otherwise. By deciding which papers to publish I can also shape the economics profession a little bit. And I get a thrill from discovering the occasional gem.

TIME MANAGEMENT

How do you divide up your working day, both in terms of quantity and timing of different kinds of work?

I usually try to use the morning for research, and I work at home then. I'll come into the office around noon and have lunch at the Social Science table, or one-on-one if I'm talking shop with somebody. And I use the afternoon for talking to students and colleagues, going to seminars, doing editorial work, or catching up with correspondence. Sometimes I'll use the evening for research, but I don't do that as often as I used to.

How do you balance multiple research projects?

That's another value of collaboration. If you let one project go for too long, your co-author might say, "Why haven't I seen a new draft?" And so the juggling problem can often be solved by restless co-authors [*laughs*].

How do you balance your personal and professional lives?

That's a difficult balance; there is real tension between the two. When my children were young, I tried to make sure that part of every day was set aside just for the family. But that time wasn't always as long as they wanted or, for that matter, as I wanted. I think it forced me to become more efficient in my work life. Still, there is no easy answer.

REFLECTIONS AND THE FUTURE OF ECONOMICS

What are the biggest challenges facing your research fields?

One big and important challenge in economic theory is to build a reasonably general, tractable, and predictive model of bounded rationality.

In the end, do you think the profession has helped to bring out and shape your research for the best?

When I started out in the late '70s, the work I was doing on mechanism design and game theory was well out of the mainstream of the economics profession. A few people tried to dissuade me from continuing in that direction. But many others gave encouragement and help. And so on balance I think the profession has treated me just fine [*laughs*].

To what extent has winning the Nobel Prize changed your life?

I think I've more or less kept to the same research agenda that I had before, and I still have the same job. On the other hand, there is a new component to my life: the public side. I now get invitations to speak to a much wider audience. For example, a couple of months ago, I was asked by the European Commission to give a talk to a large group of policymakers on the costs and benefits of intellectual property protection. That is an issue I'm interested in from a research perspective, but I don't think I would have been asked to speak to such an audience had it not been for the Nobel.

Do you have any professional regrets?

Of course, there are particular research lines that turned out to be dead ends, and I wish I hadn't spent so much time on them. But that's the way research goes. Most ideas don't work out, and you have to accept that. But when it comes to bigger decisions, I don't have any huge regrets. I've been very lucky with how my career has gone.

What are your professional ambitions?

Just to carry on with the things I'm doing. I hope that I will remain professionally and creatively active for a long time to come. I take some encouragement from the fact that my old teacher Kenneth Arrow is still intellectually lively at the age of nearly 89. I think he sets a good example, and I'd like to follow it [*laughs*].

How would you describe the state of economics today? Are you optimistic about its future?

We've come a long way in economics since I started out. Obviously we've still got a lot to learn before we can answer all the questions we want to [*laughs*]. There are some huge questions that remain open, but am I optimistic that we will find pretty good answers eventually? Yes, definitely. The record of accomplishment to date has been pretty good, and with remarkably talented, hardworking, and enthusiastic people coming into the profession, there's no reason why it shouldn't be even better in the future.

NOTES

1. See, for example, Kremer M. and E.S. Maskin (1996), 'Wage Inequality and Segregation by Skill', *NBER Working Papers* 5718, National Bureau of Economic Research; Maskin E.S., Qian, Y. and C. Xu (1997), 'Incentives, Scale Economies, and Organizational Form', *Harvard Institute of Economic Research Working Papers* 1801, Harvard – Institute of Economic Research.
2. Bénabou, R. and J. Tirole (2006), 'Belief in a Just World and Redistributive Politics', *Quarterly Journal of Economics*, Vol. 121, No. 2 (May), pp. 699–746; Bodner, Ronit and Dražen Prelec (2002), 'Self-signaling in a neo-Calvinist Model of Everyday Decision Making', in Isabelle Brocas and Juan Carillo (eds), *Psychology and Economics*, Vol. I, Oxford University Press.
3. Quattrone, G.A. and A. Tversky (1984), 'Causal versus Diagnostic Contingencies: On Self-deception and on the Voter's Illusion', *Journal of Personality and Social Psychology*, Vol. 46, No. 2 (February), pp. 237–248.
4. Donohue, III, J.J. and S.D. Levitt (2001), 'The Impact of Legalized Abortion on Crime', *Quarterly Journal of Economics*, Vol. 116, No. 2 (May), pp. 379–420.

Ellen R. McGrattan
(Federal Reserve
Bank of Minneapolis)

Ellen McGrattan was born in New London, Connecticut in 1962 and graduated with a BS in mathematics and economics from Boston College in 1984 before obtaining a PhD in economics from Stanford University in 1989. Between 1989 and 1992, she was an Assistant Professor of Economics at Duke University and then joined the Federal Reserve Bank of Minneapolis, where she has remained ever since, currently serving as Monetary Advisor in the Research Department.

Dr McGrattan's research focuses on the aggregate effects of monetary and fiscal policy, in particular the impact on GDP, investment, the allocation of hours, and the stock market. Her most-cited articles in chronological order include 'Money as a Medium of Exchange in an Economy with Artificially Intelligent Agents', *Journal of Economic Dynamics and Control* (1990), co-authored with Ramon Marimon and Thomas Sargent, 'The Macroeconomic Effects of Distortionary Taxation', *Journal of Monetary Economics* (1994), 'An Equilibrium Model of the Business Cycle with Household Production and Fiscal Policy', *International Economic Review* (1997), co-authored with Richard Rogerson and Randall Wright, 'Sticky Price Models of the Business Cycle: Can the Contract Multiplier Solve the Persistence Problem?', *Econometrica* (2000), co-authored with V.V. Chari and Patrick Kehoe, and 'Can Sticky Price Models Generate Volatile and Persistent Real Exchange Rates?', *Review of Economic Studies* (2002), co-authored with V.V. Chari and Patrick Kehoe.

Dr McGrattan is an Adjunct Professor at the University of Minnesota, a Research Economist at the National Bureau of Economic Research, and an Editor of the *Review of Economic Dynamics*.

I interviewed Ellen McGrattan in a seminar room at the Federal Reserve Bank of Minneapolis. It was early-afternoon of Friday, 28 January 2011.

BACKGROUND INFORMATION

What was your attraction to economics?

I have to say that when I went to Boston College as an undergraduate, I had no idea what the field of economics was or what an economist did. I was a math major but didn't think that was going to be my career, and so I started looking around and took a class, *Principles of Economics*. I remember it very clearly. It was taught by a professor named Richard Tresch, whose job was to get the kids excited about economics. He came in one day and said, "Today, we're going to talk about money." Then he grabbed some change from his pocket and threw it at the audience! [*Laughs*]. Of course, it was a serious class, but he sucked you in. I didn't see the math applications at that point, but you could tell there was something behind those curves being shifted around.

I pursued economics on the math-oriented track, and then when I reached my junior year, I thought, "This is cool, but I still have no idea what it means to be an economist." And so I asked one of my professors, Frank Gollop, if I could get a summer job as an RA. It turned out that somebody along the hall was a buddy of Bill Nordhaus from Yale. Bill kindly hired me to be part of his team of undergraduate RAs and it was the best summer ever. The most exciting part of the job was seeing the graduate students, like John Campbell, Andy Caplin, Steve Durlauf, and Michael Haliassos working on their theses, stressing about their topics, and going out on the job market. Another thing that was interesting was a survey of forecasters that I did for Nordhaus. I had to figure out how to get professional forecasters like Otto Eckstein and Larry Klein on the phone long enough to answer roughly 20 questions. The question in the survey that I thought was the most interesting was, "What is your modeling philosophy? Are you a monetarist, a Keynesian, or a rational expectationalist?" At first, I pronounced Keynes as it looks rather than *Canes*. Nordhaus said, "My God, where have you been educated, or should I say, not educated? The man's name is John Maynard *Keynes* [*stresses correct pronunciation*]." I did know that monetarism had something to do with Milton Friedman, but I didn't know anything about rational expectations. It sounded intriguing. When I went back to BC, I told Frank Gollop that I wanted to learn about rational expectations. He said, "Oh, good news. We just hired a guy from Minnesota. His name is Scott Freeman, a student of Neil Wallace." Scott allowed me to do the undergraduate honors thesis with him. He went to his shelf and picked up the galleys for Tom Sargent's first major book and said, "See what you can do with this."[1] I devoured it. And that's when I realized that I wanted to become an economist.

I applied to a bunch of places for graduate school, including Minnesota, because Scott said I had to go there. But some of the faculty at BC who were MIT grads said, "Minnesota? The people there are *crazy*." I didn't know what crazy meant; I thought it might have something to do with Marxism. They should have told me that they were doing all the work on rational expectations. And so I ended up going to a place that nobody had said anything bad about – Stanford. I could have gone to MIT – a subway ride away – but I sat in on classes there and didn't hear anything about rational expectations. I threw a dart at the places where I couldn't take the subway. How dumb is that?

Anyway, I ended up at Stanford and had a miserable first year because they weren't teaching what I thought was the cutting-edge material. I told this to my now-husband, who was a student in aerospace engineering at the time, and he said, "You're a first-year graduate student. You know nothing. You need to take more courses and figure it out. Give it a year before you abandon ship." And so I waited, and sure enough, Tom Sargent shows up. I didn't know it was him; I had only read his book. There was a guy walking down the hall wearing those funky glasses that turn dark when you're outside. I thought, "God, that guy has the weirdest glasses." I knew he had to be a professor because of his age and he said "hi" to me. I thought maybe he was lost and was having trouble seeing with those funky glasses [*laughs*]. I didn't realize it was him until he started teaching, and I was so excited. I showed up to his first class too early – for a few minutes, I was the only one there – and Tom was at the front. I was sitting at the back feeling awkward. Even though I had read every page of his book, I didn't know him. But then he says to me, "Scott says 'hi.'" He had gotten a letter from Scott that said, "I told this woman to go to Minnesota and work with you. Stupidly, she didn't go, but now thankfully you're at Stanford and she's there. Please look after her." That was so nice.

I remember the econometrics class that Tom taught. He said, "In this course, we're going to use a lot of linear and quadratic methods. I know many people think that's not high-tech, but it put people on the moon, and that's good enough for me." He was great. And then I worked as his RA. He'll deny this, but the only thing he ever asked me to do was to fix the latest, greatest machine in his office when it locked up. He would come in to tell me, "I've broken the machine." And I'd say, "You mean you took a hammer and smashed it?" He'd reply, "No, but it's hung again." And so I would just press the 'escape' button and, if that didn't work, I'd reboot it [*laughs*].

It was wonderful being around Tom. He would bring in people like Randy Wright, Richard Rogerson, Rody Mannelli, and Hugo Hopenhayn, which made it lively intellectually, and they were fun people, too.

As a researcher, which colleagues have been most influential or inspirational?

My career outside of the Fed was pretty short. I was at Duke for only three years, and then I got a call from the Minneapolis Fed. I realized that the number of like-minded people I would be talking to on a-day-to-day basis would be much greater than at Duke. The only problem was that I was married to a guy who worked on super high-speed fluid dynamics at North Carolina State, which has a big engineering school. So I asked him, "Graham, could you ever imagine life in Minnesota?" He said, "I went there on the job market and it's filled with Sputniks. That's code for professors hired in the 1960s." I told him to give a talk there to see if it had changed. He came back and told me, "Well, a bunch of the Sputniks have died. I could imagine giving it a try." And so we came to Minnesota, which is where most of my mentoring has taken place. Ed Prescott has been the biggest influence but, at first, I could not understand him. Not long after I had arrived at the Fed, he came into my office, without any introduction, and started talking about planetary movements and how it related to economics. He was looking at the wall as if it had a window and a view of the planets. I told him, "You know what? I have absolutely no idea what you are talking about." It was like I had turned a switch on. He said, "Oh, you don't understand that? Let me explain ... " It was if he spoke two languages: English and something I could not understand. I'll give you another example. One day he asked me, "Why should I think you're anything other than a second-rate economist?" Now that I know Ed very well, I'll translate it: "What do you think your major contribution to the science is going to be?" I remember telling Bob Lucas that story and he said, "Wow, I would have been totally intimidated!" But then I told him how I responded to Ed, which was, "Well, I don't have a good answer right now, but someday, I'm going to dazzle you." That pleased Ed.

What I learned from him was that I needed to be ready for when he came into my office, because he always wanted to know what I was working on. He'd say, "What are you doing?" followed by the hardest question, "And why?" And so I started to get used to thinking in terms of something I call the 'want operator'. What are we trying to do here? What is success and what isn't? What is the big picture? In the first slide of my presentations, I always begin with a question and some motivation for why answering it is important. Sometimes my research goes all over the place, but Ed taught me how to stay focused. I have never met anyone as good as he is at forcing me to focus. I always tell the graduate students, "Look, Ed changed my life by asking me: *Why* are you doing this? Don't wait until you get into the Fed's bag lunch seminar for me to ask that question in front of a whole group of people." And it also got me thinking about policy analysis. Do we have the right tools? Maybe not. But there is always a question in the back of my mind that I am trying to answer. That's how I plan out all my new projects, and there is no downside; perhaps, I don't get the answer that I was expecting, but I learn from it. There are many in our profession who want a detailed model of 'reality' but have no specific question in mind. Thanks to Ed, I realized early on that that's the wrong route to take.

GENERAL THOUGHTS ON RESEARCH

How would you describe the research setting at the Minneapolis Fed? How is it different to working in a traditional economics department at a university?

One nice thing about the Minneapolis Fed, relative to any other research or academic institution that I know, is that we have a lot of time for research. Most of us teach one class at the U (University of Minnesota) and we advise graduate students, but we have the luxury of coming into the office and thinking all day long.

The environment is very exciting. We have fabulous seminars, great visitors passing through, and a large concentration of researchers who are interested in related topics. And they're brutally honest. If they think you're doing something stupid, they will tell you. The feedback is incredible because it's such an interactive environment. At universities, you will often see all the doors closed; they don't want students wandering in. But at the Minneapolis Fed, everyone's door is open. In fact, people don't even say, "Hey, can I bother you for a minute?" They just come into your office and start writing on your board. That's how we communicate.

I remember being in Dave Backus' office at NYU. He and Espen Henriksen wanted to tell me about a paper they were working on. I asked them, "Where is the board?" because it's so natural for me to see someone write down an equation or sketch a graph on a blackboard. Mind you, if it's Ed, it's a T account. He cannot write equations! As far as I know, all of his intuition comes from T accounts. I might be struggling with the math, and he'll say, "Well, suppose Company A has $100 ... " I used to find these discussions completely unhelpful, but now I can follow his logic. And there are a lot of other very talented people here who have such a variety of skills and different ways of thinking.

What is the value of pure versus applied research in economics?

Everything for me is applied. Take Arrow–Debreu as an example. That established a language to solve applied questions. I interviewed (Kenneth) Arrow for our *Region* magazine, and I asked him, "Would you have ever guessed that future macroeconomists would include a reference to your work in their papers?" He told me "no" because macroeconomics when he was younger meant disequilibrium. But we use Arrow–Debreu all the time. And back in the '70s and '80s, Neil Wallace, John Kareken, and Tom Sargent were doing what was viewed at the time as pure research on money and banking. But here we are in 2011 talking about 'too big to fail', which all stems from their basic theoretical frameworks.

How would you describe the dialogue between theory and empirics in economics?

It depends on what you mean by empirics. I count myself as a quantitative theorist – I want to use theory to answer questions. And so I need the theorists who write down beautiful and elegant theories. But there are economists who do theory-free work, and claim that they have a theory in mind. Unfortunately, there are assumptions that have to be made to run their regressions. Why not write down the theory and be explicit about the assumptions?

How would you characterize your own research agenda and how has it changed through time?

Coming here and being asked, "What are you doing and why?" definitely gets you focused and out of the mindset that we have to explain the world, and into thinking that we have to ask and answer questions. Some of those questions are tough, like "Why did GDP fall so much between '29 and '33?" I've learned over time that we have to keep trying to answer these tough questions. Another thing that I've learned is to be more aware of measurement and how important it is. For example, I'm now more careful about constructing GDP in my models. GDP is an accounting measure and not necessarily the analog of output in our theories. In some cases, the distinction matters.

Do you think it is important to have broad research interests?

I think it's important to be open-minded but narrow in the sense that you're an expert in a certain area.

Do you think there is any difference in the types of work done by researchers at different stages of their careers based on tenure concerns, publication requirements or other pressures? Should there be a difference?

Yes, I think tenure concerns push young researchers into too many low-risk projects. If I were king of the world, I'd get rid of job protection for everybody. People say to me, "Oh, you're at the Fed, so you can't be fired and effectively have tenure." That's not true. If I'm not doing research, I *can* be fired or moved. I remember when Rao Aiyagari was working at the Minneapolis Fed and was considering a job at Rochester. I said to him, "But Rao, why do you want to leave? This is the perfect job." He told me, "It's so high stress. Every day, everybody asks me, 'What are you doing and why?' I'm going to retire into academia." Unfortunately, Rao died at a relatively young age, but my point is that we should scrub tenure. Patrick Kehoe had tenure at Penn and he was going to give it up to come back to the Minneapolis Fed. Somebody asked him, "Are you crazy?" He said, "No, what's crazy is being in a department with people who think they need a tenure system. I can go and get another tenured job. I want to be at a place where people are kicking butt, no matter what." I agree with Patrick. And so my suggestion would be to offer term contracts to professors because they incentivize people better.

IDEA GENERATION

Where do you get your research ideas?

I have a set of standard theories in my head and if I see things that are completely contradictory, I will ask, "What's going on?"And that usually happens when I'm trying to answer policy questions. Gary Stern [ex-President of the Minneapolis Fed] used to ask us questions like, "Why is the current account balance falling so dramatically [in the early 2000s], and should the Fed do anything? Why is unemployment rising so dramatically, and should the Fed do anything?" And there are other sources for questions. For example, between 1970 and 2000, the stock market tripled and John Campbell and Bob Shiller were saying that it would have to crash eventually. Ed came into my office and said, "Campbell and Shiller say that the stock market is overvalued. I'm worried because I have all my money in stocks." I said, "That's funny because you're the guy who says we get this huge premium from equities. But I'm in the same position too, and obviously the rise in the stock market relative to GDP can't go on forever." We started thinking about the predictions of basic theory, which tells us that the value of the stock market is the value of corporate capital. This capital includes tangibles like factories, office buildings, and machines, but it also includes intangibles like patents, brand names, and firm-specific human capital. The BEA (Bureau of Economic Analysis) doesn't put a value on these intangibles, so we had to do this by using data on corporate profits and tangible capital stocks and an estimate of the return on capital used in the corporate sector. We found that the value of capital, including its use outside the country by US subsidiaries, was about 1.8 times GNP, which was the same as the value of the stock market in the first half of 2000.[2]

Then we presented the paper in the brown bag lunch here … and our colleagues practically threw tomatoes at us. "So you think that you can do economics by showing us one point in time?" they told us. We were pretty proud of our little mechanism for coming up with the intangibles, but we realized they were right. And so that got us thinking about why corporate valuations change so much over time, which introduced taxation and regulation, and that led to another paper.[3]

At what point does an idea become a project that you devote resources to?

When you know that you have a possible answer to a good question.

IDEA EXECUTION

What makes a good theoretical paper? Can you give an example?

A good theoretical paper provides a module that everybody has at the core of their theories. An example is 'Asset Prices in an Exchange Economy' by Bob Lucas.[4]

What makes a good empirical paper? Can you give an example?

I like the interaction of theory and data. I want people to stick their neck out, and put the predictions of the models and the data in the same table or graph.

A good example is Kydland and Prescott's 'Time to Build' paper.[5] That paper was the motivation for my PhD thesis. What I loved about it was that they were willing to match up theory and data, and I hadn't seen that before. I thought, "This is it. We're going to show all the warts and pimples; figure out on what dimensions we are off." They had a model of the business cycle in which the labor market predictions were way off because the monetary and technology shocks that they included didn't affect how people intra-temporally substitute between leisure and consumption. This is needed in order to get action on the hours worked dimension. They completely missed that, but their reported statistics demonstrate that clearly.

When I was a graduate student, I would read papers for a class or listen to presentations, and sometimes the claims made no sense. I wrote a code called 'the planner', in which you could type in utility functions, production functions, and so on. It allowed me to check on their claims.

When you hit a brick wall on a project, do you continue to work on the problem or do you take a break and work on something else?

For me, a brick wall is when I'm getting an answer that makes absolutely no sense. For example, Patrick Kehoe, V.V. Chari and I wanted to demonstrate the Dornbusch view that a little bit of stickiness in prices can generate a lot of variation in real exchange rates. So, we wrote some code, put it in the computer … but got nothing. Then we went to the pad and pencil. When we wrote it out, we realized that conventional wisdom was wrong unless the model had empirically implausible production technologies or demand functions. They had never written it down; they had just assumed it. John Taylor is a brilliant guy, who can write down the correct first-order conditions, but he doesn't necessarily tie back the terms in there to the things that are fundamental. And so that brick wall turned into a paper that is probably the most cited of all of ours because we took some conventional wisdom and found that it was not right.[6] The old paper and pencil won the day.

When a project isn't going to turn out as hoped, do you scrap it or aim to send the work to a second-tier or field journal?

Sometimes I will use the failures for teaching. I say to my students, "All I'm going to do is just put a bunch of questions in your head without answers. And guess what? Think about those for your thesis. Because if you can answer any of those questions, that's what we would call a home run." They like that because it gives them brick walls that people have been hitting, or ones that they won't admit to hitting. And I also tell them, "Here's what you're going to say at the beginning: we're at a brick wall, but now I've figured it out; I've figured out why our theory and the data are so at odds, and I'm going to tell you why it's important that I get this right."

Failure is good because (a) it gives our graduate students things to think about, and (b) it keeps us very humble.

What has been the biggest change during your career in how researchers in your fields conduct research?

I think we have become more timid about doing quantitative theory. I wish economics were more like engineering where, if someone finds an important factor, people say, "Wow, that's a big deal. Yes, the model and data don't line up perfectly, but we're one order of magnitude closer." That constitutes progress in my opinion.

THE WRITING PROCESS

Which aspect of the writing process do you find most difficult?

I find it all difficult. I never learned to write as a kid. I don't know what I would have done without Kathy Rolfe, who was the editor of *The Quarterly Review* for many years. What did she teach me? Every paragraph is a theorem; it has to have a theorem statement, followed by the details, and then the summary that leads you to the next theorem. And you've got to have the paper's one main point up front.

I used to look at other people's writings. I love the way Bob Lucas writes, for example. But I can't get away with writing as he does, in such an authoritative tone.

I also read the work of the Public Affairs Department here, whose job it is to communicate our research to the world. Doug Clement is the editor of their magazine, *Region*. He wrote an article on the research Ed and I were doing on intangible capital.[7] He put the two of us into a room together so that we could have a conversation, and then he wrote the article based on it. It's so cool. He described why the work was important, how the world looks confusing when we think about stock markets and business cycles without intangible capital, and how the world isn't so confusing once we introduce it. You're just sucked in. I'm always amazed when people write that well. I just think, "Damn, I wish I could do that." [*Laughs*].

How do you divide up the writing tasks when you work with co-authors?

When I'm working with Patrick and Chari, they're like one person who writes. Patrick sits at the computer and says to Chari, "Okay, what do I write next?" Chari will say something, but Patrick will tell him, "They're not going to get that." And so Chari dictates it and Patrick paraphrases it so that everyone will get the point. It's a good combination. And I'm fine with that since I'm not the best writer in the world.

It's tricky when I'm working with Ed, because one of us has to be the primary writer. And that's usually me. He doesn't like to read and that means that I have to make sure that the main finding of the paper is in the first paragraph. But that's extremely useful because there are all sorts of impatient people out there.

And I've had other co-authors. One example would be Ravi Jagannathan. We wrote a paper on the CAPM debate because I wanted to understand it. I told him, "Pick the top three papers on that issue and I'll read them and then write the paper. You can be the second writer because you know all the fine, boring details." And that's what we did.[8]

So, it's great if I can find somebody to write beautifully for me – a Patrick-Chari team – but it's not always possible. You have to go with complementary skills, right? And with Ed, that means those damned T-accounts [*laughs*].

COLLABORATION

When you work with co-authors, how do you decide whom to work with? Is it all about those complementary skills?

I need co-authors who can deal with my bossiness. And I love it if they can do the things that I hate, like clean-up work; for example, when a referee asks you to relate your work to the other 800 papers in the literature.

I like doing the nerdy work; thinking about the theory, exploring the data, and doing the computation. And I like giving presentations. I spend a lot of time on them. For example, I had to give a plenary talk last summer at the SED (Society of Economic Dynamics) and prepared for two months. It took me the first month just to come up with the title: 'Intangible Gains to Openness'. And I did seven mini-bag lunches with my colleagues. For each one, I told them that they had to pound me into shape. And so I revamped it little by little. By the end, it went well. The preparation is a pain, but I like the feeling of getting the ideas out there. And I don't mind doing a show. In fact, I probably would be a good MBA teacher. It's just the nagging and whining that I wouldn't be able to handle.

How do you prefer to interact with your co-authors (e-mail, phone, or face-to-face)?

Face-to-face. Ed is at ASU (Arizona State University) half the year. I just flew down there for the week. My husband was upset. He said, "But it's Christmas time, we've got so much to do." And I told him, "I know, it's the perfect time to go." [*Laughs*].

What are the main challenges associated with collaborative work and how do you overcome them?

For me, collaborative work is fun. But here's one problem with Ed: sometimes I need time to just scrounge out my math and think about it, and all he wants to do is his T accounts. And so I say to him, "Go to your office and think about it your way and I'll think about it my way. Then we'll get together and figure out if we're on the same page." He'll get halfway down the hall, flip around, and tell me, "Okay, I thought about it." But I'll say, "No, go *all* the way down the hall and stay there for a while." Ed's a learning-by-talking person, and so is Chari. But sometimes I just need time with my pad and pencil.

RESEARCH ASSISTANCE AND FUNDING

How do you use research assistants?

Mostly for note-checking and tracking down things in the library.

How important is funding for getting your work done?

It's not. I work in the institution that prints the money [*laughs*].

SEMINAR PARTICIPATION AND NETWORKING

What are the benefits to attending a seminar that is closely related to your work versus one that is not closely related?

We invite people from all fields to give talks at the Fed, but most of the seminars are in macro. I get a lot out of the back-and-forth discussions with the audience.

How important is professional networking to success in research?

You might say that my profession is central banking. Our ex-Head of Research here, Art Rolnick, used to say, "I give you guys a certain amount of money to go to conferences; don't waste it." What he meant was, "Don't bother going to those 'system' conferences with only researchers from the Federal Reserve system; go to the academic conferences with researchers from everywhere." That gave us a bad reputation in the system for being jerks, but he was right. Why not just go to the main conferences? That's where the networking goes on. And because I have to edit a journal, I like to figure out who knows what. Plus, I always like to self-promote: "Don't you want to teach my paper in your class?" [*Laughs*].

COMMUNICATION OF RESEARCH

How do you find the right balance between communicating your research at an early stage versus the close-to-finished stage?

I'm always worried about 'too early'. And so I definitely don't give any talk without a paper. I'll even write up the slides as a paper just because I want some structure. The best thing is good slides. People should get the main ideas even if the presenter says nothing.

PUBLICATION

How do you decide upon the appropriate journal to send your research to?

It's tricky. If you want to increase the chances of publication, it helps to look at the kind of papers that are coming out in a particular journal, and who's on the editorial board. Do the editors know who is working on this topic when they send it out to referees, or are you just going to get some random person? Doing a little bit of research at the beginning can save time.

How would you best describe your approach to dealing with a 'revise and resubmit' request from a journal? How about an outright rejection?

A lot of people complain that referees ruin their papers. They don't. I think they're honest brokers. They're giving you their objective opinion, and that's vital. They make you go over a certain bar, which I need. And so I value the refereeing process. Do you want the blogging system where anybody gets to write nonsense?

What if you get an outright rejection? You kick some dirt and move on. That's life.

Do you think that the current structure of the publication process in economics facilitates or impedes scientific understanding and knowledge production?

I would love it if people didn't have to write so many papers. Stop counting the number of *AER*s someone has. Have they influenced the profession? Have we gone in a different direction? That's what we should be aiming for.

What has been your best and worst experience during the publication process?

I would say the only bad experience I've ever had is with an editor that felt that they had to have unanimity of the referees. Editors must be able to use their own judgment.

I recently had a good experience at the *AER* with our 'Technology Capital and the US Current Account' paper.[9] The referees basically said, "The central mechanisms at work here are A and B, but you provide no micro evidence. We want to see it." And so Ed and I had to figure it out. We got the right referees, they gave us the right bar, and we were able to jump over it, and ultimately get the paper published. Some people might have grumbled and said they made us do a boatload of work. But if it makes the paper great, I'll do it. Bring it on!

REFEREEING AND EDITING

Do you have any advice for a young scholar on being a referee?

My advice is don't do too much. And only take on things that are super-close to what you're doing. That's useful for building human capital.

Do you have any advice for a young scholar on being an editor?

My advice is don't take on any big editor jobs. I'm an editor at *RED (Review of Economic Dynamics)*, which requires less work. Usually, what I'm doing is getting a paper from a young guy whose main result shows up in Figure 8, Panel D and I'm telling him to get rid of Figures 1 through 7 and the first parts of Figure 8 so that the main result is not buried. They tend to follow my advice because they're just looking for the kind of feedback that I get from my colleagues here at the Fed.

TIME MANAGEMENT

How do you divide up your working day, both in terms of quantity and timing of different kinds of work?

Many research departments in the Fed system use a rule: X per cent of your time is for bank work and $1 - X$ is your own research time. But when our new Research Director (Kei-Mu Yi) came here, I told him, "We don't think that way. One hundred per cent of our time is policy-oriented. But a necessary input for good policy analysis is good research."

How do you balance multiple research projects?

I'm a parallel processor, so usually I have two projects going on at the same time. That helps, because if you get stuck on one of them, you can just work on the other.

How do you balance your personal and professional lives?

The trick is marrying another academic [*laughs*]. We know how the business works. But my husband is an engineer and has to do more dog-and-pony shows; he gets $4 million in grants and needs to constantly show that he is not wasting it.

We have two teenage girls. When they were younger, I asked them, "What do you say to your friends when they ask what your mom and dad do?" They said, "That you guys just sit in front of computers all day long, staring and typing." Now that they're older, they say, "It's something about the economy and space and fluids ... some boring stuff." [*Laughs*].

On weekends, I'll sometimes bring the kids to the Fed to do their homework. Many people think that I'm abusing my children by doing that, but they're fine. All I've done is turned them off to being economists [*laughs*].

REFLECTIONS AND THE FUTURE OF ECONOMICS

What have been the most important findings and contributions in your research fields during your career?

If you took the stock of papers in macro when I was a graduate student and compared it to now, you would say, "Oh, my God, we've advanced so much." The Keynesians were writing down investment or consumption equations using partial equilibrium analysis, but now we try to get the general equilibrium effects, if there are any. Bob Lucas and Tom Sargent's introduction to their 'After Keynesian Macroeconomics' article is brutal but gorgeous.[10] They had to beat up the Keynesians, but we can't get away with that now, because the New Keynesians aren't that different from the real business cycle theorists.

I could also tell there had been an enormous change when Ed wanted to do a practice for his Nobel seminar in Stockholm. He brought in some younger colleagues and started talking about how we don't do systems of equations anymore. They were thinking, "What are you talking about? We write out the first-order conditions and then we've got a system of equations that we solve." What he meant was in the past, somebody gives you the 'I' (investment) equation, somebody else gives you the 'C' (consumption) equation, and then you make a system. I said, "Ed, stop. You need to talk more explicitly about how we now write these models as fully articulated economic systems." He didn't realize he had to explain that, which was very interesting to see.

What are the strengths and weaknesses of your own research?

Strength: it's quantitative. Weakness: more micro has to come into play.

In the end, do you think the profession has helped to bring out and shape your research for the best?

I'm not sure about the profession. But my colleagues here at the Fed have completely shaped me – they're the best.

Do you have any professional regrets?

None. There's a line out of a Disney movie: "I'm a lucky bug."

What are your professional ambitions?

My professional ambition is to always remain in the trenches. I don't want to be a general because their job is boring. Tom Cooley once said to me, "Ellen, you need to become the President of the Minneapolis Fed." I told him how much I would hate it, and then Tom Sargent said I could just do it the Barbra Streisand way: hold only a few concerts that are so good that you build up a huge following. But I couldn't see it. I love being the dork sitting in the office and thinking about questions. That's so much more fun than being the general.

How would you describe the state of economics today? Are you optimistic about its future?

I am very optimistic. The only thing that I'm worried about is that we're getting a little stale. We need people saying, "You guys have it all wrong," which is why I want to be in the trenches. With the financial crisis, people have been saying that we're ruined. I think that's crazy; we knew all along that there's a lot to work on. We must remember to remain humble because there's always going to be the next revolution.

NOTES

1. Thomas J. Sargent (1979), *Macroeconomic Theory*, New York: Academic Press.
2. McGrattan, E.R. and E.C. Prescott (2000), 'Is the Stock Market Overvalued?', *Federal Reserve Bank of Minneapolis Quarterly Review*, Vol. 24, No. 4 (Fall), pp. 20–40.
3. McGrattan, E.R. and E.C. Prescott (2005), 'Taxes, Regulations, and the Value of US and UK Corporations', *Review of Economic Studies*, Vol. 72, No. 3 (July), pp. 767–796.
4. Lucas, Jr, R.E. (1978), 'Asset Prices in an Exchange Economy', *Econometrica*, Vol. 46, No. 6 (November), pp. 1429–1445.
5. Kydland, F.E. and E.C. Prescott (1982), 'Time to Build and Aggregate Fluctuations', *Econometrica*, Vol. 50, No. 6 (November), pp. 1345–1370.
6. Chari, V.V., Kehoe, P.J. and E.R. McGrattan (2002), 'Can Sticky Price Models Generate Volatile and Persistent Real Exchange Rates?', *Review of Economic Studies*, Vol. 69, No. 3 (July), pp. 533–563.
7. Clement, D. (2005), 'The Untouchables', *The Region*, December, pp. 30–33, 52–57.
8. Jagganathan, R. and E.R. McGrattan (1995), 'The CAPM Debate', *Federal Reserve Bank of Minneapolis Quarterly Review*, Vol. 19, No. 4 (Fall), pp. 2–17.
9. McGrattan, E.R. and E.C. Prescott (2010), 'Technology Capital and the US Current Account', *American Economic Review*, Vol. 100, No. 4 (September), pp. 1493–1522.
10. In light of the economic difficulties facing the US economy in the 1970s, Lucas and Sargent describe the predictions of Keynesian theory to be "wildly incorrect" and argue that, "The task now facing contemporary students of the business cycle is to sort through the wreckage, determining which features of that remarkable intellectual event called the Keynesian Revolution can be salvaged and put to good use and which others must be discarded. Though it is far from clear what the outcome of this process will be, it is already evident that it will necessarily involve the reopening of basic issues in monetary economics which have been viewed since the thirties as 'closed' and the reevaluation of every institutional framework within which monetary and fiscal policy is formulated in the advanced countries." (Robert E. Lucas, Jr and Thomas J. Sargent (1978), 'After Keynesian Macroeconomics', in *After the Phillips Curve: Persistence of High Inflation and High Unemployment*, Boston, MA: Federal Reserve Bank of Boston, pp. 49–50).

Paul Milgrom
(Stanford University)

Paul Milgrom was born in Detroit, Michigan in 1948 and graduated with an AB in mathematics from the University of Michigan in 1970 before obtaining both an MS in statistics and a PhD in business from Stanford University in 1978 and 1979 respectively. He has taught at Northwestern University, 1979–1983, Yale University, where he served as the Williams Brothers Professor of Management Studies and Professor of Economics between 1985 and 1987, and Stanford University, where he currently serves as the Shirley R. and Leonard W. Ely, Jr Professor of Humanities and Professor of Economics.

Professor Milgrom is best known for his contributions to microeconomic theory and his pioneering innovations in the practical design of multi-item auctions. His most-cited articles in chronological order include 'A Theory of Auctions and Competitive Bidding', *Econometrica* (1982), co-authored with Robert Weber, 'Rational Cooperation in the Finitely Repeated Prisoners' Dilemma', *Journal of Economic Theory* (1982), co-authored with David Kreps, John Roberts, and Robert Wilson, 'Bid, Ask and Transaction Prices in a Specialist Market with Heterogeneously Informed Traders', *Journal of Financial Economics* (1985), co-authored with Lawrence Glosten, 'The Economics of Modern Manufacturing: Technology, Strategy, and

Organization', *American Economic Review* (1990), co-authored with John Roberts, and 'Multitask Principal–Agent Analyses: Incentive Contracts, Asset Ownership and Job Design', *Journal of Law, Economics and Organization* (1991), co-authored with Bengt Holmstrom. His books include *Economics, Organization and Management* (Prentice-Hall, 1992), co-authored with John Roberts, and *Putting Auction Theory to Work* (Cambridge University Press, 2004).

Professor Milgrom's academic awards include the 2008 Erwin Plein Nemmers Prize in Economics, which is awarded every two years to recognize "work of lasting significance" in the discipline. The selection committee cited Milgrom "for contributions dramatically expanding the understanding of the role of information and incentives in a variety of settings, including auctions, the theory of the firm, and oligopolistic markets." Among his other honors, Milgrom was elected as a Fellow of the Econometric Society in 1984, a Fellow of the National Academy of Sciences in 1992, and a Fellow of the American Academy of Arts and Sciences in 2006. He was awarded an honorary doctorate from the Stockholm School of Economics in 2001. He served as Co-Editor of the *American Economic Review* from 1990 to 1993. Professor Milgrom's business activities have included designing auctions and exchanges, advising bidders, and founding an auction software company, Auctionomics.

I interviewed Paul Milgrom at the office of Auctionomics in Palo Alto, California. It was early-afternoon of Wednesday, 18 July 2010.

BACKGROUND INFORMATION

Your bachelor's and master's degrees are in mathematics and statistics respectively, and your PhD is in business. What was the eventual attraction to economics?

In retrospect, it seems so random that I wound up doing economics, or even becoming a scholar and teacher at all. My undergraduate years were in the turbulent 1960s and I had no idea about what I wanted to do. With a degree in mathematics, I was recruited for a job as an actuarial trainee and eventually became a Fellow of the Society of Actuaries. But my inclination to do research surfaced anyway. I published two award-winning papers in the *Transactions of the Society of Actuaries* about problems for which there were not yet well-established solutions.[1]

As a young actuary, I became interested in the other problems being studied around me, and headed off planning to get an MBA at Stanford. But once I was there, I found myself making suggestions to faculty about alternative methods for solving problems and got recruited after my first year in the MBA program to switch into the business doctoral program. I was exposed to operations research models for the first time by Professor Evan Porteus and found them quite exciting! I read, and was especially fascinated by, William Vickrey's paper about auctions; amazed that auctions could be so successfully studied from a mathematical point of view.[2] Next, I saw mathematical models being applied in interesting ways by young Stanford professors, including David Kreps and Michael Harrison, who engaged me in their research on the theory of financial markets. And, Robert Wilson, who became my dissertation advisor, was pushing the frontiers in the mathematical modeling of auctions.

I took a course from Wilson and decided to write my term paper intending to extend a study that he had begun about how information is reflected in the prices that emerge from auctions. What I did not know is that Wilson and Kreps had attempted and given up on the same problem, so when I made substantial progress, they were both very excited. The term paper became the main chapter of my doctoral dissertation, which I finished after just about two years in the doctoral program. I got hired into an amazing group of researchers that had come together at the MEDS (Managerial Economics and Decision Sciences) department at what is now the Kellogg Graduate School of Management. What we were working on was not mainstream economics then; the mainstream moved to us in large part as a result of the research we did.

MEDS was a very special place and became responsible for much of the influence of game theory on economics. Mark Satterthwaite, Roger Myerson, Bengt Holmstrom, David Baron, John Roberts, Nancy Stokey, and Robert Weber were young faculty there and they are now a virtual who's who of mechanism design, auctions, and applied game theory. You could write a book about this group alone!

My master's degree in statistics was not independently significant. The Statistics Department gave me credit for my actuarial studies and I took some doctoral courses in probability and stochastic processes because those seemed useful for the study of financial markets. Together, that created enough credits for my master's degree.

Why did you decide to pursue an academic career?

For me, becoming an academic is more a story of fate than one of will. Even as a young actuary, I was more curious about how to solve the new problems facing the field than doing routine and profitable consulting work. And I published my ideas in the actuary's journal.

When I went to graduate school, I thought I would become a business consultant, but the travel schedule seemed too onerous for the life I wanted to live. I liked the idea of having the freedom of a scholar to work on the puzzles that attracted me, rather than on the problems that somebody else identified.

As a researcher, which colleagues have been most influential or inspirational?

That brings us back to MEDS and the great colleagues I had there. Morten Kamien, who helped to build that group, refers to that period at MEDS in the late 1970s as the "puppy wars," because the young professors there were so competitive with one another. Imagine the setting. We have an expectation that perhaps half of a typical crop of assistant professors will get tenure, and none of us had any idea how unusual and outstanding this group was: Myerson, now a Nobel Laureate, Holmstrom, President of the Econometric Society, and Stokey, Fellow of the American Academy of Arts and Sciences. Every member of the group I've named has left an important mark on economics or game theory.

Mort, by the way, had an unusual strategy that paid huge dividends in building that group. He simply hired the smartest young people he could get, without the usual regard to field balance that constrains economics departments' hiring. Nobody else was hiring scholars doing game theory, so he could assemble the very best in one place. We learned from one another. We competed. We would go into the coffee room at MEDS and sit down to watch one colleague at the blackboard explain to another some recent research result. I'd think, "Wow! That is really good. I've got to work harder!"

GENERAL THOUGHTS ON RESEARCH

What is the value of pure versus applied research in economics?

I think the pure versus applied distinction, which is about the questions asked, is commonly confused with the empirical versus theoretical distinction, which is about the methods used.

One cannot usually do important policy-related research based on empirics alone, without developing some sort of theory based on the evidence, because policy decisions often depend on counterfactuals: what would happen to foreign investment if we cut taxes and reduced interest rates? One needs a theory based on empirical studies of the past to predict what will happen when something new is tried. One can sometimes do policy experiments to test proposed new policies, but even then, theory is what guides the decision about which proposals to test.

In the area of market design, where I do much of my own current research, theoretical studies highlight what empirical and experimental research seeks to measure. And those of us who do theoretical work are having very applied impacts, creating the market rules that have been considered and often adopted for everything from school matching (New York and Boston) to kidney exchanges (New England) to radio spectrum auctions (worldwide).

How would you describe the dialogue between theory and empirics in economics?

The quality of the dialogue between researchers using different methods – empirical, experimental or theoretical – varies among fields in economics. Certainly, in fields like macroeconomics and international trade, there is a close collaboration between those who propose theories and those who do empirical studies. In my field of market design, I see absolutely no barriers to communications among those who do theory, experiments, and empirical tests. Some of the best researchers, like Alvin Roth at Harvard, do work of all three kinds.

How has your research agenda changed over time?

As a young researcher, I didn't really have a research agenda; I just worked on the problems that I thought were fascinating. At first, I liked auction theory and found flaws in the ways that it was done, so I set out to develop methods that were more sound and felt lucky to see how well that worked out.

My training in economics at the Stanford Business School was very incomplete, so when I got to Northwestern University, I was still looking around to see what would most interest me. I was introduced to broader questions in economics by listening to seminars my colleagues gave or watching the presentations they made on the blackboard in the coffee room.

John Roberts soon became my friend and posed questions about limit pricing and organization, which we puzzled about together. Because of my training in mathematics, I was interested in why some of our models were tractable and others were not, which launched me into certain questions of game theory. I was like a kid in a candy store! It was fun!

Do you think it is important to have broad research interests?

What does 'broad' mean, after all? A researcher's interests need to be wide enough that he can generate a series of interesting research problems to stay active and productive. For some great researchers, like Alvin Roth, that is done by mixing empirical, theoretical, and experimental studies of the same policy issue. For others, the mastery of some method, whether it is experimental or dynamic stochastic theory models, is enough. For still others, like Barry Weingast, the breadth comes from mixing perspectives across disciplines; economic, political science, history, and game theory.

Do you think there is any difference in the types of work done by researchers at different stages in their careers based on tenure concerns, publication requirements or other pressures? Should there be a difference?

There are differences, but I'm not convinced they are damaging or that they are based entirely on the factors that you describe. If tenure and publication were the driving factors, we'd expect that the riskier research and biggest breakthroughs would come from senior scholars, who can better afford a dry spell with low output. But I don't think that is an accurate characterization of what we see. Most of the research that is cited by the Nobel Prize committee in economics emphasizes work done when the researcher was still young. Michael Spence and John Nash, for example, are cited essentially for the work in their doctoral theses.

A typical doctoral student becomes well read in the subject matter of her doctoral dissertation, and graduates with unfinished work to do in that area. As a new teacher, lots of time is usually eaten up in the first year or two adapting to that. Meanwhile, the young professor is attending seminars and hearing new ideas until she finally has time for a major new effort. And so career demands certainly affect research patterns. But I don't see much evidence that young economics researchers are averse to being innovative risk-takers.

You are one of the few economic theorists whose work has directly built markets. How has that affected your views on how to do research?

Theory research usually abstracts from some important aspects of a problem in order to give a better treatment of the remaining issues. Just as a beginning student in physics might solve an incline plane problem with a hypothetical uniformly sloped, frictionless surface, my colleague Bengt Holmstrom and I studied incentive contracts assuming away income and wealth effects, and assuming that the economic environment was stationary.

But when I do market design, things change. It is not enough to study the outcomes of markets when players are perfectly rational, or when they are competitive, because they might not be. And so I find myself drawn to do more comprehensive research, investigating more behavioral assumptions and more aspects of the performance of alternative market designs.

IDEA GENERATION

Where do you get your research ideas? At what point does an idea become a project that you devote resources to?

I'd say that the bigger question is one of deciding what problems to work on. When I think about something for a while, I usually find at least some angle that is worth investigating. If there are big insights to be had, they usually come later, as I look at the problem and what others have written or said about it.

I started working on auctions because I was excited by Vickrey and because my advisor, Wilson, had written about that. I tried to improve on Wilson's work, and that led to openings to do other things. I got interested in principal–agent theory from discussions with Bengt Holmstrom, and we wrote together to explore that.[3] John Roberts and I jointly read the work of a sociologist, Jay Galbraith, about how organizations adapt to uncertainty and we wondered whether it could be made meaningful in economic terms. That initiated a long line of our work.[4]

Most recently, advising actual bidders and helping to design real markets has pointed out the inadequacies of many parts of existing theory, so I've begun to work on that.[5] It is really exciting to be able to recognize new problems from applications I've worked on, rather than just by reading the work of other scholars. This period is very satisfying in that way!

IDEA EXECUTION

What makes a good theoretical paper? Can you give an example?

The papers I like best – whether theoretical, empirical or experimental – are ones that ask 'interesting' new questions and give simple, clear answers. It should go without saying that the methods used need to be sound.

For theoretical papers, I've already mentioned Vickrey's paper, which was stunningly original. It showed that certain seemingly different auctions were really the same game ('strategic equivalence') and that there is a strategy-proof mechanism for getting to efficient outcomes. Another favorite is 'College Admission and the Stability of Marriage' by Gale and Shapley.[6] That paper is so simple that it hardly seems technical, yet it introduced the concept of stability and showed that stable matches exist for certain problems (and fail to exist for others). And Akerlof's 'lemons' paper is a third.[7] Again, it asked a new question about how adverse selection affects the viability of markets and showed how it could cause a market to collapse entirely.

Among my own publications, I think the 'multitask' papers co-authored with Bengt Holmstrom are my best on that criterion.[8] We asked how incentive theory changes when the agent's task has more than one dimension and we gave some pretty simple answers that help us to account for facts about the world.

What makes a good empirical paper? Can you give an example?

The basic criterion is much the same; it is only the relevant methods that differ. One old favorite of mine is Joshua Angrist's paper about the effect of military service on veterans' earnings.[9] He used data from the Vietnam era, when there was a lottery that determined one's place in the military draft, to tease out that effect. It was an interesting question, beautifully addressed.

When you hit a brick wall on a project, do you continue to work on the problem or do you take a break from it and work on something else?

There is no one answer to that, partly because 'brick wall' is just a metaphor. Sometimes, when a theory problem is too hard, I move to a simpler but related problem. Holmstrom and I came to our multitask work when our research into the problem of common agency seemed too hard.

I don't usually consciously give up on a problem. Typically, I have several projects going, so it is not really a matter of taking a break. The old, hard problem stews in the back of my mind and, eventually, if I can't make any progress and don't want to simplify, I may forget about it for a while, hoping to come back to it later. Probably, I just forget about some of these.

Related to the previous question, when it appears that a project isn't going to turn out as hoped, do you scrap the project or aim to send the work to a second-tier or field journal?

I don't have a journal in mind when I do a project. I'm just trying to do interesting, excellent work. I scrap it if the work is not interesting to me, not just because some referee doesn't like it.

What has been the biggest change during your career in how researchers in your fields conduct research?

There have been several big changes that affected me. The use of experiments is one. I've been impressed by that and have tried my own hand in one recently. Another is the contact of microeconomic theorists with practical applications, particularly in market design. But my friend Roger Myerson has also been giving advice about constitutions and nation-building based on a deep theoretical understanding of how institutions gain strength.

THE WRITING PROCESS

Which aspect of the writing process do you find most difficult?

Getting started is the hardest part. Actually, for doing theory, writing is part of the research process. I like to write the introduction to my paper early in the process and then to rewrite it once I have my results developed. The first draft of the introduction is the way I clarify for myself the scope of my project, what I hope to achieve, and why I think it may be important. That is where I start.

What steps have you taken during your career to improve the quality of your writing?

That began early for me. When Robert Weber and I were writing our 1982 auction papers, we debated about every paragraph, every sentence, every word, every comma, and every hyphen.[10] We read Theodore Bernstein's book *The Careful Writer* and enjoyed some hilarious moments. I can still remember laughing about hyphenation examples like 'five-inch-gun crew' and 'small-business men'. Those are harder to parse without the hyphens.

I wrote a lot with John Roberts, whose style was so different from mine. For one thing, he uses much longer sentences. I joked that was because, as undergraduates, he studied history and I studied mathematics. We worked together effectively because we admired one another and were both concerned mainly with clarity and effect.

How do you split up the writing tasks among co-authors?

That depends on many things. I have had some frequent co-authors in my career and then usually one of us writes the entire first draft of a paper. When John Roberts and I wrote our book, *Economics, Organization and Management*, we divided up writing the first drafts of chapters based roughly on what we had been teaching.

COLLABORATION

When you work with co-authors, how do you decide whom to work with?

When I was new in the profession, that was easy. At Northwestern, if two of us were discussing an idea that seemed exciting, we might start work together. I found it more fun to have someone to talk to during the project, to share the excitement at every hurdle leap and every nice turn of phrase. If the work went especially well, we'd write a paper. In three cases, with Robert Weber, John Roberts, and Bengt Holmstrom, those collaborations were lots of fun and we continued to work.

Later, more co-authorships began over discussions I had with colleagues, when we had all contributed something interesting to the discussion. For example, my papers with Larry Glosten, Nancy Stokey, Ilya Segal, and Larry Ausubel developed in that way.

Is geographical proximity ever an important consideration in choosing a co-author? How has this changed in the course of your career?

Oh, yes! Again, the point for me originally was to share the excitement. Today, my co-authors are younger scholars who are probably just doing me a favor. They claim to be inspired by my ideas, but they talk more to one another and less to me.

How do you prefer to interact with your co-authors (e-mail, phone, or face-to-face)?

Today, the work proceeds by electronic means. E-mail is part of it. But the cloud and Skype play roles too. For example, my co-authors Yeon-Koo Che, Eric Budish, and Fuhito Kojima share files with me using Dropbox, which keeps files in a shared directory synchronized across our computers. If I open that folder on my computer, I'll see just what they see on theirs. I have different folders for different co-authors, and the Dropbox software ensures that all of them are always up-to-date.

What are the biggest challenges associated with collaborative work and how do you overcome them?

I've been lucky to have had three co-authors with whom I have written multiple times. But at different stages in my career, the challenges were different. Right now, for example, I'm writing with younger scholars who seem to have a lot of time and energy to work. When you're all working on solving a problem, it's nice to have a similar amount of time available, because there is competition about who's going to find the solution first. I've had to adapt as the senior scholar working with younger scholars. It still rubs me wrong to be puzzling over a problem and have someone else call me with the solution. I guess you never get over the desire to work through those things yourself. And so at this stage in my career, the fact that we work at different paces and we bring different skills is a challenge to me.

When I was really young, one of the biggest challenges was credit; the university supposedly gives credit more or less equally to co-authors or gives each co-author full credit for the work that is done. But there was an unfortunate incident when Robert Weber and I were working together. We co-authored seven papers, and somewhere late in the collaboration, we both came up for tenure and I got it and he didn't, which suggested that the committee wasn't giving us equal credit for our work. I don't know exactly what happened, but it was devastating to us as co-authors because Bob felt at that point that he obviously wasn't getting his share of the credit and couldn't continue to work with me.

I'm pretty well known. I once wrote an influential paper with Larry Glosten and people would ask me, "What was Larry's contribution in that paper?" What did they mean by that? It was collaborative work![11] But it does create some tension when people of different rank are contributing to a paper, and I'm not sure that I ever successfully dealt with that.

RESEARCH ASSISTANCE AND FUNDING

How do you use research assistants?

Last year, Marissa Beck was working with me. I had her go over papers that I had written, partly for training, but also to check that everything was correct. Sometimes, I would ask whether she could come up with a shorter proof of something that I thought was ugly. Or I might ask her to present a paper that I thought was interesting, and I would give her feedback.

I tend to think of RAs partly as apprentices. They're learning how to do the research, and my job is to get them to help me.

How important is funding for getting your work done?

I haven't had a big problem getting funding, but things have to get paid for otherwise I can't do them.

Do you have any advice for a young scholar on the funding process?

As a theorist, I always try to make it clear to the reviewers of my grant application that this is a research process, and that if I knew what the result was going to be, I wouldn't need a grant. And so if you are also doing theory, my advice is that you should show the whole flow of the research; things that you are finishing up, things that are in process and things that you hope are coming down the pike.

SEMINAR PARTICIPATION AND NETWORKING

What are the benefits to attending a seminar that is closely related to your work versus one that is not closely related?

[*Laughs*]. The reason I'm laughing is that I tend to have fairly wide interests and I partly discover what I'm interested in during seminars. I'll go to one and say, "That's a curious point. I wonder if I can develop it further or give it to a graduate student to work on." And so I think it's really important not to become narrow. I get nearly as much out of the seminars that are not closely related to my own research, because they inspire new ideas and new perspectives. But I don't need a long seminar for the ones that are closely related to my own research. The presenter could have given me a few sentences and I'd have said, "Oh, I see how that works."

How important is professional networking to success in research?

It is important to present your work in front of other people for several reasons. First, you get feedback and sometimes that feedback is surprising. Second, if you're doing good work and nobody knows about it, you're not going to get a good job. And third, sometimes you find co-authors that way; you make a presentation and somebody makes a comment and afterwards you say, "Hey, let's write a paper about that." That's happened to me a bunch of times in my career.

To what extent is the absence of departmental colleagues working in one's research area a major disadvantage?

As I've already said, I don't think you want to be too narrow. People need to learn from others and from the contributions made to other parts of economics. And so you adapt your breadth of interests somewhat to the people around you.

COMMUNICATION OF RESEARCH

How do you find the right balance between communicating your research at an early stage versus the close-to-finished stage?

That's less of a problem for a theorist. There are famous cases from science where people were racing to discover something, like the double helix, for example. But I have rarely found research to be a race such that I had to keep my work secret. And so I have always been happy to publish working papers. In fact, within theory, the earlier you publish, the more priority you have.

What are the unique challenges to giving a seminar and how do you overcome them?

I just came back from lecturing in Brazil to a group that included everybody, from students who were barely into their doctoral studies, to Roger

Myerson, who's a Nobel Laureate. Speaking to an audience like that is really difficult. You have to decide who it is you are trying to reach, and at what level, and you have to motivate them to believe that what you're doing in your research is new and interesting. And I think the difficulty of faking it is part of what inspires me to do good research. It really *does* have to be new and interesting to convince people. And so I try not to just convince myself of bs about that; I try to actually say, "Gee, I've got an audience that I have to present to next week. This better be honest and good. Let's give the best presentation I can."

PUBLICATION

How do you decide upon the appropriate journal to send your research to?

How do I decide on the appropriate journal? Sometimes, the references make it obvious; you are referring to or building on work that's already been done in a particular area. But the journals have been changing. There are more and more papers being submitted and the general journals like the *American Economic Review* have also broken up into the more specialized *AEJ Micro* and the *AEJ Macro*.

How would you best describe your approach to dealing with a 'revise and resubmit' request from a journal? How about an outright rejection?

This is something that has changed enormously over the years. These days, the referees expect a lot more control over the paper than they did 20 years ago. I find this very difficult, because I have a point of view and I like to think that one of my advantages is that I, as the author, have a *unique* point of view. And so if I get a 'revise and resubmit', the challenge is, "Well, am I going to argue with the referee or am I just going to get on with it by doing what the referee suggests?" I guess I'm a little combative because I more often do the former. I try to stay true to my vision. If the referee has an objection but I still think I'm right, I try to ask myself, "Why is the referee not convinced?" I'm not going to tell the referee what he wants to hear just to get published; I'm going to try to convince him, or at least the editor, of my point of view. And so, I look, I listen, I pay attention to what the referees say, but I don't always write what they want or expect.

My response to a rejection depends on the basis for the rejection. Recently, I got a rejection that said that the result was known, and it turned out it was. I was surprised to discover that something that I had worked on was already known, and that rejection stands. Usually, though, it is almost never the case that my work is exactly the same as what somebody did before. There might be some overlap and then I need to decide whether there is enough to focus on what's different and reshape my paper around it. In that rejected paper, there is a question about both the technical contribution and the substantive contribution. The referees were technical referees who I don't think were prepared to assess the substantive contribution. They said the method that I've emphasized has already been developed elsewhere. And so sometimes, I don't just have to say, "The referee doesn't understand what the contribution is." Instead, as with a 'revise and resubmit', I need to rewrite the paper so that it is convincing to the readers. Yet, I'm still looking for guidance, and if the referee says there's an error or that it's already been done, then that may take so much out of the paper that I have to give up on it. But I don't usually give up on such things [*laughs*].

Do you think that the current structure of the publication process in economics facilitates or impedes scientific understanding and knowledge production?

Economics is very strange. The publication lags are very long and the papers have gotten, for the most part, longer. I think there are way too many long papers. The journals encourage verbosity and the rankings of institutions and economists do so as well by having page counts in major journals as a basis of evaluation. I love some of the old papers by Lloyd Shapley or John Nash or Gerard Debreu that are very short; there's a nugget in there, you get to it quickly and that's it, you've learned something. And then you chew on it for a while. You don't read 40 pages about it the way some papers are written today. I often feel that I would have benefited from shorter papers. And so I think that the current process slows and distorts the creation of knowledge compared to what I think is ideal.

What has been your best and worst experience during the publication process?

Oh, boy! I had an unusually favorable start to my career in multiple ways, but in the publication process also. As I explained earlier, the first paper that I wrote was one that I had worked on as a term paper for a course. My dissertation advisor was very excited because, unbeknownst to me, Wilson and Kreps had worked on the same problem and hadn't made any progress on it, and so they were surprised when I did. He told me to write it up as a paper, and I submitted it to *Econometrica*. At the time, Hugo Sonnenschein was the editor and I got back a letter from him that said, "Accepted." That didn't strike me as odd at the time, but now I understand that one hardly ever has a paper that is just accepted – the referees always want some changes to be made. A wonderful first experience![12]

In my 1982 paper with Robert Weber in *Econometrica*, we pored over its structure again and again until we finally photocopied it and sent it in. One referee wrote back and said, "I can't find anything to criticize in this paper. There's not even a typo." In the early eighties with hand-typed papers, that was a big deal!

My worst experience was my book with John Roberts. That was published by Prentice-Hall, who had recently made a change in their economics editor. We were trying to get the book in shape, but our calls were unanswered and our letters were ignored. This went on for many, many months. It turned out that Prentice-Hall was concealing from authors and potential authors the fact that a key editor had quit. That was really terrible and explains why there has never been a revision of the book. Our experience with Prentice-Hall was so bad that we couldn't face up to working with them again. Work with publishers you can rely on, or you can get hurt otherwise.

REFEREEING AND EDITING

How do you decide upon whether or not to accept a refereeing job?

Most of the papers that come my way could have some interest, and I typically accept the job if I have time. But I don't accept from the journals that I don't publish in. For the most part, I don't think they are doing good work in areas that I'm interested in, and so I'm not interested in refereeing papers there either.

How has your approach to refereeing changed through time?

I find more and more that the center of my refereeing is deciding whether what's been done is interesting, and only secondarily focusing on whether the details are well executed. One thing that I've come to believe is that if a paper is not very well written the first time, it's not going to be very well written in its revision either. It's something about the author's capabilities or inclinations. And so what I am really looking for is interesting ideas.

Do you have any advice for a young scholar on being a referee?

Don't take on more than you can chew. Some young people who are very good, and turn around reports very quickly, get a lot of requests. But find out what the norm is. You may be above it, but you are not obliged to take every request that comes your way. In fact, it can pay to turn down some requests.

As former Co-Editor of the American Economic Review, *do you have any advice for a young scholar on being an editor?*

There is a lot of prominence that comes from being an editor. It gets you some name recognition within your department or within a certain group of people, people know that it involves a lot of hard work, and it means that somebody has judged you to be a reliable judge of research. On the other hand, editing jobs can be extremely demanding. Some editors make a routine out of it and do it for many years, but for some of us, three or four years is enough and we want to move on to other things. And so people should think hard about it because editing is a major commitment. It's almost like the decision to have a child. If you're going to do it well, it requires a lot of time. When people are asked to become an editor of a major journal, they very rarely say "no" – they find the honor and prestige so significant – but maybe they say "yes" more often than they should.

TIME MANAGEMENT

How do you divide up your working day, both in terms of quantity and timing of different kinds of work?

In the last year, I took a year of leave to work on commercial things. I've gotten very excited about creating theories that work and making real-world markets work better. And so the quantity and timing of different kinds of work have changed enormously. Again, I think that it's too easy to coast into doing what you are asked to do: do a certain amount of teaching and spend the rest of your time doing research. But I do try to make decisions about what I'm going to spend my time on. This year, I decided I was going to open this office that we're sitting in and actually get my research put to work.

When I worked at Northwestern University, I lived almost three miles from campus, which was close to an hour's walk home. My best work time in terms of solving problems was the walk. It was quite wonderful. I lived in

Central Park Avenue in Evanston and I would go down a street called Lincoln Beautiful that was lined with big stone houses. It was lovely all times of the year. During the day, I might be working on a problem with a co-author (especially Robert Weber at that time), but there are a lot of interruptions when you're in the office. And so those walks were an amazingly productive time; I could just focus in on a problem and think hard about it without anybody interrupting me. It became such a pattern that I would have an insight or a solution to a problem on the walk home that my co-authors started thinking, "Oh, oh, Paul just left the building – we're going to get a call in an hour." I remember that Bob used to rush to his office to work on the same problem because he didn't want me to always solve it first. And so I'd get home and make the call and he would say, "Yes, I have it too!" [*Laughs*]

How do you balance multiple research projects?

The struggle in balancing multiple research projects is deciding what I think is important and making sure I'm putting enough time into that, rather than what's being pushed on me by deadlines and by others. Ultimately, my excitement comes from doing good work; the work that I think is important. There is a lot of pressure, if you have multiple projects going on, to do other things. And so it's all about taking control and making a decision.

What is the optimal number of projects that you could be working on at any given time?

There's a question about what it means to be 'working on'. At peak periods of my productivity, I remember saying "no" to some interesting projects. For example, there is a Drew Fudenberg and Jean Tirole paper that is about a subject that I declined to work on with those guys because at the time I had four other really interesting projects going on. But usually, it's not about the optimal number of projects; there is room for one more project if it meets my standards.

How do you balance your research and non-research activities?

The biggest trend in my career has been that I've been doing more and more consulting. It's a problem for me sometimes because I wonder if I have enough time left to do a good job at my basic teaching and research.

How about the balance between your personal and professional lives?

That's been an interesting one throughout my whole life. When I was working on my book with John Roberts, I became concerned that my children were going to be ignored. A book is exhausting; it engages you totally. That called for real time management. And so one of the things I did was set aside one night of the week for each of my two children. I would take them out to dinner and just have some one-on-one time with each of them. Wives never have trouble making demands, but for your children you need to decide what's important so that you can set aside time for them.

I remember Mikhail Gorbachev coming to Stanford when the Soviet Union was collapsing, and I was invited to participate in a meeting with him. But it was one of the nights with my children. I had told them that, as long as I was in town, the priority was that the night belonged to them. And so I skipped the meeting with Gorbachev to go out to dinner with my daughter that night [*laughs*].

REFLECTIONS AND THE FUTURE OF ECONOMICS

What have been the most important findings and contributions in your research fields during your career?

I've been doing economic theory for a long time and there have been great advances in the whole idea of equilibrium and whether it makes any sense at all and, if so, *which* kind of equilibrium makes most sense. In terms of areas of theory, mechanism design came into existence during my career. When I was at Northwestern, Roger Myerson, Bengt Holmstrom, and Mark Satterthwaite, and Dave Baron were there making theoretical contributions that became fundamental in that area. It was just huge and changed the way we think about a lot of things. Some of those contributions were applications, such as understanding that the national resident matching program was using the Gale-Shapley algorithm, which is one of Al Roth's contributions to the economics of matching. And then that was used to learn lessons and create new mechanisms, such as the medical match to figure out how to treat couples and then how to adapt it to school matching in New York and Boston. People began doing economic engineering. And on the auctions side, new kinds of auctions were designed for real-world problems, which is where my own contributions in recent years have largely been.

What are the biggest challenges facing your research fields?

In the fields I've just described, there's been something of a loss of uncertainty. In the 1970s and 1980s, I was one of the people at the forefront of applying game theoretic models and equilibrium theory to new economic problems. Nash equilibrium, for example, was hardly being applied before then. And it was huge movement because it was a general method for treating all kinds of social institutions. But people don't always play Nash equilibrium; we are not sure why in some games they do and in other games they don't. And so this general method that has raised our sights and aspirations is highly imperfect and that represents a real challenge for how we should think about these things.

Certainly, there is a division right now. There are some experimenters who think they have the answer: you simulate an institution in a laboratory. I don't agree with that. Laboratory simulations are, for the most part, based on lots of assumptions. For example, there are experiments going on using auctions, which involve complex auction institutions. But which details should be modeled in the lab, what should the values of the bidders be, and how should they be related to each other? It is easy for experiments to miss the main point. For example, it turns out that we have learned from practical work that budgets are extremely important in determining some auction outcomes. But treatments based on varying budgets are almost never included in experiments. And so working out the role of experiments in economic theory is a big challenge.

What are the strengths and weaknesses of your own research?

A growing strength of my own research right now is how well grounded it is. Early on in my career, aesthetics drove my research. I still like a lot of beautiful and interesting work, but part of what I'm doing these days is designing markets and doing research about how to solve particular problems that come out of the market design question. That's a strength. But as usual when practical things are driving research, they can also be too narrowing. I approve of the pursuit of knowledge for its sake. There is something about that that just feels right, and the questions that I'm drawn to are not necessarily the deepest, most general questions. I really admire it when I see other researchers come by and present seminars that are asking those sorts of questions. I strive to have both relevance and depth, but I don't always achieve it.

In the end, do you think the profession has helped to bring out and shape your research for the best?

I'm not sure that 'the profession' is the right level of analysis, or that 'shaping' is the right objective. I was lucky. I fell into an ecosystem at Northwestern University that supported research outside what was then the mainstream, without attempting to shape it back in. I was a theorist and needed little more than opportunity, challenge, and stimulation, and I got all that just when I needed it.

And, despite the novelty of game theory applications in those years, the economics profession was fascinated and quick to reward this research. Like many of my colleagues, I got early interest from top institutions, like Harvard and Yale. I was awarded early tenure at Yale, less than three years out of graduate school, followed by an endowed chair. And I received more offers from Harvard, Princeton, Berkeley, and Stanford. I definitely felt encouraged and supported.

Do you have any professional regrets?

Yes, I do have professional regrets. This comes out of competitiveness. As I said earlier, when I was at Northwestern, there were so many people there doing mechanism design. I avoided working on it for fear of just being right in the middle of a crunch. I wanted to step out and do things that were more unusual. And so I asked other sorts of questions. But it was a mistake not to do fundamental research on what turned out to be the most important area of theory for a period of decades.

What are your professional ambitions?

That's changed over the years. When I was young, I wanted recognition. For example, I was hoping that someday I would be elected to the National Academy of Sciences. That has happened. But I don't think of those things as goals at all these days. Mostly, what I want to do is create markets that work well. I only think about formal awards and recognition when others ask about it, although when it happens, it's a great opportunity for friends to get together and celebrate.

How would you describe the state of economics today? Are you optimistic about its future?

The state of economics today? I don't stop very often to reflect on that. I would say that ten to fifteen years ago, economists were maybe a little too self-satisfied. Every graduate program taught the same thing as if we had core knowledge that was so well grounded that it could be taught like quantum physics. Our models aren't that accurate. The truth is that there are lots of things out there that we find puzzling, but now more and more research reflects the fact that economists are taking different approaches when looking for insights. That's got to be a good thing.

NOTES

1. Milgrom, P. (1975), 'On Understanding the Effects of GAAP Reserve Assumptions', *Transactions of the Society of Actuaries*, Vol. XXVII, pp. 71–88; Milgrom, P.R. (1985), 'Measuring Interest-Rate Risk', *Transactions of the Society of Actuaries*, Vol. XXXVI, pp. 241–257.
2. Vickrey, W. (1961), 'Counterspeculation, Auctions, and Competitive Sealed Tenders', *Journal of Finance*, Vol. 16, No. 1 (March), pp. 8–37.
3. See, for example, Holmstrom, B. and P.R. Milgrom (1987), 'Aggregation and Linearity in the Provision of Intertemporal Incentives', *Econometrica*, Vol. 55, No. 2 (March), pp. 303–328; Holmstrom, B. and P.R. Milgrom (1990), 'Regulating Trade Among Agents', *Journal of Institutional and Theoretical Economics*, Vol. 146, No. 1 (March), pp. 85–105.
4. See, for example, Milgrom, P.R. and J. Roberts (1988), 'An Economic Approach to Influence Activities and Organizational Responses', *American Journal of Sociology*, Vol. 94 (Supplement), July, S154–S179.
5. See, for example, Milgrom, P.R. (2011), 'Critical Issues in Market Design', *Economic Inquiry*, Vol. 48, No. 2 (April), pp. 311–320.
6. Gale, D. and L.S. Shapley (1962), 'College Admissions and the Stability of Marriage', *The American Mathematical Monthly*, Vol. 69, No. 1 (January), pp. 9–15.
7. Akerlof, G.A. (1970), 'The Market for "Lemons": Quality Uncertainty and the Market Mechanism', *Quarterly Journal of Economics*, Vol. 84, No. 3 (August), pp. 488–500.
8. Holmstrom, B. and P.R. Milgrom (1991), 'Multitask Principal–Agent Analyses: Incentive Contracts, Asset Ownership and Job Design', *Journal of Law, Economics and Organization*, Vol. 7 (September), pp. 24–52; Holmstrom, B. and P.R. Milgrom (1994), 'The Firm as an Incentive System', *American Economic Review*, Vol. 84, No. 4 (September), pp. 972–991.
9. Angrist, J.D. (1990), 'Lifetime Earnings and the Vietnam Era Draft Lottery: Evidence from Social Security Administrative Records', *American Economic Review*, Vol. 80, No. 3 (June), pp. 313–366.
10. Milgrom, P.R. and R.J. Weber (1982), 'The Value of Information in a Sealed Bid Auction', *Journal of Mathematical Economics*, Vol. 10, No. 1 (June), pp. 105–114; Milgrom, P.R. and R.J. Weber (1982), 'A Theory of Auctions and Competitive Bidding', *Econometrica*, Vol. 50, No. 5 (September), pp. 1089–1122.

11. Glosten, L.R. and P.R. Milgrom (1985), 'Bid, Ask and Transaction Prices in a Specialist Market with Heterogeneously Informed Traders', *Journal of Financial Economics*, Vol. 14, No. 1 (March), pp. 71–100.
12. Milgrom, P.R. (1979), 'A Convergence Theorem for Competitive Bidding with Differential Information', *Econometrica*, Vol. 47, No. 3 (May), pp. 679–688.

Ariel Pakes
(Harvard University)

Ariel Pakes was born in Alberta, Canada and graduated with a bachelor's degree in economics and philosophy and a master's degree in economics from The Hebrew University of Jerusalem in 1971 and 1973 respectively. He then obtained a second master's degree in economics as well as a PhD in economics from Harvard University in 1976 and 1979 respectively. Professor Pakes has taught economics at a number of universities, including The Hebrew University of Jerusalem, 1980–1986, the University of Wisconsin–Madison, 1986–1988, Yale University, where he was Professor of Economics between 1988 and 1997 and the Charles and Dorothea Dilley Professor of Economics between 1997 and 1999, and Harvard University, where he has taught since 1999, currently serving as the Steven McArthur Heller Professor of Economics.

Professor Pakes' research interests are industrial organization, the economics of technological change, and econometric theory. His most-cited articles in chronological order include 'On Patents, R&D, and the Stock Market Rate of Return', *Journal of Political Economy* (1985), 'Patents as Options: Some Estimates of the Value of Holding European Patent Stocks', *Econometrica* (1986), 'Simulation and the Asymptotics of Optimization Estimators', *Econometrica* (1989), co-authored with David Pollard,

'Automobile Prices in Market Equilibrium', *Econometrica* (1995), co-authored with Steve Berry and James Levinsohn, 'Markov-Perfect Industry Dynamics: A Framework for Empirical Work', *Review of Economic Studies* (1995), co-authored with Rick Ericson.

In 1988, Professor Pakes was elected as a Fellow of the Econometric Society, from whom he received the Frisch Medal in 1986, and was elected as a Fellow of the American Academy of Arts and Sciences in 2002. His editorial positions include being Advisory Editor at *Econometrica* and *Economics Letters*, and Associate Editor of the *Journal of the European Economic Association* and *Economics of Innovation and New Technology*. Between 1999 and 2009, he was Editor of the *RAND Journal of Economics*.

I interviewed Ariel Pakes in his office in the Department of Economics at the Stern School of Business, New York University, where he is a Visiting Scholar. It was mid-afternoon of Friday, 16 July 2010.

BACKGROUND INFORMATION

What was your attraction to economics?

I was quite good in the sciences in high school, but I was also very interested in history and society. My brother suggested I try economics. In truth, I did a lot of philosophy during my BA, and there was a period of time when I very much wanted to be an author. I did a trip around the world and tried to write a novel. It was the story of a kid like me who had traveled 5,000 miles away from home and lived in different cultures. Before I started it, I had sent away for fellowships to do graduate work in economics, in case I didn't like being an author, and I got one from Harvard. At some point on my trip, I was on an island called Tenerife, off the coast of Africa, and there were three people who were living with me in a little place there. I gave each of them a chapter of the novel, and invited them to dinner at the nearest restaurant, which was about six or seven miles away. I asked them whether I should go back to Harvard or continue writing my novel. They all said I should go back to Harvard. And so that was the end of my writing career.

As a student, which professors were most influential or inspirational?

I've thought about this periodically. I can think of people who have had an influence on me. Zvi Griliches, who was my advisor, was one such person in that there were real social science problems that he was trying to understand, and he was very good at sorting out what the problems were. On the other hand, I wasn't particularly enamored with the way he got solutions. And then there were people who got solutions, but I wasn't particularly enamored with the questions they were asking. I didn't fit into a normal categorization of student.

Why did you decide to pursue an academic career?

I can't tell if I was just gutless to go out into the real world. I had thought about a bunch of other things when I was growing up. As I said earlier, I wanted for so long to be an author. And then I told people the reason I was getting a doctorate was so I could go to *The New York Times* and not start out at a very low level. But when I started getting into research, it got more and more interesting. And my enjoyment from doing research has certainly increased over time.

I think I have also been lucky. I remember going out for a coffee with Janet Yellen, one of my teachers at Harvard, when I was in my first or second year. She asked me what I wanted to do, and I told her I wanted to put together empirical work and theory. She said that that's the hardest thing to do. But I think the truth is it got easier because both computers and datasets got better.

As a researcher, which colleagues have been most influential or inspirational?

At the beginning of my academic career, part of my problem was that I didn't fit into one group. The colleagues who had the most influence on me were those who probably didn't like me, and had good reason not to. And so my growth came mostly through negative reactions rather than through trying to emulate somebody. I would try and do something, and they would say they didn't like it. Sometimes they were right, and that had a big impact. For example, when I tried to come back to industrial organization, people would go after me for not knowing enough details about an industry. My reaction was, yes, maybe I should build models for a particular market, or institutional structure, and only think about generalizations later.

GENERAL THOUGHTS ON RESEARCH

What is the value of pure versus applied research in economics?

The disappointing part of economics is that there aren't enough people who know enough about both fields to do the crossover. As a result, both sides spend a lot of energy on things that don't make a lot of sense. Another result is that the applied group only takes a fair amount of time to learn the lessons of theory. For example, for a long time, I didn't know where the work of Drew Fudenberg, a Harvard colleague, was going. But I now realize that extensions of his concept of self-confirming equilibrium will end up being used in virtually all of dynamics, including IO and public finance.

It's a shame that there's not enough communication. The theorists don't really know what we need. And what we need is often not an analytic solution; it's things like: what's an appropriate equilibrium concept (or a rest point we can think of moving towards) for particular environments? What's an appropriate way for firms to learn? If they don't know what we're interested in, they'll go off and do something else, which may end up being relevant in 20 years, but I think there is a smaller probability of even that happening than if they would actually talk to us more.

How would you characterize your own research agenda and how has it changed through time?

My own research agenda for many, many years has been trying to figure out how to analyze market interactions. The way it's changed is that for a long time I was interested in econometrics because I thought that was missing. And now I'm just as interested in theory because I think that's what is missing. Many people would characterize me as part econometrician. I don't think anybody would characterize me as part theoretician, but I'm spending a lot of my time now on theory.

Do you think it is important to have broad research interests?

The way I went was to try and integrate broad theory and econometrics into applied work on particular problems, but I have not tried to be on top of 50 different applied fields. There are people who go the other way (focus on theory or econometrics, and then look for an applied problem that is suited to it), but I'm less enthusiastic about that because I think the right set of models and tools depends on the institutional details. That's one of the things I learned from my IO colleagues. It's great to have somebody around who's knowledgeable about the world and/or who has great methodological depth, but from the point of view of research, I would prefer you had the range of tools for a given set of institutions rather than a broader set of institutions or a broader set of tools.

Sometimes I talk to my public finance colleagues because they have a problem, and I try to understand what's going on. But I would never write a paper that said, "Here's what's going on in public finance," or "Here's what's wrong with public finance," or something similar in another field that I'm not in. I don't think it's a scholarly endeavor to try and be on top of 14 or 15 fields. And I don't know anybody who is smart enough to do it. It's a question of whether you can make progress on understanding things. Bringing tools or ideas from one field to another can be very helpful, and that's probably the biggest gain that I get from my colleagues in other fields.

I went recently to a conference in Florida, where Dan McFadden gathered a group of us from different sub-fields. I was surprised at how much we had in common about the issues. Pierre-André Chiappori is a good example. He is doing work on decision-making within the family. A lot of the issues between all our fields were similar, like the way in which people learn, and the nature of a rest point. It was also heartening to learn the extent that we can learn from each other about similar problems in different institutional environments. But I do think that each institutional environment will end up having its own empirically relevant answers.

Do you think there is any difference in the types of work done by researchers at different stages of their careers based on tenure concerns, publication requirements or other pressures? Should there be a difference?

Whether there is a difference or not depends on the person. I haven't changed my research strategy at all, but the big difference in me now is how much I learn from my students. Over the last ten or fifteen years, I have taken on many projects because my students were working on real-world problems that became challenges to me. Somebody once said to me that being a teacher of a graduate student is a two-way street. Intellectually, I get a lot of input from my students. In fact, in the last ten years, I think I've gotten more from my students than my colleagues.

IDEA GENERATION

Where do you get your research ideas?

Initially, they came from reading the newspaper or *The Economist* or just looking at the world and seeing what was missing from our models. And then more recently, as I just said, a lot of them come from students working on particular industries and realizing there is a set of institutions that we don't know how to model.

At what point does an idea become a project that you devote resources to?

What happens is first I get interested, and then at some point as a result of talking to somebody or playing with the idea at night by myself, I figure out there's really a way to attack the problem. And then I'm pretty determined [*laughs*]. I just work on it – often for years and years – until I think I've got something. I'm reasonably famous in the profession for taking a long time to finish something. That's just my style.

IDEA EXECUTION

What makes a good theoretical paper?

I'm industrial organization-centric, so I look for two kinds of things there. One is a reasonable notion of equilibrium or a rest point or a condition that the equilibrium has to satisfy, because in some sense that's what I'm going to end up taking to the data and use to estimate parameters. That's much more complicated than it sounds because in different situations what's reasonable is different. But right now that's the biggest deal problem I have in analyzing different market institutions.

The other part of theory papers I pay attention to are those that assume away the world with what I call a toy model, but bring out processes that I wouldn't have thought possible. They often also tell you when they're going to be reasonable by giving you appropriate assumptions. There's never going to be a world like the toy model, but it still helps me interpret what could go on in the world, and sometimes I need an empirical framework that will allow that to happen.

If it's a toy model where I can reverse the intuition in three seconds by making a more realistic assumption, I don't like it. But there are a lot of toy models that I think are actually quite good. Fundamentally, they help me a lot.

Can you give an example?

The work on self-confirming equilibrium by Fudenberg and Levine ends up being quite important.[1] When I started doing dynamics, the 'Markov-Perfect' work of Maskin and Tirole was also important to me.[2] And I could give you some toy models that I thought were quite helpful, like the model on entry deterrence by Dixit or the model on excess investment by Mankiw and Whinston.[3] Once you see them and realize what's going on, they're useful.

What makes a good empirical paper?

A good empirical paper is one that explains something in the real world. It can either just explain it, or it can explain it and, better yet, enable us to work out the implications of various policy scenarios. One of the early good empirical papers like that was Lanier Benkard's thesis.[4]

Also, a lot of the empirical work that I like has both empirical content and methodological content. And so I think the Olley–Pakes production function paper is a first-rate empirical piece, and I like my work on hedonic price indices also.[5] I guess I have this problem that I really like my own empirical work [*laughs*].

When you hit a brick wall on a project, do you continue to work on the problem or do you take a break and work on something else?

I go for a while, but I have to think I have a way through the wall. If I cover all bases and figure out that I can't do it that way, then I stop. But it's a bit different on empirical projects because what happens is you realize this is not the way to look at the data, and you change either the question you're looking at, or the way you're looking at the current question. I'll stop and say, "Okay, we're doing something wrong because the data is coming back saying that this is not the right way to look at the problem." And then I'll step back, and I might leave it for a while. That happens with many, many empirical problems.

Can you give a specific example?

Yes, my last hedonics paper was like that. I already had a hedonics paper in the *AER* where I was trying to show how to do a price index.[6] The way that the consumer price index is constructed is data collectors go to a store and write down the prices of goods along with their characteristics. Then they take a weighted average of the ratios of two prices for a good with the same characteristics (one in the base period when they first go to the store and one in the comparison period when they return to the store). If a good from the base period was not on the shelves in the comparison period, then it is just dropped out, and the index is constructed using a weighted average of the ratios for the remaining goods. These are called matched-model indexes. From the economics of it, it was pretty clear to me that the goods being dropped out were disproportionately ones whose prices were falling, because that's what was being taken off the shelf. And so you were left with an upward bias in the index. But hedonics could correct for this. I did it for computers, which was a huge correction, and it got published in the *AER*. The Bureau of Labor Statistics started gearing up to do it more generally, partly because of my work.

And then there was a National Academy Panel of guys older than me – which makes them quite old – who claimed that I was right that it worked on computers, but that it didn't give you anything different than a matched model on other things. I couldn't believe it. The economics were just so clean. And so I started a research paper with Tim Erickson from the BLS to work on it. We kept hitting a brick wall until finally we figured out what was wrong. We now have a joint paper, which is forthcoming in the *AER*.[7] I think we know the answer now. We were stumped for a couple of years. But I was not going to give up until I figured out what was going on [*laughs*].

When a project isn't going to turn out as hoped, do you scrap it or aim to send the work to a second-tier or field journal?

I've never stopped a project and then sent it to a second-tier journal. Sometimes if there's something very simple and small, but important, on my research program, I'll send it to a non-major journal. Robin Lee and I did some work that we could summarize in four pages. Originally, it was going to be part of my Fisher-Schultz Lecture, but I said, "This is crazy. It doesn't really fit. We should just make sure people know the answer." And so it's published in *Economics Letters*.[8]

What has been the biggest change during your career in how researchers in your fields conduct research?

Computers – no question. That's one reason why there is empirical research. They provided the impetus for doing all the econometrics and computational techniques. For example, when I was a student, you couldn't compute a reasonably complicated Nash equilibrium. But now you can do it in milliseconds.

My first major paper was about patents as options and won the Frisch Medal.[9] I was at The Hebrew University in Jerusalem, and to do the paper I took down the science building's whole computing center for a week … and I was out of the country. When I came back, the Dean came to me and said, "You can't do this again. The scientists were going nuts." With much weaker assumptions, I could do the calculations on my laptop in half an hour now! It's a different world.

THE WRITING PROCESS

Which aspect of the writing process do you find most difficult?

I'm one of those people who likes to write. I think a lot while I write. I can find it difficult to explain things to others without my knowledge of the field, but I'm getting better with age. Daron (Acemoğlu) is big on getting me to write in a way that somebody who isn't up with the techniques that I use can understand.

I used to be terrible. I have a paper with Rick Ericson – one of my most cited papers – that must be one of the worst-written papers in the history of the profession.[10] I would never write it like that now. But in those days I just thought you wrote down the answer.

What's so bad about it?

It's impossible to follow because it's just so poorly written. Part of it is I didn't understand it as well as I do now, and the other part is that Rick and I didn't spend enough time writing.

I've got to admit that Dan McFadden's first major piece, for which he deservedly won the Nobel Prize, was like that.[11] It's a paper on logit analysis, which is something I've done a lot of research on and people think I'm reasonably expert in that area. Yet, I still have trouble reading Dan's paper! I can get through it, but, boy, I can't imagine people dealing with it

30 years ago. There is an example of someone who, at that time at least, didn't know how to write either, but he is about as successful an economist as you can be.

What steps have you taken during your career to improve the quality of your writing?

I have just finished writing a paper with Daron as the editor. I think the paper is a lot better as a result of his hitting me on the head 15 times!

Who proofreads your writing?

Before I send out something, several of my colleagues or ex-students will have read it. But the problem is they think very similarly to the way I do. And so when someone from a different field reads it – like Daron – he might not quite understand it.

How do you split up the writing tasks among co-authors?

If you're honest, it's always obvious. People worry about whose name is on the paper and who writes what. But every time I've written a paper, it's always been obvious whether somebody's name should be first or second. There are parts of the paper that I will write better than you, and there are parts of the paper that you will definitely write better than me. It just gets allocated.

COLLABORATION

When you work with co-authors, how do you decide whom to work with?

With the exception of one or two people, most of the people I've worked with are those who know things that I don't know. The Ericson-Pakes paper started when I was just finishing my doctorate, and I didn't know much math. I needed help. At that time, Rick was somewhat of a probabilist, and he was interested and very smart. And I also wrote a paper with a true probabilist at Yale called David Pollard.[12] I had an econometric problem and walked into his office and said, "I don't understand this." He replied, "I'll explain it to you, but then you have to explain it in the paper."

I worked with Steve Berry at Yale because we were sitting next door to each other for ten years. We just talked. Everybody thought of him as the IO guy and me as the econometrician, but the truth is we were both both. That was the only case where my co-author had very similar interests to mine.

Do you work with your current PhD students?

No. I made a rule at a pretty early stage that the only time I would work with my PhD students was after they were reasonably established. Steve Berry was my PhD student, but I only worked with him a number of years after him getting his doctorate. And right now, I'm working with an ex-student of mine, Kate Ho, who knows a lot about hospitals.

I try not to work with my current PhD students because if you write a great paper with them, people are going to say that only I wrote it. That happened with Steve Olley, and I was always very sad about that. I thought it was a mistake. And so from then on I've never done it again.

How do you prefer to interact with your co-authors (e-mail, phone, or face-to-face)?

I think it's very hard to do collaborative work without, at some point, getting together for longish periods of time. But there are long stages in the middle of a project when people can do different parts of the work. And with e-mail and airplanes, it's just much easier now.

My farthest distance co-author is Chaim Fershtman. We have written two papers together, and I've got to admit that almost all of the real work is done when we're together in the same room.[13] But work with Kate is not so much like that because there's a much more well-defined distribution of tasks. I'll do more of the econometrics, and she'll do more of the empirical work, and you can somewhat do those separately. But when we have to actually sit down and say, "Okay, how should we look at this problem?" which is what we are doing right now, we have to get together and figure out what can be done. That's partly a function of me working with people from different fields. I don't know what you can do in your field, and you don't know what I can do in mine. Unless you're sitting down together before a blackboard or a computer screen, it's very hard to figure that out.

RESEARCH ASSISTANCE AND FUNDING

How do you use undergraduate and graduate research assistants?

I use undergraduate students for data gathering of various forms. That does require a lot of skill and smarts sometimes, but it doesn't typically require technical detail, which they don't get until they go to graduate school.

When I use graduate students, it almost always has to do with computers. And most of the graduate students that I use as an RA also do theses with me. I put them on newish methodological things, and that's part of the training.

How important is funding for getting your work done?

It hasn't been important so far. For many years after I moved to the States, I had NSF funding continually. Then when I moved to Harvard, I got this chunk of money for research, which was quite a lot, and it got replenished at some point. And I've gotten some research grants in the interim. But I have spent hardly any time in the last ten years getting research grants, partly because the NSF was down so much in funding. I was a senior guy and it seemed crazy to go to them. And I didn't have projects that were that expensive, but I'm going to have to start worrying about it again.

Do you have any advice for a young scholar on the funding process?

I don't know a hell of a lot about it relative to anybody else. Most of my grants are all straight from the NSF. I think that's probably an error on the part of our profession in the sense that there are many places with much more funding that you could explore. The NIH and the EPA (Environmental Protection Agency) should be used more, as well as grants from other nations. There are a million places, and I don't think we make enough use of them.

SEMINAR PARTICIPATION AND NETWORKING

What are the benefits to attending a seminar that is closely related to your work versus one that is not closely related?

Unfortunately, at Harvard, there are so many seminars that I seldom go to something that isn't related to my work. The times that I do go to something that is unrelated are usually if it's a junior or senior colleague of mine that I'm friendly with, or I've talked to them about their research over coffee, or they've asked me to show, which happens periodically because they think that I might have something to add. And once in a while I'll go to something that's on a topic that is big or interesting, and I think I might get something out of it.

It's a shame that I don't go to more seminars, but I have two in my field every week, plus the econometrics one, which is often given by a friend of mine. That's three seminars in a week, which is a lot. Doing more than that is hard.

How important is professional networking to success in research?

Probably more important than it should be. But it does depend on the field and what you mean by success. I think the really successful people who made a lasting contribution would have made it with or without their networks. It's the people in the middle who get sorted out by them. If you want to go by way of the Standing Committee of the AEA for something, then the networks help.

But once you write a good paper and you want to be involved, people will pay attention to you. A good example is your own John Asker. What happened to him was dramatic. He came out of graduate school at the same time as another student of mine, Matt Gentzkow. I think they were the best two guys of their generation. From Day One, Matt networked, got involved, and he's done some very good work. John disappeared to Australia and worked for a politician among other things. But then he wrote this one paper on bidding rings, and now he's in the middle of everything again.[14]

To what extent is the absence of departmental colleagues working in one's research area a major disadvantage?

It's a little bit of a disadvantage. But there are parts of it that shouldn't be overlooked. One is the fact that if nobody is doing what I'm doing, then that makes me pay attention to what they're doing. One of the biggest advantages of going to Harvard is that I've learned a lot from the questions that others in my department are asking. That includes the behavioral guys, but also people like Al Roth, Drew Fudenberg, and Oliver Hart. When I have questions about theory, it's funny how I end up walking up to either Drew or Oliver and asking them. They will have looked at a problem in a different way.

Of course, if you ask me whether I would like to have somebody I could talk to about my specific research, the answer would be "yes," and that's partly why I come here (to NYU as a visitor). When I was at Yale, I didn't spend a lot of time talking with people who were doing things that were very different conceptually. But since I've moved, I have picked up many new questions. And it seemed obvious that I had to do that if I was to survive at Harvard.

COMMUNICATION OF RESEARCH

How do you find the right balance between communicating your research at an early stage versus the close-to-finished stage?

The balance for me is when to give a seminar. I think it's better to wait. I don't like giving a seminar unless I'm sure I have something to say and I'm right about it. When I walk in, I usually think that I know more about this topic than anybody in the world. But it's inevitably true that, at the beginning, people will point out things that I didn't think about, and that helps the paper a ton. The last paper that I wrote with Chaim is a very good example. The seminars improved the paper by an incredible amount and changed the way I think about it. It's now more relevant, more general, and more thoughtful.

I gain a lot from seminars. And this is even truer for empirical work because there are often stages where you have something to say, but it's not quite right. Seminars can give you a whole different way of looking at the problem. I've had very few empirical projects that end up in the place they were supposed to when they started out. In fact, I can think of only two in my entire career.

What are the unique challenges to giving a seminar and how do you overcome them?

People say I've gotten much better. You want to put across what's important, and you want to be able to answer, in a clean way, detailed questions if they arise. That's the combination. Don't focus on the details. But if somebody asks you about a detail they've thought about, because it's got broader implications or because they want to make sure that you did it right, then you must have an answer. That's what I try to tell my students.

PUBLICATION

How do you decide upon the appropriate journal to send your research to?

I think there's a breakdown between how technical and non-technical a paper is. If it's technical, almost everything has gone to either *Econometrica* or the *Review of Economic Studies*. Earlier in my career, I sent more papers to the *Review of Economic Studies* than *Econometrica*. And then the less technical papers have gone either to the *AER*, the *JPE* or *RAND*. It's a toss of a coin between those three.

How would you best describe your approach to dealing with a 'revise and resubmit' request from a journal? How about an outright rejection?

I'm very serious about 'revise and resubmits'. If the editor is straight about what he wants, then I try to do it, otherwise it's a non-convergent cycle.

I haven't had an empirical paper rejected for a long time. It's probably a little easier for me because, compared to the rest of the profession, I write only a small number of papers.

Do you think the current structure of the publication process facilitates or impedes scientific understanding and knowledge production?

It's too slow in economics, especially for empirical work. I don't know quite how to fix it. I was an editor of *RAND* for a long time. Somebody once told me that when they get something published by me it should show up on a vita as *RAND** because I forced them to do a lot. But I was also pretty straight. If I sent a revision and you did it, the paper was going to get in.

I think editors could put more time into clarifying exactly what they want, and then accepting a paper if they got what they want and rejecting it if they didn't get what they want. They just don't put in the time. But it's hard to blame them if you get too many 'hard-to-do' papers. It would be helpful if journals like *Econometrica* increased the size of their editorial boards.

I also don't like the proliferation of journals. There's too much to read, and too many little things get written. People should write less, and we should care less about how many papers you wrote and more about the contribution of the papers that you did write. That's always been my credo.

What has been your best and worst experience with the publication process?

When I was younger, everything was dramatic. I was very worried about everything. The work out of my thesis ended up being very hard to publish. That hurt me. It was maybe my worst experience.

I felt best about my first article in *Econometrica*.[15] I still didn't have tenure, it was the lead article, and people were telling me it was very good. The editor was Gary Chamberlain, and he was very fair and very straight. It was accepted after the first revision, which was a very nice experience.

REFEREEING AND EDITING

How do you decide upon whether or not to accept a refereeing job? What are the benefits to being a referee?

For the last ten years, I've been an editor, so I've only refereed things that I could tell I was uniquely positioned in the profession to do. Now, it's a little different. If the editor is a friend, or someone who was very good to me when I was an editor, it's very hard for me to say "no." And I also feel a little responsibility to certain parts of the IO community to take on a refereeing job.

What are the benefits to being a referee?

You learn something sometimes – not always but sometimes.

How do you decide upon whether or not to accept an editing job? What are the benefits to being an editor?

It depends a lot on the personality and on the job. It was easy for me to take on *RAND* because I'm honestly interested in what happens in various industries. And it's not too detailed and technical, so it was fairly easy for me to read every paper and every proof in the journal. It would have been reasonably impossible for me to be an editor at *Econometrica* because I don't have a compartmentalized mind. It would have killed the rest of my research career.

As an editor, you are a donator for the most part. I think there is a responsibility at a certain stage in one's career to take on an editorial position. But I also learned a little about a few industries by thumbing through the papers after the referees told me what to look for.

TIME MANAGEMENT

How do you divide up your working day, both in terms of quantity and timing of different kinds of work?

Until recently, what I always did was wake up in the morning and work for three or four hours before I did anything else. I never went to the university until noon. I still tend to go in at noon, and I've been doing this since I was writing my doctoral thesis. It's so that if somebody wants to speak to me, I feel like I've already done something that I can talk about [*laughs*].

I try and go for lunch with colleagues. That's when I mostly connect with them. And then the afternoon is varied. A lot of it will be spent with students, and sometimes I'll get back to my research.

How do you balance multiple research projects?

An empirical project always gets first priority, and it always takes ten times longer than expected. I have two empirical projects right now, one with Kate and one with Allan (Collard-Wexler), and whenever they're not the focus of attention, I go back to my methodological projects.

What is the optimal number of projects that you could be working on at any given time?

On some empirical projects, it takes two years to get the data together, and I'm doing very little except for once every four months I'm sitting down with a guy who is doing the data and figuring out where we should go next. At the moment, I have three of those things going on and a couple of other papers that I'm actually writing.

How do you balance your research and non-research activities?

I spend a lot of time with my graduate students. I like that, and when I don't have graduate students, I'm unhappy. I spend very little time on administration. One of the other advantages of being in a department where very few people are like me is that I get allocated fewer administrative jobs. And so most of my time is divided between research, students, and teaching.

How about the balance between your personal and professional lives?

My kids left home in the year that I came to New York. And then Juliana, my wife, stayed here, and I went back to Cambridge. We were living separately, apart from at weekends. Tom Cooley came in one day and asked, "What's it like living on your own?" I said, "What's very strange is that all my life I just worked all the time until somebody bugged me – either one of the kids or my wife. And then if they had something they wanted to do, I would do it. But now nobody bugs me, and I don't know what it's like to not be bugged. I just work all the time, and then I get fed up." He said, "Do you mean you have to learn how to not be a student?" I said, "Yeah, that's probably right." [*Laughs*]. But now that the kids don't bug me, I'm getting better at allocating real time to the things that I like, such as reading historical novels, watching basketball, and listening to jazz.

I think the hardest time for somebody going through their professional career is 'pre-tenure with kids'. The time constraints are huge. I worked whenever I could, and somehow I kept on going for a while. They don't give you tenure until you've ruined your life, let me tell you! And I had to learn how to dis-ruin it [*laughs*].

REFLECTIONS AND THE FUTURE OF ECONOMICS

What have been the most important findings and contributions in your research fields during your career?

In my field, they were incremental by different people, and it depended on the sub-field.

It was clear that Dan McFadden's work on discrete choice was fundamental to things that came after that. And I think Olley-Pakes opened up productivity analysis and maybe Ericson-Pakes opened up dynamics, even though it was terribly written.

Rob Porter wrote a paper on collusion that was quite striking.[16] And I also like his paper with Ed Greene on collusion.[17]

If I were a little more into auctions and incentive mechanisms, the work of Myerson and Maskin and Vickery would have been very important to me. And there is also a beautiful paper by Haile and Tamer on auctions.[18]

Tim Bresnahan wrote the original paper on vertical models.[19] It was too simple and had errors in it, but it was still a very good paper. Steve Berry's

RAND article followed that, and then our joint work (also with Jim Levinsohn) on estimating demand systems.[20]

The work of Powell and Manski in econometrics was really good. They showed us different ways of looking at things that were really helpful.

In terms of dynamics, the work of Benkard and Levin and Bajari was good, and so too was my own work with Ostrovsky and Berry.

There are two papers on simulation, one by Dan McFadden and the other by David Pollard and me, which appeared back to back in *Econometrica*.[21] They had a reasonably big effect on our field.

I also think you shouldn't minimize the impact of people like Andy Postlewaite who is equally at ease with the hardest theory and empirical work, and comes to seminars and makes comments that make you rethink things. It's not only about papers; it's also about the people whom you talk to.

What are the biggest challenges facing your research fields?

How to analyze upstream markets is a totally open question and an incredibly important one for the economy. It includes all HMOs, hospitals, and retail and wholesale trade. And I think the question of how people make decisions in complicated environments that aren't based on Bayesian Markov-Perfect conditions is of huge importance as well.

Empirically, there is nothing more important than understanding what's going on in the healthcare market, including how various policies are going to affect it, and also understanding issues relating to the environment. I tell my students that if they are interested in doing something that's important to society, they should look at one of those two areas.

What are the strengths and weaknesses of your own research?

My weakness is that I don't explain things well enough. My biggest strength has been to listen to people from different fields and try to be open-minded about it. The person who was very good at that was Steve Berry. Maybe, we developed it together. I think it's very hard to overrate how important that is. Even with people who have been antagonistic towards me in my career, I will ask myself, "Do they have something to say?" Often they do.

One of the things that I'm most proud of is that, if you look across my students, they've done very different things, and they're very differentially involved in the kind of work that I'm doing. And I like to think that's reflective of the fact that I've been open to different ways of doing things.

In the end, do you think the profession has helped to bring out and shape your research for the best?

What's good about the profession is that people who do serious scholarly research eventually end up in a good place. That's the one thing that seems to work always; at least provided the researcher is persistent.

Do you have any professional regrets?

I have probably insulted people when I shouldn't have. And then I regret it afterwards, and they hold it against me forever.

What are your professional ambitions?

I'm a very happy camper right now. I like my students and I like most of my colleagues.

How would you describe the state of economics today? Are you optimistic about its future?

The problem is that theory has been developing on its own and not coming back to the empirical guys. For the first time, the empirical guys actually want to talk to the theoreticians because they can do things that are more complicated. And I've got to admit that I'm pretty disappointed in the theory guys from that point of view. If there's been a roadblock, it's that.

My gut reaction is that good theory people understand when somebody can go back and forth. And so when there's a really smart, young guy who can do that, he's going to get a lot of pats on the back from both sides and is going to progress. Somebody will break this barrier and will get ahead. That's what always happens.

NOTES

1. Fudenberg, D. and D.K. Levine (1993), 'Self-Confirming Equilibrium', *Econometrica*, Vol. 61, No. 3 (May), pp. 523–545.
2. Maskin, E.S. and J. Tirole (2001), 'Markov-Perfect Equilibrium I: Observable Actions', *Journal of Economic Theory*, Vol. 100, No. 2 (October), pp. 191–219.
3. Dixit, A. (1980), 'The Role of Investment in Entry-Deterrence', *Economic Journal*, Vol. 90, No. 307 (March), pp. 95–106; Mankiw, N.G. and M. Whinston (1986), 'Free Entry and Social Inefficiency', *RAND Journal of Economics*, Vol. 17, No. 1 (Spring), pp. 48–58.

4. Benkard, C.L. (2004), 'A Dynamic Analysis of the Market for Wide-Bodied Commercial Aircraft', *Review of Economic Studies*, Vol. 71, No. 3 (July), pp. 581–611.
5. See, for example, Olley, G.S. and A. Pakes (1996), 'The Dynamics of Productivity in the Telecommunications Equipment Industry', *Econometrica*, Vol. 64, No. 6 (November), pp. 1263–1298; Pakes, A. (2003), 'A Reconsideration of Hedonic Price Indices with an Application to PCs', *American Economic Review*, Vol. 93, No. 5, pp. 1578–1596.
6. See article in Note 5.
7. Erickson, T. and A. Pakes (2011), 'An Experimental Component Index for the CPI: From Annual Computer Data to Monthly Data on Other Goods', *American Economic Review*, Vol. 101, No. 5 (August), pp. 1707–1738.
8. Lee, R.S. and A. Pakes (2009), 'Multiple Equilibria and Selection by Learning in an Applied Setting', *Economics Letters*, Vol. 104, No. 1 (July), pp. 13–16.
9. Pakes, A. (1986), 'Patents as Options: Some Estimates of the Value of Holding European Patent Stocks', *Econometrica*, Vol. 54, No. 4 (July), pp. 755–784.
10. Ericson, R. and A. Pakes (1995), 'Markov-Perfect Industry Dynamics: A Framework for Empirical Work', *Review of Economic Studies*, Vol. 62, No. 1 (January), pp. 53–82.
11. McFadden, Daniel L. (1974), 'Conditional Logit Analysis of Qualitative Choice Behavior', in Paul Zarembka (ed.), *Frontiers in Econometrics*, Academic Press: New York, pp. 105–142.
12. Pakes, A. and D. Pollard (1989), 'Simulation and the Asymptotics of Optimization Estimators', *Econometrica*, Vol. 57, No. 5 (September), pp. 1027–1057.
13. Fershtman, C. and A. Pakes (2000), 'A Dynamic Oligopoly with Collusion and Price Wars', *RAND Journal of Economics*, Vol. 31, No. 2 (Summer), pp. 207–236; Fershtman, C. and A. Pakes (2009), 'Finite State Dynamic Games with Asymmetric Information: A Framework for Applied Work', working paper.
14. Asker, J. (2010), 'A Study of the Internal Organization of a Bidding Cartel', *American Economic Review*, Vol. 100, No. 3 (June), pp. 724–762.
15. See article in Note 9.
16. Porter, R. (1983), 'A Study of Cartel Stability: The Joint Executive Committee, 1880–1886', *Bell Journal of Economics*, Vol. 15, No. 2 (Autumn), pp. 301–314.
17. Greene, E.J. and R.H. Porter (1984), 'Noncooperative Collusion under Imperfect Price Information', *Econometrica*, Vol. 52, No. 1 (January), pp. 87–100.
18. Haile, P.A. and E. Tamer (2003), 'Inference with an Incomplete Model of English Auctions', *Journal of Political Economy*, Volume 111, No. 1 (February), pp. 1–51.
19. Bresnahan, T.F. (1987), 'Competition and Collusion in the American Automobile Market: The 1955 Price War', *Journal of Industrial Economics*, Vol. 35, No. 4 (June), pp. 457–482.
20. Berry, S.T. (1994), 'Estimating Discrete-Choice Models of Product Differentiation', *RAND Journal of Economics*, Vol. 25, No. 2 (Summer), pp. 242–262; Berry, S.T., Levinsohn, J.A. and A. Pakes (1995), 'Automobile Prices in Market Equilibrium', *Econometrica*, Vol. 63, No. 4 (July), pp. 841–890.
21. McFadden, D.L. (1989), 'A Method of Simulated Moments for Estimation of Discrete Response Models without Numerical Integration', *Econometrica*, Vol. 57, No. 5 (September), pp. 995–1026; for Pakes and Pollard paper, see Note 12.

Monika Piazzesi
(Stanford University)

Monika Piazzesi was born in Heidelberg, Germany, and graduated with a Vordiplom in economics from the University of Heidelberg, Germany in 1991 before obtaining a Diplom in economics from the University of Bonn, Germany in 1994 and a PhD in economics from Stanford University in 2000. She has taught at the Anderson School, University of California, Los Angeles, 2000–2003, the Graduate School of Business, University of Chicago, where she was a Professor of Finance and the John Huizinga Faculty Fellow between 2006 and 2008, and Stanford University, where she currently serves as the Joan Kenney Professor of Economics.

Professor Piazzesi's research focuses on financial economics, macroeconomics, and applied time series. Her most-cited articles in chronological order include 'A No-arbitrage Vector Autoregression of Term Structure Dynamics with Macroeconomic and Latent Variables', *Journal of Monetary Economics* (2003), co-authored with Andrew Ang, 'Bond Risk Premia', *American Economic Review* (2005), co-authored with John Cochrane, 'Bond Yields and the Federal Reserve', *Journal of Political Economy* (2005), 'What Does the Yield Curve Tell Us About GDP Growth?', *Journal of Econometrics* (2006), co-authored with Andrew Ang and Min Wei, and 'Housing, Consumption, and Asset Pricing', *Journal of Financial Economics* (2007), co-authored with Martin Schneider and Selale Tuzel.

Professor Piazzesi's academic awards include the Elaine Bennett Research Prize (2006), and the Bernacer Prize for the Best European Economist under the age of 40 working on Finance or Macroeconomics (2005). She is Director of the National Bureau of Economic Research's Asset Pricing Program, Affiliated Professor at the Ludwig-Maximilians-Universität München, and Co-Editor of the *Journal of Political Economy*.

I interviewed Monika Piazzesi in her office in the Department of Economics at Stanford University. It was mid-morning of Friday, 20 August 2010.

BACKGROUND INFORMATION

What was your attraction to economics?

I started out wanting to understand why some countries are well off and growing, and why others, particularly those in Africa, are doing so poorly. When I was looking for a framework that would help me think about that question, I found it in economics. Although my subsequent studies took me in another direction – I've never worked on growth theory, for example – the original motivation was to make the world a better place.

As a student, which professors were most influential or inspirational?

As an undergraduate on an exchange program at ENSAE in Paris, I had a professor called Nicole El Karoui, who taught a finance course. She had a profound impact on me because I had never seen anybody use mathematics to help understand financial markets. It was a revelation. And as a graduate student, my advisors – Darrell Duffie, Tom Sargent, John Taylor, and John Shoven – were a big influence.

Why did you decide to pursue an academic career?

I love the freedom that comes with it. I can choose my own questions, and I can try to answer them. And if I can't come up with an answer, I can move on to the next question. In the private sector, I wouldn't have this much freedom.

At the end of the day, I'm also a nerd. I have to admit that my lifestyle fits academia well. I don't think I'm very good at communicating. For example, if I had to sell a car, I would do a miserable job [*laughs*]. And so in some sense a lack of outside opportunities also drove me to academia [*laughs*].

As a researcher, which colleagues have been most influential or inspirational?

My advisors were there for me even after graduate school. They continued to encourage me, and they kept up with what I was doing. And then I had terrific colleagues at several institutions that I worked for. They were always very helpful in giving me advice on how to navigate the world of publishing and so on. At UCLA, I interacted a lot with Pedro Santa-Clara, Eduardo Schwartz, and Tony Bernardo. Then when I moved to Chicago, John Cochrane, Lars Hansen, and Pietro Veronesi always helped me in defining when a project is finished and when it is time to start a new one.

GENERAL THOUGHTS ON RESEARCH

There is an increasing emphasis in many economics departments on applied research. Is this true at Stanford?

Stanford has always had a mix of applied and theoretical research.

What is the value of pure versus applied research in economics?

A broad spectrum of research is a good thing.

How would you describe the dialogue between theory and empirics in economics?

I think there are fields, including macroeconomics and finance, which do a terrific job at managing this dialogue. There's a back and forth between writing down a model, testing which features of the model fail in the data, and then going back to the drawing board and trying to improve the theory. And this is partly what generates excitement in macroeconomics and finance; we can learn about theory from data, and about data from theory. But there are other fields where there is less interaction between theory and empirics, and I'm happy that I'm not working in one of those [*laughs*].

How would you characterize your own research agenda and how has it changed through time?

My own research agenda has always been to understand the connection between the economy and financial markets, particularly whether we can explain the volatility that we see in financial markets in terms of the fundamentals of the economy. What are the perceptions about the state of the economy? Are those perceptions generating volatility in the stock market or the bond market? Those are the types of questions that I'm interested in, loosely speaking.

I started off being interested in monetary policy and its effect on bond prices. And then I moved more towards just thinking about bond prices in general. Lately, I've been working mostly on housing markets.

Do you think it is important to have broad research interests?

[*Long pause*] Of course, I appreciate colleagues more who have broad interests, because it's easier to interact with them. But I don't think necessarily that it's important to be broad. What matters more is that the question is a good one.

Do you think there is any difference in the types of work done by researchers at different stages of their careers based on tenure concerns, publication requirements or other pressures? Should there be a difference?

I think there is a difference between research before tenure and after tenure. Right before I got tenure, I was working on projects that were 'safe' because there was limited time to get those papers published. But as soon as I knew that I would get tenure, I started some risky projects that I'd had in mind for quite some time. I'm now more relaxed in taking those risks. Ideally, institutional features should not affect what people are working on, but in reality they do.

IDEA GENERATION

Where do you get your research ideas?

There are two main sources. One is data-driven: looking at data and seeing patterns that I find puzzling. The other is model-driven: reading the literature and trying to understand why there are or aren't certain features in models. In my experience, both sources are equally productive.

At what point does an idea become a project that you devote resources to?

As soon as I get some preliminary impression that a pattern in the data is really there, or if I continue to be puzzled about something in a model for at least a week, then I consider that a project. My goal is to figure out what's going on. Sometimes the answer is boring and may not lead to a paper, but I must satisfy my curiosity.

IDEA EXECUTION

What makes a good theoretical paper? Can you give an example?

[*Long pause*] That's a tough question. A good theoretical paper may be intuitive or advance our understanding of reality, ideally by bringing out some aspect that can be tested in the data. Let me grab one example. Hanno Lustig, who was two years below me in the PhD program at Stanford, has written a paper about a model with heterogeneous agents who are facing collateral constraints.[1] I thought that paper was contributing to my understanding of asset markets, because it showed how to solve a very complicated model in a very elegant way, and also provided interesting testable implications for the data.

What makes a good empirical paper? Can you give an example?

A good empirical paper provides a new stylized fact that is interesting and challenges existing theories and/or documents something in a solid and convincing way. An example would be an old paper by Fama and Schwert that was published in 1977.[2] It was previously thought that returns on stocks and other assets are not predictable. In fact, Fama himself had advanced the idea that in efficient markets, price returns should not be predictable, and prices should behave like random walks. But, with Schwert, he was one of the first to check this restriction by running regressions of returns on nominal interest rates. And they found that nominal interest rates can actually predict returns. That paper has had a big influence on the literature not only because of the careful way that the fact was documented but also because it challenged theories that were out there.

When you hit a brick wall on a project, do you continue to work on the problem or do you take a break and work on something else?

I run against the wall until hopefully it crumbles. But I realize that is probably not the most productive way because I tend to make progress in funny situations, like on a running trail or under the shower.

Being stuck so far has mostly been on how to solve models. For example, I was once solving a model where consumers were getting utility from consumption and housing consumption. That model looked very simple at first, but it turned out to be trickier than anticipated to solve for the asset prices. It took a while for my co-authors and I to find the appropriate numerical technique.

Related to the previous question, when a project isn't going to turn out as hoped, do you scrap it or aim to send the work to a second-tier or field journal?

I scrap it. I think the publishing process itself takes rather long, and so it's better to start something new. But I realize that may not be the right strategy, because I am not the best judge of my own research. Some papers of mine that have had, by official measures, the biggest success are not the ones that I like the most.

What has been the biggest change during your career in how researchers in your fields conduct research?

The financial crisis has opened up the minds of a lot of people who thought that we had found the right model to be thinking about financial markets. I'm quite happy that the financial crisis happened, because people had to go back to the drawing board and rethink the choices that the literature had made about how people form expectations, how they're facing constraints in actual markets, how limited their possibilities for risk sharing really are, how dependent they are on financial advisors, and so on. Yes, the crisis has been bad in many ways, but it's been very good for research.

THE WRITING PROCESS

Which aspect of the writing process do you find most difficult?

I find writing a difficult process because of its repetitive nature. A paper has to be rewritten over and over again until it can be read by somebody other than my co-authors and I. That's stressful.

What steps have you taken during your career to improve the quality of your writing?

Oh, I've read all the books that are supposed to teach me about how to be a better writer, and I've gotten a lot of advice from others on what's bad about my writing. But I think the bottom line is: I'm not a very good writer. Of all the qualities in research that I could claim to have, writing is not one of them. I always blame it on English not being my mother tongue, but I don't think that's quite the reason because I know others who are not native-English speakers and they can write perfectly well [*laughs*]. I'm also not very good at writing in my mother tongue, which is German, so I'm clearly not good at writing in general. It's a skill that I appreciate a lot, and I just don't have it.

COLLABORATION

When you work with co-authors, how do you decide whom to work with?

There isn't an active decision process. I start talking with somebody about research, and then we start collaborating.

How do you prefer to interact with them (e-mail, phone, or face-to-face)?

I think e-mail is very important because it fixes things in writing, and forces me to come up with a plan of things that have to be done. Talking about it is also important because that helps in bouncing ideas back and forth. And face-to-face interaction used to be very important at the beginning of my career when it was more difficult to share equations.

What are the biggest challenges associated with collaborative work and how do you overcome them?

The biggest challenge is to find the right fit of a co-author because there are different types of people. There are those who are very excited in the initial stages of the project, but then don't finish things. And there are others who are great at finishing projects, but are reluctant to start something new until the old one is done. And so it's good to have a mix of people working on the same paper because then you make sure it gets started as well as finished [*laughs*].

RESEARCH ASSISTANCE AND FUNDING

How do you use undergraduate and graduate research assistants?

I have always worked with graduate students on projects. Typically, it starts as a pure research assistantship, and then slowly migrates into co-authorship. It's great to see them growing up into researchers.

This summer, I hired undergraduate RAs for the first time for data projects. I hope to make them see that research is not all about the glory of sitting there and daydreaming about interesting questions; it's the hard work of collecting data and running regressions.

How important is funding for getting your work done?

So far, I've always had the fortune of either working with datasets that are publicly available or ones that people are willing to give me for free. But funding has been very important for hiring graduate students.

Do you have any advice for a young scholar on the funding process?

I have to force myself to write the proposal, but it's very useful to get early feedback on the research.

SEMINAR PARTICIPATION AND NETWORKING

What are the benefits to attending a seminar that is closely related to your work versus one that is not closely related?

In terms of attending seminars that are closely related to my work, it's great to be able to talk about a topic that I care about. I can ask a lot of questions about the general research agenda and also about specific things. That's easier to do in a seminar than corresponding with the author via e-mail.

For seminars that are further away from my research agenda, I like to get an update on what's going on in another field. Those one-and-a-half hours can give you a lot of insight into how other people approach research in their field: what the important questions are, how those questions are being answered, and which new techniques are being used.

How important is professional networking to success in research?

That's such a great question. I hope somebody will write a paper about this sometime. But my own impression is that the importance of networking is vastly overblown. I think people recognize good research.

To what extent is the absence of departmental colleagues working in one's research area a major disadvantage?

It's a disadvantage. I like the fact that there are a whole bunch of people in the Economics Department here, and in the business school, working on similar questions. It's very important to talk with others about your research on a daily basis. Otherwise, we would all sit in Hawaii and work from there.

COMMUNICATION OF RESEARCH

How do you find the right balance between communicating your research at an early stage versus the close-to-finished stage?

For each of the papers that I have written so far, I have presented it very early on, either in internal lunches and brown bag seminars or elsewhere, because it's the first couple of seminars that teach you the most about how it's perceived and how convincing the argument is. And I post research immediately on my website, as long as it's comprehensible.

What are the unique challenges to giving a seminar and how do you overcome them?

The challenge is to talk to an audience that has not followed my whole research process of the last couple of months. I need several days to boil down what the main message is.

Do you have any advice for a young scholar on giving a seminar?

The key is to concentrate on what is the new point of the paper. Sometimes that's not clear even after having written the paper, and it only crystallizes after you present the material a couple of times. And so I think it's a dynamic process, where you start doing your best in formulating what the research is about and then you update it many times. But I don't have any good advice. I'm still struggling myself [*laughs*].

PUBLICATION

How do you decide upon the appropriate journal to send your research to?

There is a quite clear definition in economics about which are the good journals. And so I try them first, and then go to the next level down if I see that there's no way that my research is going to be published in the top journals.

How would you best describe your approach to dealing with a 'revise and resubmit' request from a journal? How about an outright rejection?

My approach is to get the rejection letter and sleep over it, because the first reaction is always one of anger, frustration, and the feeling that I'm not being understood. That feeling usually evaporates over the next couple of days when I realize that the paper was not good enough, and that I need to improve it. But I can't do this on the first day, because my initial reaction is always a violently negative one [*laughs*].

I usually approach 'revise and resubmits' with a bottle of champagne. And then on the second day, I realize that there's a lot of work to be done [*laughs*].

Do you think that the current structure of the publication process in economics facilitates or impedes scientific understanding and knowledge production?

I think journals have a tendency to publish work that is very close to research that has already been published. And so research that takes a big step forward typically has a hard time getting accepted by journals. Examples include Cox, Ingersoll, and Ross's 1985 paper on interest rates and Mehra and Prescott's paper on the equity premium puzzle from the same year.[3] They were really novel, innovative papers.

What has been your best and worst experience during the publication process?

I've had middle-of-the-pack experiences generally, but my worst experience was probably as a referee for a journal. After a year and a half, they asked me where my referee report was. And I had never gotten the paper or the referee request! I felt bad for the author in that instance. And on another occasion, I submitted a report to the same journal and it got lost in the system [*laughs*].

REFEREEING AND EDITING

Do you have any advice for a young scholar on being a referee?

People spend too much time on bad papers. Typically, the report ends up being long, which is to impress the editor, and it's not necessary.

For the past four years, you have been Co-Editor of the Journal of Political Economy. *How would you describe the experience?*

It's been a learning experience. Initially, I thought, "I'm not the right person to do this," but then I discovered that despite being disorganized in many aspects of my life, this happens to be an area where I'm very organized. And so I surprised myself that I can be very effective in making decisions about papers. One has to try it and then see whether it works out or not; you'll discover the answer within the first six months. But my experience has been a positive one. And one benefit has been that when I was a referee writing a favorable report, there was still a reasonable chance that the paper would not get published because the editor decided against it. Now, as the editor, if I like the paper, it gets published [*laughs*].

TIME MANAGEMENT

How do you divide up your working day, both in terms of quantity and timing of different kinds of work?

It depends on whether I'm teaching or not. I tend to bunch my teaching into one quarter, when I just work on research projects that are already under-way. It's very hard to start something new during that quarter. In the other quarters, I try to start my day with research, and only towards the end of the day do I get to administrative things, like editing.

How do you balance multiple research projects?

You're really touching on all the difficult areas of research [*laughs*]. I think I'm better at working on one particular project at a time. I've recently started to multitask, and I'm still trying to figure out whether I can do it. The big advantage of having multiple projects going on at the same time is that when one project is stuck, it's nice to have the feeling of success with the other projects. But I find it very difficult to dig deep into one question in the morning, and then immediately sink my teeth into another problem in the afternoon.

What is the optimal number of projects that you could be working on at any given time?

I would say two is the maximum. I've been working on three different projects lately, and it's too much for me. I know that other people can manage even four or five projects at the same time, but I'm not one of them.

How do you balance your personal and professional lives?

My partner is also an academic and I used to commute between Chicago and New York. Then the weekend was clearly defined and so the balance was very easy. But now that we're in the same place, it's much more difficult, because each weekend one of us defects and continues to work [*laughs*].

REFLECTIONS AND THE FUTURE OF ECONOMICS

What have been the most important findings and contributions in your research fields during your career?

The research in finance has shifted from trying to understand what average statistics in asset markets look like, such as the average premium that equities pays over bonds, or the average premium of long bonds over short bonds, towards understanding what makes prices move around. That literature is still ongoing, but I feel it's an area where much of the improvements were made in thinking about reasons why investors sometimes fear stocks and other times are happy to buy stocks, and how that is time varying as opposed to markets themselves being inherently risky at some points and not at others.

There has also been progress on the macro side in trying to investigate specifications of models that would lead to more interesting asset prices. When I did my PhD, much of the previous macro literature had completely ignored financial markets. But now I think more and more people realize that this is an important area, and there have been big advances, for example, in thinking about how monetary policy in models affects long-term interest rates. Previously in these models, long-term interest rates were almost constant, and so the Federal Reserve was not able to move them. Now with the financial crisis, people think about what could generate big movements in valuations of markets, like the housing market. What was the source of the shock that happened? And how does the model replicate this big drop in valuation? My hope is that at some point in the future, we're going to have a model that captures both the reason why asset prices move around, and can also explain episodes like the recent financial crisis in a macro model, so that we can think about policy. For example, how should the government react to distress in the housing market? And what would optimal monetary policy look like in a model that captures those things?

What are the strengths and weaknesses of your own research?

Clearly, in the types of models that I have been working with, investors think quite rationally about the markets that they're dealing with, and think quite calmly about the future. I have the impression that real decision-making takes place under much more uncertainty. And so I would say that that's a weakness, which also applies to the entire areas of finance and macro.

My strength is that I'm asking important research questions. I may not know all of the answers, but at least the questions are important.

In the end, do you think the profession has helped to bring out and shape your research for the best?

Past tenure, I would say "definitely." Before tenure, I was lucky in that I've always been quite stubborn. When I like certain ideas, I just work on them. Only in the last two years before tenure did I start thinking more heavily about my CV and how things would look on paper [*laughs*].

Do you have any professional regrets?

My life has been a ride. *Ex post*, I always feel with one or two students that I could have helped them even more on the job market; to ask them the question that they heard in their job talks but couldn't answer. But those are small regrets. Overall, I've been a very lucky person.

What are your professional ambitions?

It would be nice to get a better understanding of the deep questions about financial markets for which there are no answers at the moment. And those are important questions for policy. If we think about the policy response to the financial crisis, a lot of it has been in the darkness, without any models, just hoping that throwing money at the problem would solve it. I hope that, going forward, one can come up with better models that give answers with numbers of how much liquidity one should inject into the market, how many banks one should bail out, and whether the car makers really needed that bailout or not.

How would you describe the state of economics today? Are you optimistic about its future?

I think it's a terrific field. Even after working on it for ten years after the PhD, five years during the PhD, and even before that as an undergraduate major in economics, I still think this is the most exciting field ever.

NOTES

1. Li, Y. and H. Lustig (2010), 'The Market Price of Aggregate Risk and the Wealth Distribution', *Review of Financial Studies*, Vol. 23, No. 4 (April), pp. 1596–1650.
2. Fama, E.F. and G.W. Schwert (1977), 'Asset Returns and Inflation', *Journal of Financial Economics*, Vol. 5, No. 2 (November), pp. 115–146.
3. Cox, J.C., Ingersoll, J.E. and S.A. Ross (1985), 'A Theory of the Term Structure of Interest Rates', *Econometrica*, Vol. 53, No. 2 (March), pp. 385–407; Mehra, R. and E.C. Prescott (1985), 'The Equity Premium: A Puzzle', *Journal of Monetary Economics*, Vol. 15, No. 2 (March), pp. 145–161.

Carmen M. Reinhart
(Peterson Institute for International Economics)

Carmen Reinhart was born in Havana, Cuba in 1955 and graduated with a BA in economics from Florida International University in 1978 before obtaining an MA, an MPhil, and a PhD, all in economics, from Columbia University in 1980, 1981, and 1988 respectively. Between 1985 and 1986, she was Chief Economist at Bear Stearns, having joined the firm as an economist in its Research Department in 1982. After returning to Columbia to complete her doctorate, Professor Reinhart worked as an economist at the International Monetary Fund between 1988 and 1996. She then moved to the University of Maryland, as Associate Professor in the School of Public Policy (1996–1999), Professor in the School of Public Policy and Department of Economics (2000–2009), and Professor in the Department of Economics and Director, Center for International Economics (2009–2010). She returned to the International Monetary Fund between 2001 and 2003 as Deputy Director and Senior Policy Advisor in its Research Department. Since November 2010, she has held the position of Dennis Weatherstone Senior Fellow at the Peterson Institute for International Economics, Washington, DC.

Professor Reinhart's research interests focus on several topics in macroeconomics and international finance, including international capital flows, capital controls, inflation and commodity prices, banking and sovereign debt crises, currency crashes, and contagion. Her most-cited articles in chronological order include 'Capital Inflows and Real Exchange Rate Appreciation in Latin America: The Role of External Factors', *IMF Staff Papers* (1993), co-authored with Guillermo Calvo and Leonardo Leiderman, 'Leading Indicators of Currency Crises', *IMF Staff Papers* (1998), co-authored with Graciela Kaminsky and Saul Lizondo, 'The Twin Crises: The Causes of Banking and Balance-Of-Payments Problems', *American Economic Review* (1999), co-authored with Graciela Kaminsky, 'Crises, Contagion, and Confusion', *Journal of International Economics* (2000), co-authored with Graciela Kaminsky, and 'The Modern History of Exchange Rate Arrangements', *Quarterly Journal of Economics* (2002), co-authored with Kenneth Rogoff. Her books include *This Time is Different: Eight Centuries of Financial Folly* (Princeton University Press, 2009), co-authored with Kenneth Rogoff, which has been translated to 14 languages and has won several awards.

Professor Reinhart is a Research Associate at the National Bureau of Economic Research, a Research Fellow at the Centre for Economic Policy Research, and a Member of the Congressional Budget Office Panel of Economic Advisers and Council on Foreign Relations. She has served on several editorial boards, including the *International Journal of Central Banking*, *American Economic Review*, *The World Bank Economic Review*, *Review of International Economics*, and *Journal of International Economics*, and currently the *Journal of Economic Perspectives*. *Foreign Policy* magazine named Reinhart among the Top 100 Thinkers of 2011 for "raising the alarm about America's debt burden."

I interviewed Carmen Reinhart in her office at the Peterson Institute for International Economics, Washington, DC. It was early-afternoon of Friday, 5 August 2011.

BACKGROUND INFORMATION

What was your attraction to economics?

When I was an undergraduate, I took an economics principles course that was taught by a very old-fashioned Marxist. It was quite fascinating because he would take the trouble to explain the concepts, but then criticize them. In addition to the principles text, he assigned Douglas Dowd's book about capitalism gone wrong called *The Twisted Dream*. Being Cuban-born,

I was drawn to comparative issues. Latin America was the area that I became particularly interested in.

Why did you decide to pursue an academic career after working in the private sector?

Plain tiredness with being an impoverished student was a big factor that pushed me to the financial industry. I joined Bear Stearns immediately after I finished my field exams and married Vincent, a classmate. I really enjoyed those early years at the firm. It was a big learning curve. My very first assignment was to forecast Treasury debt issuance during the severe 1982 recession. This was a real challenge because funding needs for the government would skyrocket from one week to the next. It was quite exciting, but at the same time, it got to be frustrating because I could only look at an issue superficially and then I'd have to move on. For example, one of my other early reports was to examine price-earnings ratios during disinflation periods (as in the early 1980s) using Cowles Foundation data that went back to the late 1800s. I wanted to look at such things in more detail. I realized that I would never forgive myself if I didn't go back and finish my dissertation on commodity prices. After I was done with that, I decided that I would prefer to work at the insides of a policy place. I looked at the Federal Reserve, the World Bank, and the IMF, and wound up at the latter.

As a researcher, which colleagues have been most influential or inspirational?

Guillermo Calvo. Guillermo was a senior advisor at the IMF Research Department, and he had a big influence on my thinking and research; it was a real pleasure to sit down and talk about mutual projects with him. My first important paper was written with Guillermo and Leo Leiderman, a scholar visiting from Tel Aviv University. It looked at the role of external factors in explaining large capital flows to emerging markets, a phenomenon that is so alive and well right now.[1] Over the course of 30 plus years, I have also worked a lot and discussed economics with my husband and he has been extremely influential in my thinking.

GENERAL THOUGHTS ON RESEARCH

How would you describe the research environment at the Peterson Institute?

Excellent. It's different from a university to the extent that it is more applied and policy-oriented. But, to me, it makes no difference, as I am naturally attracted to this line of work. I'm doing the same research as I did at the University of Maryland over more than a decade.

What is the value of pure versus applied research in economics?

I think both have important roles in the education and training of economists. But as to my own research, I'm drawn to real-world questions that I would like to address in a more applied manner. That's what floats my boat.

How would you describe the dialogue between theory and empirics in economics?

Let me give you a concrete example from my early years as a researcher. I became very interested in the role of policy credibility. Studying this involved a marriage of theory and empirics. I was looking to see what produced booms, and then busts, in countries like Argentina, Brazil, and Israel that tried to stabilize inflation using the exchange rate.[2] And I found that having a theoretical framework was very appealing for trying to identify the underlying channels at work.

How would you characterize your research agenda and how has it changed through time?

In recent years, a lot of my work – most of it with Ken Rogoff (my co-author for a decade now) – has had a very historical perspective, which I find increasingly fascinating.[3] But my research agenda on financial crises began much earlier. For example, my work with Graciela Kaminsky on twin crises – how a banking sector problem can ultimately lead to an exchange rate crash – dates back to the mid-1990s.[4] I would describe it as having a strong interest in linking the past and the present, being importantly informed by data, and looking to theory for an organizing framework.

Do you think it is important to have broad research interests?

An important feature of my research is that it is interconnected. For example, my early work on the lack of credibility in inflation stabilization plans that lead to booms and busts is a special case of a broader pattern in the cycles surrounding financial crises. And my early research on commodity cycles is connected to the issue of pro-cyclicality of fiscal policy, which is a theme that I explored with Graciela Kaminsky and Carlos Végh in the mid-2000s.[5]

Do you think there is any difference in the types of work done by researchers at different stages of their careers based on tenure concerns, publication requirements or other pressures? Should there be a difference?

In the early stages of my career, I tried to flex my muscles to show that I had the skill set required to publish in top-tier journals. In other words, I was more concerned with technique for technique's sake. But in terms of topics, that's always just been driven by interest in real-world events. This definitely dates back to my early Wall Street experience.

IDEA GENERATION

Where do you get your research ideas?

I observe. My great hero is the fictional character, Sherlock Holmes. I love watching recurring patterns from a distance that somebody up close can't see.

Can you give an example?

Financial repression. I have recently written a paper, 'The Liquidation of Government Debt', with Maria Belen Sbrancia, who is a wonderful PhD student and co-author. It was motivated by the legitimate question of what are the possible ways in which high debt situations will unwind. From the end of World War II until the early '80s, financial repression was the norm for advanced economies. It is unfolding, particularly in Europe, but one has to connect the dots to see it as a part of a larger pattern.

At what point does an idea become a project that you devote resources to?

Here is where interconnectedness is important. To continue with the financial repression story, in 2003, Ken Rogoff, Miguel Savastano, and I wrote a paper called 'Debt Intolerance'.[6] One of our findings is that when the countries in question liberalized their financial systems, they lost certain revenues from financial repression and their debt servicing costs rose markedly. And so I flipped that by going back to when they had debt problems. How did financial repression help? That's an example of building a database in your mind of previous work that you've done or research that you've read. And that's the time to figure out the ideal dataset that would allow you to do serious analysis.

In some of my biggest projects, I start out without strong priors. For example, when Graciela and I began looking at the temporal pattern between banking crises and currency crashes, we sat down with some theoretical papers that suggested the causality ran from banking to currency, and others that argued the causality ran from currency to banking. In the end, we asked an empirical question: what does the data reveal? The extent of similarity in patterns of financial crises in the advanced and emerging market economies is not something that Ken Rogoff and I had expected to find a priori.

IDEA EXECUTION

What makes a good theoretical paper? Can you give an example?

I was on the editorial board of the *AER* for several years and I ran across a lot of theoretical papers that were inelegant and cumbersome. And so a good theoretical paper provides a simple framework. I would like to highlight Guillermo Calvo's temporariness hypothesis and the Diamond–Dybvig model of bank runs.[7] Those are issues that are very close to my interest and I can read them and say, "Ah-hah! Here's a way of thinking about why this happens." One big turn-off for me is when the authors make a set of assumptions that are very "cooked".

What makes a good empirical paper? Can you give an example?

A good empirical paper has a well-defined objective, which can either be testing a specific theory or characterizing the emerging patterns from the data. Originality is of course what makes a paper more memorable. I admire a paper by Eichengreen, Rose, and Wyplosz on contagious currency crises, for example.[8] They weren't testing a specific theory; rather they were casting a net to see what the stylized facts revealed. I find that kind of work very, very appealing, as opposed to when the authors run 420 regressions, report results in illegible tables, and then only discuss their favored model. Those exercises leave me pretty flat.

I also like a paper called 'Good-Bye Financial Repression, Hello Financial Crash' by Carlos Diaz-Alejandro.[9] It is quite chatty, but it makes such a big point, namely that even when government accounts look great, beware of contingent liabilities – which ultimately lead to trouble. I also find that narrative, but deep, approach very useful. But both of the papers that I have just mentioned were extremely important in getting me interested in financial crises.

When you hit a brick wall on a project, do you continue to work on the problem or do you take a break and work on something else?

I work on other components of the project until a better idea comes along on how to deal with the brick wall. That's a compromise, but it keeps me connected.

Related to the previous question, when a project isn't going to turn out as hoped, do you scrap it or aim to send the work to a second-tier or field journal?

Again, we are back to the issue of interconnectedness. Sometimes, I do a great deal of ancillary work that never makes it into the paper, let alone is sent out to a journal, but I realize that it might be quite relevant and helpful at a later stage, so I don't discard it. The world changes often enough to make it possible that the work will be relevant in the future.

What has been the biggest change during your career in how researchers in your fields conduct research?

I would say that at some point, predating my entry into the field, theoretical work in international finance was accorded a premium over empirics. The older literature, particularly pre-World War II was very applied. Also, economic history disappeared from most graduate programs as a course requirement.

THE WRITING PROCESS

Which aspect of the writing process do you find most difficult?

Writing the introduction. The toughest challenge is making the decision about which points to highlight. More generally, making your writing clear to the outsider, who hasn't spent 20 hours a day on the project, is very difficult. I am always reminded of Sherlock Holmes telling Dr Watson, "Everything is self evident, once it is properly explained."

What steps have you taken during your career to improve the quality of your writing?

Writing short summaries of papers is very useful. You stick to one or two points that are important and describe those clearly. I write summaries of my work for the blog VoxEU, for example, which is great discipline. Often, I will then go back to the original papers and revise them.

BOOK WRITING

You have recently written a very successful book with Kenneth Rogoff entitled, This Time is Different: Eight Centuries of Financial Folly. *Why did you write it?*

It dates back to the 'Debt Intolerance' paper mentioned earlier. What we hit upon was the fact that the advanced economies are not exactly pristine examples of credit history. At the time, we realized that even a long paper wouldn't be enough to address the issue in detail and that led to the idea of the book. But the day of the epiphany was when Ken and I decided, "Let's scrutinize the obscure publications of the League of Nations and UN." Voila! We found time series data on domestic debt for many countries that went back to the 1800s and earlier, which we then updated through to the present. Much of the historical literature was on external debt, which is understandable because the creditors are the financial centers like London, New York, and Paris. But what about when you default on your own people without the benefit of having involved an external creditor? Once I was able to get my hands on that rich source of data, the research agenda took on a life of its own.

How would you describe your book?

It is looking at a particular phenomenon in public finance and international macro that is more or less timeless. We've had defaults going back centuries and we are on the brink of experiencing them again today. The beauty, or even the necessity, of an historical approach is that to be able to talk about common patterns, you must have a documented body of these 'black swan' events. Kindleberger was an inspiration. And so was the lesser-known Winkler book (*Foreign Bonds: An Autopsy*).

Did you expect your book to be so successful?

No. We (Ken and I) thought it would be a very successful reference book with a long shelf life because it's intensively researched. Our role model was Friedman and Schwarz's *Monetary History of the United States*. You don't write a book with four long data appendices and expect it to hit the popular press.

Why do you think it has been so successful?

One reason is timing. And the other is that the book has universality. There is no lack of books written about the subprime crisis in the United States, but what if you are interested in Argentina's struggle with inflation over the last few decades, or Portugal's long history of defaults since 1850? We have that kind of universe, and the book has been translated to about 14 languages.

What were the biggest challenges that you faced when writing the book and how did you overcome them?

There were days when I would tell my husband, "I'm never going to be alive to see this book's publication." Many such days. I hit lots of brick walls on how to analyze a largely domestic default. And I cannot say that we ever actually overcame it because the ultimate answer is that most of those episodes coincide with external crises; pure observational cases where you have only a domestic crisis are so rare. And so what I tried to do was to say, "Okay, let's compare the twin defaults with the single external defaults and see which are worse." It was similar to when I was working with Graciela Kaminsky on contagion issues. Attempting to discriminate between the two channels of trade and finance was not a trivial exercise.

So, you didn't enjoy writing the book?

Enjoy is not the right word. There were wonderful moments associated with it, but there were miserable moments, too. Sometimes you could collapse something into the documentation of a pattern and charts would just jump out at you, which was very rewarding, but the run up to that often had a huge frustration component to it. The librarians at the Fed were very kind because they gave me liberal use of old United Nations books, but I would be tormented when I got them home and discovered that there had been changes to definitions over time again and again. In that sense, I would describe much of the work as archaeological in nature.

How has the book changed your career?

I've been working on crises issues for about 20 years. But crises were in the domain of emerging markets, and so the odds that policymakers and academics in those markets knew of my work were substantial before the current crisis. Now these issues have moved 'north' to the advanced economies, which means that interest in my research is much broader. All of a sudden, many people from different policy circles and the financial industry in advanced economies have taken notice of what I do. That's a big change. But I think what the book has certainly done for me is to confirm that the historical approach is a fruitful line of inquiry.

COLLABORATION

When you work with co-authors, how do you decide whom to work with?

I've written many papers with Guillermo Calvo, Graciela Kaminsky, and Ken Rogoff. I share common interests with them, and I get along with them in a very fundamental way. It's hard to be a co-author with somebody you don't like.

How do you prefer to interact with them (e-mail, phone, or face-to-face)?

I'm a big phone person. When you live in different cities, one-on-one meetings are much more infrequent and writing e-mails takes a long time. I'd rather sit down and write part of the paper than exchange a long series of e-mails.

What are the biggest challenges associated with collaborative work and how do you overcome them?

One big challenge is finding the right timing because schedules are very complicated. Mine is a mess, as you know. And the other issue is when you have legitimate differences in opinion. You need to find a way to word things so that you are still happy without having made the other person miserable. For example, Ken Rogoff is much more positive about the benefits of capital mobility than I – we have been having that discussion for ten years now. And so we have to work with those differences.

Do you like doing collaborative work?

If you read *The Silver Blaze* by Conan Doyle, you will discover that horses are gregarious creatures. I am like that. I enjoy talking with people about work; they bring in angles and ideas that may be complementary or even very different. So, yes, I like collaboration very much.

RESEARCH ASSISTANCE

How do you use research assistants?

Not as efficiently as I should is the short and truthful answer. But because I often work with many countries, the research involves repetition, and so I am able to use RAs. Maybe I'm deluding myself, but I try to make sure that they learn something in the process.

SEMINAR PARTICIPATION AND NETWORKING

What are the benefits to attending a seminar that is closely related to your work versus one that is not closely related?

I am not, and never have been, as judicious as I should be about going to seminars. I keep telling myself that I should attend more, but there are always so many more to attend.

How important is professional networking to success in research?

Professional networking is very important. I think that is something that some of the 'early-blooming' stars in the profession did well, such as being part of the NBER network at an early stage in one's career.

COMMUNICATION OF RESEARCH

How do you find the right balance between communicating your research at an early stage versus the close-to-finished stage?

I tend to communicate at a later stage because it takes me time to digest and evolve the work I do.

What are the unique challenges to giving a seminar and how do you overcome them?

Anticipating questions is tough, and pacing yourself is difficult, too. I try to find out about the audience as much as possible; how engaging they are likely to be, and the topics that might be of most interest to them. The discipline of writing short summaries of papers applies to presentations, also. It's very important that the main message isn't lost, and so I place the big question(s) asked in the paper and main findings at the beginning of the presentation.

PUBLICATION

How do you decide upon the appropriate journal to send your research to?

Certain topics are more appealing to a general journal while others are tailor-made for a specialization journal. The extent to which the work is original, as opposed to being derivative, is also an important consideration.

How would you best describe your approach to dealing with a 'revise and resubmit' request from a journal? How about an outright rejection?

There are some rejections that are harder to take than others. I hate it when you get a report back that is a couple of paragraphs long, which reflects the fact that the referee probably didn't get past the first page. My response to those hasn't gotten better over the years and might have even gotten worse [*laughs*].

I'm obsessive with 'revise and resubmits'. I take them very seriously. I provide a detailed guide to my responses, which is a sign of respect for the editor and for the referees who do take time to read my work.

Do you think that the current structure of the publication process in economics facilitates or impedes scientific understanding and knowledge production?

Look, it's a real crapshoot. Your guess is as good as mine.

What has been your best and worst experience during the publication process?

My worst was receiving a referee report that called me every name under the sun. It was written in a very adversarial tone, if not always for the right reasons, which is more irksome.

My best is having an editor like a working paper and then approach me and ask for it to be submitted to the journal. That's a great sign, and I've been lucky enough that that's happened more than once.

TIME MANAGEMENT

How do you divide up your working day, both in terms of quantity and timing of different kinds of work?

I'm cyclical. There are days when I cannot put two sentences together for the life of me, but I will focus intensely on something else that is not economics, like redecorating my house. And there are other days that will involve very little sleep because I am working so hard on an 'economics project'. For example, when I was putting together the massive databases for the book, the concept of time disappeared. This has always been a pattern with me. I think it's about rest. I often find that when I take some time away from work, I will return to it fresh and be much more productive.

How do you balance multiple research projects?

Not that well. Ultimately, what it involves is becoming delinquent in some of the projects and hiding from co-authors [*laughs*]. There's a limit to how many things I can dive into at one time.

How do you balance your personal and professional lives?

It's not often been balanced, but again it depends on when you ask. I've had periods in which I've been much more predisposed to leisure and other times when I've worked intensely. The demands on my time have certainly risen, but it's happened at a good time in my life-cycle, because my son is off to college. And so I'm now able to do more traveling to give talks and seminars.

REFLECTIONS AND THE FUTURE OF ECONOMICS

What have been the most important findings and contributions in your research fields during your career?

I think my work has helped to inform academics, policymakers, financial markets, and the public at large on many dimensions of financial crises. Inflation crises, banking crises, sovereign crises, and currency crises are different animals, but broadly defined, I have helped in our understanding of their long-run antecedents, their underlying causes, the factors that amplify them, what they look like, what they smell like, what their shadow is …

What are the biggest challenges facing your research fields?

International finance as a field would do well to become more integrated with "mainstream" macroeconomics. After the recent financial crisis, there were many articles about how macroeconomists had got things so badly wrong. But if you look at the international finance literature, you will see a lot of work that is very germane to what we have seen since 2007 on credit cycles, capital flows, and contagion.

What are the strengths and weaknesses of your own research?

A definite strength is being able to discern recurring patterns. It's almost like a clinical diagnosis of a disease; even if you have the same disease, the patterns are different if you are 15 years old than if you are 80 years old. The descriptive side of my work is very richly developed, but I need to improve the accompanying analysis of the whys. Specifically, political economy issues and behavioral economics considerations could complement and enrich my line of analysis on the whys.

In the end, do you think the profession has helped to bring out and shape your research for the best?

I've done my research because I'm interested in these issues. I don't know what role, if any, the profession has had.

Do you have any professional regrets?

As a researcher, it probably took me too long to get to academia. The experiences at Wall Street and the IMF were very enriching, but I had a longer route to get to academia, and I think I pay a penalty to this day. The top-tier universities decide who is part of that elite group at an early stage in one's career.

What are your professional ambitions?

To do as well in the next few years as I have recently. It's been very rewarding to have my research reach a broad audience.

How would you describe the state of economics today? Are you optimistic about its future?

I don't think we're on the verge of a great overhaul. Each economist has built up their own very specific human capital and they're not going to become different people overnight. But I would hope that the overshooting that went on in the last couple of decades, as regards downplaying the importance of history in the curriculum, gets corrected. When I went to graduate school you still needed a history class, and Ken Rogoff was taught by Charles Kindleberger. And so I do think that a curriculum that places a greater weight on history would be a good thing in the formation of a new generation of economists.

NOTES

1. Calvo, G.A., Leiderman, L. and C.M. Reinhart (1993), 'Capital Inflows and Real Exchange Rate Appreciation in Latin America: The Role of External Factors', *IMF Staff Papers*, Vol. 40, No. 1 (March), pp. 108–151.
2. See, for example, C.M. Reinhart and P. Wickham (1994), 'Commodity Prices: Cyclical Weakness or Secular Decline', *IMF Staff Papers*, Vol. 41, No. 2 (June), pp. 175–213.
3. See, for example, Reinhart, C.M. and K.S. Rogoff (2004), 'The Modern History of Exchange Rate Arrangements: A Reinterpretation', *Quarterly Journal of Economics*, Vol. 119, No. 1 (February), pp. 1–48; Reinhart, C.M. and K.S. Rogoff (2008), 'Is the 2007 US Sub-prime Financial Crisis So Different? An International Historical Comparison', *American Economic Review*, Vol. 98, No. 2 (May), pp. 339–344; Reinhart, V.R. and C.M. Reinhart (2009), 'When the North Last Headed South: Revisiting the 1930s', *Brookings Papers on Economic Activity*, Vol. 40, No. 2 (Fall), pp. 251–276.
4. Kaminsky, G.L. and C.M. Reinhart (1999), 'The Twin Crises: The Causes of Banking and Balance-of-Payments Problems', *American Economic Review*, Vol. 89, No. 3 (June), pp. 473–500.
5. See, for example, C.M. Reinhart and P. Wickham (1994), 'Commodity Prices: Cyclical Weakness or Secular Decline', *IMF Staff Papers*, Vol. 41, No. 2 (June), pp. 175–213; Kaminsky, G.L., Reinhart, C.M. and C.A. Végh (2004), 'When It Rains, It Pours: Procyclical Capital Flows and Macroeconomic Policies', in *NBER Macroeconomics Annual*, Vol. 19, pp. 11–82.
6. Reinhart, C.M., Rogoff, K.S. and M.A. Savastano (2003), 'Debt Intolerance', *Brookings Papers on Economic Activity*, Vol. 34, No. 1 (Spring), pp. 1–74.
7. Calvo, G.A. (1986), 'Temporary Stabilization: Predetermined Exchange Rates', *Journal of Political Economy*, Vol. 94, No. 6 (December), pp. 1319–1329; Diamond, D.W. and P.H. Dybvig (1983), 'Bank Runs, Deposit Insurance, and Liquidity', *Journal of Political Economy*, Vol. 91, No. 3 (June), pp. 401–419.
8. Eichengreen, B.J., Rose, A.K. and C. Wyplosz (1996), 'Contagious Currency Crises: First Tests', *Scandinavian Journal of Economics*, Vol. 98, No. 4 (December), pp. 463–484.
9. Diaz-Alejandro, C. (1985), 'Good-Bye Financial Repression, Hello Financial Crash', *Journal of Development Economics*, Vol. 19, Nos 1–2 (September–October), pp. 1–24.

Thomas J. Sargent
(New York University)

Thomas Sargent was born in Pasadena, California in 1943 and graduated with a BA from the University of California, Berkeley in 1964 before obtaining a PhD in economics from Harvard University in 1968. Professor Sargent has taught at the University of Pennsylvania, 1970–1971, the University of Minnesota, 1971–1987, the University of Chicago, 1991–1998, Stanford University, 1998–2002, and New York University, where he currently serves as the Berkley Professor of Economics and Business. Since 1987, he has been a Senior Fellow at the Hoover Institution, Stanford University.

Professor Sargent's research fields are macroeconomics, monetary economics, and time series econometrics. He is perhaps best known as one of the pioneers of the rational expectations revolution in macroeconomics in the 1970s. His most-cited articles in chronological order include '"Rational Expectations", the Optimal Monetary Instrument, and the Optimal Money Supply Rule', *Journal of Political Economy* (1975), co-authored with Neil Wallace, 'Estimation of Dynamic Labor Demand Schedules under Rational Expectations', *Journal of Political Economy* (1978), 'Some Unpleasant Monetarist Arithmetic', *Federal Reserve Bank of Minneapolis Quarterly Review* (1981), co-authored with Neil Wallace, 'Convergence of Least

Squares Learning Mechanisms in Self-referential Linear Stochastic Models', *Journal of Economic Theory* (1989), co-authored with Albert Marcet, and 'The European Unemployment Dilemma', *Journal of Political Economy* (1998), co-authored with Lars Ljungqvist. His books include *Macroeconomic Theory* (Academic Press, second edition, 1987), *Dynamic Macroeconomic Theory* (Harvard University Press, 1987), *Rational Expectations Econometrics* (Westview Press, 1991), co-authored with Lars Hansen, *Bounded Rationality in Macroeconomics* (Oxford University Press, 1993), *The Conquest of American Inflation* (Princeton University Press, 1999), *The Big Problem of Small Change* (Princeton University Press, 2002), co-authored with François Velde, *Recursive Macroeconomic Theory* (MIT Press, second edition, 2004), co-authored with Lars Ljungqvist, and *Robustness* (Princeton University Press, 2008), co-authored with Lars Hansen.

Professor Sargent's academic awards include the Mary Elizabeth Morgan Prize for Excellence in Economics (1979) from the University of Chicago, and the Erwin Plein Nemmers Prize in Economics (1996) from Northwestern University. He holds honorary doctorates from the Stockholm School of Economics (2003), and the European University Institute (2008). He was elected as a Fellow of the Econometric Society in 1976 and a Fellow of both the National Academy of Sciences and the American Academy of Arts and Sciences in 1983. He was awarded the Nobel Prize in Economic Sciences in 2011, along with Christopher Sims, "for their empirical research on cause and effect in the macroeconomy."

I interviewed Thomas Sargent in his office in the Department of Economics of the Stern School of Business at New York University. It was late-morning of Thursday, 23 December 2010.

BACKGROUND INFORMATION

What was your attraction to economics?

I was very interested in the Great Depression because it affected my family members, and they talked about it a lot. And when I first studied economics, it just seemed intrinsically fascinating. You got to look at problems in society using some math and history, and even a little psychology.

As a student, which professors were most influential or inspirational?

I had a bunch of professors who were influential. When I was a freshman at Berkeley in the early '60s, I took a class in economics from Benjamin Ward. Berkeley was a very intellectual place at that time, and Ward would often get standing ovations after some of his lectures. George Archibald, Hyman Minsky, and James Pierce were also wonderful professors, and I was helped by a very inspirational TA called Jerry Kenley.

When I went to graduate school at Harvard, John Meyer was my advisor, and I took his econometrics class. It was quite disorganized, and I didn't really understand any of the ideas when he was teaching them, but somehow they stuck. He was a great teacher.

Why did you decide to pursue an academic career?

It's what I'm best suited for. I get paid to do things during the week that I'd do in my free time anyway, like reading books and thinking about hard problems. Not only are those problems intellectually hard, but they are occasionally of use to making society and the economy better off. Also, I have the opportunity to interact with some very talented students, which means you get to give back.

As a researcher, which colleagues have been most influential or inspirational?

When I got out of graduate school, I didn't know very much math at all, and so I was very lucky early on to meet people like Neil Wallace, Bob Lucas, Ed Prescott, and Ned Phelps, who knew more than I did. But I've also worked with some of my students, such as Lars Hansen and Albert Marcet, who have been extremely influential to me. And there are others, like Chuck Whiteman, Marty Eichenbaum, and Larry Christiano, with whom I haven't worked, but whose research has fed into my own. I continue to learn from my students to this day.

GENERAL THOUGHTS ON RESEARCH

What is the value of pure versus applied research in economics?

Most research falls on its face, even if you publish a paper. It just doesn't turn out to be fruitful for other people to build on to understand the world.

But if you look at the basic tools that applied researchers use today, you find that they were supplied by theory that was viewed as very abstract 50 or 60 years ago. Expected utility is one example; it is used everywhere.

How would you describe the dialogue between theory and empirics in economics?

In macroeconomics and monetary economics, there is an intimate relationship between theory and empirics. For example, our general equilibrium theories are designed to explain how markets work in normal times or during crises. And it's always been true that getting models to more or less fit the data has been something we've aspired to. The reason I say "more or less" is that there's a longstanding tension between theory and rational expectations econometrics, which imposes tremendous discipline on empirical work. I've heard friends of mine, like Bob Lucas and Ed Prescott, say it imposes too much discipline because it rejects too many 'good theories'. And it has. One reaction in the '80s was that many people backed off using, say, maximum likelihood techniques, and proceeded to lower the bar for doing successful empirical work. In particular, they gave up trying to obtain good fits in the sense of the likelihood function, and instead engaged in calibration.

What has happened in the last ten years is that we are again focusing on the likelihood function, because the economics itself drives you to do that if you are going to do serious empirical work. But the tension is still there because the likelihood function is a cruel master. Are you fitting or over-fitting the data? That is a big-time issue in applied macroeconomics. Some people have proliferated shocks and frictions in attempts to fit the data and they've been successful in some ways, but the hazard of over-fitting the data is that you sacrifice your ability to extrapolate outside the sample. But this continuing tension has been very fruitful, because in the endeavor to repair poor fits, new theoretical boundaries have been pushed, which is how it should be.

How would you characterize your own research agenda and how has it changed through time?

Joseph Schumpeter said that nobody over 30 ever had an original idea. Having studied many economists, he argued that we form our view of how the economy is put together at an early age. I think that's probably true of me. My overriding vision of the economy has always been one in which individuals confront dynamic, stochastic problems.

When you're doing research on a day-to-day basis, things have a momentum of their own. That's true both in empirical and in theoretical work. Just as you solve one problem, you learn that another one has popped up. I'm not sure you would describe that as a research agenda.

Do you think it is important to have broad research interests?

That's a tough call. Adam Smith talked about the benefits of specialization, and we are seeing more and more economists doing just that. But the downside is that you have specialists within a department who can't talk to each other. And so, in some ways, it has been an adverse development.

Do you think there is any difference in the types of work done by researchers at different stages of their careers based on tenure concerns, publication requirements or other pressures? Should there be a difference?

That's interesting. There's a fraction of people my age and younger who, whether they admit it or not, quit doing hard work at the frontier. But that's not true of my close friends in the profession, like Neil Wallace, Chris Sims, Bob Lucas, and Ed Prescott. They are in their late 60s or early 70s, but when they give a talk, young people listen, and it's not purely out of respect. Their papers are technically demanding because I don't think any of those guys are capable of changing their research technology.

IDEA GENERATION

Where do you get your research ideas?

If you read and participate in the research process, your work has a life of its own. Questions open up, and you pick one. I don't think there's much of a mystery to it. The way people tend to get started in research is they read both the literature and the newspaper. But, in macroeconomics, there's not much difference between those two sources, because there are concerns in the headlines that are also frontline questions in our models. How can we measure inequality? How do we explain inequality? How can we influence inequality? Can economic policy pronouncements be trusted? How should those pronouncements be made? Those are pressing problems and our answers to them are always imperfect. We have a benchmark model with complete markets and no frictions that is still very useful to apply in various contexts. But once we add frictions, all hell breaks loose. One friction doesn't look like another, frictions can interact, and people inside the models and those in the real world do things to get around them. There is a whole catalogue of problems. We could write them down right now and do some pattern recognition. Around 50 of them would keep coming up in different ways. But there is a lot of commonality in the tools that macro-economists use to attack those problems, at least relative to when I was a kid.

At what point does an idea become a project that you devote resources to?

It's hard to tell, because I've started a whole bunch of projects, put them away, thought they were dead, and then some time later realized, "I think I know how to fix the problem." I have a theory that your brain is working on something when you don't think it is. That's a lot of fun.

Can you give an example?

Yes. In the early '70s, I read a paper by Phillip Cagan on hyperinflation.[1] I then tried to build a rational expectations version of it. I worked on it for months and months, but I didn't get anywhere, and I remember putting the file in a drawer. About a year later, I was jogging in a field in Minnesota when, suddenly, I just had an idea that would cut through things, and I was then able to write the paper in a very short amount of time.[2] What I did was to figure out how the world would have to look if Cagan's adaptive expectations mechanism was to be rational. I reverse engineered it! I had been trying too hard before.

IDEA EXECUTION

What makes a good theoretical paper?

That question reminds me of when I go to the art museum and I am asked why I like something. There is art in economics papers. A theoretical paper can be beautiful, but that can also mean that it is useful.

Can you give an example?

Abreu, Pearce, and Stacchetti wrote two papers on repeated games with private information.[3] At the time, that didn't seem to be of much direct interest to macroeconomists, but it turns out that the key elements of a financial crisis are found in their model. The papers are not terribly well written, but they are very rigorous mathematically and close a bunch of theoretical problems, like whether there is a worse sub-game perfect equilibrium.

I also like a paper about ambiguity aversion that was written by two exquisite theorists, Itzhak Gilboa and David Schmeidler, who have highly practical interests. It is short, deep, and seamless. In fact, you wouldn't change a word in the paper, and you just have to admire their command of the English language.[4]

What makes a good empirical paper?

Again, it is beautiful, but here that can mean it is shedding light on which theories we should be pursuing or how we should be making policy.

Can you give an example?

Hansen and Jagannathan's work on bounds on stochastic discount factors.[5] That's a great paper for its sophisticated understanding of both the basic theory and econometrics. And it's a very clever and enduring characterization of asset pricing puzzles that has opened up lots of doors. Hansen also has a recent paper with Heaton and Li on measuring long-run risk.[6] It puts together theory and empirical work in a very elegant way.

When you hit a brick wall on a project, do you continue to work on the problem or do you take a break and work on something else?

I have great co-authors, so when I hit a wall, which happens all the time, I will make a phone call. When I am working on something by myself, and I run into a problem, I will put it away for a while. Sometimes that can be effective, as I alluded to earlier.

When I interviewed Randy Wright, he described you as a "real grinder." Is that how you would describe your approach to day-to-day research?

Yes. You come in each day with your lunch pail, put it down, and get to work, even when you don't feel like it.

Related to the previous question, when a project isn't going to turn out as hoped, do you scrap it or aim to send the work to a second-tier or field journal?

In macroeconomics, field journals are very good. In some sense, more serious work is published in those than in the more prestigious journals like the *AER*. But my vision of research is that you just have to make a marginal contribution. For me, it's enough to work something out that I didn't quite understand before. If you try to bunt and get to first base, every once in a while things are going to work out.

What has been the biggest change during your career in how researchers in your fields conduct research?

The biggest change in macroeconomics occurred when rational expectations was introduced in the '70s. As a researcher, you now needed to know a lot more about stochastic processes and dynamic programming. And that put people out of business, particularly those who came out of graduate school when I did, because it took great effort to re-tool. I have not seen anything like it since then. David Levine calls it normal science nowadays, taking a line from Kuhn. You could say some of the work on ambiguity aversion is quite different from rational expectations, but that's not really true; in terms of the tools and perspective, they are very close. And I think developments should be fairly continuous. Actually, I could teach a macroeconomics course in which I use nothing written after 1980, and it would still be challenging and pertinent.

What would be your response to those who argue that too much math is being used in economic theory today?

It's hard to know what's in their minds. Would you say that about physics? Or engineering? No. Economics is a quantitative discipline. Our colleagues in statistics and math are developing things that are potentially useful to us. I don't know how you could say you don't like it. It's true that it takes some effort to learn math; there is a negative sign on the utility of effort, I'll grant that. But take someone like Paul Milgrom. He's a very gifted applied mathematician who has an eye for spotting where a piece of theoretical mathematics can be used to push forward an intractable problem, like in auctions, for example. He does it over and over again. Who in his or her right mind would say that Paul Milgrom uses too much math?

THE WRITING PROCESS

Which aspect of the writing process do you find most difficult?

Writing is difficult. I try to be clear, but it's a struggle for me. I know some very talented writers, like David Kreps and Bob Lucas, who could have been real writers. I have no idea whether they work hard at it, or if it just comes easily, but they are certainly gifted.

What steps have you taken during your career to improve the quality of your writing?

I had some great classes at Berkeley on how to write an argument. But that doesn't teach you how to write something that is at the next level. I wish I could do that.

COLLABORATION

When you work with co-authors, how do you decide whom to work with?

That's easy. I have longstanding friends whom I write with. During a conversation, an idea will come up and we'll decide to nail it.

How do you prefer to interact with them (e-mail, phone, or face-to-face)?

I do like face-to-face discussions. But if I am working with someone like Lars Ljungqvist, who is in Sweden, we can exchange e-mails and use Skype.

What are the main challenges associated with collaborative work?

It's always hard to do collaborative work. In a sense, it's like a marriage, because it involves a lot of trust. And some days you do more than the other person, and other days they do more than you. But you must figure out the fairness in effort, whether it's explicit or not. And you also have to be on the same wavelength as your co-author. You can get into disputes about which position to take in a paper and how to state it. That can be fun, but in my experience, there are sources of tension all the way along the process. I hate to be in the audience when my co-authors are giving a paper, because I think they're screwing up. And I'm sure they feel exactly the same about me.

How do you resolve conflict?

Sometimes I say something fairly directly and, if it's ignored, I will say it again. But I've had a bunch of co-authors with whom I've repeatedly written. We end up approaching problems the same way, and if there is any tension, it tends to be productive.

RESEARCH ASSISTANCE

How do you use undergraduate and graduate research assistants?

I have used graduate students for many years. The empirical regularity is that the meaner I am, in terms of my demands, the better it is for them on the job market.

Last summer, I hired undergraduate RAs for the first time. It worked out very well. I had been teaching a hard course and, at the end, three or four of the students said they wanted to do some work in the summer. They collected data on 19th-century bond prices and helped to build an econometric model. They were doing real research, and they said they enjoyed it.

SEMINAR PARTICIPATION AND NETWORKING

What are the benefits to attending a seminar that is closely related to your work versus one that is not closely related?

I tend to go to a wide range of seminars. But macroeconomics is very imperialistic, and so even if you just go to those, you get exposed to lots of wonderful and promising research. I find that exhilarating.

How important is professional networking to success in research?

Networking is everything. I'm not sure I like the phrase, but there is the sociology of research in which groups of people tend to work on the same thing. That creates a bunch of energy and enthusiasm. But the downside is that if someone is doing something a little different, they may feel neglected and have a tough time. And I would say history shows that advances come mostly from those who are going down a new line.

To what extent is the absence of departmental colleagues working in one's research area a major disadvantage?

Indifference is a killer. If you're in a department where people think what you're working on is dead wrong, and they're passionate about it, that can be fun, because they're going to talk to you about it. You tend to thrive when there is a critical mass in your area, unless you're a loner.

COMMUNICATION OF RESEARCH

How do you find the right balance between communicating your research at an early stage versus the close-to-finished stage?

My rule is that a person will only read a paper one time. And so if you write a bad early draft, don't count on anybody coming back to read a second one. You must polish anything that you put out there.

What are the unique challenges to giving a seminar and how do you overcome them?

Nowadays, everybody has to use slides. I must confess that, in the right hands, they are a great technology for communication. But I haven't mastered how to use them as much as I should. I'm just a dinosaur in that respect.

PUBLICATION

How do you decide upon the appropriate journal to send your research to?

My basic algorithm is that I start at the top and go down, and I don't get upset until it's been rejected five times.

How would you best describe your approach to dealing with a 'revise and resubmit' request from a journal? How about an outright rejection?

The refereeing process in economics is way out of control. In particular, editors are too intrusive. They tell you how to structure and write your paper, and some even say what should be in it. I don't think that's any of their business. You feel better when you get a referee report where it looks like the person knows more about the problem than you do, but I can give you examples of where the refereeing process has made my paper worse. Sometimes you just have to go along with it.

In terms of a rejection, nobody likes to get that letter. That's just the human condition.

What has been your best and worst experience during the publication process?

I submitted a couple of papers to the *JPE* in the '90s and received fantastic referee reports. One of the papers was written with a friend on the macro-economics of the French Revolution and it was hard to referee.[7] But we got very sophisticated comments from someone who, as I found out years later, is not an economic historian. In the other paper, I also figured out who the referee was, but only on the day after he died. That really upset me, because he was a friend of mine. I couldn't touch the paper for two years. We ended up making him a co-author, although he might not like it wherever he is.[8]

I've had papers outright rejected for stupid reasons. I once wrote a paper with Lars Hansen that got into *Econometrica*, but they made us take out all the interesting economic theory and focus solely on a very narrow technical issue that would interest almost no one.[9] The editor wouldn't overrule the referees, who insisted that we make the changes. That's an example of where the refereeing process made a good paper into a boring one.

BOOK WRITING

You have written several books. Why do you write them?

Sometimes, I've been trying to figure out something when teaching a class, and my notes have grown into a book. But I have also written books that are monographs about a particular subject. That gives you more freedom than writing a paper, and I am trying to learn something along the way. In the introduction of Paul Johnson's *A History of the American People*, he says that he wrote it because he didn't know any American history, and wanted to learn some. I feel the same way when I write my monographs.

Do you enjoy writing books?

I wouldn't do it otherwise. A few years ago, I wrote a book called *The Conquest of American Inflation*. It was fun putting it together, because it was like writing an essay in college. I had to structure the argument.

TIME MANAGEMENT

How do you divide up your working day, both in terms of quantity and timing of different kinds of work?

I have a cabin in Montana in the summer. I work all day, and then at 5:00 or 6:00, I go out to a stream and fish until dark. That is perfect. But during the academic year, just like Randy Wright said, I come in with my lunch pail and work.

How do you balance multiple research projects?

I like to have more than one project going on at the same time because I get too bored with one. Switching is fun. Other people might stick to one and finish it, and that's probably a better work habit, but I have a limited attention span.

How do you balance your research and non-research activities?

I hate administrative duties. I devote a lot of time to teaching my students. In fact, I spend more time doing that than research nowadays.

How do you balance your personal and professional lives?

That's not a problem. My wife's father is a very distinguished physics professor. And so she's used to the lifestyle. Also, she works and has her own interests.

REFLECTIONS AND THE FUTURE OF ECONOMICS

What are the biggest challenges facing your research fields?

Relative to the '30s, the last few years have been better. But we've had two decades of very high unemployment in Europe, and we're into the second or third year of high unemployment in the United States, which is unacceptable and important to get straight. There is a tension between unemployment insurance and incentives, and in some ways, I think the Europeans are ahead of us. For example, Sweden is reforming its system for compensating people for not working, at exactly the time that we are extending unemployment compensation. They are trying to get out of a trap and I worry about us getting into one. But the interesting thing about macroeconomics is that the questions don't really change; they are damn hard questions. And we only get marginally more insights about how to look at them.

What are the strengths and weaknesses of your own research?

I view this as like a matching process: you have to accept at some point what you can do and can't do, and then make the best use of your skills. And so I think one of my strengths is that I know what I can do and can't do. And I probably do work right at the niche that I'm supposed to be at.

I have all sorts of weaknesses. My theory's not rigorous enough, my empirical work's not ambitious enough, and my writing's not clear enough. I'm aware of all those things. I'm just trying to make a marginal contribution.

In the end, do you think the profession has helped to bring out and shape your research for the best?

I've never cared much about that. I think it was William James who said that differences in philosophy come down to differences in personality. The people whom I know well within the profession have strong instincts about how to set up a problem. Take Neil Wallace and Chris Sims, who are both extremely smart. Wallace is much closer to being a pure theorist, because he seizes on a couple of observations that he thinks are very critical and then goes after them relentlessly. Sims is closer to being a raw empiricist, because he wants to account for many factors simultaneously. They are always going to do work like that since they are committed to it, and it's hardwired.

Do you have any professional regrets?

No. I can't think of a more fun business to be in. We're really lucky in what we're paid to do. It's a privilege. And it's not just being a professor; it's being a professor in a field where you get to think all day about what's in 50 per cent of any first-rate newspaper.

What are your professional ambitions?

When I was 20, I probably had some unrealistic ambitions. But right now, I just want to get out of some committees and finish my next few papers.

How would you describe the state of economics today? Are you optimistic about its future?

It doesn't matter whether I'm optimistic, because people have to study economics, and I don't just mean those at university. If you're a regulator or a market participant or someone who is thinking of reforming social institutions, you're going to have to roll up your sleeves and study things that are right at the frontier of macroeconomics.

NOTES

1. Cagan, P.G. (1956), 'The Monetary Dynamics of Hyperinflation', in Milton Friedman (ed.), *Studies in the Quantity Theory of Money*, Chicago: University of Chicago Press, pp. 25–117.
2. Sargent, T.J. and N. Wallace (1973), 'Rational Expectations and the Dynamics of Hyperinflation', *International Economic Review,* Vol. 14, No. 2 (June), pp. 328–250.
3. Abreu, D., Pearce, D. and E. Stacchetti (1986), 'Optimal Cartel Equilibria with Imperfect Monitoring', *Journal of Economic Theory*, Vol. 39, No. 1 (June), pp. 251–269; Abreu, D., Pearce, D. and E. Stacchetti (1990), 'Towards a Theory of Discounted Repeated Games with Imperfect Monitoring', *Econometrica*, Vol. 58, No. 5 (September), pp. 1041–1063.
4. Gilboa, I. and D. Schmeidler (1989), 'Maximin Expected Utility with Non-Unique Prior', *Journal of Mathematical Economics*, Vol. 18, No. 2 (April), pp. 141–153.

5. Hansen, L.P. and R. Jagannathan (1991), 'Implications of Security Market Data for Models of Dynamic Economies', *Journal of Political Economy*, Vol. 99, No. 2 (April), pp. 225–262.
6. Hansen, L.P., Heaton, J.C. and N. Li (2008), 'Consumption Strikes Back? Measuring Long-Run Risk', *Journal of Political Economy*, Vol. 116, No. 2 (April), pp. 260–302.
7. Sargent, T.J. and F.R. Velde (1995), 'Macroeconomic Features of the French Revolution', *Journal of Political Economy*, Vol. 103, No. 3 (June), pp. 474–518.
8. Aiyagari, S.R., Marcet, A., Sargent, T.J. and J. Seppälä (2002), 'Optimal Taxation without State-Contingent Debt', *Journal of Political Economy*, Vol. 110, No. 6 (December), pp. 1220–1254.
9. Hansen, L.P. and T.J. Sargent (1983), 'The Dimensionality of the Aliasing Problem in Models with Rational Spectral Densities', *Econometrica*, Vol. 51, No. 2 (March), pp. 377–388.

Joseph E. Stiglitz
(Columbia University)

Joseph Stiglitz was born in Gary, Indiana in 1943, and received a liberal arts education (originally majoring in physics, but switching to mathematics and economics) at Amherst College. He left Amherst to obtain a PhD at the Massachusetts Institute of Technology in 1963, was awarded a BA by Amherst in 1964, left MIT a year later to study at the University of Cambridge, under a Fulbright Scholarship, and, after completing his MIT doctoral dissertation, taught there as an assistant professor during the academic year 1966–1967. Shortly after arriving at Cambridge, he was appointed as a Tapp Junior Research Fellow at Gonville and Caius College, a position which he held until 1970. He taught at Yale University from 1967 to 1974, and was promoted to full Professor there in 1970. He has also taught at Stanford University, 1974–1976 and 1988–2001, Oxford University, 1976–1979, Princeton University, 1979–1988, and Columbia University, where he currently serves as University Professor.

Professor Stiglitz is best known for his research on the economics of information, in particular exploring the consequences of informational asymmetries and pioneering the concepts of adverse selection and moral hazard. He has also made major contributions to macroeconomics and monetary theory, to development economics and trade theory, to public and corporate finance, to the theories of industrial organization and rural organization, and to the theories of welfare economics and of income and wealth distribution. His most-cited articles in chronological order include 'Equilibrium in Competitive Insurance Markets: An Essay on the Economics of Imperfect Information', *Quarterly Journal of Economics* (1976), co-authored with Michael Rothschild, 'Monopolistic Competition and Optimum Product Diversity', *American Economic Review* (1977), co-authored with Avinash Dixit, 'On the Impossibility of Informationally Efficient Markets', *American Economic Review* (1980), co-authored with Sanford Grossman, 'Credit Rationing in Markets with Imperfect Information', *American Economic Review* (1981), co-authored with Andrew Weiss, and 'Equilibrium Unemployment as a Worker Discipline Device', *American Economic Review* (1984), co-authored with Carl Shapiro. His books include *Globalization and Its Discontents* (W.W. Norton, 2001), *The Roaring Nineties* (W.W. Norton, 2003), *Towards a New Paradigm in Monetary Economics* (Cambridge University Press, 2003), co-authored with Bruce Greenwald, *Fair Trade for All* (Oxford University Press, 2005), co-authored with Andrew Charlton, *Making Globalization Work* (W.W. Norton and Penguin/Allen Lane, 2006), *The Three Trillion Dollar War: The True Cost of the Iraq Conflict* (W.W. Norton and Penguin/Allen Lane, 2008), co-authored with Linda Bilmes, and *Freefall: America, Free Markets, and the Sinking of the World Economy* (W.W. Norton and Penguin/Allen Lane, 2010).

Professor Stiglitz was elected as a Fellow of the Econometric Society in 1972, a Fellow of the American Academy of Arts and Sciences in 1983, and a Corresponding Fellow of the British Academy in 1993 and of the Royal Society in 2009. He was awarded the John Bates Clark Medal in 1979 and received the Nobel Prize in Economic Sciences, along with Michael Spence and George Akerlof, in 2001, "for laying the foundations for the theory of markets with asymmetric information." He was a lead author of the 1995 report on climate change of the Intergovernmental Panel on Climate Change (IPCC), which shared the 2007 Nobel Peace Prize with Albert Gore.

Professor Stiglitz was a member of President Clinton's Council of Economic Advisers, 1993–1995, and served as its Chairman, 1995–1997. He then became Chief Economist and Senior Vice-President of the World Bank, 1997–2000. In 2008, he was asked by the French President, Nicolas Sarkozy, to chair the Commission on the Measurement of Economic Performance and Social Progress. In 2009, he was appointed by the

President of the United Nations General Assembly as Chair of the Commission of Experts on Reform of the International Financial and Monetary System.

I interviewed Joseph Stiglitz in a café on the Upper West Side of Manhattan, New York City. It was mid-morning of Saturday, 2 October 2010.

BACKGROUND INFORMATION

Why did you decide to pursue an academic career in economics?

I grew up in Gary, Indiana, where the poverty, the discrimination, and the sporadic unemployment certainly made me think about why those problems existed, and what we could do about them. But a critical part of my development was being a member of the debating society in high school. Most of the issues that we talked about were related to economics. In fact, one that I remember in particular is something that we are debating more than 50 years later, which is our agricultural support program.

GENERAL THOUGHTS ON RESEARCH

What is the value of pure versus applied research in economics?

I make less distinction than some people do because my own research strategy is largely to look at concrete problems that raise deep theoretical issues. An obvious example was my paper on sharecropping.[1] Here was an applied problem: why do we have sharecropping contracts? You might say that that's a very nitty-gritty development economics question. But I saw it as a puzzle, because economic theory talks about the importance of incentives and yet sharecropping attenuates them since 50 per cent of the output is taken by the landlord. And so if you begin with the presumption of some sort of efficiency in economic relations, you have to ask: why would there be a persistent contractual arrangement that was seemingly inefficient? The answer I provided had to do with imperfections in risk markets and asymmetries of information. A huge literature on incentives and asymmetric information grew out of this very concrete problem. At the end of the paper, I noted that it was relevant to not only sharecropping, but also to many other things, including executive compensation and corporate governance. Now, an applied economist might have simply stopped at the issue of sharecropping. But as a theorist, I want to know what the underlying economic principles are that can be applied elsewhere. Then I can think about why the labor market is different from the capital market, for example. Answering this question will, in turn, give some insight into their critical properties. It is true that as you get deeper and deeper into understanding a particular market application, some might say that this takes you deeper and deeper into the weeds, but even then there is almost always a set of principles that emerges that can help you think about broader issues.

How would you describe your current research agenda?

My work style always entails pushing forward on several frontiers at one time. The financial crisis has raised a lot of issues about macroeconomics.[2] In a way, though, it has validated the macro agenda that I have been engaged in for the last 25 years. And it has led me to go deeper into certain issues. For instance, one issue that the crisis brought out was systemic risk; in particular, how the failure of one bank can lead to the failure of others. I had identified that as a crucial issue, five years before it came to light in the current crisis, in my 2003 book with Bruce Greenwald, *Towards a New Paradigm in Monetary Economics*. More recently, I have applied the tools of network analysis to Japanese data on debt-credit networks. This is relevant to the issue of financial stability, since the failure of a firm that is heavily indebted to a bank may have consequences for the bank itself, which, in turn, may transfer this adverse shock to other firms.[3] And I have also been working on the issue of economic architecture that relates, for example, to the nature of risk-sharing relationships between countries, which then raises the question of what is the *optimal* degree and form of financial integration.[4]

A second line of work relates to the fact that standard macro models have no financial sector. The traditional LM curve is totally inadequate. You can't summarize the financial sector in a money demand equation. What you need is both a banking sector and a non-banking sector. Bruce Greenwald and I made some progress with this in our 2003 book and in our subsequent research.

A third, very different strand of work, is in the area of development economics. Karla Hoff and I have been thinking about how so-called cognitive frames, or ideologies, shape perceptions, which, in turn, affect choices. Our view is that this perspective may help explain why institutional change can be difficult and societies so rigid.[5] This research is also related to a book that I am finishing with Bruce Greenwald that looks at how we can analyze economies as learning institutions.

And finally, I am continually working on some old problems, which, 40 years after I first approached them, remarkably remain unresolved. In particular, there is the question of how we can construct economic models that integrate both moral hazard and adverse selection.

How did your work as Chairman of the President's Council of Economic Advisers and as Chief Economist at the World Bank change your views on (a) how academic research in economics is conducted and (b) the use of academic research in economics?

There were several observations. First, the gap between what economists do, and what we need to design laws and policies, was pretty big. One very fascinating example was the design of legislation for dealing with toxic waste. That involved environmental economics, but you also had to have an understanding of law, land markets, and some science. But academic research tends to be more siloed. And so a policymaker could read the literature of law and economics, for example, but he would have to pull it all together himself, and that's hard when you're trying to address simultaneously the myriad of other problems confronting the country and the world.

There were other instances when I was shocked by how superficial and inadequate research was on the key questions that we faced. One of the first tasks I faced after assuming the job as chief economist of the World Bank was how to deal with the East Asian crisis. The IMF said the response was to raise interest rates. I asked the question, "Where is the theory or evidence indicating that is an appropriate response?" The answer was not to resort either to theory or evidence, so much as to previous custom: "We always respond in this way." They described what they had done in previous crises, but I wanted to know the theory that said this would work, and for whom, and what were the general equilibrium consequences. The level of sophistication was, quite honestly, disappointing.

The IMF came out trying to change the rules of global capital markets by pushing capital market liberalization. But again, where was the evidence and theory suggesting that capital market liberalization leads to more stability? I have written a paper showing that it led to more instability.[6] At the time, there was only *one* research paper, by Dani Rodrik, that argued that it did not lead to more stability empirically.[7] There was very little research and what research there was tended to be more ideologically driven, using models with perfect capital markets which were clearly inappropriate for developing countries.

What was striking to me, particularly in development, was the religious nature of the beliefs in the neo-classical model; the distance between the assumptions made and the world that we live.

Do you think that academic research in economics today is more or less valuable than when you started your career?

I'd say equally valuable. When I started my career, I think that there was some arrogance in the profession. We had developed Keynesian economics and thought we knew the right model. But over time, we became aware of how little we knew: new problems presented themselves, like inflation, for which the old models didn't provide adequate answers. We became more sensitive to the disparity between the assumptions we made in micro-economics (as we studied individual firms and households) and macro-economics (where we study aggregate behavior). Beginning with the late 1960s and early 1970s, there was a major change in the paradigm (in which I played some role), from the perfect information model to one that recognized that an important aspect of human behavior is the response to imperfect information. That was a very fundamental and very deep trans-formation in economics, one that made it clear that the return to further research was extremely valuable. But then we went through a period when, again, there was a little bit of arrogance in the air. Some macroeconomists thought that they had developed better models describing aggregate behav-ior ('representative agent', new classical, and real business cycle models). But these models not only didn't predict the recent financial crisis, they suggested such crises couldn't occur. They didn't provide much under-standing of what had happened or what to do about it. In fact, many economists believe that the crisis arose partly because too many policymak-ers followed the dictums of these theories. And so at this juncture, I would say that there is recognition that that model clearly was inadequate. This has had a whole set of ramifications. Advocates of these models might say, "Well, accidents happen and our model works most of the time." My response would be, "But you need it to work when it's important." Financial crises may not occur every year, but when they do, the social costs are enormous.

In response to the crisis, the Institute of New Economic Thinking has been established to help support research exploring alternative paradigms. I believe that such research is invaluable, if we are to have a more stable, more efficient, economy – let alone one in which the fruits of economic growth are better distributed.

IDEA GENERATION

Where do you get your research ideas?

Talking, reading, looking. Take the question of sharecropping. Why did I get interested in that? It's obviously a very important institution, and one that more people have worked in than any other. It was a mystery to me why more people hadn't studied it before, because it was so anomalous. A young economist at Chicago, Steven Cheung, had written a paper in which he argued that sharecropping does not affect incentives for workers, but he made some very unpersuasive assumptions, particularly in relation to information, and so that provided an opportunity for me to apply a different analytic approach.[8]

Another source of ideas comes from the interaction between theoretical puzzles and policy. Take the question of how to construct a model that integrates moral hazard and adverse selection, together with the major policy issue of how to run health insurance in the US. For many years, the theories of moral hazard and adverse selection have been studied separately, but if you look at something like health insurance, then it becomes clear that you should be thinking about them together. For example, you can propose to deal with moral hazard by providing big deductions, but that can lead to cream skimming and undermine the extent of risk pooling. And so as a theorist, you say, "Wow, unless we address this theoretical lacuna – how to analyze markets in which moral hazard and adverse selection are both present – then we're never going to be able to answer the question of how to design our health insurance system."

IDEA EXECUTION

What makes a good theoretical paper?

It's one that begins with a good problem without any obvious answers. By the time you finish it, you often say that the answer now seems pretty obvious, but then you realize *why* it wasn't so obvious [*laughs*]. And, quite often, a good theoretical paper will also go down a line that wasn't easy. One nice example is a paper by one of my former students, Dilip Abreu, which provides a framework for studying how co-operation can be enforced in infinitely repeated games with discounting.[9] In this set-up, a strategy has the potential to be very complicated since it may involve infinitely repeated punishments and history-dependent prescriptions. However, Abreu shows that much of this complexity is unnecessary, because under fairly weak conditions, the 'good' equilibrium can be achieved with a 'simple' strategy. Using very elegant mathematics, he proves that an 'optimal penal code' will exist, so that a player who is considering any kind of deviation can always be deterred by the threat of a worse punishment.

I also like my recent theoretical paper on optimal economic architecture. It brings out the importance of a very simple mathematical observation, which is the fact that most macro models assume convexity. In that case, risk sharing always pays. But the world is full of non-convexities. For example, bankruptcy introduces a very important non-convexity. The bankruptcy of one firm affects the likelihood of the bankruptcy of those to whom it owes money, its suppliers, and those who may rely upon it for supplies. In short, actions that affect one firm's likelihood of bankruptcy have adverse effects on other parties. What I like about my paper, in particular, is that once we drop the assumption of convexity, which has formed the basis of both policy and research for 60 years, it leads to very different views about the desirability of different economic architectures and the consequences of diversification. In so doing, it outlines a future research program. And I would say that's another aspect of a good theoretical paper: it's not the end of a line of work, it's the beginning.

What makes a good empirical paper?

Most econometricians or statisticians would say that it uses convincing data to test an important hypothesis in a rigorous way. Part of the standard format today for an empirical paper is to begin with hypotheses 'derived' from a theoretical structure. For the most part, I think that's all for the good, but the problem is that much of the theory that is at the beginning of an empirical paper tends to be very hokey. I'll give you an example. There were some very nice papers in the '60s by Dale Jorgenson and others testing the neo-classical investment equation, which was held up as the model of 'good econometrics' of that period.[10] But it turned out to have two fundamental flaws. First, it assumed that the Modigliani–Miller Theorem – the value of a firm is independent of how it is financed – was correct. They assumed that there were perfect capital markets. But research exploring the implications of information asymmetries explained why the Modigliani–Miller Theorem in general doesn't hold and why capital markets are often very imperfect. Andrew Weiss and I showed that with imperfect information, credit constraints could become important; a firm may not be able to borrow as much as it would like.[11] The amount it may be able to borrow, and therefore how much it may be able to invest, will depend upon the size of the firm's equity. Second, when you take a problem like investment and apply it to the real world, there are messy complications, such as taxes. And those econometric papers typically mis-specified the tax implications for the cost of capital. In the absence of taxation, financial structure did not matter, but with taxation it did. The calculated after-tax cost of equity capital appeared to be different from the after-tax cost of debt. It should be obvious that, depending on which was lower, firms could be financed either by debt or by equity. And with debt cheaper, firms should have been wholly financed with debt, but somehow, there were limits to the debt-equity ratio that were totally inconsistent with the spirit of the Modigliani–Miller Theorem.

COLLABORATION

When you work with co-authors, how do you decide whom to work with?

Much of my research is motivated by talking. I'll be speaking with someone about the work that I, or they, have done recently, and I'll start thinking, "Golly, there are some important questions that this work raises, and we should be able to formulate a new model here … " But I work with various people in many different ways. Some of my co-authors are bubbling up with ideas, others are very meticulous in dotting the i's and crossing the t's, and there are those who bring certain mathematical skills to the table, which is true of the younger co-authors with whom I'm working right now.

COMMUNICATION OF RESEARCH

What are the unique challenges to giving a seminar and how do you overcome them?

I always feel that the most important part is conveying the intuition of how I went about doing the work – and why I undertook the research project. Young economists are very much into models, but I think in words and translate into equations, and other people in my generation often think in geometry. Different minds work in different ways and so that's the challenge. For instance, I remember one of the first seminars that I gave, which was at the University of Chicago. I explained why risk markets were inefficient. This goes back to the idea that you've got a sufficient condition for market efficiency when there exists a complete set of what we call Arrow-Debreu securities.[12] That led to the question that was posed in the '50s of whether that is necessary or, under plausible assumptions, would financial markets be inefficient if there weren't many of these securities, and what was the nature of the bias? Several people in subsequent years tried to provide an answer to that question. For example, Peter Diamond wrote a very influential paper proving that financial markets were efficient in a second-best sense.[13] But I didn't believe it, and showed in a paper that he had made a number of extreme assumptions that were not, in general, true.[14] For instance, he assumed that even when firms are not perfectly correlated, they would believe that doubling their scale would double their market value, that there was no bankruptcy, and only a single commodity. Anyway, I was giving a version of this work at Chicago and Milton Friedman was there. He said, "I don't understand. There are markets for variances and markets for means? You can always express things in mean and variance and therefore, in effect, there is a full set of markets?" Friedman was a great intuitive thinker but in some cases, intuition can only take you so far, and I knew he was wrong here. (There were, in effect, a number of assumptions underlying his 'intuition', and it's not always easy to uncover these assumptions). He had his vocabulary and I had my model, and so I had to figure out how to translate my model into his language. I failed [*laughs*]. I realized afterwards how to do it, but when you are under the time pressure of a seminar, you have to be able to relate to people who have different ways of understanding.

TIME MANAGEMENT

How do you divide up your working day, both in terms of quantity and timing of different kinds of work?

My life is very chaotic and so it's a working life rather than a working day. I would describe it as having lots of constraints. For example, on Thursday of this week, I testified in Congress, and on Tuesday, I had a meeting with the Department of Justice. Those are things where I don't have discretion and I try to use all the available time that's not committed otherwise to my research. But it's a continual battle to carve out that time.

The boundary to my research and writings are also porous in the sense that when I'm writing my more popular books, I'm always thinking about the deeper theoretical issues. It might seem like I am just popularizing my work, but it's absolutely part of the research program. And I enjoy writing those books. You could say that Keynes was trying to solve the problem of the Great Depression in his *General Theory*. It wasn't quite written for the average layman, but clearly it was more accessible than mathematical argument. And so in my books I think I can make some of the analysis accessible, and then put on the table a research agenda, those questions that are not finished. In most of my work, I always try to see what are the underlying theoretical assumptions that people have not understood. For example, when I look at what's happened in the financial crisis and issues of excessive bank leverage, I think about the Modigliani–Miller Theorem, arguing that increased leverage doesn't create more 'value', it simply shifts risk around. When I'm serving on commissions, I will often realize that the current literature on theory might not address a big problem, but I will then begin work on it. I served, for instance, on an Advisory Commission for the SEC-CFTC on the Flash Crash. Given the Flash Crash, I asked myself, how would I go about re-writing Grossman-Stiglitz?[15] I see the various parts of my professional life as thus really complementary.

REFLECTIONS AND THE FUTURE OF ECONOMICS

What are the biggest challenges facing your research fields?

I think one of the biggest challenges facing economics today is in macro-economics, where various versions of the 'perfect market' (neo-classical) have predominated. But there are several aspects of the behavior of the economy that were clearly inconsistent with any model predicated on rationality. Let me give you two examples. First, it is easy to write down a model of an optimal incentive structure that incorporates information about performance of the firm and other firms in the industry. But few of the observed compensation schemes for executives at the heart of the financial crisis were consistent with what the model predicts. It was obvious that they were designed to encourage shortsighted behavior and excessive risk taking. Everybody should have seen that.

Second, it is difficult to reconcile the recent behavior of financial institutions within a model of rationality. Even though they are supposed to understand risk, there seemed to be no understanding of the Modigliani–Miller Theorem. They pushed for more leverage because that gave a higher return on equity. But risk was simply being created elsewhere, and as the risk of bankruptcy increased, the value of the firm should have been decreasing. Interest rates paid on debt therefore should have increased. Neither those running these financial institutions, their regulators, nor their investors, really grasped the import of the Modigliani–Miller Theorem, which, incidentally, is taught at the beginning of every finance class in the world.

What are the strengths and weaknesses of your own research?

All research involves trade-offs. Models involve simplification, and the question is what do you simplify? Good research simplifies things that are irrelevant and keeps the core. I would like to believe that I made the right choices in my models. But obviously what is uncomplicated and manageable depends on one's ability to formulate general mathematical models. Take the Greenwald-Stiglitz macro model in our 2003 book. We formulated that as a two or three period model and analyzed how banks would behave and what macroeconomics would look like. I would like to have done that in the context of an infinite period model, which is the convention today, but my own judgment is that the insights you get from that type of model are not worth the complexity that it adds, and the simplifications typically made to make these long-run models tractable often leave out all the interesting issues. As I say, it's a question of trade-offs.

The second point relates to my earlier one about the limits to economics. My research over the last 40 years has been very good in showing the limits of the perfect information model. And while I've demonstrated that the imperfect information model can contribute a great deal, and explain things that the perfect information model can't, there are still many puzzles to be solved when you go beyond rationality. I've worked out a few things, but I think they've been more useful in terms of framing the issue than in making a major breakthrough in our understanding.

Do you have any professional regrets?

There have been one or two sentences in a couple of my books and articles that have inflamed some people, and I probably regret having articulated the ideas that way. But in one case, I made it very clear that this was not intended to reflect on any particular person, but on the system. It was about the importance of having systems that are designed to ensure that individuals don't face conflicts of interest because that undermines their operation or, at the least, confidence in them. The positive side of my statement was that it called more attention to a very big issue than if I had just said, in the usual language, that there are problems associated with multiple principal–agent scenarios that lead to conflicts of interest. That would have just been like water off a duck's back. Everybody's heard about the issue of revolving doors, and while that may be more 'understandable' than discussions of multiple principal–agent problems, such discussions haven't sufficed to motivate changes in rules or behavior. On the other hand, it had the negative effect of distracting attention away from a substantive point to the defense of a particular individual. That's a trade-off you always face. But I think I made the wrong decision, as suggested by what is remembered from these battles. What's so interesting is that people remember the battle as one of personalities. They forget that the IMF conceded that, for instance, on the substantive issue of capital controls, I was right. Just after my book came out, they produced papers basically saying that there was no evidence that capital market liberalization was good for growth or stability. More recently, they have even come out in favor of capital controls, under suitable conditions. In the end, you can move the institutions and the profession, but what people remember is the personal debates.

Are you optimistic about the future of economics?

Yes, I am, but not totally. I've been a little shocked because I would have thought that having seen the failure of the standard macroeconomic model, people would say we really have to change it. As far as I can tell, a significant fraction of the profession hasn't done so, which suggests to me that it is taken almost as religion. To me, it would seem that if you have a data point that is so 'large' in a sense and so inconsistent with your model, any scientist would change his mind, or at least express concern about the applicability of his model.

Economics is about prediction. Most of the economics profession didn't predict the most important event in 75 years in spite of 'the advances of economic science'. And yet, anyone not wedded to the notion that markets were perfect could have seen the storm coming, and some did. Something is wrong, because not only did we not predict the crisis, we (that is to say, the 'mainstream' of the profession) said it couldn't happen.

NOTES

1. Stiglitz, J.E. (1974), 'Incentives and Risk Sharing in Sharecropping', *Review of Economic Studies*, Vol. 41, No. 2 (April), pp. 219–255.
2. See Stiglitz, J.E. (2011), 'Rethinking Macroeconomics: What Went Wrong and How to Fix It', *Global Policy*, Vol. 2, No. 2 (May), pp. 165–175; Stiglitz, J.E. (2011), 'Rethinking Macroeconomics: What Failed and How to Repair It', *Journal of the European Economic Association*, Vol. 9, No. 4 (August), pp. 591–645.
3. De Masi, G., Fujiwara, Y., Gallegati, M., Greenwald, B. and J.E. Stiglitz (2011), 'An Analysis of the Japanese Credit Network', *Evolutionary and Institutional Economics Review*, Vol. 7, No. 2, pp. 203–232.
4. Stiglitz, J.E. (2010), 'Risk and Global Economic Architecture: Why Full Financial Integration May Be Undesirable', *American Economic Review*, Papers and Proceedings, Vol. 100, No. 2 (May), pp. 388–392; Stiglitz, J.E. (2010), 'Contagion, Liberalization, and the Optimal Structure of Globalization', *Journal of Globalization and Development*, Vol. 1, No. 2 (December), pp. 19–36.
5. Hoff, K. and J.E. Stiglitz (2010), 'Equilibrium Frictions: A Cognitive Approach to Societal Rigidity', *American Economic Review*, Papers and Proceedings, Vol. 100, No. 2 (May), pp. 141–146.
6. Stiglitz, J.E. (2000), 'Capital Market Liberalization, Economic Growth, and Instability', *World Development*, Vol. 28, No. 6 (June), pp. 1075–1086; Stiglitz, J.E. (2004), 'Capital-Market Liberalization, Globalization and the IMF', *Oxford Review of Economic Policy*, Vol. 20, No. 1 (Spring), pp. 57–71.
7. Rodrik, D. (1998), 'Who Needs Capital-account Convertibility?', *Essays in International Finance* 207, International Finance Section, Department of Economics, Princeton University (May), pp. 55–65.
8. Cheung, S.N.S. (1968), 'Private Property Rights and Sharecropping', *Journal of Political Economy*, Vol. 76, No. 6 (November), pp. 1107–1122.
9. Abreu, D. (1988), 'On the Theory of Infinitely Repeated Games with Discounting', *Econometrica*, Vol. 56, No. 2 (March), pp. 383–396.
10. Jorgenson, D.W. (1963), 'Capital Theory and Investment', *American Economic Review*, Papers and Proceedings, Vol. 53, No. 2 (May), pp. 247–259; Hall R.E. and D.W. Jorgenson (1967), 'Tax Policy and Investment Behavior', *American Economic Review*, Vol. 59, No. 3 (June), pp. 319–414.
11. Stiglitz, J.E. and A.M. Weiss (1981), 'Credit Rationing in Markets with Imperfect Information', *American Economic Review*, Vol. 71, No. 3 (June), pp. 393–410.
12. Arrow, K.J. (1964), 'The Role of Securities in the Optimal Allocation of Risk Bearing', *Review of Economic Studies*, Vol. 31, No. 2 (April), pp. 91–96; Gerard Debreu (1959), *The Theory of Value*, New York: John Wiley and Sons.
13. Diamond, P.A. (1967), 'The Role of a Stock Market in a General Equilibrium Model with Technological Uncertainty', *American Economic Review*, Vol. 57, No. 4 (September), pp. 759–776.
14. Stiglitz, J.E. (1972), 'On the Optimality of the Stock Market Allocation of Investment', *Quarterly Journal of Economics*, Vol. 86, No. 1 (February), pp. 25–60; Stiglitz, J.E. (1982), 'The Inefficiency of the Stock Market Equilibrium', *Review of Economic Studies*, Vol. 49, No. 2 (April), pp. 241–261.
15. The Flash Crash refers to the US stock market crash that took place on 6 May 2010. The Dow Jones Industrial Average plunged by almost 1000 points before partially recovering within 20 minutes; Grossman, S.J. and J.E. Stiglitz (1980), 'On the Impossibility of Informationally Efficient Markets', *American Economic Review*, Vol. 70, No. 3 (June), pp. 393–408.

E. Roy Weintraub
(Duke University)

E. Roy Weintraub was born in Brooklyn, New York in 1943 and graduated with an AB in mathematics from Swarthmore College in 1964, before obtaining both an MS and a PhD in applied mathematics from the University of Pennsylvania in 1968 and 1969 respectively. Professor Weintraub taught economics at Rutgers College, The State University of New Jersey between 1968 and 1970, and then moved to Duke University, where he has remained ever since, currently serving as Professor of Economics.

Professor Weintraub's research interests are life writing and the history of economics, historiography of economics, and the history of the mathematization of economics. His most-cited articles in chronological order include '"Uncertainty" and the Keynesian Revolution', *History of Political Economy* (1975), 'The Microfoundations of Macroeconomics: A Critical Survey', *Journal of Economic Literature* (1977), 'On the Existence of a Competitive Equilibrium: 1930–1954', *Journal of Economic Literature* (1983), 'Axiomatisch Mißverständnis', *Economic Journal* (1998), and 'Methodology Doesn't Matter, but the History of Economic Thought Might', *Scandinavian Journal of Economics* (1989). His books include *General Equilibrium Theory* (Macmillan, 1974), *Conflict and Cooperation in Economics* (Macmillan, 1975), *Microfoundations: The Compatibility of*

Microeconomics and Macroeconomics (Cambridge University Press, 1979), *Mathematics for Economists: An Integrated Approach* (Cambridge University Press, 1982), *General Equilibrium Analysis: Studies in Appraisal* (Cambridge University Press, 1985), *Stabilizing Dynamics: Constructing Economic Knowledge* (Cambridge University Press, 1991), *Towards a History of Game Theory* (Duke University Press, 1992), *The Future of the History of Economics* (Duke University Press, 2002), *How Economics Became a Mathematical Science* (Duke University Press, 2002), and *Economists' Lives: Biography and Autobiography in the History of Economics* (Duke University Press, 2007), co-edited with Evelyn L. Forget.

Professor Weintraub's academic awards include the Best Monograph Prize from the European Society for the History of Economic Thought and the Joseph J. Spengler Prize for the Best Book in the History of Economics from the History of Economics Society, which were both received in 2005. He is a former President of the History of Economics Society, and currently he is Associate Editor of the *History of Political Economy* and the *Economics Bulletin*. In 2011, he was named a Distinguished Fellow of the History of Economics Society.

I interviewed Roy Weintraub in his office in the Department of Economics at Duke University, Durham, North Carolina. It was mid-afternoon of Friday, 14 January 2011.

BACKGROUND INFORMATION

You are trained as a mathematician. How did you end up as an economics professor?

The short story is that when I was a second-year graduate student in mathematics, a new PhD program was created that allowed you to write a dissertation in an applied area. At the time, I was struggling to complete my preliminary examinations, and it was becoming clear that I wasn't going to turn into the kind of mathematician who would have a major career. And so I started talking to people around the university who were affiliated with the program. This led to a call from Larry Klein in Economics. He had heard from my father, who taught economics, that I was on the loose, and he asked me to talk to him, because he had some problems that he thought I might be interested in working on. Klein was a family friend, but of course he was also an economist of great stature, and so I decided to write my dissertation in the area of mathematical economics under his co-supervision.

As a student, which professors were most influential or inspirational?

I didn't have any professors who were influential or inspirational. I grew up around them, and so my relationship with them was different from the norm. Being a professor was simply not a big deal. In fact, I used to joke that I was seven years old before I realized that not everybody carried the first honorific of 'doctor'.

Was an academic career therefore the default profession to enter into?

Sure. When I was in high school, I was even typecast as a professor of geology for the play *Our Town* by Thornton Wilder [*laughs*].

As a researcher, which colleagues have been most influential or inspirational?

The one colleague who's been enormously helpful to me over the years is Neil De Marchi. We're very good friends – I introduced him to his future wife – and he has the kind of broad intellectual interests and engagements that I resonate with. He's always been the best critic of my work, and the person I give my papers to first. As for inspirational, it has to be Barbara Herrnstein Smith, of Duke's Program in Literature, who models for me what intellectual honesty and integrity should mean.

GENERAL THOUGHTS ON RESEARCH

There is an increasing emphasis in many economics departments on applied research. Is this true at Duke?

Yes, over the last decade, we've moved very strongly into that area, and certainly with the encouragement of almost everybody in the department.

What is the value of pure versus applied research in economics?

I don't know what that means anymore. There are many different categories of research in economics, and standards evolve over time. Someone from outside a particular research community doesn't really have a good idea of what constitutes good and bad work. And so you have to learn to trust, which is the basis of all scientific work.

There seems to be little dialogue between theory and the history of ideas in economics, though perhaps that is starting to change a bit in light of the current economic crisis. Do you think that there is now the potential for an increase in such dialogue?

The job of a historian of economics is to narrate the past, not to go back and find raisins in the 1870s that improve today's pudding. I don't think there's anything in the past that will make economics better. The only thing that will make economics better is by actually producing better economics, because 'better' is a word that's only relevant within a particular research community. They're the ones who judge, award credit, and make those kinds of decisions. Most historians of economics disagree, and believe it can be written in the service of improving the discipline. I think that's nuts in the same way that a historian of physics would never think of changing the nature of physics research. But those individuals think of the history of economics from the perspective of an economist, because many of them teach introductory economics courses and socialize with those from the mainstream of the profession; they don't fully engage with the historians' community, with the history of science community, and with the science studies community. In my view, they are quite amateurish historians.

How would you characterize your own research agenda and how has it changed over time?

I began as a mathematician teaching mathematics to economics students at Rutgers. Next I became a mathematical economist, and then evolved into a theorist who was interested primarily in general equilibrium theory. That led to an engagement in the early '80s with the philosophy of science literature because I wanted to understand how one appraises that kind of scientific work. During this period, I realized that nobody knew very much about the history of specific work in modern economics. And so I started to develop a history of general equilibrium theory, and I quickly became fascinated with pursuing historical research. With the help of a year spent at the National Humanities Center, where I hung out with historians, philosophers, literary scholars, and the like, I began to turn myself into a historian.

Do you think it is important to have broad research interests?

I'm reminded of the sentence in Isaiah Berlin's essay, 'The Hedgehog and the Fox': "The fox knows many things, but the hedgehog knows one big thing." I would say you have to find a way to be authentic in terms of your personality structure, your socialization patterns, and the work that you do; otherwise, you're going to run into a lot of trouble.

IDEA GENERATION

Where do you get your research ideas?

From my past research. When I'm working on a project, it's always the case that questions remain unanswered, and I can return to them in the future. And when I'm completing a project, I will often have new ideas that will move my research in a different direction. I remember speaking to Joe Spengler at a Christmas party here many years ago. Joe was a former President of the AEA and, in my view, the creator of the fields of economic demography and the history of economics. He was about to leave the party early, and I asked him where he was going. He told me, "I have to deal with the page proofs for a book that I have written on Persian economic thought." I said, "Geez, how did you ever get interested in that?" "Well," he replied, "I was doing a book on *Indian* economic thought and one thing led to another ... " And that's exactly how I work. For example, my research on the existence of competitive equilibrium led me to think about whether the work on the stability of general equilibrium was consistent and coherent. Using autobiographical accounts in some of my histories, I began thinking about the nature of autobiographical memory, and so on.

At what point does an idea become a project that you devote resources to?

I can't separate ideas and projects. I do it all simultaneously. Sometimes when a project is moving ahead, I'll realize that it is time to make commitments that force me to bring it to a conclusion, such as finding a book contract, or a conference to give a paper, or inviting myself to Paris or London or Rome to give a seminar to my friends.

IDEA EXECUTION

What makes a good theoretical paper? Can you give an example?

One that I spent a lot of time trying to understand where it came from was Arrow and Debreu's 1954 paper on competitive equilibrium.[1] What makes it a good paper? It depends on who is asking the question. The profession seemed to like it because it solved some problems that were longstanding and connected to important traditions. But it was also valued for particular kinds of techniques within a particular small community out of which it emerged, namely Cowles at Chicago during the 1950 to 1953 period. And so, as a historian, I think it nonsense to believe that you can provide an answer to your question that stands outside of time. The concept of a good paper is local and contingent. And it's the same for an empirical paper. The profession has questions that are open, and papers try to solve those problems. But are those problems the most important ones? How the hell would we know? We couldn't recognize that if it came up and struck us in the face. There is no view from outside the local and contingent circumstances of particular intellectual communities.

Is there a particular empirical paper that you like?

One that gave some drive to my own doctoral dissertation, at least in the mind of my advisor, was the Adelman–Adelman paper, which subjected the early Klein–Goldberger model to random shocks in order to see whether they could induce realistic business cycles in a macro model.[2] That was an interesting paper.

What advice would you give a young scholar on writing a paper relating to the history of economic thought?

I don't use the phrase 'history of economic thought', because it makes it seem that those thoughts are 'out there' and disconnected from people. But history isn't 'out there'; people write history. I think a *history of economics* paper is useful and convincing if it constructs an interesting historical argument and employs real historical evidence; in other words, research has been undertaken. I find text-based, exegetical exercises very uninteresting; for example, when someone says, "Let's go back and see what Adam Smith really meant in Chapter 4 of the *Wealth of Nations* … " A history paper is narrative; you're telling stories about the past. And to make your reader empathize with the past, you have to make the stories as compelling as possible.

Until about a decade or two ago, most historians of economics didn't do much historical research in the same sense that history departments require doctoral students to do. There were folks like Joe Dorfman and Bob Coats who of course did, but they were rather isolated. But at Duke, we now have the Economists' Papers Project archive, which is an immense collection of papers of distinguished economists. This includes professional correspondence, as well as the notes, drafts, and manuscripts of major works. For example, for a long time, people have been writing about Paul Samuelson's *Principles* book, but it's been the same story over and over again, because the primary source is the text. But we now have access to the files and documents concerning the process by which Samuelson developed, wrote, and revised his book. When you use those archival materials, you get a much richer story; a sense that, "Yeah, that's what was *really* going on," which is every historian's ideal: you find new materials as a result of your research that allow you to illuminate and reinterpret a story that was pretty uninteresting or very straightforward and not as complex as human experience generally is.

When you hit a brick wall on a project, do you continue to work on the problem or do you take a break and work on something else?

I do both. Generally, though, I have several large projects going on at once, and so it takes a while to disengage emotionally and intellectually from a project. You are going to experience losses in walking away, because streams of thought will no longer be as active on your behalf. But I find I do work in curious ways. My wife will often say, "What are you doing?" I'll reply, "Oh … ", and then she'll say, "You're working, aren't you?" to which I'll respond, "I guess I am." And so I probably work 24 hours a day. Of course, I'm not writing when I'm in my sleep, but there are problems that I'm thinking about subconsciously.

I don't know what 'taking a break' means. Just as thoughts of my wife, my children, and my grandchildren are always with me, so are the elements of my research. You can't just put them away. It would be like saying, "Today, I'm not going to think about my family while I work." [*Laughs*].

What has been the biggest change during your career in how researchers in your fields conduct research?

I have seen the efforts that I, and a few others, have made to change the values of the history of economics community. Back in the early '80s, when I was beginning to think about the history of general equilibrium theory, Arjo Klamer was Neil De Marchi's and my PhD student. He wanted to write about new classical economics. I said to him, "Arjo, the people who you are writing about, like Bob Lucas and Tom Sargent, are living. Why don't you just go and talk with them?" Nobody had previously done such an oral history, and so we sent him off to conduct some interviews.[3] What an opportunity! But my getting impatient with Arjo came about because, in gathering the evidence for my work on the history of general equilibrium theory, I had thought to write to many of the folks who were still alive, like Arrow, Debreu, McKenzie, Koopmans, Chipman, Georgescu-Roegen, Tintner, Menger, and Simon. They were all absolutely delighted to have questions asked about their past work. I developed fairly long correspondence files with them and used those self-reports as part of my paper that got into the *JEL*, which was different from any other paper that I had ever seen people write in history.[4] And it got me thinking that maybe I and others could do this more systematically, which led me to persuade people at Duke to construct the Economists' Papers Project. So I've seen the history of economics move in this different direction; very different from the kind of history of economics that George Stigler thought was important. I'm very pleased that I've helped to create a major resource for historians of economics to do what I consider to be more interesting work; one that is closer to the history of contemporary science.

What is your view on the increased use of mathematics in economic theory papers today?

You could ask the same question in 1880, 1890, 1900, 1910 ... this has been going on for a long time.

When I spoke with Chuck Manski, he expressed concern that young theorists today feel the need to show off their math skills, whereas he values 'simple insight'?

I heard exactly the same complaints on the part of faculty members at the University of Pennsylvania in Economics in the 1960s. They would say, "He came in and started proving theorems. What the hell did that have to do with economics?" As I say, this is a continuous complaint, and some of it is changing fashions, but also changing conversations within these particular communities. What the community takes as acceptable, useful, relevant, and important changes over time. There isn't a correct way to write an economics paper, but Manski's comment suggests there is. There are folks who want to make that judgment a philosophical or even a moral issue, but my argument is that it is always a historical question. How did those tastes change? What was it in the service of? What were the people thinking?

What were they doing? How did it work? Those are the questions that interest me as a historian. Only an active scientist could ask your question; one who has no historical sensibility whatsoever.

THE WRITING PROCESS

Which aspect of the writing process do you find most difficult?

For me, the absolutely hardest part is the first draft. If you go back to the *Paris Review* interviews with famous writers, one of the major questions that was almost always asked was whether they edited during writing or after they had finished. Hemingway, for instance, couldn't write sentence number two unless he was absolutely satisfied with sentence number one. Others just let it rip and then threw away most of it. I'm in the latter category. But in the mid-'80s, I figured out that since I talk much faster than I write, it would be best to dictate the material and send it to a typist. And so I generally dictate somewhere between five to ten pages at a shot, and there might be one useful page that makes it into the draft. The other material isn't wasted; it goes into an outtakes file, sits there, and I may come back to draw on it years later.

I don't begin with an outline for the first draft, because if I did, I probably would never have found the issue interesting in the first place. I need to figure it out, which involves constructing the arguments. At the first draft stage, I have only partial, maybe mutually contradictory, arguments with weak evidence in support. At some point, though, that draft has enough structure that I can begin the most complex, most challenging, and most fun part of writing, cutting and editing the draft and shaping it. I can edit the draft, or a section of it, each day, put it away, and come back to it over and over to ask questions like: "Why is that word there?" "Does this really answer the rhetorical question asked in the previous sentence?" "How is this argument functioning?" I'm trying to make the work speak in a convincing fashion. I love it.

What do you think of the standard of writing by economists?

Oh, economists can't write. Almost none of them have any ear for the English language. There's no sense of a rhythm in their writing, and no particular style that would identify them as the author compared to someone else. There are only a few folks whose writing approaches a level of literary competence that would lead you to read them even if you weren't an economist.

Such as whom?

I think Deirdre McCloskey writes well even though I'm not as intrigued by her arguments as I was in the past. Mary Morgan writes with a really authentic voice, and I have to attend very carefully to what Mary says, because she writes in a very understated fashion, but there's tremendous power in much of her work. Philip Mirowski writes in a very distinctive manner. I'm not always happy with what I'm reading, because it's too argumentative for me, but it's certainly well written, and there is no question of who the author is.

Who proofreads your writing?

I proofread it, and if De Marchi is around, I'll give it to him, but he's increasingly busy. When you write books, you must have a very good relationship with the general editor, and then you need to be very accommodating and cooperative with the copy editor. I've been fortunate, because the folks whom I've worked with at Cambridge University Press and Duke University Press have been great. Currently, I'm doing a piece that's going to appear in the Spring issue of the *Journal of Economic Perspectives*.[5] Their editorial work on papers is much better than any I've found in professional journals because they have a different audience. The managing editor, Tim Taylor, is very, very good and helpful. Who else? I had one absolutely spectacular copy editor for a paper I did a while ago for the *South Atlantic Quarterly*.[6] That's a literary journal, but it was just wonderful to have an experience of working with someone whose language sense was so good.

COLLABORATION

Most of your work is sole-authored, whereas much of the work conducted by the other interviewees in this book is collaborative. What are the pros and cons of your approach?

When I was Acting Dean of the Faculty here, I was problem solving all the time. I tend to have many ideas, and can produce ten different solutions to a problem very quickly. Eight of them are totally stupid, one of them is half-stupid, and the other one is worth thinking about. The function of my staff at the time was to critique my solutions. And I would say that in collaborative research, you see those two roles at work; one person produces different ideas, and the other sets out to test them. That's how my very early theoretical work with Daniel Graham was done; I would have ideas that he would attempt to prove and disprove, and vice versa. That was very useful. In fact, I'm sure that none of those technical papers could have been written individually by either of us.[7]

I haven't done collaborative work on my historical projects, but I'm about to co-author a book on the history of existence of general equilibrium with a young German researcher, Till Düppe. He and I have been corresponding back and forth because he's unearthed, and has access to, the Debreu papers, which include lengthy interviews with members of the Debreu extended family. I'd been planning to make my McKenzie material into a book, because I have so much of it, and I started thinking, "God, I wish I had the Debreu papers ... " I wrote to him asking whether he was the least bit interested in my McKenzie material. He jumped at it! And so we are going to write the book together. It should be interesting, because it's my first attempt at joint work on a historical project. As you get older, sometimes you want to try something different. Can we bring this off? I don't know. It may just crash and burn, but at the moment it seems like fun.

SEMINAR PARTICIPATION AND NETWORKING

What are the benefits to attending a seminar that is closely related to your work versus one that is not closely related?

There are different ways of taking in information. When I was a student, I couldn't both attend to what the professor was saying and take notes. It was one or the other, and I decided to screw it; I was more interested in getting a sense of what was going on and gave up on notes. My older son, who like me has some ADHD issues and specific learning disabilities, takes in information by ear; not by sight, not by reading, but if he hears it, he knows it, and he has figured out strategies over his life to get that kind of information to do it. It's just breathtaking to watch. And so, for him, going to a seminar would be great. For me, it is almost worthless. I can watch the performance and get a sense of the theatre, but I need to read the paper several times, otherwise I don't understand it.

How important is professional networking to success in research?

There's a sense in which it's so important that it's almost not worth talking about, because professional success *is* success in a network. That's how science is done; you have to be in networks, you have to convince people, and you have to learn from others. The community is where the science is embedded; it's not in a paper somewhere. Who's your audience? Who thinks what work in this area may or may not be worthwhile? That's what I think of as a network.

I've been on many promotion and tenure committees, and ultimately the one question you're trying to ask is: is this person a player? And the answer is entirely network-based. You can't be a hermit and be very interesting or successful at the same time. Wittgenstein may have been anti-social, but he was at the center of a large number of other philosophers and scholars at King's College, Cambridge for a long period of time.

COMMUNICATION OF RESEARCH

How do you find the right balance between communicating your research at an early stage versus the close-to-finished stage?

I've never much cared about holding back work. We've got lots of informal ways of having internal conversations here, like lunch seminars, and I no longer feel embarrassed about going on the road with work that's not completely finished. I'm interested in talking to people and having them think with me. If I get comments such as, "That doesn't make any sense at all," I will deal with it, because it doesn't harm me to be criticized. I don't go to places where I know I'm going to have a hostile audience, but there aren't many such places. I'm very easy to like [*laughs*].

What are the unique challenges to giving a seminar and how do you overcome them?

What I generally do is talk about the context of the paper, which means historicizing it in terms of my own interests in projects, outline the major issues and questions that it opens up, and then turn the seminar into a conversation with as much of the audience as is interested. I'm fairly gregarious, and I don't regard public speaking as a chore; I find it interesting.

PUBLICATION

How do you decide upon the appropriate journal to send your research to?

I don't write articles with an idea for a particular journal. The project gets going, and if it's good enough, it'll find one. My paper on McKenzie started getting bigger and bigger, becoming more interesting, and opening up a number of different issues, so I decided to send a short, more general interest piece of it off to the *Journal of Economic Perspectives*. There was a detective story involved in the research, because I uncovered a big-time surprise, namely that the referee for the McKenzie general equilibrium paper turned out to be Gerard Debreu. That came as a shock to a lot of people. The *JEP* hasn't published much in the history of economics that has been interesting historically, but I got an incredibly positive response from the editors – they said they couldn't put it down.

For about five years, I've been working on a manuscript called, 'Charismatic Scholars, Intellectual Communities, and the Allegation of Anti-Semitism', which features case studies of Jung, De Man, Marx, Keynes, and Hayek. I have had some very positive responses from readers, but some of the different presses thought it was way too interdisciplinary. A reader who was a sociologist thought there wasn't enough sociology. The literary studies reader basically said, "Who the hell is this economist dragging his feet all over Paul De Man? What does he know?" Well, I know a lot more than the guy thought. Anyway, at present I've ended up extracting the material on Keynes and it's been accepted at a history of economics journal.[8] But I'll be back to the large project again, sometime.

How would you best describe your approach to dealing with a 'revise and resubmit' request from a journal? How about an outright rejection?

By and large, referees are serious people who take themselves seriously, so I address their comments carefully. As you get older, you tend to insulate yourself against rejections by finding ways to anticipate that a particular journal won't be interested in a particular topic. And so I'm not going to send my work to the *AER*.

Do you think that the current structure of the publication process in economics facilitates or impedes scientific understanding and knowledge production?

Journals are increasingly irrelevant for the transmission of knowledge. Work is seen, thought about, and talked about, by the established communities long before it appears in a journal. Getting it published is only serving the function of validating credit in certain ways; senior people are not publishing in journals as much as they used to – they're submitting their work to collections or giving it as addresses – and this is effectively leaving the publications for junior faculty in order to make reputations and gain tenure. The AEA's creation of a bunch of new journals is a reflection of the fact that there needed to be more avenues through which junior faculty members could be certified.

What has been your best and worst experience during the publication process?

Many years ago, I had one very bad experience with a very prestigious journal. There was simply no response whatsoever to the submission, even for a year any acknowledgement that it had been received. What I was able to put together from a couple of conversations some years later was that there was some embarrassment at the journal, and it was quite possibly associated with the paper having gone to an anti-Semitic referee in Germany.

I've had exceptional good fortune with several papers. Both of my papers in the *Journal of Economic Literature* were magnificent intellectual exchanges with the editor, Mark Perlman.[9] I felt really, really aided and quite pleased to be part of such a co-operative process.

BOOK WRITING

You have written several books. Why do you write them?

Because I have to! [*Laughs*]. Don't scholars write books? I thought they did! [*Laughs*]. Sometimes the story is large and complex, and that's what a book is.

Do you enjoy writing books?

I love it. It's a very satisfying process because you can always be working on it. But it takes a long time to write a good book because it is very, very difficult to sustain an argument over several hundred pages. I've written three really good, 'mature', single-authored books, but what I also am pleased about is that every book that I've done is, in my view, better than the one before it. That's why I'm apprehensive about doing the present one, because I thought my last book, *How Economics Became a Mathematical Science*, was terrific! I had to interweave many different stories so that they mutually supported one another. That was hard, and it took ten years to do, but it was very satisfying to bring off something as large and complex. Why do you think people write symphonies rather than works for solo piano? [*Laughs*].

Books have long been a staple of the history of economics literature. Yet, the book publishing industry seems to be in a state of flux, and the increasing prominence of 'impact factors' and the like are pushing the profession increasingly toward journal articles as the means for professional advancement. What advice would you give to a young scholar in the field about book writing versus journal article writing?

For history of economics, I think you have to be doing both. In institutions and countries where there are comprehensive research assessment exercises, you have to write journal articles, and if you want to be taken seriously as a scholar of such-and-such, then you have to write a book on it. For example, probably the best scholars of Jevons are Harro Maas, Margaret Schabas, Sandra Peart, and Michael White. Michael has written many magnificent articles on Jevons, but he has not written his book on Jevons, and I hope he does it.

What are your thoughts on the future of book publishing in economics?

Books have been around for a very long time, and I don't think they're going to disappear. Some arguments are long and complicated; they can't be tweeted [*laughs*].

REFEREEING AND EDITING

Do you have any advice for a young scholar on being a referee?

No. It would only be the same kind of advice if I were asked a question like, "How can you become a better human being?"

My wife is a marital therapist, and she tells me that one way to improve communication in a couple is to ask one party, before responding to statements, what the other has said, to make sure there is a baseline of respect for the other. That is helpful to think about when you are refereeing. And so I've tried to keep it a practice of attempting to restate the major points and the argument of a paper in the first paragraph of my report in such a way that I can convince myself that the author would agree with me. The author is seeing that I do understand what he or she is saying, and I'm already forcing myself to be in a position of asking how this paper can be stronger, or what are its weaknesses that either can or can't be repaired. That strategy removes my persona to some degree from the refereeing.

TIME MANAGEMENT

How do you divide up your working day, both in terms of quantity and timing of different kinds of work?

I don't. When I'm walking on the indoor track, I'm thinking about work. I can't compartmentalize anything.

How do you balance multiple research projects?

It's just something you do.

Some of the interviewees in this book prefer to complete one project at a time …

I can't do that. I read five or six books at a time. Look, here are some that I cleared off my desk for you today. [*Shows me several, weighty history of economics volumes*].

How about the balance between your research and non-research activities?

I really like teaching. I'm teaching small classes of juniors and seniors who are interested in the courses that I teach. I find the students utterly delightful and very smart, and I like engaging with them; it keeps me connected. If you have to convince people that what you do is interesting and enjoyable, you're also confirming that for yourself. And so if I can't do that to a class of juniors and seniors, I think I should retire, because I would no longer believe in what I'm doing.

As you get older, your energy level is lower for doing all kinds of other things, but I've done everything here at Duke. I was Director of Graduate Studies for a dozen years, Chair of the department for four years, Chair of a second department at the same time for a year, twice Chair of the Academic Council, and Acting Dean of the Faculty of Arts and Sciences for two years. I've been very involved with the life of the university. These days, I've withdrawn from most of it, but I'll probably be pulled out of retirement to sit on an august committee to give advice to an important person [*laughs*].

How about the balance between your personal and professional lives?

Part of my marriage contract with my second wife over 20 years ago was to take seriously "whither thou goest, I will go." And so we go to all conferences together. That's a balance.

I was very, very active physically – playing tournament tennis and squash – but that had its own toll. I now have a badly damaged shoulder, so I just can't do some sports anymore. But it's better than being dead [*laughs*].

REFLECTIONS AND THE FUTURE OF ECONOMICS

What have been the most important findings and contributions in your research fields during your career?

I've shown the history of economics community that the technical economics of the post-World War II period can be historicized; one does not have to keep writing about Smith or Ricardo or Keynes or Hayek. More importantly, I've both shown and argued that such historicizing should be based on both archival material and oral histories. Almost nobody was doing this before me. And so I've helped to inaugurate a new era in the history of economics.

My other lasting contribution is the Economists' Papers Project. I hope I'm thought of like Bob Gallman, who collected an enormous set of pre-Civil War plantation records across the South to get a full and complete picture of southern slaveholding, and those records have been used by American economic historians ever after. Gallman is lionized. I was the initiator and internal force of the Duke archival facility, and I'm very proud of it.

What are the biggest challenges facing the history of economics?

Figuring out what it's supposed to be doing; whether it's economics or it isn't.

What are the strengths and weaknesses of your own research?

Something that others, particularly Mark Blaug and Philip Mirowski, have claimed as a weakness, but I see as a strength, is that I don't use the history to promote one or another view of how economics might be improved. It's a constant criticism that I'm too neutral; that I have no position on whether general equilibrium theory is a good or bad thing, for example. But I criticize Mirowski's work for being too engaged in writing history in the service of particular kinds of intellectual positions.

On the other hand, I've always been pleased that people comment on how well written and how engaging my narratives are, and that the range of my scholarship is a model for how one can approach historical writing in economics.

In the end, do you think the profession has helped to bring out and shape your research for the best?

I don't have much contact with a 'profession'. I haven't much listened to others. I make enough money, I have fun teaching, I enjoy my colleagues, I seem to be productive, and I do work that others find engaging, which always surprises me.

Do you have any professional regrets?

I don't much like counterfactual history. I'm sorry, though, that I'm not going to live for another hundred years; it's so much fun to be doing what I'm doing. That said, God knows what shape my body would be in by that time! [*Laughs*].

What are your professional ambitions?

To keep working on the kinds of projects that I've developed, showing that it can be done.

How would you describe the state of economics today? Are you optimistic about its future?

I don't really consider myself an economist in the sense of being a member of the mainstream economics community anymore. Unlike many who write in the history of economics, I like economists, I respect them, and I think by and large they're doing very interesting work. I'm enthralled by the work of my junior colleagues. I can't open issues of major journals these days without just being tremendously impressed at the topics that people are engaging with and the arguments that are being employed. It's wonderful.

NOTES

1. K.J. Arrow and G. Debreu (1954), 'Existence of an Equilibrium for a Competitive Economy', *Econometrica*, Vol. 22, No. 3 (July), pp. 265–290.
2. Adelman, I. and F.L. Adelman (1959), 'The Dynamic Properties of the Klein–Goldberger Model', *Econometrica*, Vol. 27, No. 4 (October), pp. 596–625.
3. Klamer, Arjo (1984), *Conversations with Economists: New Classical Economists and Opponents Speak Out on the Current Controversy in Macroeconomics*, Totowa: Rowman and Littlefield.
4. Weintraub, E.R. (1983), 'On the Existence of a Competitive Equilibrium: 1930–1954', *Journal of Economic Literature*, Vol. 21, No. 1 (March), pp. 1–39.
5. Weintraub, E.R. (2011), 'Lionel W. McKenzie and the Proof of the Existence of a Competitive Equilibrium', *Journal of Economic Perspectives*, Vol. 25, No. 2 (Spring), pp. 199–215.
6. Weintraub, E.R. (1995), 'Is "Is a Precursor of" a Transitive Relation?', *South Atlantic Quarterly*, Vol. 95, No. 2, pp. 571–589.
7. Graham, D.H., Jacobson, E. and E.R. Weintraub (1972), 'Transaction Costs and the Convergence of a "Trade Out of Equilibrium" Adjustment Process', *International Economic Review*, Vol. 13, No. 1 (June), pp. 123–131; Graham, D.H. and E.R. Weintraub (1975), 'On Convergence to Pareto Allocations', *Review of Economic Studies*, Vol. 42, No. 3 (July), pp. 469–472.
8. Weintraub, E.R. (2012), 'Keynesian Historiography and the Anti-Semitism Question', *History of Political Economy*, Vol. 44, No. 1 (Spring), pp. 41–67.
9. See article in Note 4 and Weintraub, E.R. (1977), 'The Microfoundations of Macroeconomics: A Critical Survey', *Journal of Economic Literature*, Vol. 15, No. 1 (March), pp. 1–23.

Justin Wolfers
(University of
Pennsylvania)

Justin Wolfers was born in Papua New Guinea in 1972 and graduated with a bachelor's degree in economics from the University of Sydney in 1994 before obtaining both an AM and a PhD in economics from Harvard University in 2000 and 2001 respectively. He was an Assistant Professor of Economics at the Graduate School of Business, Stanford University between 2001 and 2005 and then moved to the Wharton School, University of Pennsylvania, where he currently serves as the Class of 1965 Wharton Term Associate Professor of Business and Public Policy.

Professor Wolfers' research interests include law and economics, labor economics, social policy, political economy, behavioral economics, and macroeconomics. His most-cited articles in chronological order include 'The Role of Shocks and Institutions in the Rise of European Unemployment: The Aggregate Evidence', *Economic Journal* (2000), co-authored with Olivier Blanchard, 'Prediction Markets', *Journal of Economic Perspectives* (2004), co-authored with Eric Zitzewitz, 'Uses and Abuses of Empirical Evidence in the Death Penalty Debate', *Stanford Law Review* (2005), co-authored with John Donohue, 'Did Unilateral Divorce Laws Raise Divorce Rates? A Reconciliation and New Results', *American Economic Review* (2006), and 'Economic Growth and Subjective Well-being:

Reassessing the Easterlin Paradox', *Brookings Papers on Economic Activity* (2008), co-authored with Betsey Stevenson. He is also a contributor to *The New York Times*, where he writes for the *Freakonomics* blog, and to *The Wall Street Journal*.

Professor Wolfers is a Research Associate at the National Bureau of Economic Research and at the Centre for Applied Macroeconomic Analysis (Australian National University), as well as being a Senior Fellow at the Brookings Institution. Since 2009, he has been Editor of the *Brookings Papers on Economic Activity*.

I interviewed Justin Wolfers in his office at the Wharton School, University of Pennsylvania. It was early-afternoon of Monday, 14 June 2010.

BACKGROUND INFORMATION

What was your attraction to economics?

The first economics course I took was in high school in Australia in 1989 through 1990. It was an amazing time because the Australian economy was just recovering, and the unemployment rate got down as low as 6 per cent. As a high school student, I used to track these things in real time and it would feel weird to say 6.3 versus 6.1. That sounds small, but when you converted it into people, it seemed really big. And so it felt like the task of an economist was big and important. Then a recession hit, and I watched ten years of hard work in lowering the unemployment rate go down the drain almost overnight. Therefore, economics was a subject that immediately captured my interest in terms of an emerging social conscience; it was about the world we actually lived in and it appeared to matter.

As a student, which professors were most influential or inspirational?

My high school teachers were terrific in allowing me to think about different issues and encouraging me to do so. It's unusual to think of one's high school mentors so fondly, but in fact they're thanked in the introduction of my PhD thesis.

My professors as an undergraduate at the University of Sydney were amazing. They had remarkably open doors and encouraged me to go on to the Reserve Bank of Australia, and I was happy to follow their advice because I was totally captured by policy questions. I had a wonderful mentor at the central bank, an economist called Jackie Dwyer, who mentored a surprisingly large number of now quite prominent US economists.

At graduate school, I was primarily a student of Larry Katz. Any time you want to talk to him about anything that's remotely social science, Larry's willing to do it, and he loves doing it. Larry's just amazing in terms of the time he devotes to his students. His view that an economist should be an economist is something that's really stuck with me.

The other person whom I worked very closely with during graduate school was Olivier Blanchard from MIT. Olivier was Larry's advisor, and as much as Larry was hands on, Olivier was hands off … and very French. It's a funny education process at Harvard. The students generally do very well, but then you try and figure out why. We read the same books as the students at, say, the Australian National University, so what is it that's different? Well, Olivier told us that you're here to write papers and when you're finished writing a paper, you send it to the *AER*. That's where you should try and get your work published.

Olivier and I wrote a little together, and he advised me even when I started working on family economics. I would take him my latest work on the family, and he'd say, "Tell me about it." I would tell him, and he would nod and, in a very French way, say, "Yes," and then, "We're done." That was advising. So I'd get on my bike, ride home, and think, "Wow, was that good enough? Maybe I should work harder next time."

Olivier's continued to be involved in my career ever since. One of the nicest things he did for me was, maybe three or four years ago, he sent an e-mail completely out of the blue about a paper I had written, just saying, "I do not care for this. This is not you. This is not how you should work." He was right. I was trying to do something that was trendy rather than useful. It wasn't true to my training, and it wasn't true to myself. But it was an enormous compliment that five or six years after my leaving his care, he was happy to set me on the straight and narrow.

The other thing that was really important for me at Harvard was being part of a group called the Multidisciplinary Program on Inequality and Social Policy. It was a program run out of the Kennedy School, which brought together sociologists, political scientists, and economists. My mentor coming out of that was a sociologist, Sandy Jencks, who ended up on my thesis committee. I think that's how I learned how to hear, understand, and read sociology and political science. I always joked with Sandy that sociologists have terrific questions and economists have terrific answers. He was polite enough never to kick me out of his office for saying that, but there are just wonderful questions sitting in those fields to pick up and work with, and I'm happy to bring my economist's toolkit to those questions.

Why did you decide to pursue an academic career?

When I came to the US, it was with every intention of going back home to Australia, because I wanted to have an influence on public policy. But I remember very well one moment that really changed my mind. In my first year at Harvard, Greg Mankiw invited me to the NBER monetary economics meeting. I went to a relatively small conference room, and there were 30 people in the room, but they were 30 of the 40 leading monetary economists I had ever heard of. We were discussing whatever papers were being presented that day, but I also understood – having been at the Reserve Bank of Australia – that those papers would come out as little yellow books from the NBER, and then researchers at the research department at the Reserve Bank of Australia would take those ideas developed in Cambridge, Massachusetts and apply them to Australian data, and that would inform Australian monetary policy. That's probably true in well over one hundred countries around the world. And so rather than being in one of those research departments replicating those papers, I thought it would be much more interesting and exciting if I could be one of the 30 people in that room talking about how we should analyze monetary policy. I walked out convinced that I could have a bigger influence on public policy by being in a US academic institution.

As a researcher, which colleagues have been most influential or inspirational?

At Stanford, Eddie Lazear was a spectacular guy to be around. One of the things that I learned from Eddie is that, despite being an amazingly successful Stanford professor, he still regards himself as a Chicago guy at heart. So, any time we were ever in a seminar talking about anything, he could immediately bring all of the insights of the Chicago tradition to a new issue. Having grown up as a Cambridge guy, these were a set of insights that were not always obvious to me.

The colleague whom I get a lot out of interacting with since I've taken over editing the *Brookings Papers on Economic Activity* is David Romer. David is just an amazing co-editor. He has enormous breadth in the set of things he understands and has tremendous insight and wonderful intuition. He also has remarkable integrity. Of the people whom I've mentioned so far, one of the common threads that I continually admire about them is their integrity. It's an integrity about how you do economics; we're here to tell the truth, not to win ideological battles, and economics has a purpose, and that purpose is way bigger than us and our careers.

GENERAL THOUGHTS ON RESEARCH

What is the value of pure versus applied research in economics?

It's certainly easy to see the social value of applied research. If you figure out a way to run a more effective monetary policy, one hopes the Fed picks it up. So, in some sense, one definition of 'applied' is that it has a clear link to an existing problem, whether it's one that's faced by policymakers or businesses or individual consumers.

It's too easy for applied economists then to pooh-pooh pure theory. The reach of pure theory is far greater than that of any applied paper. Think about the information economics revolution and George Akerlof's contribution on adverse selection. That fundamentally changes how we think about any market, and it doesn't just change how professors of economics think about it; it changes all the way through to how we teach first-year economics, so therefore it changes even how freshmen – who then go on to run businesses or run for Congress – think about how markets work. We have this deep insight that in many cases, due to informational problems, markets aren't going to hit the right outcomes.

Home runs for the theorists completely change everything; it's hard to imagine an applied paper having that big of an impact.

How would you describe the dialogue between theory and empirics in economics?

There should be a strong link between theory and measurement, but we see a lot of variance across fields. Labor economics and public finance, for example, are very much focused on getting measurement right. But the downside of those fields is that there is a weaker focus on theory. And then there is a bunch of fields that are very much more focused on theory than measurement. In IO and macro, for example, there is an enormous emphasis on technique. But today we are living in a world where data are plentiful, and it seems too often that complicated models are being used to fill in for data that could be obtained by tenaciously calling firms or policymakers.

Do you think it is important to have broad research interests?

I think it's critically important. First of all, it sustains you. If you're going to have a career as an economics researcher, it's going to last a long time. So, if you simply do the theory of the firm for 40 years, you'll eventually become tired. The second observation is that all fields and all scholars need to renew and refresh. What's the source of new ideas? Again, take the theory of the firm. Some of the new ideas in that sub-field have come from political science and the law, and previous to that, the game theory revolution fundamentally changed how we think about what firms do.

I also think it's likely that as an economist you're going to have a responsibility to think broadly. A company may bring you in as an expert on the theory of the firm and ask you about something that you haven't been thinking about, such as executive compensation. But the basic tools we have yield insight into that.

How would you characterize your own research agenda?

Depending on whether you liked me or not, you would use different language. If you were not predisposed to like my work, I think you would call a lot of it economic imperialism, in the sense that very little of it is about production and consumption. Instead, my work shares an interface with sociology, psychology, political science, and law. My hope is that an economist can actually add some insight to those fields, so a positive description would be intellectual arbitrage. I want to apply the economic method to where it's going to have the greatest returns. And it turns out that it's being applied tirelessly to thinking about production and consumption, but very little to thinking about marriage and divorce, happiness, crime, and politics.

Do you think there is any difference in the types of work done by researchers at different stages of their careers based on tenure concerns, publication requirements or other pressures? Should there be a difference?

I can think of three differences. One is ambition. The younger scholar needs to make sure that the paper is at least going to hit a journal, but the older scholar can afford to swing for the fences and occasionally miss.

The second difference is focus; a footprint in some sense. I remember I was given a lot of advice, "Justin, you've got to stop writing in many fields because after seven years, we need to be able to say to the Provost that you are the expert at X." That is a dreadful idea, but it's one that's incredibly widespread. To use a baseball analogy, one homerun and a couple of singles appear to be better than seven triples and eight doubles if one is across different fields. But the truth is everyone's a world expert in something the moment you define it narrowly enough. If you're the 487th best applied microeconomist, but the first best at the applied theory of the firm in the cornflakes industry, that turns out to be a much better tenure case compared to the guy who is making contributions across 12 different fields. So, there's a lot of pressure on young scholars to restrict their attention to one or two issues and that's very destructive, partly because I think there is real value in intellectual arbitrage.

The third difference you see is one's interest in engaging the broader public in a bunch of different ways; whether it's engaging the public literally as a policymaker like Ben Bernanke, or writing op-eds, or answering the phone when a reporter calls you, or being an informal or formal advisor to policymakers in Washington, DC. One sees a much larger number of tenured people doing this because, again, younger scholars would receive very little formal career credit.

Normatively, I think it would be useful if people were ambitious throughout their careers. Be the best economist you can be. Therefore, if we provide incentives otherwise, that is a very destructive thing. But in terms of one's broader engagement with the public – and this includes teaching – I don't have a strong view. Many people think it's good that we wait until we're older to do that, and maybe they're right. But I do think that we should, at the very least while we're young, still learn how to communicate to those broader publics, so if they happen to be interested in what we're doing, there'll be some way for them to understand what it is we're doing.

IDEA GENERATION

Where do you get your research ideas?

If you think about economics through a post-Beckerian lens – economics is everywhere – it's great practice then to walk around wearing those glasses and actually try and understand everything you see. It's a lot of fun. My significant other, Betsey, is also an economist, and so it's not even socially awkward to be out somewhere and say, "Why do you think it is that … ?" By thinking about it through the economic lens, you'll come up with a completely different explanation than people otherwise had. But you'll soon discover also that there are things that are more puzzling than we once thought. For example, it's completely unclear why prejudice against African-Americans has declined over the past 30 years. There is not a single, deep, obvious driving force that would cause people's attitudes to change. The laws haven't changed, African-American economic progress has been surprisingly slow, and desegregation hasn't really made that much further progress. And so there is an economic question: what explains declining prejudice against African-Americans?

I think generating ideas is mostly about thinking about economics, thinking about economics, and thinking about economics … and after that, talking about it, talking about it, and talking about it. What do I do with my friends? I talk about economics. I ask them what they're working on, and they ask me what I'm working on. They're in a completely different field to me, so when I give them input, it'll be a set of insights they've not thought about and vice versa. You can often write a bad paper and spend some time talking about it, and through that figure out the good paper that's hidden within it. It's an iterative process.

I had a wonderful experience the other day with a graduate student who came into my office. He had worked really hard on a conference presentation, but it still wasn't clear when he went away and gave the paper. Then he met people – during coffee or in the elevator – who asked him, "What's your paper about?" He must have given his five-minute pitch about 40 times. He came back and told me, "Now I understand what I'm doing." That's a very common thing; it happens when you talk about your ideas.

The one other thing that is useful is to go to an enormous quantity of seminars. Through this, you can be exposed to things that are at the front of someone else's mind, and clearly you'll be exposed to literatures that you're not aware of. Doing this across disciplines can be particularly important, because then you get a sense, for instance, that there is a demand in sociology to understand what's going on with the family. There's not a huge demand within economics, but then you realize there are some insights that economists have – boom, there's your paper.

At what point does an idea become a project that you devote resources to?

I have a very different working process than most people. I will never devote any substantial resources until I can see in my mind what a finished paper would look like: what is the first table? How should that table be interpreted? What are the problems with that interpretation, and so what are the second, third, and fourth tables? What is the model that is generating the results? That is purely background processing. I will then go for a long run and, over the course of a couple of hours, I will see very clearly the first, second, third, fourth, and fifth sections of the paper. At that point, it will move from a conversation with Betsey to one with my colleagues where I try and get a sense of whether other people have worked on this and why it might be interesting. Then I start writing.

IDEA EXECUTION

What makes a good theoretical paper?

A good theoretical paper tells me something that I didn't know and that I wanted to know. Claudia Goldin once told me that you know that a model is worth including in a paper when it speaks back to you. If all you do is chug from a set of uninteresting axioms to a set of uninteresting implications, then I learn more about your math skills than your economic skills.

Can you give an example?

George Akerlof's paper on the market for 'lemons'.[1] The underlying idea is elegant and simple, and there is no attempt in the paper to make it anything other than elegant and simple. And as I said earlier, it is so powerful that it transformed just about every field in economics. Incidentally, it is also a paper that was rejected by several leading economics journals.

What makes a good empirical paper?

A good empirical paper also tells me something that I didn't know and that I wanted to know. With empirics, I also require that it's true; that it's actually true in your data and usefully true in other contexts. With theory, I guess it also has to be true in the extremely narrow sense of whether or not the conclusions follow from the axioms. But that's an uninteresting true. A more interesting true is whether or not those axioms are actually relevant in the world in which we live.

Can you give an example?

Mankiw, Romer, and Weil looking at the relationship between economic development and an extended version of the Solow model that includes human as well as physical capital.[2] The model is very simple but wonderful, and gives them structure as they approach the data. The empirics are very straightforward but have remarkable power to explain which countries are rich and which are poor. And that model has informed my own research. In the economics of happiness, one of the most widely believed results has been something called the Easterlin Paradox. Betsey Stevenson and I revisited the data on the relationship between economic development and happiness.[3] We looked at it in straightforward and simple terms, using scatter plots rather than regressions, and it turned out that the stylized facts (rich countries aren't happier than poor countries, or that as countries get richer, they don't become happier) were just false. And that has reasonably large implications about how you think about economic development.

When you hit a brick wall on a project, do you continue to work on the problem or do you take a break from it and work on something else?

I persist. For an empiricist, it is a little easier. If the data aren't co-operating, your job is to find the golden thread that runs through the data and report it; there always exists one. For a theorist, it can be harder because you're writing down a model and the math can be difficult. But as an empiricist, I don't see a lot of brick walls because I'm not seeking a conclusion. What I'm trying to do is learn something.

Related to the previous question, when it appears that a project isn't going to turn out as hoped, do you scrap the project or aim to send it to a second-tier or field journal?

I do get cases where the data won't tell a simple, clear, concise story, or estimates that are very imprecise. If they're so imprecise that they can't tell us much, I'll scrap the project. But, more generally, my working style is not to come to the plate looking to hit a homerun. I usually start a project thinking, "Well, the last one worked out okay. I'll just take a breather and do something real simple," and that I'm going to hit a double. But, every time, I end up being surprised by how far I can go with it.

What has been the biggest change during your career in how researchers in your fields conduct research?

I think there are greater returns to collecting your own data. The output of the Census Bureau and the Bureau of Economic Analysis has barely changed through my research career, but the quantity of things in the world that are being measured has grown exponentially. Economists are starting to use some of those data. For example, I've worked with data from Google, Gallup, and all sorts of corporations.

When I was in graduate school, sociologists used to express enormous frustration that economists had no interest in data collection. It's still rarely the case that we're writing seminars about it, but what we are doing is being more tenacious about going out there and discovering the data that actually exist.

THE WRITING PROCESS

Which aspect of the writing process do you find most difficult?

I like it all. It's easy to bitch and moan about how difficult writing is. But then you do it and get it right, and it's wonderful.

I used to do what you would call the research up front – collect data, write regressions, write down models – and then later on try and write it. That's a terrible way to work because what you're doing is putting off until later all the things that as an economist you don't enjoy … but that are absolutely critical if the paper's ever going to get published. So, now I literally reverse the process; I start by writing. Only after I've written, do I allow myself to put together a slide deck for a presentation. I put the cost up front and the fun stuff at the other end. Typically, one window's open in Word and the other window's open in Stata. In the physical sciences, writing a paper is something you do after the science. I try to integrate the two when I'm doing economics. That may just be about my self-control problems – if I don't integrate them, then I'll never get around to doing the writing – but I suspect that it may be a useful thing to do as a social scientist.

What steps have you taken during your career to improve the quality of your writing?

I've worked really hard at it. I entered graduate school as a terrible writer. One thing is to read critically the work of people whose writing you admire. That involves figuring out whom you admire, and so there are also some real value judgments. For instance, Greg Mankiw is a wonderful communicator and one of his dictums is that every paper can be boiled down to one graph. Everyone says, "That would be true if you had simple ideas like Greg, but mine are complicated." I think people who say that are wrong. They're just refusing to spend the time to understand really deeply their ideas. Therefore, understanding the value of clear communication actually requires this enormous value judgment and a leap that many graduate students aren't willing to make, which is to realize that their job is to communicate, not to be complicated scientists. Graduate students will often try and write in the most technical and obfuscatory way, and in LaTeX so that it looks like they're physical scientists. They'll refer to the people in their models as agents rather than people. The list goes on. What they're trying to do is win an intellectual weight lifting competition.

Learning to write well is about making hard ideas easy. If the cost of that is people think that you're simple because your ideas are simple, then you've got to have the courage of your convictions. A year ago, I was working with a writing coach, and I probably should do more of it again.

Relative to most economists, I started engaging with the media much earlier in my career. During graduate school, I was writing op-eds in the Australian press, and I've kept that up ever since. That's been a tool that I've used to teach myself how to communicate. I take a complicated economic idea and I find a way of expressing it in 800 words, which is much shorter than you think. Then you send it off to an op-ed page where it's edited by someone whose job is to be an editor – someone who really knows how to write in a way that an economist doesn't. It's a wonderful learning experience. I've had people from *The Wall Street Journal* or *The New York Times* teach me how to write, and all I have to do is provide them with some economics along the way.

I also write for the *Freakonomics* blog. I do, say, 400 words in a culture where most people read two lines and get bored. So, you've got to be snappy and fun. Writing for that general audience is very different to writing for fellow economists, but it helps you develop skills that are going to be helpful for hitting the general economists. Again, very few of the people whom I want to communicate with in the dusty old economics journals are exact specialists in what I'm doing; they're economists from other fields, and so I need to be able to make my ideas interpretable.

Who proofreads your writing?

Me, Betsey Stevenson, and my very talented undergraduate RAs. It seems like American undergraduates have superb writing skills if you find the right ones.

How do you split up the writing tasks among co-authors?

In many of the co-authorships, I begin the relationship as the stronger writer. I'll either write the first draft and the last draft, or I'll tear a first draft to pieces and still write the last draft. The control freak in me is the part that finds it difficult to let the co-authors do the writing. But there are a few exceptions. Betsey Stevenson is a very strong writer and Eric Zitzewitz is a co-author where we've been equals throughout. He still jokes about how anal I can be on a final draft, and that's probably true. I've also had a couple of very successful partnerships with graduate students, like Erik Snowberg.[4] In those cases, I'll often have them write the first draft largely as a teaching exercise. I'll tear it to pieces, we'll write a proper first draft, and then move forward.

I once wrote a paper with Joe Price where he wrote a first draft, and then he came to Philadelphia. We sat in my study and I said, "Joe, now let's write a proper introduction. We have 60 minutes. You write on your computer, I'll write on mine. We'll see what we can come up with." Sixty minutes later, we came up with two introductions. He compared the two and said he preferred mine. He analyzed why he liked better the introduction I had written. That was a writing lesson for Joe. Then he wrote the first draft of the rest of the paper, and it was absolutely splendid.[5]

COLLABORATION

When you work with co-authors, how do you decide whom to work with?

Happenstance is a big part of it. I've worked with friends and with people I've never met before. A slightly different question is: how should one do it? It's too easy to think that what one should do is find a really good match – someone who thinks like me – because then we'll never have any conflict. But the Ricardian model of trade tells us that different factor endowments lead to greater trade. So, what you really want is someone who's good at the things you're bad at, and you're good at the things they're bad at. I've started using that Ricardian criterion a lot more recently.

Is geographical proximity ever an important consideration in choosing a co-author?

The only Philadelphia-based co-author I have is Betsey Stevenson, who's also in the same house. All of my other co-authors are all around the world.

How do you prefer to interact with your co-authors (e-mail, phone, or face-to-face)?

Very early on, when you're trying to sketch out the bare bones of a paper, something face-to-face or on the phone is going to be helpful. Doing the empirical analysis is then easy; someone collects the data, puts together a 'do' file, and we just share all that electronically. We can also check and replicate each other's work if we like, but Ricardian trade suggests that I should trust you to do something, and you should trust me to do something. Writing is also fairly easy. Again, I'm a control freak, so I'll take a firm hand at some point, but my co-authors will certainly get a chance to change things.

It's never been a question I've even thought to ask, because you and I grew up in a time where electronic communication is simple, cheap, and free. For intellectual exchanges, sometimes being forced to sit down and write down what it is you're thinking about means you don't waste your co-author's time, which you may have done if they were just in your office next door.

The one co-authoring relationship where the tyranny of distance is not present is the one with Betsey. She will work in her study on the third floor of our house, and I'll work in my study on the first floor. Our work flow looks exactly the same as when I'm working with Andrew Leigh in Australia. We'll e-mail files backwards and forwards. Despite the fact that we live in the same house and have adjoining offices, the whole process is exactly the same as when I have co-authors on the other side of the world.

RESEARCH ASSISTANCE AND FUNDING

How do you use undergraduate and graduate research assistants?

I work with my undergraduates fairly intensively. I often use them for exploratory analysis, where they find some data or literature for me. I also use them a lot in my writing; I want them to improve it.

Working with graduate research assistants can be a little harder, partly because you want to be a nice guy, which means making sure that your demands of them are not knocking off their research progress. As a result, at the moment I'm only working with graduate students on co-authored papers because then that guilt goes away. And I try to remember the way Olivier treated me, which was to pose a problem and assume that the student is smart enough to figure it out.

How important is funding for getting your work done?

The endogenous answer is that I have lots of ideas but not tons of money, so I just pursue the ones that are cheap. But funding has so far been quite unimportant. I've been remarkably successful at getting companies to give me data that would otherwise cost hundreds of thousands of dollars. I have a horse racing dataset that the Jockey Club gave me, and Gallup provided access to the Gallup World Post, which is a wonderful resource. If you're entrepreneurial about getting on the phone to people and explaining what you're trying to do, then at worst you're not a threat, and at best you're a complement to what they're doing. For instance, the work that I've done with the Gallup data has gotten it a lot of attention, and they're pleased with that.

Entrepreneurial spirit can be a substitute for funding. I wish I was better funded, but I've never spent a lot of time trying to get large amounts of funding, because every day I wake up I've got tons of research to do and not enough time to write more research grants.

Do you have any advice for a young scholar on the funding process?

I think a more important thing than learning how to get funding is learning how to make funding a complement to, rather than a substitute for, research. It's easy to let time spent writing grants crowd out time spent doing research. The difficult skill is trying to use that money constructively. Therefore, the way that I think about this is: what's the optimal firm size for producing economic research? Most economists tend to believe that the optimal firm size is one. If that's the case, then you don't need any funding, because your wage is already being paid for. If you believe that the optimal firm size is four, then you need to get funding for three research assistants and make sure that your firm of four is producing more than a firm of one would produce. I wasted a lot of time earlier in my career trying to run a firm of four and not being very good at it. But it's almost certainly the case that the optimal firm size is well above one, and I would love to figure out how to make funding a deeper complement to research.

SEMINAR PARTICIPATION AND NETWORKING

What are the benefits to attending a seminar that is closely related to your work versus one that is not closely related?

I get way more benefit out of attending something unrelated to my work. If something's closely related to my work, I may not know the insight of that particular author, but I can probably sort out the exact contribution of that author in ten minutes. If I go to something in a field unrelated to mine, I not only learn about the author's specific contribution, but I also learn about the literature into which they're contributing, and about how it is that one does research in that field. There are much, much greater gains.

How important is professional networking to success in research?

Critically important is the positive statement and too important is the normative statement. People make judgments about you and your work based on very little information. It's not rare that I've sat in a hiring meeting and someone will suggest a candidate, and someone else will say, "I saw them give a seminar once. It was terrible." That one interaction was enough to kill that candidate.

The other reason that I think it's really important is we might think that publication is about taking a paper, putting it in a journal, and then everyone sitting at their desks and reading it. It's just not true – no one reads journals. What we do is we attend seminars, and sometimes our friends say, "This is a very important paper. You should read it." Then you go and look it up. Publication is about getting people to read your paper, and they'll do that because they know you. Knowing and being known by other economists is surprisingly important.

How does the researcher without extensive networks succeed?

The kids coming out of the top few programs – Harvard, MIT, Chicago, and so on – know many, many economists. If you come out of a small program, then it is true that you begin without that network, but you just start aggressively getting out and meeting people. Yes, your network will still never be as easily formed as some. For example, I look at my friends who started as American undergraduates, and they can still talk to their under-graduate advisors who are famous economists. They start a step ahead, but communicating your ideas to the community of economists is just as important for them as it is for anyone else, and it's just as doable.

To what extent is the absence of departmental colleagues working in one's research area a major disadvantage?

All things considered, it would be better to be in a department with lots of people who are complementary to you. But again, think about the model of Ricardian trade. You're going to get more from trading ideas with people who are some 'distance' from you.

COMMUNICATION OF RESEARCH

How do you find the right balance between communicating your research at an early stage versus the close-to-finished stage?

A lot of people I know, when they come up with an idea that they're going to start working on, are then very secretive about it. They're worried that people will steal their ideas. I'm exactly the opposite. Sunlight's the best disinfectant, so if I tell everyone in the world what I'm working on, then if someone comes along and steals the idea, there are hundreds of economists who know that was my idea first. The best advice is that when you're in the process of thinking about an issue, be as public as you can.

But one can't publish an idea; one publishes a paper. When you're at the point in your research that you've convinced yourself that the paper is right – and you've convinced others – then communicate it broadly. I would not put out a paper that's plausibly wrong. People talk about one part of the process being putting out a working paper and then learning from that so that the final paper is much, much better. I'm early enough in my career that the hit to my reputation of putting out a working paper that was incorrect would be just too great.

What are the unique challenges to giving a seminar and how do you overcome them?

The challenge is to understand that the most important person in the room is not you; it's the guy at the back who's not even convinced he needs to know the answer to what you're going to give. But I don't really think of a seminar as challenging; I think of it as fun. You've worked hard on your idea and now get to display it. It's like a coming out party for a research paper. Enjoy it, be gracious, and listen.

PUBLICATION

How do you decide upon the appropriate journal to send your research to?

I spend very little time thinking about this because I think very little scholarly communication occurs through journals. But being completely honest, where I send things ends up being dictated largely by the strategic career interests of either myself or of my co-author. So, if I have a paper with someone who's about to go for tenure, we'll send it to the *QJE* because they have the fastest turnaround time. Having published quite a lot in the *QJE,* I was pleased recently to send something to the *JPE* just to show that I can be published in another major journal instead.

But the truth is no psychologist on earth reads the *American Economic Review*; just like no economist reads the *American Sociological Review* or the *American Political Science Review*. This is where communicating with the general public is helpful. If *The New York Times* decides to write up one of your papers, it turns out that psychologists and sociologists also read *The New York Times*. As I mentioned earlier, Betsey and I had a paper looking at happiness and income, which is an issue that's of quite some interest to psychologists. We published it in an economics journal, but it was written up by *The New York Times*, and as a result really got picked up by the psychologists. The channels for cross-disciplinary communication are very weak and maybe the media is the best of them. That's another reason why I worry less about which journal masthead a paper is on.

How would you best describe your approach to dealing with a 'revise and resubmit' request from a journal? How about an outright rejection?

I spend too much time turning around 'revise and resubmits', particularly if it comes back from a top journal. I revise the hell out of it so that you give the referees and the editor no choice. That can mean that I end up working three times harder to move from a 99 per cent chance to a 100 per cent chance. For someone early in their career, I strongly advise that.

I tend to submit a paper only when I'm confident that the result is true. So, when a paper is rejected, it's for one of two reasons: I haven't clearly enough articulated how and why it's true, or for some reason exogenous to the execution – you're not from the right school of thought, or they think that this is not for a general interest journal. If that's the case, there's very little to learn. Put the paper in an envelope and send it straight back out the next day. Try not to over-interpret what was an idiosyncratic draw of referees.

Do you think the current structure of the publication process in economics facilitates or impedes scientific understanding and knowledge production?

There are two parts of the process that impede progress. One is that the formal journal system rewards incremental improvements; I have had the greatest success with my less ambitious papers. The other part is that hiring committees essentially outsource their decision-making processes to journal editors. Many, many schools will simply count up how many *QJE*s, *AER*s, and *JPE*s you have. I think that's insane; you can have a splendid paper that, for better or worse, was published elsewhere. So, the problem is how people choose to consume the signal that comes from a publication. I think if you want to hire someone, you should read their work and figure out if it's good. That's your answer.

REFEREEING AND EDITING

How do you decide upon whether or not to accept a refereeing job?

In the first half of my career, I accepted everything sent my way. That was almost certainly a mistake because it involved a lot of refereeing for journals that I have nothing to do with and will never publish in. I took on a greater load than I should have, and I needed to prioritize my own research. Today, I reject very close to 100 per cent of requests with a few exceptions, as I'm a journal editor.

What are the benefits to refereeing versus being a journal editor?

Early in one's career as a referee, you can figure out why it is that you're recommending that papers are rejected, and that can become part of the writing lesson when it's time for you to construct your own papers. After that, refereeing is a service that one does for the community of scholars because one is a member of that community.

The editorial position that I accepted is an unusual one. It's the *Brookings Papers on Economic Activity*, which runs two major conferences per year, and we solicit papers rather than accepting them. That means as an editor, I have some ability to influence because these are papers that would not otherwise be written. I can approach you and say, "I think this is a very important question. I really wish a top-tier economist like you was working on this problem. I have a lot of money to pay you to write this paper for me." I have a wonderful platform where the Brookings Institution will do everything they can to bring attention to your paper, and that turns out to be a great deal.

The *Brookings Papers* over the years have had a tradition of policy relevance, so this is also a way for me to stay up to date with the policy debate. The job I took over was previously done by Doug Elmendorf, who's now head of the CBO, by Larry Summers, who is head of the NEC, and by Greg Mankiw, who used to be chair of the CEA. I was woefully under qualified compared to those three, and when you're under qualified for something, it's probably a good idea to do it.

TIME MANAGEMENT

How do you divide up your working day, both in terms of quantity and timing of different kinds of work?

I'm probably not very good at it. I recently became a father and that's added a constraint. So, now the way I find extra hours in the day is to wake up at 5:00 am and get writing done. It's very easy for us to believe that Matlab, Mathematica, and Stata are the most important programs on our computers, but it turns out that the only one that writes papers is Word.

Beyond that, the truth is I really enjoy being an economist, and maybe the only part of time management that I get right is to follow the things that I love doing. That means that I get a whole lot of time management wrong, I'm sure. Papers sit there half done waiting for me to get excited about them again, but excitement's such a complement to productivity so that may be the right thing to do.

How do you balance multiple research projects?

I have co-authors who kick me in the bum when something needs to get done.

What is the optimal number of projects that you could be working on at any given time?

Maybe half a dozen. I would say that one is too few. I know many economists who knock them out one at a time, but you need to be excited and engaged. The other problem with doing one is that it's not clear when you finish that one project what the next one's going to be. We talked earlier about the importance of working across lots of areas of economics. If you're doing one, you're obviously only working on one area of economics, and the opportunities for intellectual arbitrage go away.

There was a point when I was working on 20 at the same time. I would come in every week and make epsilon progress on all 20, which then means that any of them would take infinite time to finish. That was too many.

How do you find the right balance between your research and non-research activities?

One thing that's important is not to confuse work and leisure. For instance, when I blog, that's leisure. I need to be very clear that if I write a splendid blog today, I didn't get any work done.

I try to minimize the non-research distractions, but it is a value judgment for each person. Thinking about what communities you want to affect should be the thing that drives your time allocation. So, if you want to be part of the community of scholars, you should do some refereeing. If you want to affect public policy, you should write some op-eds. If you want to transform the way economics is taught at your university, you should be an active part of hiring.

How about the balance between your personal and professional lives?

My personal and professional lives are completely blended. My favorite co-author is my significant other. I co-teach with Betsey as well. We teach a large core course here at Wharton, and normally when you teach a core class at a business school, there are interminable teaching meetings, but we talk about the material on the drive home. And when we're writing a paper together, we'll talk about it when we're feeding our daughter Matilda.

Ten of my best friends in the United States are economists. When I see them I say, "How are you? How are your kids? What are you working on?" A barbeque with friends will look a lot like a seminar.

I think it would be very hard to be successful as an economist without having that degree of passion for what you do.

REFLECTIONS AND THE FUTURE OF ECONOMICS

What have been the most important findings and contributions in your research fields during your career?

One critically important publication was Gary Becker's *Treatise on the Family*.[6] That was published when I was about three years old, but its impact may have been felt most strongly in the last 20 years. In particular, there is a coherent and substantive field of inquiry called the economics of the family that is informed by standard Chicago price theory and involves serious empirical work looking at issues surrounding the family. And when you put the *Treatise* together with his work on crime and discrimination, Gary's great success has been to launch economics into new and broader lines of inquiry. Impolitely, it's called economic imperialism and Gary calls it social economics. I just think of it as economics, and that's the difference – my generation of economists grows up with sets of results that use basic economic theory to understand politics, crime, marriage and divorce. It's respectable for us to pick up any social phenomenon and try to examine it.

What are the biggest challenges facing your research fields?

There is enormous unfinished business in trying to link the economic approach to substantial areas of inquiry that have traditionally been outside economics. It's still the case that when people think about family phenomena, they often feel they should be calling a sociologist. Sociology is a useful case study because it is the domain where economists have been most successful, in that some of their theoretical and empirical insights have been accepted within the field. But psychology has been one field where I think economics, on the whole, has been a net importer. There is unfinished business in the behavioral economics revolution. So far, it has all been about judgment and decision-making. But, emotion, for example, is a very important issue in psychology and one imagines that economists could have something useful to say about emotional states. And, strikingly, economists have had very little impact on how psychologists do their business.

What are the strengths and weaknesses of your own research?

My strengths are that I am tenacious in seeking out the data to answer the research question at hand, and I try to sniff out questions that I think will be important.

My weaknesses are that I sometimes get distracted by questions that are fun but not important, and I think I could do a better job at using economic theory rather than just data.

Do you have any professional regrets?

I wish I had been better at time allocation earlier in my career. The thing I've learned is that there are enormous payoffs for being really good at something, and enormous distractions on the way there. If I had understood quite how large the payoffs are from being the best economist I can be, I would have found time management a lot easier. It's incredibly flattering if someone wants to fly you halfway across the country to talk to a crowded room of people who are on the edge of their seats to hear what you're going to say, but it doesn't actually help you achieve the things you care about.

What are your professional ambitions?

One ambition is that I hope that I don't become worried about counting up notches on my belt about what I have and haven't achieved in my career. One sees a lot of very miserable, old economists talking about how they "coulda been a contender." I've been given opportunities that I never dreamed I would be given, and I don't want to lose that sense of excitement and wonder. Coming from Australia, I never expected to get to meet and learn from great economists. That sense of excitement and wonder gives me a special joy from doing economics that I really hope I can retain.

How would you describe the state of economics today? Are you optimistic about its future?

Economics is the queen of the social sciences. The economic method is increasingly central to how all of us think about every aspect of our lives. The President consults a Council of Economic Advisers. He does not have a Council of Poets, a Council of English Scholars, or even a Council of Sociologists. And so I think economics is in a wonderful, wonderful place.

Am I optimistic about the future? Absolutely. Economics is now the *lingua franca* of the policy world. That tells you we're in a pretty good state.

NOTES

1. Akerlof, G.A. (1970), 'The Market for "Lemons": Quality Uncertainty and the Market Mechanism', *Quarterly Journal of Economics*, Vol. 84, No. 3 (August), pp. 488–500.
2. Mankiw, N.G., Romer, D. and D.N. Weil (1992), 'A Contribution to the Empirics of Economic Growth', *Quarterly Journal of Economics*, Vol. 107, No. 2 (May), pp. 407–437.
3. Stevenson, B. and J. Wolfers (2008), 'Economic Growth and Subjective Well-Being: Reassessing the Easterlin Paradox', *Brookings Papers on Economic Activity*, Economic Studies Program, The Brookings Institution, Vol. 39, No. 1 (Spring), pp. 1–102.
4. See, for example, Snowberg, E.C., Wolfers, J. and E. Zitzewitz (2007), 'Partisan Impacts on the Economy: Evidence from Prediction Markets and Close Elections', *Quarterly Journal of Economics*, Vol. 122, No. 2 (May), pp. 807–829; Snowberg, E.C. and J. Wolfers (2010), 'Explaining the Favorite-Long Shot Bias: Is it Risk-Love or Misperceptions?', *Journal of Political Economy*, Vol. 118, No. 4 (August), pp. 723–746.
5. Price, J. and J. Wolfers (2010), 'Racial Discrimination Among NBA Referees', *Quarterly Journal of Economics*, Vol. 125, No. 4 (November), pp. 1859–1887.
6. Gary S. Becker (1981), *A Treatise on the Family*, Harvard University Press.

Randall Wright
(University of
Wisconsin –
Madison)

Randall Wright was born in Winnipeg, Manitoba, Canada in 1956 and graduated with a BA in economics from the University of Manitoba in 1979 before obtaining a PhD in economics from the University of Minnesota in 1986. He was an Assistant Professor of Economics at Cornell University between 1984 and 1987 and then moved to the University of Pennsylvania where he became Professor of Economics in 1996. In 2009, he took up a joint position at the University of Wisconsin – Madison as the Ray Zemon Professor of Liquid Assets in the Department of Finance, Investment and Banking at the Wisconsin School of Business, and in the Department of Economics.

Professor Wright's research focuses on monetary and macroeconomics, and he is perhaps best known for his work on the microfoundations of monetary theory. His most-cited articles in chronological order include 'On Money as a Medium of Exchange', *Journal of Political Economy* (1989), co-authored with Nobuhiro Kiyotaki, 'Why is Automobile Insurance in Philadelphia so Damn Expensive?', *American Economic Review*, co-authored with Eric Smith, 'A Search-Theoretic Approach to Monetary Economics', *American Economic Review* (1993), co-authored with Nobuhiro Kiyotaki, 'A Unified Framework for Monetary Theory and Policy Analysis', *Journal of Political Economy* (2005), co-authored with Ricardo

Lagos, and 'Money in Search Equilibrium, in Competitive Equilibrium, and in Competitive Search Equilibrium', *Econometrica* (2005), co-authored with Guillaume Rocheteau.

Professor Wright is a Consultant to the Federal Reserve Bank of Minneapolis, the Federal Reserve Bank of Chicago, and the Bank of Canada. He is a Research Associate at the National Bureau of Economic Research, an Associate Editor of the *Journal of Economic Theory*, and an Advisory Editor of *Macroeconomic Dynamics* and the *North American Journal of Economics and Finance*. He edited the *International Economic Review* between 1998 and 2008. In 1997, he was elected as a Fellow of the Econometric Society.

I interviewed Randall Wright in his office in the Department of Finance, Investment and Banking at the Wisconsin School of Business, Madison. It was mid-afternoon of Friday, 25 June 2010.

BACKGROUND INFORMATION

What was your attraction to economics?

I didn't grow up wanting to be an economist. People might grow up wanting to be an athlete or a musician, but being an economist was not something I always imagined as a dream job. I went to the University of Manitoba and did well in my introductory economics course, so thought I'd pursue it, and the more I did it, the more I found it intriguing and challenging.

As a student, which professors were most influential or inspirational?

There was a great guy called Jim Selden at the University of Manitoba. He taught me rigorous undergraduate economics and, along with Jim Dean, encouraged me to apply to graduate school in the US. I applied to Minnesota, because it was close to (and warmer than) Winnipeg, and I got in. There, Neil Wallace became my advisor and mentor. Much of the way in which I approach economics comes from him. He instilled in me the idea that it's important to be rigorous, careful, and logical, but still think about important issues like inflation and unemployment.

Tom Sargent was another big influence. He's passionate about economics and a hard worker – a real grinder. I loved his teaching style. He'd come in and write equations on the board for 90 minutes. It was extremely hard to follow; indeed, it was difficult even to copy them down. But he liked those equations, and he thought we could learn something from them. I agree. We don't want to get hung up on technique, but you need to be able to specify your model with equations. Tom used to also say that you have to imagine what it would be like to be an agent living in the model. I always think that way now.

Edward Prescott came along in my second year of graduate school, and he was a big inspiration as well. He taught me that it's important to integrate theory and measurement. Even though I'm mostly a monetary theorist, I also do some quantitative work, and I was inspired by Prescott to do that.

On the pure theory side, at Minnesota, I have to say Leo Hurwicz was great. He was one of the deepest of economists of the last century. He won the Nobel Prize a couple of years ago, and very deservedly. Leo also had a real passion for economics.

Why did you decide to pursue an academic career?

I sort of just fell into academia – it wasn't like I planned it. Once one gets close to completion in graduate school, the system steers you ahead to the job market, and I went along with it.

As a researcher, which colleagues have been most influential or inspirational?

After leaving graduate school, my first job was at Cornell, which was great. I got to learn a different kind of economics than I had learned at Minnesota. It was a hotbed of search theory. Ken Burdett and Dale Mortensen, who was visiting Cornell during my first year, taught me a lot.

Richard Rogerson has also been a very important colleague, collaborator, and friend over the years. We entered graduate school at Minnesota at the same time. We would study together, and then we were colleagues at the University of Pennsylvania for several years. He was a big inspiration. I've always looked up to people with more technical ability, and he knows a lot of math, but he never seems to do mathematics for its own sake; he always has an eye for important real-world problems. We did some good work together, which I really enjoyed, and hopefully we will do some more.

I've also worked a lot with Nobuhiro Kiyotaki over the years. We first met at Wisconsin 23 years ago, when he was an assistant professor and I was visiting for a term. He was a big influence. He taught me about being diligent and hardworking. Of course, it helps to be smart, as he is. He also has a vision, a broad perspective on economic issues.

GENERAL THOUGHTS ON RESEARCH

What is the value of pure versus applied research in economics?

The purest of all academic research is probably number theory, which studies the most arcane and irrelevant properties of numbers. There is something called Ruth-Aaron numbers, named after the baseball players. If you're interested, look up what those are, and you'll see how ridiculous number theory is. It turns out, however, that much to people's surprise, number theory has recently become one of the most practical theories or approaches to mathematics, because it is used in encryption (the design of codes to make it hard to hack into computer networks).

Even if that's an apocryphal story, it still shows that something that appears to be arcane and irrelevant may be very useful years later. This is somewhat true of economics too, which is why I don't like to see people being dismissive of pure theory. In terms of my own work, I have been told sometimes, "That's all very elegant, but tell us something to make a better monetary policy today." I think almost the opposite; too many people are all too inclined to make policy recommendations on the basis of poorly grounded theory. The profession needs a mix of pure and applied work.

Bob Hall has said to me, "I don't carry much cash, so why do we think monetary economics is interesting?" If I was a paleontologist, would he say, "I haven't seen a dinosaur in years ... "? Except for some of his colleagues, but that's another story. I think academic research for its own sake is well worthwhile. And we have to be patient – I am glad that no one shut down number theory years ago.

How would you describe the dialogue between theory and empirics in economics?

As Prescott says, good theory and good measurement go together. At the same time, some people will specialize in one and some in the other. This is desirable. But we need people in-between, too, to intermediate between the purists.

How would you characterize your own research agenda and how has it changed over time?

I've always thought about problems related to the macroeconomy, and my approach has always been the same as it was as a graduate student: try to find something interesting and try to model it in an appealing way, which means logically consistent, but also beautiful. I may not always succeed, but I want my papers to be elegant as well as relevant.

Do you think it is important to have broad research interests?

I think that the day of the Renaissance man is over. The world is so complicated, and the issues are so intricate, that if you don't specialize, you're going to be a masquerader, walking around giving all your opinions, but they're not worth very much. I understood Adam Smith when he said that if you specialize, you'll become good, and that will promote social efficiency.

Do you think there is any difference in the types of work done by researchers at different stages in their careers based on tenure concerns, publication requirements or other pressures? Should there be a difference?

Over time, one gains more experience and a better perspective. That's useful. What one doesn't want to do is end up like an old fart who says, "I once had coffee with Schumpeter." You still want to be active and be grinding away. You can see from the board here in my office that algebra and theorem proving is still a big part of what I do.

A lot of people get very worried about manipulating their career decisions to make sure things go well. I got tenure at Penn without thinking about how to manipulate the system strategically. Like I said earlier, I've always approached research the same way. But one thing to say for sure – and I've consciously thought about this – is that you should have a diversified portfolio; not every paper can be in the very best journal. You should work on several projects at the same time, because some will pan out better than others, obviously.

IDEA GENERATION

Where do you get your research ideas?

I can tell you how we came up with Kiyotaki-Wright. When I was visiting Madison, he would knock on my door about once a week and ask me questions. One day, he said, "What about unemployment?" Coming from Cornell and Minnesota, I had some ideas that I shared with him. The next week, he said, "What about stochastic dominance?" I replied, "Well, here's what I read in this book." But then one day, he came in and said, "What about money?" I replied, "I don't know. Why don't we sit down and try to come up with something?" In about 20 minutes, we came up with the idea and the basic framework, which didn't change in the many months of working on the project. So that was just somebody asking a question, and then for whatever reason, something popped into my head and we worked it out.[1]

And that has happened to me other times. Once, Bruce Smith gave a seminar on why firms lay off workers as opposed to reducing hours per worker. In the faculty club afterwards, I said to Ken Burdett, "It seems obvious to me that if you reduce hours per worker, you don't get any subsidy from the government. But if you lay off somebody, he gets unemployment insurance and that's not taxed at a fair rate when they tax firms." Burdett said, "That's interesting." I was thinking, "No, that must be obvious and something that's been done before." He'd been involved in organizing some sessions on contract theory and unemployment for a conference, and told me, "No, no, maybe people have thought of the idea, but they haven't really fleshed it out." So we did it, and it came out in the *JPE*.[2]

Ricardo Lagos and I have a paper in the *JPE* from five years ago that extends monetary theory in a way that is much more tractable and empirically relevant and policy relevant.[3] How did we get started? We were sitting in Doobie's (a pub in Philadelphia) with Ken Burdett working on the economics of crime. Lagos hadn't worked on monetary economics before that, but around midnight he looked at me and said, "You guys work on money. Why don't you do this?" By "this" he meant, well, look at the paper. We had been there for several hours. Lagos doesn't drink, although Ken and I do, and we were a bit weary, but it immediately clicked in my head that Ricardo's idea would work. And it sure did.

So a lot of it is dumb luck. You talk to people, hang out, have a few beers, and chat. Every so often, somebody says something brilliant. The key is recognizing it!

At what point does an idea become a project that you devote resources to?

When people talk to me about ideas in monetary economics, I know most of what's been done, because it's a fairly narrow field of expertise. When something new comes along, something different, I get interested. I start working on it, and I can tell pretty quickly whether it's going to pan out, because I know lots of techniques and tricks. At least in my narrow area I know a lot, because I specialize.

IDEA EXECUTION

What makes a good theoretical paper?

A good theoretical paper should have some contact with reality; it should be empirically or policy relevant. The best theoretical papers often say, "Here's an interesting economic problem, but no one's really thought of a good way to do it. Here is one way to approach it."

Can you give an example?

Uh, I'll pick Nash's paper on the bargaining problem.[4] It's brilliant. Back when I was an undergraduate, I remember people saying, "We know how to solve the perfect competition and monopoly problems, but we do not know what to do in the case of bilateral monopoly. Theory has nothing to say." It turns out that Nash had a lot to say. The math is easy – the proof is basically one little diagram – and the results are powerful and very useful. Much applied research in macro-labor and in monetary economics uses bargaining theory. The follow-up work by many people has taught us many more details about bargaining, but Nash's paper is short and sweet – something like six pages. It takes a problem that is known to be important and solves it. Is there any empirical content in that? Maybe not directly, except for the fact that the real world has people bargaining all the time, just like our models. Anyway, I like that paper.

What makes a good empirical paper?

When you look at data, and it's not consistent with standard theory, that's good empirical work because it tells theorists they have to change the model, or that something else has to be done to reconcile theory and data. The equity-premium puzzle of Mehra and Prescott is interesting.[5] We observe these facts about returns to different assets. Could you write down a simple theoretical model consistent with that? Well, you could, but it would take crazy parameter values to match the data. So it's a bit of a puzzle. That's also nice empirical work because these are not facts that you have to do a lot of complicated statistical analysis to uncover; you just go out there and measure it.

When you hit a brick wall on a project, do you continue to work on the problem or do you take a break from it and work on something else?

I have to tell this story from the movie *Cannery Row*. Nick Nolte is living as a bum in Cannery Row, but he has a PhD in marine biology, and is trying to study the mating habits of a particular type of octopi. He's explaining this to another bum, and he says, "It's really hard, because I want to photograph them mating, but they only mate in the dark, so I can't." The other bum says, "Why don't you just give up?" I was looking for him to propose some brilliant solution, but he said, "Just give up." That's funny.

Sometimes when you're working on economic problems, it would be easy just to give up, or worse, to take a shortcut. If you keep working on things, maybe years later something will come of it. Perhaps you take some shortcuts in the short run. The monetary economics that I work on is a case in point. It's pretty clear to me that Bob Lucas was always interested in getting money into equilibrium macro, or to say it differently, building an equilibrium theory of money. Somehow he decided at some point that it's not worth all the effort, and we can instead simply assume there is a cash-in-advance constraint. I respect Lucas as much as any economist there ever was, but that was a shortcut. Shortcuts can be useful in the short run, as I said, but I don't think we should give up on a problem forever just because there's a way around it that avoids the work.

Sargent told me he considers his publications to be progress reports on his research program. You type up your results and say, "Here's what we've got so far. It's not the last word," and you continue. When Kiyotaki and I first started doing monetary economics, we didn't know how to set up the bargaining problem, let alone solve it. What did we do? We could have worked on that for decades. But we said, "Okay, let's assume goods are indivisible. There's no question now about how many apples you give me for a banana: one apple for one banana is the only feasible trade." This allowed us to make progress on describing and studying the *process* of trade without getting bogged down figuring out the terms of trade.

So we took a shortcut. But then later when I worked with Alberto Trejos, we discovered a way to put bargaining in and hence determine the terms of trade endogenously. It wasn't that hard, and it led to new insights.[6] Kiyotaki and I could have stopped and said, "We just don't know how to get prices into the model." We did say, "For years, price theorists have been proceeding without knowing how to get money in the model. It's only fair to let monetary theorists proceed for a while without knowing how to get prices in the model." But we still had a longer-term perspective that said, "We'll get it eventually, or someone will get it eventually."

Related to the previous question, when it appears that a project isn't going to turn out as hoped, do you scrap the project or aim to send the work to a second-tier or field journal?

I typically won't scrap anything. All the things I work on are related to the bigger model of the exchange process. And by the way, I want to be absolutely clear that, even though I call it monetary economics, we're not studying money per se; we're studying the process of exchange, which may involve barter, credit, or intermediation. Money just happens to be a relatively simple version of an institution that facilitates the exchange process. If you can't figure out a theoretical model that explains why people use currency, how can you claim to be able to, say, solve the recent financial crisis? So we're trying to understand institutions in general that help facilitate the process of exchange.

Maybe a paper won't come out of most of the ideas that I work on, but it'll be an input into my thinking about what the bigger problem is. And because it's still a fairly new area, each little idea may be of some tangential interest to somebody. I don't mind writing it up. I don't throw things in the garbage. They're all on a piece of paper somewhere or at least in the back of my head. These ideas or projects are a bit like your children: some may be more successful than others, but you love them all.

What has been the biggest change during your career in how researchers in your fields conduct research?

The work that came out of Kydland and Prescott and real business cycle theory. This brought theory and measurement in macro closer together. Before that, macro was a bunch of people doing dinky, static models and proclaiming they know how to solve all the world's problems, and other people running regressions with very little serious basis in theory, and claiming something similar.

Macroeconomists used to make far too many sloppy assumptions. Expectations were arbitrary, for example. Then, over the years, more discipline was instilled – expectations should be rational. I prefer the discipline imposed by strict hypotheses like rational expectations, market clearing, and optimization. Economics is no fun without rules. To use an analogy, it's easy to do the crossword puzzle if you don't read the clues; just insert arbitrary letters. Reading the clues imposes a lot of discipline, and it makes it more of a challenge.

Something that's a disappointment to me is that there's been a fairly big retreat from microfoundations in macro. Many macroeconomists are very willing to impose ad hoc assumptions like sticky prices, and they do so without apology. A large fraction of the profession says, "We don't know why prices are sticky. We don't even care. We're just going to assume they are and proceed to tell central banks what to do." That's unfortunate, because I think the reasons why prices may be or at least appear sticky, and the implications of this for policy, are important issues that deserve more thought. I am working on this now, and I think the results may surprise some people.

THE WRITING PROCESS

Which aspect of the writing process do you find most difficult?

In principle, I have no problem writing for 12 or 18 hours, except that it's physically challenging. I never learned how to type, and I have bad posture, so I end up being a complete physical wreck.

I remember as a graduate student, Neil Wallace saying he would rewrite his introductions 20 times. I thought that must have been a gross exaggeration, but I am sure now that it was not. I'm continually revising my papers.

I like typing up the equations, and I like the way they look on paper. I enjoy the writing process a lot, taking these vague ideas and making them precise. When you do things on the board, you maybe skip a few steps, but when you type it up, and there's a logical gap, you often notice it.

What steps have you taken during your career to improve the quality of your writing?

Practice makes perfect, or at least practice leads to improvements. Also, you develop a style; I have a basic algorithm. I remember telling this to Prescott many years ago because he said, "Randy, you seem to write pretty well. What's your secret?" I don't remember it exactly, but it was something like this: Number one, what's the idea? Number two, why is it interesting? Number three, what has been done before and why do you think this approach is better? Number four, talk about the literature briefly, making sure you don't slight anybody. Then go right to work laying out the model.

You can apply that basic guideline to lots of different papers, from empirical work to proofs of uniqueness.

Who proofreads your writing?

Hopefully, my co-authors but nobody else. I think I know what I want to say. When I worked at the Minneapolis Fed for a year back in the early 1990s, their copy editors would go over anything we wrote with a fine toothed comb. I hated it because they were changing things in the interest of style, and style is a matter of opinion. I wanted them to check the grammar and spelling, but they wanted to write a different paper in their own style.

How do you split up the writing tasks among co-authors?

On most papers I've done, I take on the job of writing it. In a recent paper with Rob Shimer and Veronica Guerrieri, we would take turns.[7] Sometimes I would delete a paragraph and insert one that Rob deleted in the previous round, and we would go around in circles. It was fun, but generally it's good to have somebody in charge.

COLLABORATION

When you work with co-authors, how do you decide whom to work with?

First of all, here's a fact you may or may not know: I have more co-authors than anybody else in economics. Some guys in network theory with empirical applications took about 20,000 economists in a social science index and modeled it as a graph. Every economist was a node, so if you and I wrote a paper, there would be a line emanating from me to you. I have the most lines emanating from my node apparently.[8] It's nothing to be proud of. It's like if you have the most ex-wives; maybe you're a very bad husband.

I really learn a lot from working with these smart people like Shimer and Guerrieri. They're a little bit imposing, but they're younger than me, so I can handle that. I learn a lot from working with Neil Wallace or Dale Mortensen, too, but I'm scared of those guys; maybe less so now than previously, but still a bit.

I work with graduate students because they're enthusiastic and hardworking. If they have good ideas, it's your job to help them. If an idea is panning out and you're learning something, you say, "Let's work on this together."

We call economics a social science because we study social institutions, but it's also a social science because we interact. Writing joint papers is great fun.

How do you prefer to interact with them (e-mail, phone, or face-to-face)?

I don't like talking on the phone. It just seems impersonal, and at the same time, sometimes you want to say something quickly and it may come out wrong. E-mail is good, but it's more typing, and again that's dreary. It's very important to travel. Summers are just constant traveling for me.

I'm working with an ex-student of mine, Ben Lester, who's now at Western Ontario, and Andy Postlewaite, an ex-colleague from Penn. Andy wants to talk all the time, and I don't; if anything, I prefer to say, "Let's just prove the result." As my Mom says, and she said it well before Nike, "Don't talk about it. Just do it." Now, of course, you need both in economics. Ben, being our ex-student, is caught in-between Andy and me. He doesn't know whether to do the algebra or think about the big picture. It's amusing to watch. But they are terrific co-authors.

How do you overcome the challenges encountered during collaborative work?

Just do it.

RESEARCH ASSISTANCE AND FUNDING

How do you use undergraduate and graduate research assistants?

I use undergraduate students rarely, although my first co-authored paper was with an undergraduate named Janine Loberg when I was at Cornell, and that was quite a fun experience.[9]

In terms of graduate RAs, I shouldn't say this, but it's not clear that people who I pay work more than people who I don't pay. I regard the payment to a graduate student to be an RA as just like some bonus money to help them get through school. I think they would want to work with me even if I wasn't paying them, and I would want to work with them even if they weren't my RA. It's not an employer–employee relationship; we're colleagues working together.

How important is funding for getting your work done?

It's not important. I think economists are very confused, or maybe dishonest, about it. I remember many years ago, I was having dinner after a seminar or at a conference, and somebody was asked what they were working on. They said, "Well, I want to work on this if I can just get a grant to do it." We don't need grants, unless we're buying data. If you have an idea, work on it. I would do the same thing if I didn't have grants. If you told me they were going to take away my NSF grant tomorrow, would I scrap these projects? Absolutely not. If you told me I couldn't hire an RA, would I say to the students, "We can't work together"? No.

But I think the grant-giving institution is good for a variety of reasons. One, knowledge is a public good, so it should be subsidized. Two, although most economists wouldn't change their daily research habits if they didn't get a grant, it tops up our salary, so it makes the profession more attractive, and we end up getting better minds and harder-working people in economics because of it. So maybe it's important in the long run for getting the best people involved, but it is less important in the short run for getting individuals to do their job.

Do you have any advice for a young scholar on the funding process?

Not particularly. Well, I remember in my first job at Cornell, Ken Burdett was Chairman, and he said, "We'll give you summer money for the first year. In the second year, I'll look around to see if there's summer money available." I thought that was great. At the end of my second year, I knocked on his door and I said, "You claimed you'd look around to see if there's any money available." He looked around the office and said, "Nope, there's none." So, here's some advice: get it in writing.

SEMINAR PARTICIPATION AND NETWORKING

What are the benefits to attending a seminar that is closely related to your work versus one that is not closely related?

I attend every talk I can in monetary theory. I also attend macro workshops more generally and sometimes labor or pure theory. At the Minneapolis Fed, Pat and Tim Kehoe, V.V. Chari, Ellen McGrattan and others ask penetrating and pertinent questions, and I like to watch them in action.

When I was at Penn, we had a great macro workshop. It was a tough place to give a seminar. Victor Ríos-Rull would sit on one side of the room and I'd sit on the other. I was very harsh and picky with all the speakers, but I was an angel compared to Victor, who was more like a shark. He would attack them on theory, on numbers, on the big picture, on methodology; everything but the clothes they wore. Victor would make comments on monetary theory about which he knows something, but not that much, and I'd make comments on the income distribution about which I know virtually nothing. But I learned a lot from Victor's comments on monetary economics, and maybe he learned something from me. Hopefully, the speaker got something out of this, too.

So, I enjoy seminars. It's part of the social aspect of economics. And I also learn a lot. Some of what I learn is about the big picture, and some of what I learn is about the minutiae of pure monetary theory. I find that great.

How important is professional networking to success in research?

You don't necessarily need networks to do well in research. I think economics is quite fair. I know from being a journal editor, we are not more inclined to take a paper by a famous person than a graduate student. But being in networks is quite useful, and the ones I'm involved in are almost always open shops. The monetary economics group that I run with Ed Nosal at the Chicago Fed and the macro-labor group that I run with Rogerson and Shimer for the NBER welcome all kinds of people, as long as they contribute. There are ways to get ostracized, like showing up on Tuesday to present your own paper and not coming to hear anybody else. Then you're going to be out; you might get away with that once, but not twice, because we don't want bad citizens. But we also want to say, "Anybody who's a good citizen is welcome to participate."

Here's some advice that someone once told me: when you get a job, insist on being able to run the seminar series. I invited Costas Azariadis to Cornell and then he invited me to Penn. A lot of good came of that: Penn gave me a job. You don't need to be a rocket scientist to figure out that if you invite somebody, he might invite you back.

To what extent is the absence of departmental colleagues working in one's research area a major disadvantage?

It's good to have colleagues in the next office who do what you do because you can interact. But it's not critical; you can travel or have people come to visit. Also, you don't want to end up in a department where everybody thinks the same way because then, as Prescott once put it, the rest of the world will ignore you. You have to do a bit of missionary work. Go to a place that maybe isn't the epicenter of search theory, for example, and take your message there.

COMMUNICATION OF RESEARCH

How do you find the right balance between communicating your research at an early stage versus the close-to-finished stage?

I don't tend to distribute my work too much in working papers. I e-mail my friends, or we chat over a meal or something. Word-of-mouth in my area seems to get the message across pretty well.

What are the unique challenges to giving a seminar and how do you overcome them?

Giving seminars has changed over time. They used to be on the blackboard. I remember Lucas giving them with a piece of chalk in one hand, and a cigarette in the other. Sometimes he'd mix up which was which. But I liked the old-fashioned way of putting things on the board. With PowerPoint or related presentation software, too many economists are presenting their seminars like they are teaching an MBA class. It is not good to be too slick. I say we should grab some chalk and think on our feet.

The audience is aware there's a trade-off between style and substance. If somebody has animation and beautiful graphics on their slides, my tendency is to think, "Hmm, maybe they spent too much time on their presentation and not enough on the substance." I prefer a minimalist approach.

I don't get nervous giving seminars. If you have spent two years working on a problem, you ought to know something, and you shouldn't be that shy about talking about it. Over the years, you get to be able to handle questions. It'd be great to know all the answers, but sometimes you get things you can't answer, so you have to bluff your way through it, or preferably say, "I don't know the answer to that," or "We'll come back to it." You can't get derailed. You see speakers who get derailed in a seminar start to deteriorate and the people in the audience begin talking to each other. You can't lose your audience; otherwise, the whole thing goes really badly.

PUBLICATION

How do you decide upon the appropriate journal to send your research to?

You want to get things in highly regarded journals to establish some credibility. But you also have to be somewhat realistic, and, again, you should diversify your portfolio. Don't take everything you write and send it to *Econometrica*, because they're not all likely to get in.

I don't want to make this sound ridiculous, but we're also writing it down for posterity. It's not our goal to be in the front page of *The Wall Street Journal* any particular week; the intended audience is textbook-readers many years down the road. How does it filter its way in? We have to communicate to the graduate students, and to our peers who pass it on, until eventually, instead of being this lunatic fringe – for instance, like search models of money – it becomes part of the mainstream, and then becomes the received wisdom.

In micro-founded monetary economics, we know we're right. These ideas go back to Jevons, Menger, Wicksell, Smith, and the ancient frickin' Greeks. Those guys didn't have dynamic programming, or search theory, or game theory, or general equilibrium theory, so it's a much easier job for us to formalize what they had in mind. Of course, we're not going to convince everybody overnight. The old farts aren't going to start teaching this material; they're going to teach what they've been teaching for the last 40 years.

How would you best describe your approach to dealing with a 'revise and resubmit' request from a journal? How about an outright rejection?

I always feel like a door-to-door salesman getting 'revise and resubmits'. Once you get your foot in the door, you got 'em. All but two of my many 'revise and resubmits' eventually got in. The best thing you can hope for is they say, "This is interesting, but you haven't actually completely nailed it. To have a big success, you'd have to do 'this'." Then you write back in a year, and say, "Okay, I did 'this'." It's almost like they're obliged to take it. They gave you a very difficult task and you pulled it off – done deal. So, I like 'revise and resubmits'.

In terms of a pure rejection, you've got to pick yourself up off the mat and keep fighting. Lagos-Wright got rejected at *Econometrica*, even though they solicited it. So what? It came out in the *JPE*, and it's a much better paper for having gone through another round of iterations. Also, Nancy

Stokey, who was the editor, did a very admirable, beyond the call-of-duty, job of helping us whip it into shape.

Here's an example of what not to do. Kiyotaki and I published our first paper in the *JPE*. It went in pretty much straightaway in the first round. Then what's important is the follow-up paper, so people don't think it was a fluke. So, we write this paper, send it to *Econometrica*, and they rejected it. Kiyotaki said, "Yeah, I guess we're wrong. This problem isn't interesting, and we're not making any progress." He wanted to tear up the paper. He said we'd have to come up with a completely new research idea. I said, "No. The referees are confused. Or at least wrong. Let's split this rejected paper in two, put the technical stuff in one and the big idea in the other, and send one to *JET* and one to the *AER*." They both got in straightaway.[10] At the end of the day, you have to have some belief in your own work. You should not necessarily give up just because some random person, who often enough doesn't understand it or didn't even try, recommends a rejection.

Do you think the current structure of the publication process facilitates or impedes scientific understanding and knowledge production?

It's not easy getting articles published; it takes a long time. But remember that commercial for Bally Fitness where Cher said, "If it were easy, everybody would have a great body"? You have to lift weights and do aerobics and diet or, in her case, have plastic surgery. If it were easy, everybody would have ten *Econometrica*s. It's supposed to be hard. Anything that's worthwhile has to be a bit of a challenge, and I'm not really aware of too many cases where people didn't get tenure, or their careers were ruined, because of an isolated event. In economics, we write a fair number of papers and the law of large numbers kicks in. Hopefully, I'm not being too sanguine about this, but on average I think things tend to work in the profession.

What has been your best and worst experience in the publication process?

Any time a paper gets accepted, you feel happy. Some of my best publications, in terms of journal ranking, have been rejected elsewhere. I haven't had too many bad experiences, except one at the *Review of Economic Studies* recently. We made some really hard revisions and, after two-and-a-half years, even though two referees recommended publication, the editor rejected the paper on a whim. That is totally fair in two or three days, but after two or three years, it's unprofessional and irresponsible. It's no fun talking about your worst experience, but since you asked, that's the sincere truth.

REFEREEING AND EDITING

How do you decide upon whether or not to accept a refereeing job? What are the benefits to being a referee?

I used to accept them all, especially when I was young. As you get older or more established, you get more and more requests. At some point, about a dozen years ago, I became the editor of the *IER* (*International Economic Review*). That went on for a decade, and the upside was two-fold. One, I wouldn't get so many referee requests because people knew I was an editor. Two, when I got papers to referee that I wasn't particularly interested in, I'd send them back and say, "Because I'm the editor of the *IER*, I'm only refereeing papers in my own area of interest." Steve Levitt sent me something from the *JPE* to referee. I sent him back a letter saying, "I'm happy to do it, although as the editor of the *IER*, I try not to referee too much for other journals. But I'll be happy to do this out of respect for the *JPE* and your work. And by the way, I'll send you something to referee from the *IER*. If you want me to referee this, just let me know." He never let me know.

You can get away with not refereeing if you're an editor, because you're already taking on your share of the responsibility. But I still would do some, and sometimes I felt the benefit; I learned something. I think also you can make constructive comments that make the paper better. It's not that hard. It's not that I'm smarter than the person who wrote it; I just look at it from a different angle. Then we're all better off.

TIME MANAGEMENT

How do you divide up your working day, both in terms of quantity and timing of different kinds of work?

Hunter S. Thompson said once he didn't recommend drugs and violence as a lifestyle, but it sure worked for him. All I mean by this is that different approaches work for different people. I'm totally chaotic. If I'm teaching at 1 in the afternoon, I might wake up at 3 or 4 in the morning for no good reason. I just couldn't sleep; either equations are going through my head, or maybe some musical passage. Then the next thing I know, I'm going to be late for class. Where did those N hours go? I don't know. Maybe I was checking e-mail, having a cappuccino, watching TV, practicing guitar, doing some exercise, or proving a theorem. Who knows? I'm totally disorganized in terms of time. Yet, it seems to work for me.

I used to say that I had a theory to explain it, and Bob Hall likes it: a person only has time for two things in life, but there are three things I want to do. I want to socialize, exercise, and be very serious about economics. At Cornell, sometimes I'd exercise and do economics for several months, but just never go out. Other times, I would go to the gym or play soccer and then go to the bar every night. For those two months, I would have no time for economics. When I started to get back into music again, I now had four things. I could do three of them, but not all four. Bob Hall says I should just pick one other thing that I don't like and not do that, but that's cheating. And now I have two little kids, William Jack and Jamie, aged three and six! So, I am fairly pressed for time.

I'm actually getting into gardening a bit now that I live in Wisconsin. Yes, really. Why? Because then you can go outside and work on your suntan and claim you're working. But in some sense, almost everything I do is economics. When I'd socialize – especially in Philly – it was almost all economics. I'd go to the pub with Ken Burdett and have a few beers and talk. What did we talk about? Search theory.

Gwen Eudey, the mother of my children, is an economist. Sometimes we talk about economics but we should do even more. We could go out on a date, say, and talk about what we'd write if we were writing the definitive textbook for undergraduate macro.

Lagos and I decided once that the secret to life was fast transitions. When we are working really hard on a problem and trying to solve it, at some point, say 9:00 pm, we say, "Okay, we can't work anymore. We need something to eat." We want to be eating at 9:05; none of this nonsense where you pack up, turn off your computer, and change your shoes. Turnaround time is critical. You want to eliminate all the downtime. It's a bit stressful, but if you want to be serious and good at economics, it is time-consuming. Time is precious – don't waste it.

One thing people have to understand is that the production of economics is like any other production process. It takes inputs, and time is a big input. You want to write more or better papers? Work harder. It's as simple as that.

How do you balance multiple research projects?

A couple of months ago, I counted that I was working with 21 co-authors on different projects. Luckily, a lot of those papers are at least using similar techniques, so it's not like I'm jumping from applied econometrics to game theory. I do feel, if not overstressed, at least excessively in demand. But the nice thing about the area I'm working on – monetary economics with microfoundations – is that it's relatively new and there's much to be done. Hence, I can get excited about work.

What is the optimal number of projects that you could be working on at any given time?

What I'm doing now is not even feasible, let alone optimal.

How do you balance your research and non-research activities?

Things like editing, organizing conferences, or going to conferences, is part of research to me. I'm getting input into my own creative process, and it's the same with teaching. I teach what I know. I'm teaching an undergraduate course in the business school at Wisconsin called 'Markets with Frictions'. I also taught this in my penultimate year at Penn, and I got close-to-perfect teaching evaluations. Why? Because it's different. We don't merely talk about supply and demand; we talk about marriage, credit cycles, unemployment, money and banking – things that are not easy to model using classical economic theory. We use search theory.

I was recently trying to lecture in this class on a paper that I was writing with Fabrizio Mattesini and Cyril Monnet on banking, but I forgot exactly how the equations worked. I wasn't prepared. I thought I remembered, but I didn't. So, I made it up. What I made up was different from the paper, and actually a lot better. We completely re-tooled the model using this new approach. So, even my undergraduate business course is a big input into my research.

How about the balance between your personal and professional lives?

It's a big juggling act, standing with one foot on a tightrope trying to keep eight balls in the air. But it helps that Gwen is an economist, and a lot of our friends are economists. We also play in a band (The Contractions) with other people who are economists.[11] Like I said before, I don't get so nervous when I give a seminar, but if you've got Lucas and Stokey there, of course

I'm a little nervous. Being in a band helps you get over stage fright, and develop some skills in communication and presentation.

Anyway, you learn to combine your family life with your economics and your hobbies, and hopefully it all stays in the air and doesn't come crashing down.

REFLECTIONS AND THE FUTURE OF ECONOMICS

What have been the most important findings and contributions in your research fields during your career?

The development of the real business cycle research program by Finn Kydland and Ed Prescott and all their followers was a big paradigm shift. All the work of Neil Wallace in monetary economics, and economics more generally, has been important. Again, the development of microfoundations in macro has been huge. Macro is no longer just a bunch of sloppy assumptions and equations; it's got to hang together logically, and it's got to be empirically relevant. Lucas, of course, gets a lot of credit for these developments, too.

What are the biggest challenges facing your research fields?

To pick one, I think that it is important to try to understand financial intermediation better. We're making some progress, but it's a hard job, and I don't want to take shortcuts. Take Mike Woodford. He's one of the best, and I respect him immensely, but his basic textbook model has no role for money or banks or related institutions. If he wants to talk about these institutions, he'll say something like, "Imagine a bank is like any other firm. It has inputs and let's call these inputs deposits." I am not trying to quote him verbatim here, but I think he would agree that he might take this approach. He's not the first one to do this. I like Mike a lot, but I don't like that kind of shortcut. I recognize different people should do different things, but what I am trying to say here is that I don't think a bank is just another firm.

'New Monetarist Economics' is the name that Steve Williamson and I recently came up with for what we are doing. It's all about trying to understand the exchange process at a deeper level. The adjective 'deep' is maligned because people think it means we're studying how many angels could dance on the head of a pin. But I don't understand the way some economists wear their shallowness as a badge of honor, when say they actually prefer cash-in-advance models to those that strive for better micro-foundations. On banking, we're not there yet, but we really want to understand financial intermediation in more detail, and hopefully it'll be useful for thinking about the world, and maybe even trying to make it a better place. First, you have to figure it out.

What are the strengths and weaknesses of your own research?

Hopefully, people can at least admire the sweat that went into it; we try not to cheat, by taking too many shortcuts, when we can avoid it. I think the work has some novelty, but of course we're standing on the shoulders of giants like Peter Diamond and many others.

People might ask why I am so focused on this narrow area of monetary economics, when we have a banking crisis to sort out. My own view is that we're never going to sort out the crisis in any permanent, meaningful way unless we understand better the basic theory of the exchange process, of credit markets, and of intermediation. People may think that I am narrow, but I don't mind that too much. I choose to be narrow; it's the only way to get depth.

In the end, do you think the profession has helped to bring out and shape your research for the best?

I think so, in more ways than one. My role models may be very different from other people's. I'm just a poor Canadian kid who went from Winnipeg to Minnesota. I never had the 'luxury' of going to Princeton or Harvard. So I identify with people like Ken Burdett and Boyan Jovanovic. They're regular lads – hardworking, insightful, and great fun.

That's also true of the guys I hung out with at the Minneapolis Fed in the '80s: Dave Backus, Pat and Tim Kehoe, Gary Hansen, Richard Rogerson, Victor Ríos-Rull, Larry Christiano, and Marty Eichenbaum. I saw what they were doing and it inspired me to work hard. We were competitive because we all wanted to do just as well as the next guy, and I really enjoyed that.

Do you have any professional regrets?

Tom Sargent told me once that if I'd get a haircut and stop wearing an earring, I'd be able to get a job at _____. Do I regret not cutting my hair or not getting rid of my earrings? Nah. I explained to Tom that that would be like asking somebody to change religion so they can improve in terms of the social or academic ladder, and he seemed to agree. One thing I like about economics is that people and papers are evaluated based on their merit. Maybe I'm naive, but I don't think a person's gender or the color of their skin, or the way they dress, or the length of their hair, is that important when judging them for promotion or hiring or for deciding whether their work is useful.

I don't regret that I didn't, say, get to go to Princeton as an undergraduate and Harvard as a graduate student. I didn't apply. I never even knew where those places were. I am pretty happy with my education. I learned so much at Minnesota – I couldn't imagine a better graduate training – and I did get a lot out of my undergraduate training, too. But I do sometimes wonder what it would be like to start off on the elite fast track.

What are your professional ambitions?

In the short run, we're trying to build up Wisconsin. We have tremendous resources and the desire to get better. I want to continue working with graduate students. I'm very proud of my students and I've learned as much from them as they've learned from me. I've got a new crop here. As I said, it's my first year here after 23 years at Penn, so I've got to get them tooled up and thinking the way I think, and then start working with them.

For the longer run, I'm going to continue to work on New Monetarist Economics and I want to see what people think about it. We don't always have the smartest people in our group, or the people with MIT PhDs. We do not have the power of sheer numbers, like the New Keynesians, and we're typically not the favorite sons of the central bankers. But at least we have integrity. And if you don't have integrity, what have you got?

How would you describe the state of economics today? Are you optimistic about its future?

The state of economics is good. We know so much about so many things that a few decades ago were mysterious. Paul Krugman did the profession a big disservice when he went public with his ideas that we should go back to Keynesian economics. I don't think that style of economics gives us a good explanation for the cause, or any reasonable candidates for the cure, of this recent financial crisis. We should keep working hard on the things we're working on. We should have people working on many different things – as Jovanovic says, "A garden should let many kinds of flowers bloom." (Boyan always was a bit like Peter Sellers in *Being There*). Economics is a hard science; I mean a difficult science. The issues are complicated, but we're making progress. If you want to know more about what I think the fruitful areas are for future research, I suggest looking at the two recent survey-type articles Steve Williamson and I wrote on New Monetarist Economics. They're easy to find – search.

NOTES

1. Kiyotaki, N. and R. Wright (1989), 'On Money as a Medium of Exchange', *Journal of Political Economy*, Vol. 97, No. 4 (August), pp. 927–954.
2. Burdett, K. and R. Wright (1989), 'Unemployment Insurance and Short-Time Compensation: The Effects on Layoffs, Hours per Worker, and Wages', *Journal of Political Economy*, Vol. 97, No. 6 (December), pp. 1479–1496.
3. Lagos, R. and R. Wright (2005), 'A Unified Framework for Monetary Theory and Policy Analysis', *Journal of Political Economy*, Vol. 113, No. 3 (June), pp. 463–484.
4. Nash, Jr, J.F. (1950), 'The Bargaining Problem', *Econometrica*, Vol. 18, No. 2 (April), pp. 155–162.
5. Mehra, R. and E.C. Prescott (1985), 'The Equity Premium: A Puzzle', *Journal of Monetary Economics*, Vol. 15, No. 2 (March), pp. 145–161.
6. Trejos, A. and R. Wright (1995), 'Search, Bargaining, Money and Prices', *Journal of Political Economy*, Vol. 103, No. 1 (February), pp. 118–141.
7. Guerrieri, V., Shimer, R. and R. Wright (2009), 'Adverse Selection in Competitive Search Equilibrium', *NBER Working Papers* 14915, National Bureau of Economic Research.
8. Krichel, T. and N. Bakkalbasi (2006), 'A Social Network Analysis of Research Collaboration in the Economics Community', *Journal of Information Management and Scientometrics*, Vol. 3, No. 2. Available at http://openlib.org/home/krichel/papers/nancy.pdf.
9. Wright, R. and J. Loberg (1987), 'Unemployment Insurance, Taxes, and Unemployment', *Canadian Journal of Economics*, Vol. 20, No. 1 (February), pp. 36–54.
10. Kiyotaki, N. and R. Wright (1991), 'A Contribution to the Pure Theory of Money', *Journal of Economic Theory*, Vol. 83, No. 1 (March), pp. 215–235; Kiyotaki, N. and R. Wright (1993), 'A Search-Theoretic Approach to Monetary Economics', *American Economic Review*, Vol. 83, No. 1 (March), pp. 63–77.
11. See http://contractions.marginalq.com/.

Index

Printed and bound by CPI Group (UK) Ltd, Croydon, CR0 4YY

16/04/2025

14658378-0004